D0904432

THE
TRADITIONAL GAMES

OF

ENGLAND, SCOTLAND, AND IRELAND

WITH

TUNES, SINGING-RHYMES, AND METHODS OF PLAYING
ACCORDING TO THE VARIANTS EXTANT AND
RECORDED IN DIFFERENT PARTS
OF THE KINGDOM

COLLECTED AND ANNOTATED BY

ALICE BERTHA GOMME

INTRODUCTION BY

DOROTHY HOWARD

IN TWO VOLUMES
VOLUME I

DOVER PUBLICATIONS, INC.
NEW YORK

Copyright © 1964 by Dover Publications, Inc.

All rights reserved under Pan American and International Copyright Conventions.

Published simultaneously in Canada by McClelland and Stewart, Limited.

Published in the United Kingdom by Constable and Company, Limited, 10 Orange Street, London W. C. 2.

This Dover edition, first published in 1964, is an unabridged and corrected republication of the work first published by David Nutt, London, as Part I of the *Dictionary of British Folk-Lore*. Volume I was first published in 1894, and Volume II was first published in 1898.

This edition also contains a new Introduction, especially prepared for this Dover edition by Dorothy Howard.

Library of Congress Catalog Card Number: 63-21811

Manufactured in the United States of America

Dover Publications, Inc.
180 Varick Street
New York 14, N. Y.

TO

MY HUSBAND

Introduction to Dover Edition

The Traditional Games of England, Scotland, and Ireland, published in 1894–1898 in two volumes and long out of print, 'has been, for years, practically unobtainable by scholars searching second-hand bookstores on both sides of the Atlantic. Why no publisher prior to Dover Publications, Inc. chose to re-issue this two volume study, the standard work in its field for more than half a century, is an unfathomable mystery.

A new edition at this time invites: (1) a restatement of important facts about Alice Bertha Gomme (collector and annotator) and her noted editor-husband, Sir George Laurence Gomme; (2) an assessment of the significance of her work in her own time and since; and (3) some analysis of her field of research—its status in folklore circles and in the market places in the British Isles and in the United States during the years when the romantic 19th century was hurrying the world of good Queen Victoria over the brink of the 20th into the age of world wars, depressions, Freud, baby-sitters and juvenile delinquents.

Members of the discipline know that folklorists of various vintages and brands agree (with many ifs and buts) that the name *Gomme* has a permanent place in the history of folklore scholarship; that Lady Alice Bertha and Sir George Laurence each, separately, made a unique and important contribution to knowledge; and that together, as a husband and wife team, they have held the distinction of being the most important if not the only team of its kind in England until the middle of the present century.

The list of Lady Alice's published works is short[1] when compared to that of her husband.[2] Sir Laurence ranged over a

---

[1]Her published books include: *Children's Singing Games* (London, 1894), 2 volumes, in collaboration with C. J. Sharp; *The Traditional Games of England, Scotland, and Ireland* (London, 1894–1898), 2 volumes; *Games for Parlour and Playground* (London, 1898); *Old English Singing Games* (London, 1900); and *British Folk Lore, Folk Songs and Singing Games* (London, n.d. [1916]), in collaboration with her husband. A listing of miscellaneous articles published by her in *Folk-Lore* (London, 1890 to date), may be found in Wilfrid Bonser, *A Bibliography of Folklore* (London, 1961), items numbered 3, 304, 1033, 1106, 1159, 1195, 1277, 1368, 1995, 2361, 2573, and 2577. Obituaries for her, written by M. Gaster and F. Boas, may be found in *Folk-Lore* 49 (1938), pp. 93–94.

[2]For a bibliography of the writings of G. Laurence Gomme on folklore and anthropology, see *Folk-Lore* 27 (1916), pp. 408–413.

wide field in subject matter, whereas Lady Alice limited her studies almost entirely to children's games, a proper limitation for a Victorian lady and wife of an eminent scholar whose light was not obscured by even half a bushel. In a list of 19th-century British collectors of nursery rhymes and play lore, Lady Alice's name stands last in historical sequence and first in importance: Joseph Strutt, *Sports and Pastimes of the People of England* (London, 1801); Robert Chambers, *Popular Rhymes of Scotland* (first edition Edinburgh, 1826); James Orchard Halliwell, *The Nursery Rhymes of England* (London, 1842) and *Popular Rhymes and Nursery Tales* (London, 1849); G. F. Northall, *English Folk Rhymes* (London, 1892); and last, *The Traditional Games of England, Scotland, and Ireland*, two volumes (London, 1894–1898), collected and annotated by Alice Bertha Gomme, and edited by G. Laurence Gomme as Part I of *A Dictionary of British Folk-Lore* (the present work is hereafter referred to as the 'Gomme *Dictionary*').

In comparing the Gomme *Dictionary* with preceding works, it should be noted that Lady Alice sought to distinguish children's games from adult games, and playground lore from nursery lore; she did not limit her study to verbal aspects of children's play; she was more systematic than any of her predecessors in geographic location of items; and finally, her undertaking was more comprehensive than any preceding study. "I had hoped to have covered in my collection the whole field of games as played by children in the United Kingdom . . ." (Vol. I, p.xv), said she. Her collection, therefore, stands as a culminating work of the 19th century. As folklorists know, it was a part of her husband's larger plan for a dictionary of British folklore; it survives as a remnant of a plan which was never carried through.

Among 20th-century scholars, Lady Alice holds the position of predecessor whose limitations, shortcomings, and inadequacies must be pointed out in order to justify further research. But, at the same time, the mistake should not be made of judging her in the context of American and British mores of 1963 instead of in her own British Victorian habitat, or of blaming her for having lived and worked in her own time instead of in ours.

No student of children's playlore can now or ever ignore the Gomme *Dictionary*. No monumental study equal to hers has yet appeared anywhere. In the United States scattered studies of limited scope have appeared as articles in folklore journals, as sections in sundry anthologies, as chapters in volumes of regional lore, as doctoral theses, and in two small books published seventy years apart: W. W. Newell's *Games and Songs of American Children* (New York, 1883);[1] and Paul Brewster's *American Non-Singing Games* (Norman, Oklahoma, 1953). In the United States no scholar or group of scholars has yet given the time and attention to a study with the dimensions of the Gomme *Dictionary*. In British nations the accomplishments and outlook are better.

Iona and Peter Opie, with their scholarly *Oxford Dictionary of Nursery Rhymes* (published in London in 1951 and still selling steadily) and *The Lore and Language of Schoolchildren*, (published in London in 1959 and immediately becoming *the* best seller of its ilk), are now working on a study of children's games of the British Isles; and their work, when completed and published, *promises* to be the *definitive* study in children's folklore of the 20th century.

Also in 1959, *The Games of New Zealand Children* by Brian Sutton-Smith was published by the University of California Press. Dr. Sutton-Smith, working in a folklorist's paradise (two small isolated islands with a total population of two million people) spent two years (1949, 1950) in that equable climate traveling, sleeping in a sleeping bag, watching children play and recording what he saw and heard. The study is a unique gem. Dr. Sutton-Smith, a psychologist now living in the United States, hopes to return to New Zealand some years hence to restudy play customs. Meanwhile he is giving his attention to qualitative analysis of American children's play customs, and it is to be hoped that he and his psychologist colleagues can alter an amorphous situation and ultimately give direction and shape to studies in American children's playlore.

In 1954 and 1955, as an American Fulbright scholar, I spent a year in Australia, collecting and studying Australian children's traditional play ways. Material from that study has appeared in folklore-journal articles in the United States and England; and hopes are still held that the entire study may yet be published as a book.

In Canada, the collection of children's playlore appears to be incidental with folklorists who are primarily interested in folksongs and folk tales. The small amount of published material is to be found in periodicals and in small miscellaneous sections of studies dedicated to other categories.

In order to assess the historical significance of the Gomme *Dictionary*, it is necessary, first, to return to its date of publi-

---

[1] Reprinted by Dover Publications in 1963.

cation, 1894–1898, to the society in which Lady Alice lived
and worked, and to examine: the position of women and
children in late-Victorian England; the status of women in
academic and scholarly compounds; the prestige of folklore
study in academic and popular life; and—most important—
the big umbrella of folklore theory which Lady Alice's husband held over a group of active scholars and in the shadow
of which Lady Alice happily worked.

Sir Laurence's Darwinian theory of unilinear cultural evolution, with emphasis on survivals, is a basic assumption in
the entire two-volume *Dictionary* and is distinctly implied in
Lady Alice's own statement about her method of collection:
"The bulk of the collection has been made by myself, greatly
through the kindness of many correspondents . . ." (Vol. I,
p. xiv). Later in the same paragraph she lists her most important correspondents (all of whom were obviously adults).
The games in her *Dictionary*, it must therefore be inferred, are
games belonging to Lady Alice's childhood or earlier and not
necessarily current among children at her time of reporting;
the descriptions came from the memories (accurate or otherwise) of adults and not from observation of children at play.
The games reported represent the play life (or part of the
play life) of articulate, "proper" Victorian adults (of Queen
Victoria's youth) reporting on "proper" games. Lady Alice,
if she had any inkling of improper games lurking in the memories of her literate adult informants, gave no hint of it. And
she chose to ignore the games of Dickens' illiterate back alleys
and tenements though she could hardly have been unaware
that they existed. Since, according to statistics, Dickens'
children far outnumbered well-fed-and-housed Victorian children and since psychological excavators have dug up evidence
to indicate that nice Victorian children were often naughty,
we can only conjecture that Lady Alice's *Dictionary* might
have run to twenty volumes, had she undertaken a different
study with a different point of view.

There is no need to lament the limitations of the Gomme
study. We should accept it for what it is and be grateful,
mindful that sixty-five years hence—in the year 2028—our
own limitations as scholars may be lamented by those who
follow us. In this year of 1963 (the era of Kinsey, transistor
tape recorders and triumphant juvenile delinquents) we should
consider what would have been the fate of Alice Bertha
Gomme, woman-scholar extraordinary of her day, had she
been still more extraordinary; had she attempted to sit on
curbstones listening to children play and to record the un-

varnished facts. Her findings would never have seen the light of print; and Alice would have been shoved permanently down some rabbit hole; she would never have become *Lady* Alice; and we would not, today, have her two-volume *Dictionary* to reissue.

Alice Bertha Gomme accepted the circumscriptions of society (as any woman must in any society in any historical age), and operated efficiently within the prescribed dicta. The circumscriptions of Victorian English society included children who "should be seen and not heard," who "should speak when spoken to," and who, when they did speak out of turn, were "sent out to play," often beyond the hearing and sight of adults into a secret world of their own making, considered trivial and inconsequential by serious and erudite grown-ups. The Gomme study of games, undertaken in this milieu, constitutes an act of distinct independent scholarship. Today it seems happily ironic that her two-volume study, which was to have served as introductory units in her husband's gigantic undertaking of Baconian dimensions, has survived alone to be reissued for folklore scholars.

Scholars interested in children represent many disciplines; and the increasing interest in the study of children's behavior cannot be credited as much to folklorists as to psychologists and sociologists—to those seeking to understand human behavior of individuals and of groups of individuals (including children).

Children today, the world over, unlike the children of Alice Bertha Gomme's day, are seen and heard speaking out of turn. With the world-wide increasing birth-rate and decreasing death-rate, the children who are inheriting the earth have not descended from heaven in trailing clouds of glory but daily make the newspaper headlines for earthly reasons. By their increasing numbers they become an increasing nuisance to adults; and the adults are worried. Out of the dire necessity of this worry have come the attempts to understand children's behavior, permitted and unpermitted. Suddenly (historically speaking) what children do and say in this secret world of unsupervised play in city slums and country lanes is no longer considered trivia to be ignored. The physical-educationists were the first academicians to come up with an answer and a remedy. Their answer was rule books for the old games (modified); and their remedy was an adaptation of a jail set-up called "supervised play." Supervisors and supervised playgrounds have increased as the children increase in numbers and are herded into urban areas. But the worry has also increased because the nuisance value of children in orderly society has increased. Consequently psychologists and sociologists explore libraries for every bit of information on children's behavior in past ages and eavesdrop with transistor tape recorders, and undertake to explore the psyches, ids and egos of children for data to feed IBM machines, which in a matter of moments, they hope, can disgorge answers like the magic music of a Pied Piper to lure the herds of noisy children somewhere, though *where* still needs more definition.

Among American folklore scholars, attention to children's traditional play ways has increased slowly. The absorbing interests of our scholars have been and still are: the folksong, the folk-tale, the proverb and related linguistic categories. In 1883, W. W. Newell's *Games and Songs of American Children* followed the Francis James Child pattern by emphasizing verbal aspects of children's play. As late as 1938, academic dicta in one of the largest, old American universities prescribed that a doctoral candidate undertaking a study in children's folklore could not stray outside the verbal corral into the wild sagebrush of play custom where the words and sounds had a life and being before they were herded into the compound for branding, taming and sorting into adult-prescribed pens.

In popular trade publications (especially in the United States), children's folklore and folklore for children (much of it "fakelore") have been exploited in recent years in appeals to nostalgic adults remembering their childhood days through rose-colored memory; to over-worked schoolteachers seeking "supplemental reading material" for slow readers; to uninspired physical-educationists appropriating old games and revamping them to fit supervised play programs; and to misguided missionaries undertaking to transmit by book the old games and play ways which children have transmitted to children on playgrounds for hundreds of years.

The reissue by an American scholarly publisher of Alice Bertha Gomme's *Dictionary* is a sign and signal, it is to be hoped, that children's folklore is climbing the ladder of academic and scholarly respectability on this side of the ocean. When Lady Alice died in 1938, twenty-two years after the death of her more famous husband (she was born in 1852), her death went almost unnoticed by the press in England and America except for obituaries in folklore periodicals. Yet any pretense at scholarship in her field has required and will continue to require early citation of her work. Lady

Alice, it is true, hitched her sturdy wagon full of facts to a theoretical star which promptly descended below the horizon of academic respectability; but the wagon full of facts still sits detached from its fallen star. Her collection and study, placed in historical perspective and reinterpreted, can be of permanent value to any and all scholars seeking to understand human behavior.

No student of children's playlore can escape indebtedness to Alice Bertha Gomme: her gargantuan accumulation of facts, her organization of material (whether adopted, adapted, or departed from), and her unrealized hopes for a definitive study. These remain constant facts to help or haunt aspiring scholars who play "Giant Steps" on Alice Bertha's staked playground.

DOROTHY HOWARD

Frostburg State College
Frostburg, Maryland
March, 1963

PREFACE

SOON after the formation of the Folk-lore Society in 1878 my husband planned, and has ever since been collecting for, the compilation of a dictionary of British Folk-lore. A great deal of the material has been put in form for publication, but at this stage the extent of the work presented an unexpected obstacle to its completion.

To print the whole in one alphabet would be more than could be accomplished except by the active co-operation of a willing band of workers, and then the time required for such an undertaking, together with the cost, almost seemed to debar the hope of ever completing arrangements for its publication. Nevertheless, unless we have a scientific arrangement of the enormously scattered material and a close comparison of the details of each item of folk-lore, it is next to impossible to expect that the full truth which lies hidden in these remnants of the past may be revealed.

During my preparation of a book of games for children it occurred to me that to separate the whole of the games from the general body of folk-lore and to make them a section of the proposed dictionary would be an advantageous step, as by arranging the larger groups of folk-lore in independent sections the possibility of publishing the contemplated dictionary again seemed to revive. Accordingly, the original plan has been so far modified that these volumes will form the first section of the dictionary, which, instead of being issued in one alphabet throughout, will now be issued in sections, each section being arranged alphabetically.

The games included in this collection bear the important qualification of being nearly all Children's Games: that is to say, they were either originally children's games since developed into games for adults, or they were the more serious avocations of adults, which have since become children's games only. In both cases the transition is due to traditional circumstances, and not to any formal arrangements. All invented games of skill are therefore excluded from this collection, but it includes both indoor and outdoor games, and those played by both girls and boys.

The bulk of the collection has been made by myself, greatly through the kindness of many correspondents, to whom I cannot be sufficiently grateful. In every case I have acknowledged my indebtedness, which, besides being an act of justice, is a guarantee of the genuineness of the collection. I have appended to this preface a list of the collectors, together with the counties to which the games belong; but I must particularly thank the Rev. W. Gregor, Mr. S. O. Addy, and Miss Fowler, who very generously placed collections at my disposal, which had been prepared before they knew of my project; also Miss Burne, Miss L. E. Broadwood, and others, for kindly obtaining variants and tunes I should not otherwise have received. To the many versions now printed for the first time I have added either a complete transcript of, where necessary, or a reference to, where that was sufficient, printed versions of games to be found in the well-known collections of Halliwell and Chambers, the publications of the Folk-lore and Dialect Societies, Jamieson's, Nares', and Halliwell's Dictionaries, and other printed sources of information. When quoting from a printed authority, I have as far as possible given the exact

words, and have always given the reference. I had hoped to
have covered in my collection the whole field of games as
played by children in the United Kingdom, but it will be seen
that many counties in each country are still unrepresented;
and I shall be greatly indebted for any games from other places,
which would help to make this collection more complete. The
tunes of the games have been taken down, as sung by the
children, either by myself or correspondents (except where
otherwise stated), and are unaltered.

The games consist of two main divisions, which may be called
descriptive, and singing or choral. The descriptive games are
arranged so as to give the most perfect type, and, where they
occur, variable types in succession, followed, where possible,
by any suggestions I have to make as to the possible origin
of the game. The singing games are arranged so as to give,
first, the tunes; secondly, the different versions of the game-
rhymes; thirdly, the method of playing; fourthly, an analysis
of the game-rhymes on a plan arranged by my husband, and
which is an entirely novel feature in discussing the history
of games; fifthly, a discussion of the results of the analysis
of the rhymes so far as the different versions allow; and
sixthly, an attempt to deduce from the evidence thus collected
suggestions as to the probable origin of the game, together
with such references to early authorities and other facts bearing upon the subject as help to elucidate the views expressed.
Where the method of playing the game is involved, or where
there are several changes in the forms, diagrams or illustrations,
which have been drawn by Mr. J. P. Emslie, are inserted in
order to assist the reader to understand the different actions,
and in one or two instances I have been able to give a facsimile reproduction of representations of the games from early
MSS. in the Bodleian and British Museum Libraries.

Although none of the versions of the games now collected
together are in their original form, but are more or less fragmentary, it cannot, I think, fail to be noticed how extremely
interesting these games are, not only from the point of view
of the means of amusement (and under this head there can
be no question of their interest), but as a means of obtaining an insight into many of the customs and beliefs of our
ancestors. Children do not invent, but they imitate or mimic
very largely, and in many of these games we have, there is
little doubt, unconscious folk-dramas of events and customs
which were at one time being enacted as a part of the serious
concerns of life before the eyes of children many generations
ago. As to the many points of interest under this and other
heads there is no occasion to dwell at length here, because the
second volume will contain an appendix giving a complete
analysis of the incidents mentioned in the games, and an
attempt to tell the story of their origin and development,
together with a comparison with the games of children of
foreign countries.

The intense pleasure which the collection of these games
has given me has been considerably enhanced by the many
expressions of the same kind of pleasure from correspondents
who have helped me, it not being an infrequent case for me to
be thanked for reviving some of the keenest pleasures expe-
rienced by the collector since childhood; and I cannot help
thinking that, if these traditional games have the power of
thus imparting pleasure after the lapse of many years, they
must contain the power of giving an equal pleasure to those
who may now learn them for the first time.

ALICE BERTHA GOMME.

BARNES COMMON, S.W.,
   Jan. 1894.

LIST OF AUTHORITIES

ENGLAND.

Halliwell's *Nursery Rhymes.*
Halliwell's *Dictionary,* ed. 1889.
Holloway's *Dictionary,* ed. 1838.
Strutt's *Sports and Pastimes,* ed. 1831.
Brand's *Popular Antiquities,* ed. 1875.
Nares' *Glossary,* ed. 1872.

Grose's *Dictionary,* 1823.
Notes and Queries.
Reliquary.
English Dialect Society Publications.
Folk-lore Society Publications, 1878–1892.

BEDFORDSHIRE—
    Luton . . . . . Mrs. Ashdown.
    Roxton . . . . . Miss Lumley.
BERKSHIRE . . . . . Lowsley's *Glossary.*
    Enborne . . . . Miss Kimber.
    Fernham, Longcot . . . Miss I. Barclay.
    Newbury . . . . Mrs. S. Batson, Miss Kimber.
    Sulhampstead . . . Miss Thoyts (*Antiquary,* vol. xxvii.)
CAMBRIDGESHIRE—
    Cambridge . . . . Mrs. Haddon.
CHESHIRE . . . . . { Darlington's, Holland's, Leigh's, and Wilbraham's *Glossaries.*
    Congleton . . . . Miss A. E. Twemlow.
CORNWALL . . . . . *Folk-lore Journal,* v., Courtney's *Glossary.*
    Penzance . . . . Miss Courtney, Mrs. Mabbott.
CUMBERLAND . . . . Dickinson's *Glossary.*
DERBYSHIRE . . . . { *Folk-lore Journal,* vol. i., Mrs. Harley, Mr. S. O. Addy.
    Dronfield, Eckington, Egan . Mr. S. O. Addy.
DEVONSHIRE . . . . Halliwell's *Dictionary.*
DORSETSHIRE . . . . Barnes' *Glossary, Folk-lore Journal,* vol. vii.
DURHAM . . . . . Brockett's *North Country Words,* ed. 1846.
    Gainford . . . . Miss Eddleston.
    South Shields . . . Miss Blair.
ESSEX—
    Bocking . . . . . *Folk-lore Record,* vol. iii. pt. 2.
    Colchester . . . . Miss G. M. Francis.
GLOUCESTERSHIRE . . . Holloway's *Dictionary, Midland Garner.*
    Shepscombe, Cheltenham . Miss Mendham.
    Forest of Dean . . . Miss Matthews.
HAMPSHIRE . . . . . Cope's *Glossary,* Miss Mendham.
    Bitterne . . . . . Mrs. Byford.
    Liphook . . . . Miss Fowler.

HAMPSHIRE—
    Hartley, Winchfield, Witney .   Mr. H. S. May.
    Southampton .   .   .   Mrs. W. R. Carse.
ISLE OF MAN   .   .   .   Mr. A. W. Moore.
ISLE OF WIGHT—
    Cowes .   .   .   .   Miss E. Smith.
KENT .   .   .   .   .   Pegge's *Alphabet of Kenticisms.*
    Bexley Heath   .   .   Miss Morris.
    Crockham Hill, Deptford   .   Miss Chase.
    Platt .   .   .   .   Miss Burne.
    Wrotham   .   .   .   Miss D. Kimball.
LANCASHIRE   .   .   .   { Nodal and Milner's *Glossary*, Harland and Wilkinson's *Folk-lore*, ed. 1882, Mrs. Harley.
    Monton .   .   .   .   Miss Dendy.
LEICESTERSHIRE .   .   .   Evan's *Glossary.*
    Leicester   .   .   .   Miss Ellis.
LINCOLNSHIRE   .   .   .   { Peacock's, Cole's, and Brogden's *Glossaries*, Rev. — Roberts.
    Anderby, Botterford, Brigg, Frodingham, Horncastle, North Kelsey, Stixwould, Winterton .   .   .   } Miss Peacock.
    East Kirkby .   .   .   Miss K. Maughan.
    Metheringham   .   .   Mr. C. C. Bell.
MIDDLESEX .   .   .   .   Miss Collyer.
    Hanwell   .   .   .   Mrs. G. L. Gomme.
    London .   .   .   .   { Miss Chase, Miss F. D. Richardson, Mr. G. L. Gomme, Mrs. G. L. Gomme, Mr. J. P. Emslie, Miss Dendy, Mr. J. T. Micklethwaite (*Archæological Journal*, vol. xlix.), *Strand Magazine*, vol. ii.
NORFOLK   .   .   .   { Forby's *Vocabulary*, Spurden's *Vocabulary*, Mr. J. Doe.
    Sporle, Swaffham .   .   Miss Matthews.
NORTHAMPTONSHIRE .   .   { Baker's *Glossary*, *Northants Notes and Queries*, *Revue Celtique*, vol. iv., Rev. W. D. Sweeting.
    Maxey .   .   .   .   Rev. W. D. Sweeting.
NORTHUMBERLAND   .   .   Brockett's *Provincial Words*, ed. 1846.
    Hexham   .   .   .   Miss J. Barker.
NOTTINGHAMSHIRE   .   .   Miss Peacock.
    Long Eaton .   .   .   Miss Youngman.
    Nottingham .   .   .   Miss Winfield, Miss Peacock.
    Ordsall .   .   .   .   Miss Matthews.
OXFORDSHIRE   .   .   .   Aubrey's *Remains*, ed. 1880.
    Oxford .   .   .   .   Miss Fowler.
    Summertown .   .   .   *Midland Garner*, vol. ii.
SHROPSHIRE   .   .   .   Burne's *Shropshire Folk-lore.*
    Madeley, Middleton   .   Miss Burne.
    Tong .   .   .   .   Miss R. Harley.

SOMERSETSHIRE	Elworthy's *Dialect, Somerset and Dorset Notes and Queries,* Holloway's *Dictionary.*
Bath	Miss Large.
STAFFORDSHIRE—	
Hanbury	Miss E. Hollis.
Cheadle	Miss Burne.
Tean, North Staffordshire Potteries	Miss Keary, Miss Burne, Mrs. T. Lawton.
Wolstanton	Miss Keary.
SUFFOLK	Moor's *Suffolk Words,* Forby's *Vocabulary,* Lady C. Gurdon's *Suffolk County Folk-lore.*
SURREY—	
Barnes	Mrs. G. L. Gomme.
Clapham	Miss F. D. Richardson.
Hersham	*Folk-lore Record,* vol. v.
Redhill	Miss G. Hope.
SUSSEX	Parish's *Dialect,* Holloway's *Dictionary,* Toone's *Dictionary.*
Hurstmonceux . . .	Miss Chase.
Shipley, Horsham, West Grinstead	Miss R. H. Busk (*Notes and Queries*).
Ninfield	Mr. C. Wise.
WARWICKSHIRE	Northall's *Folk Rhymes, Notes and Queries, Northants Notes and Queries,* Mr. C. C. Bell.
WILTSHIRE—	
Marlborough, Manton, Ogbourne	Mr. H. S. May.
WORCESTERSHIRE . . .	Chamberlain's *Glossary.*
Upton-on-Severn . . .	Lawson's *Glossary.*
YORKSHIRE	Atkinson's, Addy's, Easther's, Hunter's, Robinson's, Ross and Stead's *Glossaries,* Henderson's *Folk-lore,* ed. 1879.
Almondbury	Easther's *Glossary.*
Epworth, Lossiemouth . .	Mr. C. C. Bell.
Earls Heaton, Haydon, Holmfirth	Mr. H. Hardy.
Settle	Rev. W. S. Sykes.
Sharleston	Miss Fowler, Rev. G. T. Royds.
Sheffield	Mr. S. O. Addy, Miss Lucy Garnett.
Wakefield	Miss Fowler.

SCOTLAND.

Chambers' *Popular Rhymes,* ed. 1870.
Mactaggart's *Gallovidian Encyclopædia,* ed. 1871.

Jamieson's *Etymological Dictionary,* ed. 1872-1889.
Folk-lore Society Publications.

ABERDEEN—	
Pitsligo	Rev. W. Gregor.

BANFFSHIRE—
   Duthil, Keith, Strathspey   .   Rev. W. Gregor.
ELGIN—
   Fochabers   .   .   .   .   Rev. W. Gregor.
KIRKCUDBRIGHT—
   Auchencairn -.   .   .   .   Prof. A. C. Haddon.
LANARKSHIRE—
   Biggar   .   .   .   .   .   Mr. Wm. Ballantyne.
   Lanark   .   .   .   .   .   Mr. W. G. Black.
NAIRN—
   Nairn   .   .   .   .   Rev. W. Gregor.

IRELAND.

Folk-lore Society Publications.   *Notes and Queries.*

ANTRIM AND DOWN   .   .   .   Patterson's *Glossary.*
CLARE—
   Kilkee   .   .   .   .   .   G. H. Kinahan (*Folk-lore Journal,* vol. ii.)
CORK—
   Cork   .   .   .   .   .   Mrs. B. B. Green, Miss Keane.
DOWN—
   Ballynascaw   .   .   .   .   Miss C. N. Patterson.
   Belfast   .   .   .   .   Mr. W. H. Patterson.
   Holywood   .   .   .   .   Miss C. N. Patterson.
DUBLIN—
   Dublin   .   .   .   .   .   Mrs. Lincoln.
LOUTH—
   Annaverna, Ravendale   .   .   Miss R. Stephen.
QUEEN'S COUNTY—
   Portarlington .   .   .   .   G. H. Kinahan (*Folk-lore Journal,* vol. ii.)
WATERFORD—
   Lismore .   .   .   .   .   Miss Keane.

WALES.

Byegones.   Folk-lore Society Publications.

CARMARTHENSHIRE—
   Beddgelert   .   .   .   .   Mrs. Williams.

LIST OF GAMES

Accroshay.
All-hid.
All a Row.
All in the Well.
All the Birds in the Air.
All the Boys in our Town.
All the Fishes in the Sea.
All the Soldiers in the Town.
Allicomgreenzie.
Alligoshee.
Almonds and Reasons.
Angel and Devil.
Auntieloomie.

Babbity Bowster.
Bad.
Baddin.
Badger the Bear.
Bag o' Malt.
Ball.
Ball and Bonnets.
Ball in the Decker.
Ball of Primrose.
Baloon.
Bandy-ball.
Bandy-cad.
Bandy-hoshoe.
Bandy-wicket.
Banger.
Bar.
Barbarie, King of the.
Barley-break.
Barnes (Mr.).
Base-ball.
Basket.
Battledore and Shuttlecock.
Bedlams or Relievo.
Beds.
Bell-horses.
Bellie-mantie.
Belly-blind.

Bend-leather.
Betsy Bungay.
Bicky.
Biddy-base.
Biggly.
Billet.
Billy-base.
Bingo.
Bird-apprentice.
Birds, Beasts, and Fishes.
Bittle-battle.
Bitty-base.
Black Man's Tig.
Black Thorn.
Blind Bell.
Blind Bucky Davy.
Blind Harie.
Blind Hob.
Blind Man's Buff.
Blind Man's Stan.
Blind Nerry Mopsy.
Blind Palmie.
Blind Sim.
Block, Hammer, and Nail.
Blow-point.
Bob Cherry.
Boggle about the Stacks.
Boggle-bush.
Bonnety.
Booman.
Boss-out.
Boss and Span.
Boys and Girls.
Branks.
Bridgeboard.
Broken-down Tradesmen.
Brother Ebenezer.
Bubble-hole.
Bubble-justice.
Buck, Buck.
Buck i' t' Neucks.

Buckerels.
Buckey-how.
Buff.
Buk-hid.
Bull in the Park.
Bulliheisle.
Bummers.
Bun-hole.
Bunch of Ivy.
Bung the Bucket.
Bunting.
Burly Whush.
Buttons.
Buzz and Bandy.

CACHE-POLE.
Caiche.
Call-the-Guse.
Camp.
Canlie.
Capie-Hole.
Carrick.
Carry my Lady to London.
Carrying the Queen a Letter.
Cashhornie.
Castles.
Cat and Dog.
Cat-Beds.
Cat's Cradle.
Cat-gallows.
Cat i' the Hole.
Cat after Mouse.
Catchers.
Chacke-Blyndman.
Chance Bone.
Change Seats.
Checkstone.
Cherry Odds.
Cherry-pit.
Chicamy.
Chickidy Hand.
Chinnup.
Chinny-mumps.
Chock or Chock-hole.
Chow.
Chuck-farthing.
Chuck-hole.
Chucks.
Church and Mice.

Click.
Click, Clock, Cluck.
Clowt-clowt.
Clubby.
Coal under Candlestick.
Cob.
Cobbin-match.
Cobble.
Cobbler's Hornpipe.
Cob-nut.
Cock.
Cock-battler.
Cock-fight.
Cock-haw.
Cock-stride.
Cockertie-hooie.
Cockle-bread.
Cockly-jock.
Cock's-headling.
Cock-steddling.
Codlings.
Cogger.
Cogs.
Common.
Conkers.
Conquerors.
Contrary, Rules of.
Cop-halfpenny.
Corsicrown.
Cots and Twisses.
Course o' Park.
Crab-sowl.
Crates.
Cricket.
Crooky.
Cross and Pile.
Cross-bars.
Cross-questions.
Cross Tig.
Cry Notchil.
Cuck-ball.
Cuckoo.
Cuddy and the Powks.
Cudgel.
Curcuddie.
Curly Locks.
Currants and Raisins.
Cushion Dance.
Cutch a Cutchoo.
Cutters and Trucklers.

DAB.
Dab-an-thricker.
Dab-at-the-hole.
Dalies.
Davie-drap.
Deadily.
Diamond Ring.
Dibbs.
Dinah.
Dip o' the Kit.
Dish-a-loof.
Doddart.
Doncaster Cherries.
Dools.
Down in the Valley.
Drab and Norr.
Draw a Pail of Water.
Drawing Dun out of the Mire.
Drop Handkerchief.
Dropping the Letter.
Duck under the Water.
Duck at the Table.
Duck Dance.
Duck Friar.
Ducks and Drakes.
Duffan Ring.
Dumb Crambo.
Dumb Motions.
Dump.
Dumps.
Dust-point.

ELLER Tree.
Ezzeka.

FATHER'S Fiddle.
Feed the Dove.
Find the Ring.
Fippeny Morrell.
Fire, Air, and Water.
Fivestones.
Flowers.
Follow my Gable.
Follow my Leader.
Fool, Fool, come to School.
Foot and Over.
Football.
Forfeits.
Fox.
Fox and Goose (1).

Fox and Geese (2).
Fox in the Fold.
Fox in the Hole.
French Jackie.
French and English.
French Blindman's Buff.
Friar-rush.
Frincy-francy.
Frog-lope.
Frog in the Middle.

GAP.
Garden Gate.
Gegg.
Genteel Lady.
Ghost at the Well.
Giants.
Giddy.
Gilty galty.
Gipsy.
Gled-wylie.
Glim-glam.
Gobs.
Green Grass.
Green Gravel.
Green Grow the Leaves (1).
Green Grow the Leaves (2).
Gully.

HAIRRY my Bossie.
Half-Hammer.
Han'-and-Hail.
Hand in and Hand out.
Handy-Croopen.
Handy Dandy.
Hap the Beds.
Hard Buttons.
Hare and Hounds.
Harie Hutcheon.
Hark the Robbers.
Hats in Holes.
Hattie.
Hawkey.
Headicks and Pinticks.
Heads and Tails.
Hecklebirnie.
Hen and Chicken.
Here comes a Lusty Wooer.
Here comes One Virgin.
Here I sit on a Cold Green Bank.

Here stands a Young Man.
Here we go around, around.
Here's a Soldier.
Hewley Puley.
Hey Wullie Wine.
Hickety, Bickety.
Hickety-hackety.
Hick, Step, and Jump.
Hide and Seek (1).
Hide and Seek (2).
Hinch-Pinch.
Hinmost o' Three.
Hirtschin Hairy.
Hiry-hag.
Hiss and Clap.
Hitch, Jamie, Stride and Loup.
Hitchapagy.
Hitchy Cock Ho.
Hity Tity.
Hoatie, Hots.
Hob-in-the-Hall.
Hockerty Cokerty.
Hockey.
Hoges.
Ho-go.
Hoilakes.
Holy Bang.
Honey Pots.
Hood.
Hoodle-cum-blind.
Hoodman Blind.
Hooper's Hide.
Hop-crease.
Hop-frog.
Hop-score.
Hop-scotch.
Hop, Step, and Jump.
Hornie.
Hornie Holes.
Horns.
Hot Cockles.
How many Miles to Babylon.
Howly.
Huckie-buckie   down the Brae.
Huckle-bones.
Hummie.
Hundreds.
Hunt the Hare.
Hunt the Slipper.
Hunt the Staigie.

Hunting.
Hurling.
Hurly-burly.
Huss.
Hustle Cap.
Hynny-pynny.

ISABELLA.

Jacks = Fivestones

JACK's Alive.
Jack, Jack, the Bread's a-burning.
Jack upon the Mopstick.
Jackysteauns.
Jauping Paste-eggs.
Jenny Jones.
Jenny Mac.
Jib-Job-Jeremiah.
Jiddy-cum-jiddy.
Jingle-the-bonnet.
Jingo-ring.
Jinkie.
Jock and Jock's Man.
Jockie Blind-man.
Joggle along.
Johnny Rover.
Jolly Fishermen.
Jolly Hooper.
Jolly Miller.
Jolly Rover.
Jolly Sailors.
Jowls.
Jud.

KEELING the Pot.
Keppy Ball.
Kibel and Nerspel.
King by your leave.
King Cæsar.
King Come-a-lay.
King of Cantland.
King o' the Castle.
King Plaster Palacey.
King William.
King's Chair.
Kirk the Gussie.
Kiss in the Ring.
Kit-cat.
Kit-cat-cannio.
Kittlie-cout.
Knapsack.

Knights.
Knocked at the Rapper.
Knor and Spell.

LAB.
Lady of the Land.
Lady on the Mountain.
Lady on Yonder Hill.
Lag.
Lammas.
Lamploo.
Lang Larence.
Leap Candle.
Leap-frog.
Leap the Bullock.
Leaves are Green.
Lend Me your Key.
Letting the Buck out.
Level-coil.
Libbety-lat.
Limpy Coley.
Little Dog, I call you.
Lobber.
Loggats.
London.
London Bridge.
Long-duck.
Long Tag.
Long-Tawl.
Long Terrace.
Loup the Bullocks.
Lubin.
Lug and a Bite.
Luggie.
Luking.

MAG.
Magic Whistle.
Magical Music.

Malaga Raisins.
Marbles.
Mary Brown.
Mary mixed a Pudding up.
Merrils.
Merritot.
Merry-ma-tansa.
Milking Pails.
Mineral, Animal, and Vegetable.
Minister's Cat.
Mollish's Land.
Monday, Tuesday.
Moolie Pudding.
More Sacks to the Mill.
Mother, may I go out to Play?
Mother Mop.
Mother, Mother, the Pot boils over.
Mount the Tin.
Mouse and the Cobbler.
Muffin Man.
Mulberry Bush.
Munshets.
Musical Chairs.

NACKS.
Namers and Guessers.
Neighbour.
Neivie-nick-nack.
Nettles.
New Squat.
Nine Holes.
Nine Men's Morris.
Nip-srat-and-bite.
Nitch, Notch, No-Notch.
Not.
Noughts and Crosses.
Nur and Spel.
Nuts in May.

CHILDREN'S GAMES.

Accroshay

A cap or small article is placed on the back of a stooping boy by other boys as each in turn jumps over him. The first as he jumps says "Accroshay," the second "Ashotay," the third "Assheflay," and the last "Lament, lament, Leleeman's (or Leleena's) war." The boy who in jumping knocks off either of the things has to take the place of the stooper.—Cornwall (*Folk-lore Journal*, v. 58).

See "Leap-frog."

All-hid

"A meere children's pastime" (*A Curtaine Lecture*, 1637, p. 206). This is no doubt the game of "Hide and Seek," though Cotgrave apparently makes it synonymous with "Hoodman Blind." See Halliwell's *Dictionary*. It is alluded to in Dekker's *Satiromastix*, "Our unhansomed-fac'd Poet does play at Bo-peepes with your Grace, and cryes All-hidde, as boyes doe." Tourneur, *Rev. Trag.*, III., v. 82, "A lady can at such Al-hid beguile a wiser man," is quoted in Murray's *Dictionary* as the first reference.

All a Row

All a row, a bendy bow,
Shoot at a pigeon and kill a crow ;
Shoot at another and kill his brother ;
Shoot again and kill a wren,
And that 'll do for gentlemen.
—Northall's *English Folk Rhymes*, p. 386.

This is a marching game for very little children, who follow each other in a row.

(*b*) Halliwell gives the first two lines only (*Nursery Rhymes*, No. dxv., p. 101), and there is apparently no other record of this game. It is probably ancient, and formerly of some significance. It refers to days of bows and arrows, and the allusion to the killing of the wren may have reference to the Manx and Irish custom of hunting that bird.

All in the Well

A juvenile game in Newcastle and the neighbourhood. A circle is made, about eight inches in diameter, termed the well, in the centre of which is placed a wooden peg four inches long, with a button balanced on the top. Those desirous of playing give buttons, marbles, or anything else, according to agreement, for the privilege of throwing a short stick, with which they are furnished, at the peg. Should the button fly out of the ring, the player is entitled to double the stipulated value of what he gives for the stick. The game is also practised at the Newcastle Races and other places of amusement in the North with three pegs, which are put into three circular holes made in the ground about two feet apart, and forming a triangle. In this case each hole contains a peg about nine inches long, upon which are deposited either a small knife or some copper. The person playing gives so much for each stick, and gets all the articles that are thrown off so as to fall on the outside of the holes.—Northumberland (Brockett's *North Country Glossary*).

All the Birds in the Air

A Suffolk game, not described (Moor's *Suffolk Glossary*). Jamieson also gives it without description. Compare the rhyme in the game " Fool, fool, come to School," "Little Dog, I call you."

All the Boys in our Town

I.   All the boys in our town
      Shall lead a happy life,
      Except 'tis ——, and he wants a wife.
      A wife he shall have, and a-courting he shall go,
      Along with ——, because he loves her so.
      He huddles her, he cuddles her,
      He sits her on his knee ;
      He says, My dear, do you love me ?
      I love you, and you love me,

And we shall be as happy
As a bird upon a tree.

The wife makes the pudding,
And she makes it nice and soft—
In comes the husband and cuts a slice off.
Tas-el-um, Tos-el-um, don't say Nay,
For next Monday morning shall be our wedding day;
The wife in the carriage,
The husband in the cart.
                    —Hampshire (from friend of Miss Mendham).

II.   All the boys in our town
       Leads a happy life,
       Excepting [Charley Allen],
       And he wants a wife;
       And a-courting he shall go
       Along with [girl's name],
       Because he loves her so.

       He kisses her, he cuddles her,
       He sets her on his knee,
       And says, My dearest darling,
       Do you love me?
       I love you and you love me;
       We'll both be as happy
       As birds on the tree.

       Alice made a pudding,
       She made it nice and sweet,
       Up came Charley, cut a slice off—
       A slice, a slice, we don't say No;
       The next Monday morning the wedding goes
               (or "is our wedding day").
       I've got knives and forks,
       I've got plates and dishes,
       I've got a nice young man,
       He breaks his heart with kisses.

       If poor Alice was to die,
       Wouldn't poor Charley, he *would* cry.

He would follow to the grave
With black buttons and black crape,
And a guinea for the church,
And the bell shall ring.

Up came the doctor, up came the cat,
Up came the devil with a white straw hat.
Down went the doctor, down went the cat,
Down went the devil with a white straw hat.*
                              —Deptford (Miss Chase).

III.   Up the heathery mountains and down the rushy glen
       We dare not go a-hunting for Connor and his men ;
       They are all lusty bachelors but one I know,
       And that's [Tom Mulligan], the flower of the flock ;
       He is the flower of the flock, he is the keeper of the glen,
       He courted [Kate O'Neill] before he was a man ;
       He huggled her, he guggled her, he took her on his knee,
       Saying, My bonnie [Kate O'Neill], won't you marry me ?

       So —— made a pudding so nice and so sweet,
       Saying, Taste, love, taste, and don't say no,
       For next Sunday morning to church we will go.

       With rings on our fingers and bells on our toes,
       And a little baby in her arms, and that's the way she goes.
       And here's a clap, and here's a clap, for Mrs. ——'s
         daughter.   —Belfast (W. H. Patterson).

       IV.   Up the plain and down the plain,
               As stippy [slippery] as a glass,
             We will go to Mrs. ——
               To find a pretty lass.

             [Annie] with her rosy cheeks,
               Catch her if you can,
             And if you cannot catch her
               I'll tell you who's the man.

             [Annie] made a pudding,
               She made it very sweet ;

* Miss Chase says, " I think the order of verses is right ; the children hesitated
a little."

She daren't stick a knife in
Till George came home at neet [night].

Taste [George], taste, and don't say Nay!
Perhaps to-morrow morning 'll be our wedding day.
[The bells shall ring, and we shall sing,
And all clap hands together.] *
                                   —Earls Heaton (Herbert Hardy).

(b) A full description of this game could not be obtained in
each case. The Earls Heaton game is played by forming a ring,
one child standing in the centre. After the first verse is sung, a
child from the ring goes to the one in the centre. Then the rest
of the verses are sung. The action to suit the words of the verses
does not seem to have been kept up. In the Hampshire version,
after the line " As a bird upon a tree," the two children named
pair off like sweethearts while the rest of the verse is being sung.

(c) The analysis of the game rhymes is as follows :—

	Hants.	Deptford (Kent).	Belfast.	Earls Heaton (Yorks.).
1.	Village life.	Village life.	Hunting life.	Roving life.
2.	All the boys happy.	All the boys happy.	All lusty bachelors.	—
3.	Except [ ], who wants a wife.	Except [ ], who wants a wife.	Except [ ], who courts [ ].	—
4.	He shall court [ ].	He shall court [ ].	He courted [ ].	Seeks for a bride.
5.	Huddles and cuddles, and sits on his knee.	Kisses and cuddles, and sits on his knee.	Huggled and guggled, and took on his knee.	—
6.	—	—	—	Catch the bride.
7.	Mutual expressions of love.	Mutual expressions of love.	—	—
8.	—	—	Asking to marry.	—
9.	Wife makes a pudding.	Girl makes a pudding.	Girl makes a pudding.	Girl makes a pudding.
10.	Husband cuts a slice.	Boy cuts a slice.	Asks boy to taste.	Asks boy to taste.
11.	Fixing of wedding day.	Fixing of wedding day.	Fixing of wedding day.	Fixing of wedding day.
12.	Wife in carriage, husband in cart.	Wife with domestic utensils.	Bride with rings on fingers and bells on toes.	—
13.	—	Grief if wife should die.	—	—
14.	—	—	Bride with a baby.	—
15.	—	Doctor, cat, and devil.	—	—
16.	—	—	Applause for the bride.	Applause for the bride.

* Mr. Hardy says, " This was sung to me by a girl at Earls Heaton or Soothill
Nether. Another version commences with the last verse, continues with the first, and
concludes with the second. The last two lines inserted here belong to that version."

It appears by the analysis that all the incidents of the Hants version of this game occur in one or other of the versions, and these incidents therefore may probably be typical of the game. This view would exclude the important incidents of bride capture in the Earls Heaton version; the bride having a baby in the Belfast version, and the two minor incidents in the Deptford version (Nos. 13 and 15 in the analysis), which are obviously supplemental. Chambers, in his *Popular Rhymes of Scotland*, pp. 119, 137, gives two versions of a courtship dance which are not unlike the words of this game, though they do not contain the principal incidents. Northall, in his *English Folk Rhymes*, p. 363, has some verses of a similar import, but not those of the game. W. Allingham seems to have used this rhyme as the commencement of one of his ballads, " Up the airy mountain."

(*d*) The game is clearly a marriage game. It introduces two important details in the betrothal ceremony, inasmuch as the "huddling and cuddling" is typical of the rude customs at marriage ceremonies once prevalent in Yorkshire, the northern counties, and Wales, while the making of the pudding by the bride and the subsequent eating together, are clearly analogies to the bridal-cake ceremony. In Wales, the custom known as " bundling " allowed the betrothing parties to go to bed in their clothes (Brand, ii. 98). In Yorkshire, the bridal cake was always made by the bride. The rudeness of the dialogue seems to be remarkably noticeable in this game.

See " Mary mixed a Pudding up," " Oliver, Oliver, follow the King."

All the Fishes in the Sea

A Suffolk game, not described.—Moor's *Suffolk Glossary*. See " Fool, fool, come to School," " Little Dog, I call you."

All the Soldiers in the Town

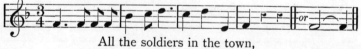

All the soldiers in the town,
They all bop down.
—Sporle, Norfolk (Miss Matthews).

The children form into a ring and sing the above words.
They "bop down" at the close of the verse. To "bop" means
in the Suffolk dialect "to stoop or bow the head."—Moor.

Allicomgreenzie

A little amusing game played by young girls at country
schools. The same as "Drop Handkerchief," except that the
penalty for not following exactly the course of the child pursued is to "stand in the circle, face out, all the game afterwards; if she succeed in catching the one, the one caught
must so stand, and the other take up the cap and go round
as before" (Mactaggart's *Gallovidian Encyclopedia*). No explanation is given of the name of this game.

See "Drop Handkerchief."

Alligoshee

I.   Betsy Blue came all in black,
     Silver buttons down her back.
     Every button cost a crown,
     Every lady turn around.
     Alligoshi, alligoshee,
     Turn the bridle over my knee.
          —Middleton (Burne's *Shropshire Folk-lore*, p. 523).

II.   Barbara, Barbara, dressed in black,
     Silver buttons all up your back.
     Allee-go-shee, allee-go-shee,
     Turn the bridle over me.
          —Shepscombe, Gloucestershire (Miss Mendham).

III.   All-i-go-shee, alligoshee,
     Turn the bridle over my knee.
     My little man is gone to sea,
     When he comes back he'll marry me.
          —Warwickshire (Northall's *Folk Rhymes*, p. 394).

IV.   Darby's son was dressed in black,
     With silver buttons down his back.
     Knee by knee, and foot by foot,
     Turn about lady under the bush.
          —Hersham, Surrey (*Folk-lore Record*, v. 87).

V.   Darby and Joan were dressed in black,
Sword and buckle behind their back.
Foot for foot, and knee for knee,
Turn about Darby's company.
—Halliwell's *Nursery Rhymes*, p. 121.

(*b*) The children form pairs, one pair following the other, with their arms linked behind.   While the first four lines are repeated by all, they skip forward, and then skip back again. At the end of the last line they turn themselves about without loosing hands.

(*c*) Miss Burne includes this among obscure and archaic games; and Halliwell-Phillips mentions it as a marching game. The three first versions have something of the nature of an incantation, while the fourth and fifth versions may probably belong to another game altogether.   It is not clear from the great variation in the verses to which class the game belongs.

Almonds and Reasons

An old English game undescribed.—*Useful Transactions in Philosophy*, 1709, p. 43.

Angel and Devil

One child is called the "Angel," another child the "Devil," and a third child the "Minder."   The children are given the names of colours by the Minder.   Then the Angel comes over and knocks, when the following dialogue takes place.

Minder: "Who's there?"
Answer: "Angel."
Minder: "What do you want?"
Angel: "Ribbons."
Minder: "What colour?"
Angel: "Red."

Minder retorts, if no child is so named, "Go and learn your A B C."   If the guess is right the child is led away.   The Devil then knocks, and the dialogue and action are repeated.— Deptford, Kent (Miss Chase).

See "Fool, fool, come to School."

Auntieloomie

The children join hands, and dance in a circle, " with a front step, a back step, and a side step, round an invisible May-pole," singing—

Can you dance the Auntieloomie?
Yes, I can; yes, I can.

Then follows kissing.—Brigg, Lincolnshire (Miss Peacock).

Babbity Bowster

—Biggar (Wm. Ballantyne).

Wha learned you to dance,
  You to dance, you to dance?
Wha learned you to dance
  Babbity Bowster brawly?

My minnie learned me to dance,
  Me to dance, me to dance;
My minnie learned me to dance
  Babbity Bowster brawly.

Wha ga'e you the keys to keep,
  Keys to keep, keys to keep?
Wha ga'e you the keys to keep,
  Babbity Bowster brawly?

My minnie ga'e me the keys to keep,
  Keys to keep, keys to keep;
My minnie ga'e me the keys to keep,
  Babbity Bowster brawly.

One, twa, three, B, ba, Babbity,
  Babbity Bowster neatly;
Kneel down, kiss the ground,
  An' kiss your bonnie lassie [or laddie].
                    —Biggar (W. H. Ballantyne).

(*b*) Mr. Ballantyne describes the dance as taking place at the end of a country ball. The lads all sat on one side and the girls on the other. It began with a boy taking a handkerchief and dancing before the girls, singing the first verse (fig. 1). Selecting one of the girls, he threw the handkerchief into her lap, or put it round her neck, holding both ends himself. Some spread the handkerchief on the floor at the feet of the girl. The object in either case was to secure a kiss, which, however, was not given without a struggle, the girls cheering their companion at every unsuccessful attempt which the boy

Fig 1   Fig 2

Fig 3   Fig 4

made (fig. 2). A girl then took the handkerchief, singing the next verse (fig. 3), and having thrown the handkerchief to one of the boys, she went off to her own side among the girls, and was pursued by the chosen boy (fig. 4). When all were thus paired, they formed into line, facing each other, and danced somewhat like the country dance of Sir Roger.

(*c*) Chambers' *Popular Rhymes*, p. 36, gives a slightly different version of the verses, and says they were sung by children at their sports in Glasgow. Mactaggart alludes to this game as "'Bumpkin Brawly,' an old dance, the dance which always ends balls; the same with the 'Cushion' almost."

Wha learned you to dance,
You to dance, you to dance,
Wha learned you to dance
A country bumpkin brawly?

My mither learned me when I was young,
When I was young, when I was young,
My mither learned me when I was young,
The country bumpkin brawly."

The tune of this song is always played to the dance, says Mactaggart, but he does not record the tune. *To bab*, in Lowland Scottish, is defined by Jamieson to mean "to play backward and forward loosely; to dance." Hence he adds, "Bab at the bowster, or Bab wi' the bowster, a very old Scottish dance, now almost out of use; formerly the last dance at weddings and merry-makings." Mr. Ballantyne says that a bolster or pillow was at one time always used. One correspondent of *N. and Q.*, ii. 518, says it is now (1850) danced with a handkerchief instead of a cushion as formerly, and no words are used, but later correspondents contradict this. See also *N. and Q.*, iii. 282.

(*d*) Two important suggestions occur as to this game. First, that the dance was originally the indication at a marriage ceremony for the bride and bridegroom to retire with "the bowster" to the nuptial couch. Secondly, that it has degenerated in Southern Britain to the ordinary "Drop Handkerchief" games of kiss in the ring. The preservation of this "Bab at the Bowster" example gives the clue both to the origin of the present game in an obsolete marriage custom, and to the descent of the game to its latest form. See "Cushion Dance."

Bad

A rude kind of "Cricket," played with a bat and a ball, usually with wall toppings for wickets. "Bad" seems to be the pronunciation or variation of "Bat." Halliwell says it was a rude game, formerly common in Yorkshire, and probably resembling the game of "Çat." There is such a game played now, but it is called "Pig."—Easther's *Almondbury Glossary*.

Baddin

The game of "Hockey" in Cheshire.—Holland's *Glossary*.

Badger the Bear

A rough game, sometimes seen in the country. The boy who personates the Bear performs his part on his hands and knees, and is prevented from getting away by a string. It is the part of another boy, his Keeper, to defend him from the attacks of the others.—Halliwell's *Dictionary*.

This is a boys' game, and is called "Buffet the Bear." It may be taken part in by any number. One boy—the Bear—goes down on all fours, and lowers his head towards his breast as much as possible. Into his hand is placed one end of a piece of cord, and another boy, called the Keeper, takes hold of the other end in one hand, while he has in the other his cap. The other boys stand round, some with their caps in hand, and others with their neckties or pocket-handkerchiefs, and on a given signal they rush on the Bear and pelt him, trying specially to buffet him about the ears and face, whilst the Keeper does his best to protect his charge. If he happens to strike a boy, that boy becomes the Bear, and the former Bear becomes the Keeper, and so on the game goes.—Keith, Banff-shire (Rev. W. Gregor).

I saw this game played on Barnes Green, Surrey, on 25th August 1892. The boys, instead of using their hats, had pieces of leather tied to a string, with which they struck the Bear on the back. They could only begin when the Keeper cried, "My Bear is free." If they struck at any other time, the striker became the Bear. It is called "Baste the Bear."—A. B. Gomme.

Chambers (*Popular Rhymes*, p. 128) describes this game under the title of "The Craw." It was played precisely in the same way as the Barnes game. The boy who holds the end of the long strap has also a hard twisted handkerchief, called the *cout;* with this cout he defends the Craw against the attacks of the other boys, who also have similar couts. Before beginning, the Guard of the Craw must call out—

Ane, twa, three, my Craw's free.

The first one he strikes becomes the Craw. When the Guard wants a respite, he calls out—

> Ane, twa, three, my Craw's no free.

(*b*) Jamieson defines "Badger-reeshil" as a severe blow; borrowed, it is supposed, from the hunting of the badger, or from the old game of "Beating the Badger."

> Then but he ran wi' hasty breishell,
> And laid on Hab a badger-reishill. —*MS. Poem.*

Mr. Emslie says he knows it under the name of "Baste the Bear" in London, and Patterson (*Antrim and Down Glossary*) mentions a game similarly named. It is played at Marlborough under the name of "Tom Tuff."—H. S. May.

See "Doncaster Cherries."

Bag o' Malt

> A bag o' malt, a bag o' salt,
> Ten tens a hundred.
> —Northall's *English Folk Rhymes*, p. 394.

Two children stand back to back, linked near the armpits, and weigh each other as they repeat these lines.

See "Weigh the Butter."

Ball

> I. Stottie ba', hinnie ba, tell to me
> How mony bairns am I to hae?
> Ane to live, and ane to dee,
> And ane to sit on the nurse's knee!
> —Chambers' *Pop. Rhymes of Scotland*, p. 115.

> II. Toss-a-ball, toss-a-ball, tell me true,
> How many years I've got to go through!
> —Burne's *Shropshire Folk-lore*, p. 530.

(*b*) Children throw a ball in the air, repeating the rhyme, and divine the length of their lives by the number of times they can catch it again. In some places this game is played with a cowslip ball, thence called a "tissy-ball."

(*c*) I have heard other rhymes added to this, to determine whether the players shall marry or not, the future husband's calling, dress to be worn, method of going to church, &c. (A. B.

Gomme). Strutt describes a handball game played during the Easter holidays for Tansy cakes (*Sports*, p. 94). Halliwell gives rhymes for ball divination (*Popular Rhymes*, p. 298) to determine the number of years before marriage will arrive. Miss Baker (*Northamptonshire Glossary*) says, "The May garland is suspended by ropes from the school-house to an opposite tree, and the Mayers amuse themselves by throwing balls over it. A native of Fotheringay, Mr. C. W. Peach," says Miss Baker, "has supplied me with the reminiscences of his own youth. He says the May garland was hung in the centre of the street, on a rope stretched from house to house. Then was made the trial of skill in tossing balls (small white leather ones) through the framework of the garland, to effect which was a triumph."

See "Cuck Ball," "Keppy Ball," "Monday."

Ball and Bonnets

This is a boys' game. The players may be of any number. They place their caps or bonnets in a row. One of the boys takes a ball, and from a fixed point, at a few yards' distance from the bonnets, tries to throw it into one of the caps (fig. 1).

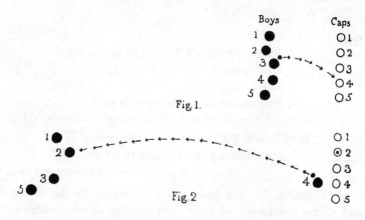

If the ball falls into the cap, all the boys, except the one into whose cap the ball has fallen, run off. The boy into whose cap the ball has been thrown goes up to it, lifts the ball from it, and calls out "Stop!" The other boys stop. The boy with the ball tries to strike one of the other boys (fig. 2).   If he does so, a small stone is put into the cap of the boy struck.   If he misses, a stone is put into his own cap.   If the boy who is to pitch the ball into the cap misses, a stone is put into his own cap, and he makes another trial.   The game goes on till six stones are put into one cap.   The boy in whose cap are the six stones has to place his hand against a wall, when he receives a certain number of blows with the ball thrown with force by one of the players.   The blows go by the name of " buns."   The game may go on in the same way till each player gets his " buns."—Nairn (Rev. W. Gregor).

See "Hats in Holes."

Ball in the Decker

A row of boys' caps is set by a wall.   One boy throws a ball into one of the caps.   The owner of the cap runs away, and is chased by all the others till caught.   He then throws the ball. —Dublin (Mrs. Lincoln).

Ball of Primrose

We'll wear yellow ribbons, yellow ribbons, yellow ribbons,
We'll wear yellow ribbons at the Ball of Primrose;
We'll all go a-waltzing, a-waltzing, a-waltzing,
We'll all go a-waltzing at the Ball of Primrose.
—Epworth, Doncaster; and Lossiemouth, Yorkshire
(Charles C. Bell).

(*b*) The children form a ring, joining hands, and dance round singing the two first lines.   Then loosing hands, they waltz in couples, singing as a refrain the last line.   The game is continued, different coloured ribbons being named each time.

(*c*) This game was played in 1869, so cannot have arisen from the political movement.

Baloon

A game played with an inflated ball of strong leather, the ball being struck by the arm, which was defended by a bracer of wood.—Brand's *Pop. Antiq.*, ii. 394.

(*b*) It is spelt "balloo" in Ben Jonson, iii. 216, and "baloome" in Randolph's *Poems*, 1643, p. 105. It is also mentioned in Middleton's *Works*, iv. 342, and by Donne.

> " 'Tis ten a clock and past; all whom the mues,
> *Baloun*, tennis, diet, or the stews
> Had all the morning held."
> —Donne's *Poems*, p. 133.

Toone (*Etymological Dict.*) says it is a game rather for exercise than contention; it was well known and practised in England in the fourteenth century, and is mentioned as one of the sports of Prince Henry, son of James I., in 1610. Strutt (*Sports and Pastimes*, p. 96) gives two illustrations of what he considers to be baloon ball play, from fourteenth century MSS.

Bandy-ball

A game played with sticks called "bandies," bent and round at one end, and a small wooden ball, which each party endeavours to drive to opposite fixed points. Northbrooke in 1577 mentions it as a favourite game in Devonshire (Halliwell's *Dict. of Provincialisms*). Strutt says the bat-stick was called a "bandy" on account of its being bent, and gives a drawing from a fourteenth century MS. book of prayers belonging to Mr. Francis Douce (*Sports*, p. 102). The bats in this drawing are nearly identical with modern golf-sticks, and "Golf" seems to be derived from this game. Peacock mentions it in his *Glossary of Manley and Corringham Words*. Forby has an interesting note in his *Vocabulary of East Anglia*, i. 14. He says, "The bandy was made of very tough wood, or shod with metal, or with the point of the horn or the hoof of some animal. The ball is a knob or gnarl from the trunk of a tree, carefully formed into a globular shape. The adverse parties strive to beat it with their bandies through one or other of the goals."

Bandy Cad or Gad

A game played with a nurr and crooked stick, also called "Shinty," and much the same as the "Hockey" of the South of England. "Cad" is the same as "cat" in the game of "Tip-cat;" it simply means a cut piece of wood.—Nodal and Milner's *Lancashire Glossary*.

Bandy-hoshoe

A game at ball common in Norfolk, and played in a similar manner to "Bandy" (Halliwell's *Dictionary*). Toone (*Etymological Dictionary*) says it is also played in Suffolk, and in West Sussex is called "Hawky."

Bandy-wicket

The game of "Cricket," played with a bandy instead of a bat (Halliwell's *Dictionary*). Toone mentions it as played in Norfolk (*Dict.*), and Moor as played in Suffolk with bricks usually, or, in their absence, with bats in place of bails or stumps (*Suffolk Words*).

Banger

Each boy provides himself with a button. One of the boys lays his button on the ground, near a wall. The other boys snap their buttons in turn against the wall. If the button drops within one span or hand-reach of the button laid down, it counts two (fig. 2); if within two spans, it counts one.

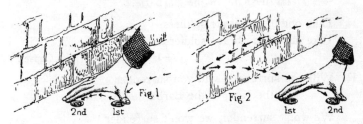

When it hits the button and bounces within one span, it counts four (fig. 1); within two spans, three; and above three spans, one. Each player snaps in turn for an agreed number; the first to score this number wins the game.—Deptford, Kent, and generally in London streets (Miss Chase).

This game is known in America as "Spans."—Newell, p. 188.

Bar

To play at "Bar," a species of game anciently used in Scotland.—Jamieson.

This game had in ancient times in England been simply denominated "Bars," or, as in an Act of James IV., 1491, edit. 1814, p. 227: "That na induellare within burgh . . . play at bar," "playing at Bars."

See "Prisoner's Base."

Barbarie, King of the

I. O will you surrender, O will you surrender
    To the King of the Barbarie?

We won't surrender, we won't surrender
    To the King of the Barbarie.

I'll go and complaint, I'll go and complaint
    To the King of the Barbarie.

You can go and complaint, you can go and complaint
    To the King of the Barbarie.

Good morning, young Prince, good morning, young Prince,
    I have a complaint for you.

What is your complaint?
What is your complaint?

They won't surrender, they won't surrender
    To the King of the Barbarie.

Take one of my brave soldiers,
Take one of my brave soldiers.
                                        —Deptford, Kent (Miss Chase).

II. Will you surrender, will you surrender
    To the King of the Barbarines?

We won't surrender, we won't surrender
    To the King of the Barbarines.

We'll make you surrender, we'll make you surrender
    To the King of the Barbarines.

You can't make us surrender, you can't make us surrender
    To the King of the Barbarines.

We'll go to the King, we'll go the King,
 To the King of the Barbarines.

You can go to the King, you can go to the King,
 To the King of the Barbarines.
   —Clapham, Surrey (Miss F. D. Richardson).

III. Will you surrender, will you surrender
  The Tower of Barbaree ?

We won't surrender, we won't surrender
 The Tower of Barbaree.

We will go and tell the Queen,
Go and tell the Queen of Barbaree.

Don't care for the Queen, don't care for the Queen,
 The Queen of Barbaree.

Good morning, young Queen, good morning, young Queen,
 I have a complaint to thee.

Pray what is your complaint to me ?

They won't surrender, they won't surrender
 The Tower of Barbaree.

Take one of my brave soldiers.
  —Lady Camilla Gurdon's *Suffolk County Folk-lore*, p. 63.

IV. You must surrend' me, you must surrend' me
  To the Queen of Barbaloo.

No, we'll not surrend' you, no, we'll not surrend' you
 To the Queen of Barbaloo.

We'll complain, we'll complain, &c.
 [To the Queen of Barbaloo.]

You can complain, you can complain, &c.
 [To the Queen of Barbaloo.]
   —Penzance (Mrs. Mabbott).

(*b*) Two children stand together joining hands tightly, to personate a fortress ; one child stands at a distance from these to personate the King of Barbarie, with other children standing behind to personate the soldiers (fig. 1). Some of the soldiers

go to the fortress and surround it, singing the first verse (fig. 2).
The children in the fortress reply, the four first verses being
thus sung alternately.   The soldiers then go to the King
singing the fifth verse (fig. 3), the remaining verses being thus
sung alternately.   One of the soldiers then goes to the fortress
and endeavours by throwing herself on the clasped hands of
the children forming the fortress to break down the guard

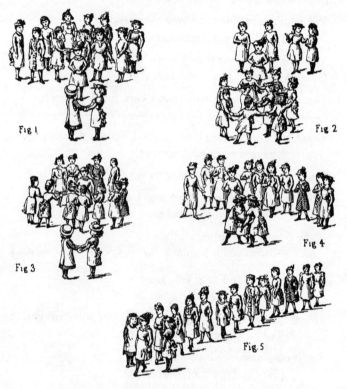

(fig. 4).   All the soldiers try to do this, one after the other;
finally the King comes, who breaks down the guard.   The whole
troop of soldiers then burst through the parted arms (fig. 5).

This is the Deptford version.   The Clapham version is
almost identical; the children take hold of each others' skirts
and make a long line.   If the brave soldier is not able to break
the clasped hands he goes to the end of the line of soldiers.

The soldiers do not surround the fortress. In the Suffolk version the soldiers try to break through the girls' hands. If they do they have the tower. The Cornwall version is not so completely an illustration of the capture of a fortress.

Barley-break

Barley-break, or the Last Couple in Hell, was a game played by six people, three of each sex, who were coupled by lot. A piece of ground was then chosen, and divided into three compartments, of which the middle one was called Hell. It was the object of the couple condemned to this division to catch the others who advanced from the two extremities (figs. 1, 2), in which case a change of situation took place, and Hell was filled by the couple who were excluded by pre-occupation from

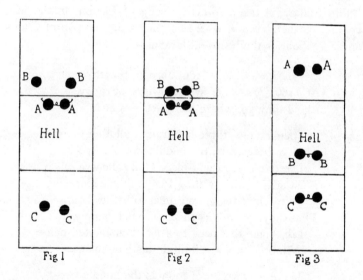

Fig 1   Fig 2   Fig 3

the other place (fig. 3). In this catching, however, there was some difficulty, as by the regulations of the game the middle couple were not to separate before they had succeeded, while the others might break hands whenever they found themselves hard pressed. When all had been taken in turn, the last couple was said to be "in Hell," and the game ended.— Dekker's *Works*, iv. 434.

Jamieson calls this "a game generally played by young people in a corn-yard. Hence called *barla-bracks about the stacks*, S. B." (*i.e.*, in the North of Scotland). "One stack is fixed on as the *dule* or goal; and one person is appointed to catch the rest of the company, who run out from the *dule*. He does not leave it till they are all out of sight. Then he sets off to catch them. Any one who is taken cannot run out again with his former associates, being accounted a prisoner; but is obliged to assist his captor in pursuing the rest. When all are taken the game is finished; and he who was first taken is bound to act as catcher in the next game. This innocent sport seems to be almost entirely forgotten in the South of Scotland. It is also falling into desuetude in the North."

(*b*) The following description of Barley-break, written by Sir Philip Sidney, is taken from the song of Lamon, in the first volume of the *Arcadia*, where he relates the passion of Claius and Strephon for the beautiful Urania :—

> She went abroad, thereby,
> At *barley-brake* her sweet, swift foot to try. . . .
> Afield they go, where many lookers be.
>
> Then couples three be straight allotted there,
> They of both ends, the middle two, do fly ;
>   The two that in mid-place Hell called were
> Must strive, with waiting foot and watching eye,
>   To catch of them, and them to hell to bear,
> That they, as well as they, may hell supply ;
>   Like some that seek to salve their blotted name
>   Will others blot, till all do taste of shame.
>
> There may you see, soon as the middle two
> Do, coupled, towards either couple make,
>   They, false and fearful, do their hands undo ;
> Brother his brother, friend doth friend forsake,
>   Heeding himself, cares not how fellow do,
> But of a stranger mutual help doth take ;
>   As perjured cowards in adversity,
>   With sight of fear, from friends to friends do fly.

Sir John Suckling also has given a description of this pastime with allegorical personages, which is quoted by Brand. In Holiday's play of the *Marriages of the Arts*, 1618, this sport is introduced, and also by Herrick (*Hesperides*, p. 44). Barley-break is several times alluded to in Massinger's plays: see the *Dramatic Works of Philip Massinger*, 1779, i. 167. "We'll run at barley-break first, and you shall be in hell" (Dekker's *The Honest Whore*). "Hee's at barli-break, and the last couple are now in hell" (Dekker's *The Virgin Martir*). See Gifford's *Massinger*, i. 104, edit. 1813. See also Browne's *Britannia's Pastorals*, published in 1614, Book I., Song 3, p. 76.

Randle Holme mentions this game as prevailing in his day in Lancashire. Harland and Wilkinson believe this game to have left its traces in Yorkshire and Lancashire. A couple link hands and sally forth from *home*, shouting something like

> Aggery, ag, ag,
> Ag's gi'en warning,

and trying to tick or touch with the free hand any of the boys running about separately. These latter try to slip behind the couple and throw their weight on the joined hands to separate them without being first touched or ticked; and if they sunder the couple, each of the severed ones has to carry one home on his back. Whoever is touched takes the place of the toucher in the linked couple (*Legends of Lancashire*, p. 138). The modern name of this game is "Prison Bars" (*Ibid.*, p. 141). There is also a description of the game in a little tract called *Barley Breake ; or, A Warning for Wantons*, 1607. It is mentioned in Wilbraham's *Cheshire Glossary* as "an old Cheshire game." Barnes, in his *Dorsetshire Glossary*, says he has seen it played with one catcher on hands and knees in the small ring (Hell), and the others dancing round the ring crying "Burn the wold witch, you barley breech." Holland (*Cheshire Glossary*) also mentions it as an old Cheshire game.

See "Boggle about the Stacks," "Scots and English."

Barnes (Mr.)

> Mr. Barnes is dead and gone,
> And left his widder,

Three poor children in her arms;
What will you give her?

Where did you come from?
—Played about 1850 at Hurstmonceaux,
Sussex (Miss Chase).

This is probably a forfeit game, imperfectly remembered.
See "Old Soldier."

Base-ball

An undescribed Suffolk game.—Moor's *Suffolk Words*.
See "Rounders."

Basket

—London (A. B. Gomme).

In this game the children all follow one who is styled the
"mother," singing:

I'll follow my mother to market,
To buy a silver basket.

The mother presently turns and catches or pretends to beat
them.—Dorsetshire (*Folk-lore Journal*, vii. 231).

We'll follow our mother to market,
To buy herself a basket;
When she comes home she'll break our bones,
We'll follow our mother to market.
—Hersham, Surrey (*Folk-lore Record*, v. 84).

A version familiar to me is the same as above, but ending
with

For tumbling over cherry stones.

The mother then chased and beat those children she caught.
The idea was, I believe, that the children were imitating or
mocking their mother (A. B. G.). In Warwickshire the four

lines of the Surrey game are concluded by the additional
lines—

> We don't care whether we work or no,
> We'll follow our mother on tipty-toe.

When the mother runs after them and buffets them.—Northall's
English Folk Rhymes, p. 393.

Battledore and Shuttlecock

See "Shuttlefeather."

Bedlams or Relievo

A number of boys agree to play at this game, and sides are
picked. Five, for example, play on each side. A square is
chalked out on a footpath by the side of a road, which is called
the "Den;" five of the boys remain by the side of the Den, one
of whom is called the "Tenter;" the Tenter has charge of the
Den, and he must always stand with one foot in the Den and the

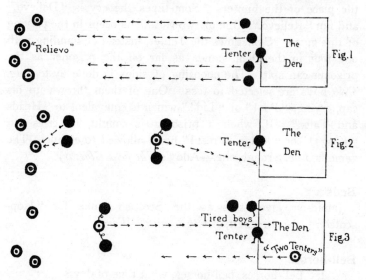

other upon the road; the remaining five boys go out to field,
it being agreed beforehand that they shall only be allowed
to run within a prescribed area, or in certain roads or streets
(fig. 1). As soon as the boys who have gone out to field have
reached a certain distance—there is no limit prescribed—they

shout "Relievo," and upon this signal the four boys standing by the side of the Den pursue them, leaving the Tenter in charge of the Den (fig. 2). When a boy is caught he is taken to the Den, where he is obliged to remain, unless the Tenter puts both his feet into the Den, or takes out the one foot which he ought always to keep in the Den. If the Tenter is thus caught tripping, the prisoner can escape from the Den. If during the progress of the game one of the boys out at field runs through the Den shouting "Relievo" without being caught by the Tenter, the prisoner is allowed to escape, and join his comrades at field. If one of the boys out at field is tired, and comes to stand by the side of the Den, he is not allowed to put his foot into the Den. If he does so the prisoner calls out, "There are two Tenters," and escapes if he can (fig. 3). When all the boys out at field have been caught and put into the Den, the process is reversed—the boys who have been, as it were, hunted, taking the place of the hunters. Sometimes the cry is "Delievo," and not "Relievo." One or two variations occur in the playing of this game. Sometimes the Tenter, instead of standing with one foot in the Den, stands as far off the prisoner as the prisoner can spit. The choosing of sides is done by tossing. Two boys are selected to toss. One of them throws up his cap, crying, "Pot!" or "Lid!" which is equivalent to "Heads and Tails." If, when a prisoner is caught, he cries out "Kings!" or "Kings to rest!" he is allowed to escape. The game is a very rough one.—Addy's *Sheffield Glossary*.

Beds

Jamieson gives this as the Scottish name for "Hop-scotch;" also Brockett, *North Country Words*.

Bell-horses

I.   Bell-horses, bell-horses, what time of day?
      One o'clock, two o'clock, three, and away!
      Bell-horses, bell-horses, what time of day?
      Two o'clock, three o'clock, four, and away!
      Five o'clock, six o'clock, now time to stay!
          —Stanton Lacey (Burne's *Shropshire Folk-lore*, p. 520).

II.   Bellasay, bellasay, what time of day ?
       One o'clock, two o'clock, three, and away.
                        —Halliwell's *Nursery Rhymes*, p. 283.

(*b*) The children form long trains, standing one behind the
other.   They march and sing the first four lines, then the fifth
line, when they stand and begin again as before.

(*c*) Miss Burne suggests a connection with the old pack-
horses.   Mr. Addy (*Sheffield Glossary*) gives the first two
lines as a game.   He says, " The first horse in a team conveying lead to be smelted wore bells, and was called the bell-
horse."   I remember when a child the two first lines being
used to start children a race (A. B. G.).   Chambers (*Pop.
Rhymes*, p. 148) gives a similar verse, used for starting a race :—
       Race horses, race horses, what time of day ?
       One o'clock, two o'clock, three, and away ;
and these lines are also used for the same purpose in Cheshire
(Holland's *Glossary*) and Somersetshire (Elworthy's *Glossary*).
Halliwell, on the strength of the corrupted word " Bellasay,"
connects the game with a proverbial saying applied to the family
of Bellasis ; but there is no evidence of such a connection
except the word-corruption.   The rhyme occurs in *Gammer
Gurton's Garland*, 1783, the last words of the second line
being " time to away."

Bellie-mantie

The name for " Blind Man's Buff " in Upper Clydesdale.   As
anciently in this game he who was the chief actor was not
only hoodwinked, but enveloped in the skin of an animal.—
Jamieson.

See " Blind Man's Buff."

Belly-blind

The name for " Blind Man's Buff " in Roxburgh, Clydesdale, and other counties of the border.   It is probable that the
term is the same with " Billy Blynde," said to be the name of a
familiar spirit or good genius somewhat similar to the brownie.—
Jamieson.

See " Blind Man's Buff."

Bend-leather

A boys' phrase for a slide on a pond when the ice is thin and bends. There is a game on the ice called playing at "Bend-leather." Whilst the boys are sliding they say "Bend-leather, bend-leather, puff, puff, puff."—Addy's *Sheffield Glossary*.

Betsy Bungay

Hi, Betsy Bungay, all day on Sunday;
You're the lock and I'm the key,
All day on Monday.   —Kent (J. P. Emslie).

Two children cross their hands in the fashion known as a "sedan chair." A third child sits on their hands. The two sing the first line. One of them sings, "You're the lock," the other sings, "and I'm the key," and as they sang the words they unclasped their hands and dropped their companion on the ground. Mr. J. P. Emslie writes, "My mother learned this from her mother, who was a native of St. Laurence, in the Isle of Thanet. The game possibly belongs to Kent."

Bicky

In Somersetshire the game of "Hide and Seek." *To bik'ee* is for the seekers to go and lean their heads against a wall, so as not to see where the others go to hide.—Elworthy's *Dialect*.

See "Hide and Seek."

Biddy-base

A Lincolnshire name for "Prisoner's Base."—Halliwell's *Dictionary;* Peacock's *Manley and Corringham Glossary;* Cole's *S. W. Lincolnshire Glossary*.

Biggly

Name for "Blind Man's Buff."—Dickinson's *Cumberland Glossary*.

Billet

The Derbyshire name for "Tip-cat."—Halliwell's *Dictionary*.

Billy-base

A name for "Prisoner's Base."—Halliwell's *Dictionary*.

Bingo

—Leicestershire.

—Hexham.

—Derbyshire.

—Earls Heaton, Yorks.

—Enborne.

I.   The miller's mill-dog lay at the mill-door,
     And his name was Little Bingo.
     B with an I, I with an N, N with a G, G with an O,
     And his name was Little Bingo.

The miller he bought a cask of ale,
And he called it right good Stingo.
S with a T, T with an I, I with an N, N with a G,
    G with an O,
And he called it right good Stingo.

The miller he went to town one day,
And he bought a wedding Ring-o!
R with an I, I with an N, N with a G, G with an O,
And he bought a wedding Ring-o!
                              —Monton, Lancashire (Miss Dendy).

II.   A farmer's dog lay on the floor,
           And Bingo was his name O!
       B, i, n, g, o, B, i, n, g, o,
           And Bingo was his name O!

       The farmer likes a glass of beer,
           I think he calls it Stingo!
       S, t, i, n, g, o, S, t, i, n, g, o!
           I think he calls it Stingo!
       S, t, i, n, g, O!   I think he calls it Stingo!
               —Market Drayton, Ellesmere, Oswestry (Burne's
                   Shropshire Folk-lore, p. 513).

III.   There was a jolly farmer,
       And he had a jolly son,
       And his name was Bobby Bingo.
       BINGO, BINGO, BINGO,
       And Bingo was his name.
           —Liphook, Hants ; Wakefield, Yorks (Miss Fowler).

IV.   There *was* a farmer *had* a dog,
       His name was Bobby Bingo.
       B-i-n-g-o, B-i-n-g-o, B-i-n-g-o,
       His name was Bobby Bingo.
     —Tean, Staffs. ; and North Staffs. Potteries (Miss Keary).

V.   The farmer's dog lay on the hearth,
       And Bingo was his name oh !
       B-i-n-g-o, B-i-n-g-o, B-i-n-g-o,
       And Bingo was his name oh !
                              —Nottinghamshire (Miss Winfield).

VI.   The miller's dog lay on the wall,
And Bingo was his name Oh!
B-i-n-g-o,
And Bingo was his name Oh!
—Maxey, Northants (Rev. W. D. Sweeting).

VII.   The shepherd's dog lay on the hearth,
And Bingo was his name O.
B i n g o, Bi, n, g, o, Bi-n-g-o,
And Bingo was his name O.
—Eckington, Derbyshire (S. O. Addy).

VIII.   Pinto went to sleep one night,
And Pinto was his name oh!
P-i-n-t-o, P-i-n-t-o,
And Pinto was his name oh.
—Enbourne, Berks (Miss Kimber).

(*b*) In the Lancashire version, one child represents the Miller. The rest of the children stand round in a circle, with the Miller in the centre. All dance round and sing the verses. When it comes to the spelling part of the rhyme, the Miller points at one child, who must call out the right letter. If the child fails to do this she becomes Miller. In the Shropshire version, a ring is formed with one player in the middle. They dance round and sing the verses. When it comes to the spelling part, the girl in the middle cries B, and signals to another, who says I, the next to her N, the third G, the fourth "O! his name was Bobby Bingo!" Whoever makes a mistake takes the place of the girl in the middle. In the Liphook version, at the fourth line the children stand still and repeat a letter each in turn as quickly as they can, clapping their hands, and at the last line they turn right round, join hands, and begin again. In the Tean version, the one in the centre points, standing still, to some in the ring to say the letters B.I.N.G; the letter O has to be sung; if not, the one who says it goes in the ring, and repeats it all again until the game is given up. In the other Staffordshire version, when they stop, the one in the middle points to five of the others in turn, who have to say the letters forming "Bingo," while the one to whom O comes has to sing it on the note on which the others left off. Any one who says the wrong letter, or fails to sing the O right, takes the place of the middle one. The Northants version follows the Lancashire version, but if the answers are all made correctly, the last line is sung by the circle, and the game begins again. In the Metheringham version the child in the centre is blindfolded. When the song is over the girls say, "Point with your finger as we go round." The girl in the centre points accordingly, and whichever of the others happens to be opposite to her when she says "Stop!" is caught. If the blindfolded girl can identify her captive they exchange places, and the game goes on as before. The Forest of Dean and the Earls Heaton versions are played the same as the Lancashire. In the West Cornwall version, as seen played in 1884, a ring is formed, into the middle of which goes a child holding a stick; the others with joined hands run round in a circle, singing the verses. When they have finished singing they cease running, whilst the one in the centre, pointing with his stick, asks them in turn to spell Bingo. If they all spell it correctly they again move round singing; but should either of them make a mistake, he or she has to take the place of the middle man (*Folk-lore Journal*, v. 58). In the Hexham version they sing a second verse, which is the same as the first with the name spelt *backwards*. The Berks version is practically the same as the Tean version. The Eckington (Derbyshire) version is played as follows:—A number of young women form a ring. A man stands within the ring, and they sing the words. He then makes choice of a girl, who takes his arm. They both walk round the circle while the others sing the same lines again. The girl who has been chosen makes choice of a young man in the ring, who in his turn chooses another girl, and so on till they have all paired off.

(*c*) The first verse of the Shropshire version is also sung at Metheringham, near Lincoln (C. C. Bell), and Cowes, I.W. (Miss E. Smith). The Staffordshire version of the words is sung in Forest of Dean, Gloucestershire (Miss Matthews), West Cornwall (*Folk-lore Journal*, v. 58), Earls Heaton, Yorkshire (H. Hardy), Hexham, Northumberland (Miss Barker),

Leicester (Miss Ellis).   Miss Peacock says, "A version is known in Lincolnshire." Tunes have also been sent from Tean, North Staffs. (Miss Keary), and Epworth, Doncaster (Mr. C. C. Bell), which are nearly identical with the Leicester tune; from Market Drayton (Miss Burne), similar to the Derbyshire tune; from Monton, Lancashire (Miss Dendy), which appears to be only the latter part of the tune, and is similar to those given above. The tune given by Rimbault is not the same as those collected above, though there is a certain similarity.

The editor of *Northamptonshire Notes and Queries*, vol. i. p. 214, says, "Some readers will remember that Byngo is the name of the 'Franklyn's dogge' that Ingoldsby introduces into a few lines described as a portion of a primitive ballad, which has escaped the researches of Ritson and Ellis, but is yet replete with beauties of no common order." In the *Nursery Songs* collected by Ed. Rimbault from oral tradition is "Little Bingo." The words of this are very similar to the Lancashire version of the game sent by Miss Dendy. There is an additional verse in the nursery song.

Bird-apprentice

A row of boys or girls stands parallel with another row opposite. Each of the first row chooses the name of some bird, and a member of the other row then calls out all the names of birds he can think of. If the middle member of the first row has chosen either of them, he calls out "Yes," and all the guessers immediately run to take the place of the first row, the members of which attempt to catch them. If any succeed, they have the privilege of riding in on their captives' backs.—Ogbourne, Wilts (H. S. May).

Birds, Beasts, and Fishes

$$B \times \times \times \times \times \times \times h = Bullfinch$$
$$E \times \times \times \times \times \times t \quad = Elephant$$
$$S \times \times \times \times \times \times \times h = Swordfish$$

This is a slate game, and two or more children play. One writes the initial and final letters of a bird's, beast's, or fish's name, making crosses (×) instead of the intermediate letters of the word, stating whether the name is that of bird, beast, or fish. The other players must guess in turn what the name is. The first one who succeeds takes for himself the same number of marks as there are crosses in the word, and then writes the name of anything he chooses in the same manner. If the players are unsuccessful in guessing the name, the writer takes the number to his own score and writes another. The game is won when one player gains a certain number of marks previously decided upon as "game."—Barnes (A. B. Gomme).

Bittle-battle

The Sussex game of "Stoolball." There is a tradition that this game was originally played by the milkmaids with their milking-stools, which they used for bats; but this word makes it more probable that the stool was the wicket, and that it was defended with the bittle, which would be called the bittle-bat.—Parish's *Sussex Dialect*.

See "Stoolball."

Bitty-base

Bishop Kennet (in *MS. Lansd.* 1033) gives this name as a term for "Prisoner's Base."—Halliwell's *Dictionary*.

Black Man's Tig

A long rope is tied to a gate or pole, and one of the players holds the end of the rope, and tries to catch another player. When he succeeds in doing so the one captured joins him (by holding hands) and helps to catch the other players. The game is finished when all are caught.—Cork (Miss Keane).

Black Thorn

—Earls Heaton, Yorks.

I.   Blackthorn!
     Butter-milk and barley-corn;

How many geese have you to-day?
As many as you can catch and carry away.
—Monton, Lancashire (Miss Dendy).

II.   Blackthorn! Blackthorn!
Blue milk and barley-corn;
How many geese have you to-day?
More than you can catch and carry away.
—Harland and Wilkinson's *Lancashire Folk-lore*, p. 150.

III.   Blackthorn!
New milk and barley-corn;
How many sheep have you to sell?
More nor yo can catch and fly away wi'.
—Addy's *Sheffield Glossary*.

IV.   Blackthorn!
Butter-milk and barley-corn;
How many sheep have you to-day?
As many as you catch and carry away.
—Earls Heaton, Yorkshire (Herbert Hardy).

(*b*) One set of children stand against a wall, another set stand opposite, facing them. The first set sing the first line, the others replying with the second line, and so with the third and fourth lines. The two sides then rush over to each other, and the second set are caught. The child who is caught last becomes one of the first set for another game. This is the Earls Heaton version. The Lancashire game, as described by Miss Dendy, is: One child stands opposite a row of children, and the row run over to the opposite side, when the one child tries to catch them. The prisoners made, join the one child, and assist her in the process of catching the others. The rhyme is repeated in each case until all are caught, the last one out becoming "Blackthorn" for a new game. Harland and Wilkinson describe the game somewhat differently. Each player has a mark, and after the dialogue the players run over to each other's marks, and if any can be caught before getting home to the opposite mark, he has to carry his captor to the mark, when he takes his place as an additional catcher.

(*c*) Miss Burne's version (*Shropshire Folk-lore*, p. 521) is practically the same as the Earls Heaton game, and Easther in his *Almondbury Glossary* gives a version practically like the Sheffield.   Mr. Hardy says it is sometimes called "Black-butt," when the opposite side cry "Away we cut."   Miss Dendy quotes an old Lancashire rhyme, which curiously refers to the different subjects in the Lancashire game rhyme.   It is as follows :—

> Little boy, little boy, where were you born ?
> Way up in Lancashire, under a thorn,
> Where they sup butter-milk in a ram's horn.

Another version is given in *Notes and Queries*, 3rd Series, vii. 285.

(*d*) This is a dramatic game, in which the children seem to personate animals, and to depict events belonging to the history of the flock.   Miss Burne groups it under her "dramatic games."

Blind Bell

A game formerly common in Berwickshire, in which all the players were hoodwinked except the person who was called the Bell.   He carried a bell, which he rung, still endeavouring to keep out of the way of his hoodwinked partners in the game.   When he was taken, the person who seized him was released from the bandage, and got possession of the bell, the bandage being transferred to him who was laid hold of.— Jamieson.

(*b*) In "The Modern Playmate," edited by Rev. J. G. Wood, this game is described under the name of "Jingling."   Mr. Wood says there is a rougher game played at country feasts and fairs in which a pig takes the place of the boy with the bell, but he does not give the locality (p. 7).   Strutt also describes it (*Sports*, p. 317).

Blind Bucky-Davy

In Somersetshire the game of "Blind Man's Buff."   Also in Cornwall (see Couch's *Polperro*, p. 173).   Pulman says this means "Blind buck and have ye" (Elworthy's *Dialect*).

Blind Harie
A name for "Blind Man's Buff."—Jamieson.

Blind Hob
The Suffolk name for "Blind Man's Buff.—Halliwell's *Dictionary;* Moor's *Suffolk Glossary.*

Blind Man's Buff
I. Come, shepherd, come, shepherd, and count your sheep.
I canna come now, for I'm fast asleep.
If you don't come now they'll all be gone.
What's in my way?
A bottle of hay.
Am I over it?
            —Shrewsbury (Burne's *Shropshire Folk-lore*, p. 525).

  II. How many fingers do I hold up?
  Four, three, &c. [at random in reply].
  How many horses has your father?
  Three [fixed reply].
  What colour?
  White, red, and grey.
  Turn you about three times;
  Catch whom you may!   —Deptford (Miss Chase).

III. How many horses has your father got in his stables?
Three.
What colour are they?
Red, white, and grey.
Then turn about, and twist about, and catch whom you
  may.
            —Cornwall (*Folk-lore Journal*, v. 57, 58).

IV. Antony Blindman kens ta me
Sen I bought butter and cheese o' thee?
I ga' tha my pot,
I ga' tha my pan,
I ga' tha a' I hed but a rap ho'penny I gave a poor oald
  man.   —Cumberland (Dickinson's *Glossary*).

(*b*) In the Deptford version one of the players is blindfolded. The one who blindfolds ascertains that the player cannot see by putting the first question. When the players are satisfied that the blindfolding is complete, the dialogue follows, and the blind man is turned round three times. The game is for him to catch one of the players, who is blindfolded in turn if the blind man succeeds in guessing who he is. Players are allowed to pull, pinch, and buffet the blind man.

(*c*) This sport is found among the illuminations of an old missal formerly in the possession of John Ives, cited by Strutt in his *Manners and Customs*. The two illustrations are fac-similes from drawings in one of the Bodleian MSS., and they

indicate the complete covering of the head, and also the fact that the game was played by adults. Gay says concerning it—

> As once I play'd at *blindman's-buff*, it hap't,
> *About my eyes the towel thick was wrapt.*
> *I miss'd the swains, and seiz'd on Blouzelind.*

And another reference is quoted by Brand (ii. 398)—

> Sometyme the one would goe, sometyme the other,
> Sometymes all thre at once, and sometyme neither;
> Thus they with him play at boyes blynde-man-bluffe.
>   —*The Newe Metamorphosis*, 1600, MS.

Other names for this game are "Belly Mantie," "Billy Blind," "Blind Bucky Davy," "Blind Harie," "Blind Hob," "Blind Nerry Mopsey," "Blind Palmie," "Blind Sim," "Buck Hid,"

" Chacke Blynd Man," " Hoodle-cum-blind," " Hoodman Blind,"
" Hooper's Hide," " Jockie Blind Man."

(*d*) There is some reason for believing that this game can
be traced up to very ancient rites connected with prehistoric
worship. The name " Billy Blind " denoted the person who
was blindfolded in the game, as may be seen by an old poem
by Lyndsay, quoted by Jamieson :

War I ane King
I sould richt sone mak reformatioun
Farlyeand thairof your grace sould richt sone finde
That Preistis sall leid yow lyke ane bellye blinde.

And also in Clerk's *Advice to Luvaris :*

Sum festnit is and ma not flé,
Sum led is lyk the belly blynd
With luve, war bettir lat it be.

" It is probable," says Jamieson, " that the term is the same
as Billy Blynde, said to be the name of a familiar spirit or good
genius somewhat similar to the brownie." Professor Child
identifies it with Odin, the blind deity. Another name in Scotland is also " Blind Harie," which is not the common Christian name " Harry," because this was not a name familiar in
Scotland. Blind Harie may therefore, Jamieson thinks, arise
from the rough or hairy attire worn by the principal actor.
Auld Harie is one of the names given to the devil, and also
to the spirit Brownie, who is represented as a hairy being.
Under " Coolin," a curious Highland custom is described by
Jamieson, which is singularly like the game of " Belly Blind,"

and assists in the conclusion that the game has descended from a rite where animal gods were represented. Sporting with animals before sacrificing them was a general feature at these rites. It is known that the Church opposed the people imitating beasts, and in this connection it is curious to note that in South Germany the game is called *blind bock*, i.e., "blind goat," and in German *blinde kuhe*, or "blind cow." In Scotland, one of the names for the game, according to A. Scott's poems, was "Blind Buk":

> Blind buk! but at the bound thou schutes,
> And them forbeirs that the rebutes.

It may therefore be conjectured that the person who was hoodwinked assumed the appearance of a goat, stag, or cow by putting on the skin of one of those animals.

He who is twice crowned or touched on the head by the taker or him who is hoodwinked, instead of once only, according to the law of the game, is said to be *brunt* (burned), and regains his liberty.—Jamieson.

Blind Man's Stan

A boys' game, played with the eggs of small birds. The eggs are placed on the ground, and the player who is blindfolded takes a certain number of steps in the direction of the eggs; he then slaps the ground with a stick thrice in the hope of breaking the eggs; then the next player, and so on.—Patterson's *Antrim and Down Glossary*.

Blind Nerry-Mopsey

The Whitby name for "Blind Man's Buff.—Robinson's *Glossary*.

Blind Palmie or Pawmie

One of the names given to the game of "Blindman's Buff."—Jamieson.

Blind Sim

Suffolk name for "Blind Man's Buff."—Forby's *Vocabulary of East Anglia*.

Block, Haimmer (Hammer), and Nail

This is a boys' game, and requires seven players. One boy, the Block, goes down on all fours ; another, the Nail, does the same behind the Block, with his head close to his *a posteriori* part. A third boy, the Hammer, lies down on his back behind the two. Of the remaining four boys one stations himself at each leg and one at each arm of the Hammer, and he is thus lifted. He is swung backwards and forwards three times in this position by the four, who keep repeating "Once, twice, thrice." When the word "Thrice" is repeated, the *a posteriori* part of the Hammer is knocked against the same part of the Nail. Any number of knocks may be given, according to the humour of the players.—Keith (Rev. W. Gregor).

A fellow lies on all fours—this is the Block ; one steadies him before—this is the Study ; a third is made a Hammer of, and swung by boys against the Block (Mactaggart's *Gallovidian Encyclopædia*). Patterson (*Antrim and Down Glossary*) mentions a game, "Hammer, Block, and Bible," which is probably the same game.

Blow-point

Strutt considers this to have been a children's game, played by blowing an arrow through a trunk at certain numbers by way of lottery (*Sports*, p. 403). Nares says the game was blowing small pins or points against each other, and probably not unlike "Push-pin." Marmion in his *Antiquary*, 1641, says : "I have heard of a nobleman that has been drunk with a tinker, and of a magnifico that has played at blow-point." In the *Comedy of Lingua*, 1607, act iii., sc. 2, Anamnestes introduces Memory as telling "how he played at blowe-point with Jupiter when he was in his side-coats." References to this game are also made in *Apollo Shroving*, 1627, p. 49 ; and see Hawkins' *English Drama*, iii. 243.

See "Dust-Point."

Bob Cherry

A children's game, consisting in jumping at cherries above their heads and trying to catch them with their mouths (Halliwell's *Dictionary*). It is alluded to in Herrick's

Hesperides as "Chop Cherry." Major Lowsley describes the
game as taking the end of a cherry-stalk between the teeth,
and holding the head perfectly level, trying to get the cherry
into the mouth without using the hands or moving the head

(*Berkshire Glossary*). It is also mentioned in Peacock's
Manley and Corringham Glossary. Strutt gives a curious
illustration of the game in his *Sports and Pastimes*, which is
here reproduced from the original MS. in the British Museum.

The Staffordshire St. Clement Day custom (Poole's *Staffordshire Customs, &c.*, p. 36) and the northern Hallowe'en custom
(Brockett's *North-Country Words*) probably indicate the origin
of this game from an ancient rite.

Boggle about the Stacks

A favourite play among young people in the villages, in
which one hunts several others (Brockett's *North-Country
Words*). The game is alluded to in one of the songs given by
Ritson (ii. 3), and Jamieson describes it as a Scottish game.

See "Barley-break."

Boggle-bush

The child's play of finding the hidden person in the company.
—Robinson's *Whitby Glossary*. See "Hide and Seek."

Bonnety

This is a boys' game. The players place their bonnets or caps in a pile. They then join hands and stand in a circle round it. They then pull each other, and twist and wriggle round and round and over it, till one overturns it or knocks a bonnet off it. The player who does so is hoisted on the back of another, and pelted by all the others with their bonnets.
—Keith, Nairn (Rev. W. Gregor).

Booman

—Norfolk.

Dill doule for Booman, Booman is dead and gone,
Left his wife all alone, and all his children.

Where shall we bury him? Carry him to London;
By his grandfather's grave grows a green onion.

Dig his grave wide and deep, strow it with flowers;
Toll the bell, toll the bell, twenty-four hours.

—Norfolk, 1825–30 (J. Doe).

(b) One boy lies down and personates Booman. Other boys form a ring round him, joining hands and alternately raising and lowering them, to imitate bell-pulling, while the girls who play sit down and weep. The boys sing the first verse. The girls seek for daisies or any wild flowers, and join in the singing of the second verse, while the boys raise the prostrate Booman and carry him about. When singing the third verse the boys act digging a grave, and the dead boy is lowered. The girls strew flowers over the body. When finished another boy becomes Booman.

(c) This game is clearly dramatic, to imitate a funeral. Mr. Doe writes, "I have seen somewhere [in Norfolk] a tomb with a crest on it—a leek—and the name Beaumont," but it does not seem necessary to thus account for the game.

Boss-out

A game at marbles.   Strutt describes it as follows:—" One bowls a marble to any distance that he pleases, which serves as a mark for his antagonist to bowl at, whose business it is to hit the marble first bowled, or lay his own near enough to it for him to span the space between them and touch both the marbles.   In either case he wins.   If not, his marble remains where it lay, and becomes a mark for the first player, and so alternately until the game be won."—*Sports*, p. 384.

Boss and Span

The same as " Boss-out."   It is mentioned, but not described, in Baker's *Northamptonshire Glossary*.

Boys and Girls

—*The Dancing Master*, 1728, vol. ii., p. 138.

> Boys, boys, come out to play,
> The moon doth shine as bright as day;
> Come with a whoop, come with a call,
> Come with a goodwill or don't come at all ;
> Lose your supper and lose your sleep,
> So come to your playmates in the street.
> —*Useful Transactions in Philosophy*, p. 44.

This rhyme is repeated when it is decided to begin any game, as a general call to the players.   The above writer says

it occurs in a very ancient MS., but does not give any reference
to it. Halliwell quotes the four first lines, the first line reading
" Boys and girls," instead of " Boys, boys," from a curious
ballad written about the year 1720, formerly in the possession
of Mr. Crofton Croker (*Nursery Rhymes*). Chambers also
gives this rhyme (*Popular Rhymes*, p. 152).

Branks

A game formerly common at fairs, called also " Hit my Legs
and miss my Pegs."—Dickinson's *Cumberland Glossary*.

Bridgeboard

A game at marbles. The boys have a board a foot long,
four inches in depth, and an inch (or
so) thick, with squares as in the diagram ; any number of holes at the
ground edge, numbered irregularly.

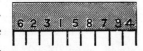

The board is placed firmly on the ground, and each player
bowls at it. He wins the number of marbles denoted by the
figure above the opening through which his marble passes. If
he misses a hole, his marble is lost to the owner of the Bridgeboard.—Earls Heaton (Herbert Hardy). [The owner or keeper
of the Bridgeboard presumably pays those boys who succeed
in winning marbles.]

See " Nine Holes."

Broken-down Tradesmen

A boys' game, undescribed.—Patterson's *Antrim and Down
Glossary*.

Brother Ebenezer

Ebenezer is sent out of the room, and the remainder choose
one of themselves. Two children act in concert, it being
understood that the last person speaking when Ebenezer goes
out of the room is the person to be chosen. The medium left in
the room causes the others to think of this person without letting
them know that they are not choosing of their own free will.
The medium then says, " Brother Ebenezer, come in," and asks
him in succession, " Was it William, or Jane," &c., mentioning

several names before saying the right one, Ebenezer saying
"No!" to all until the one is mentioned who last spoke.—
Bitterne, Hants (Mrs. Byford).

Bubble-hole
A child's game, undescribed.—Halliwell's *Dictionary*.

Bubble-justice
The name of a game probably the same as " Nine Holes."—
Halliwell's *Dictionary*.

Buck, Buck
A boy stoops so that his arms rest on a table ; another boy
sits on him as he would on a horse.   He then holds up (say)
three fingers, and says—

> Buck, buck, how many horns do I hold up ?

The stooping boy guesses, and if he says a wrong number
the other says—

> [Two] you say and three there be ;
> Buck, buck, how many horns do I hold up ?

When the stooping boy guesses rightly the other says—

> [Four] you say and [four] there be ;
> Buck, buck, rise up.

The boy then gets off and stoops for the other one to mount,
and the game is played again.—London (J. P. Emslie).

Similar action accompanies the following rhyme :—

> Inkum, jinkum, Jeremy buck,
> Yamdy horns do au cock up ?
> Two thà sès, and three there is,
> Au'll lea'n thee to la'ke at Inkum.
> > —Almondbury (Easther's *Glossary*).

A different action occurs in other places.   It is played by
three boys in the following way :—One stands with his back
to a wall ; the second stoops down with his head against the
stomach of the first boy, " forming a back ; " the third jumps on
it, and holds up his hand with the fingers distended, saying—

> Buck shee, buck shee buck,
> How many fingers do I hold up ?

Should the stooper guess correctly, they all change places, and the jumper forms the back. Another and not such a rough way of playing this game is for the guesser to stand with his face towards a wall, keeping his eyes shut.—Cornwall (*Folklore Journal*, v. 59).

In Nairn, Scotland, the game is called Post and Rider. One boy, the Post, takes his stand beside a wall. Another boy stoops down with his head touching the Post's breast. Several other boys stoop down in the same way behind the first boy, all in line. The Rider then leaps on the back of the boy at the end of the row of stooping boys, and from his back to that of the one in front, and so on from back to back till he reaches the boy next the Post. He then holds up so many fingers, and says—

Buck, buck, how many fingers do I hold up?

The boy makes a guess. If the number guessed is wrong, the Rider gives the number guessed as well as the correct number, and again holds up so many, saying—

[Four] you say, but [two] it is;
Buck, buck, how many fingers do I hold up?

This goes on till the correct number is guessed, when the guesser becomes the Rider. The game was called "Buck, Buck" at Keith. Three players only took part in the game—the Post, the Buck, and the Rider. The words used by the Rider were—

Buck, buck, how many horns do I hold up?

If the guess was wrong, the Rider gave the Buck as many blows or kicks with the heel as the difference between the correct number and the number guessed. This process went on till the correct number was guessed, when the Rider and the Buck changed places.—Rev. W. Gregor.

(*b*) Dr. Tylor says: "It is interesting to notice the wide distribution and long permanence of these trifles in history when we read the following passage from Petronius Arbiter, written in the time of Nero:—'Trimalchio, not to seem moved by the loss, kissed the boy, and bade him get up on his back. Without delay the boy climbed on horseback on him, and slapped him on the shoulders with his hand, laughing and calling out,

"Bucca, bucca, quot sunt hic ? " '—*Petron. Arbitri Satiræ*, by Buchler, p. 84 (other readings are *buccæ* or *bucco*)."—*Primitive Culture*, i. 67.

Buck i' t' Neucks

A rude game amongst boys.—Dickinson's *Cumberland Glossary*.

Buckerels

"A kind of play used by boys in London streets in Henry VIII.'s time, now disused, and I think forgot" (Blount's *Glossographia*, p. 95). Hall mentions this game, temp. Henry VIII., f. 91.

Buckey-how

For this the boys divide into sides. One "stops at home," the other goes off to a certain distance agreed on beforehand and shouts "Buckey-how." The boys "at home" then give chase, and when they succeed in catching an adversary, they bring him home, and there he stays until all on his side are caught, when they in turn become the chasers.—Cornwall (*Folk-lore Journal*, v. 60).

Buff

1st player, thumping the floor with a stick : "Knock, knock!"
2nd ditto : "Who's there ? "
1st : "Buff."
2nd : "What says Buff ? "
1st : "Buff says Buff to all his men,
    And I say Buff to you again ! "
2nd : "Methinks Buff smiles ? "
1st : "Buff neither laughs nor smiles,
    But looks in your face
    With a comical grace,
    And delivers the staff to you again " (handing it over).
    —Shropshire (Burne's *Shropshire Folk-lore*, p. 526).

Same verses as in Shropshire, except the last, which runs as follows :—

Buff neither laughs nor smiles,
But strokes his face
With a very good grace,
And delivers his staff to you.
—Cheltenham (Miss E. Mendham).

Same verses as in Shropshire, except the last, which runs
as follows :—

Buff neither laughs nor smiles,
But strokes his face for want of grace,
And sticks his staff in the right place.
—London (J. P. Emslie).

(*b*) Five or six children stand in a row. Another child
comes up to the first of the row, and strikes smartly on the
ground with a stick. The child facing him asks the first
question, and the one with the stick answers. At "strokes
his face" he suits the action to the words, and then thumps
with his stick on the ground at the beginning of the last line.
The object of all the players is to make Buff smile while going
through this absurdity, and if he does he must pay a forfeit.

Another version is for one child to be blindfolded, and
stand in the middle of a ring of children, holding a long wand
in his hand. The ring dance round to a tune and sing a
chorus [which is not given by the writer]. They then stop.
Buff extends his wand, and the person to whom it happens to
be pointed must step out of the circle to hold the end in his
hand. Buff then interrogates the holder of the wand by grunt-
ing three times, and is answered in like manner. Buff then
guesses who is the holder of the wand. If he guesses rightly,
the holder of the stick becomes Buff, and he joins the ring
(*Winter Evening's Amusements*, p. 6). When I played at this
game the ring of children walked in silence three times only round
Buff, then stopped and knelt or stooped down on the ground,
strict silence being observed. Buff asked three questions (anything he chose) of the child to whom he pointed the stick, who
replied by imitating cries of animals or birds (A. B. Gomme).

(*c*) This is a well-known game. It is also called "Buffy
Gruffy," or "Indian Buff." The Dorsetshire version in *Folk-
lore Journal*, vii. 238, 239, is the same as the Shropshire
version.

Halliwell (*Nursery Rhymes*, cclxxxii.) gives a slight variant. It is also given by Mr. Addy in his *Sheffield Glossary*, the words being the same except the last two lines, which run—

But shows his face with a comely grace,
And leaves his staff at the very next place.

Buk-hid

This seems to be an old name for some game, probably "Blindman's Buff," Sw. "Blind-bock," q. "bock" and "hufwud head" (having the head resembling a goat). The sense, however, would agree better with "Bo-peep" or "Hide and Seek." —Jamieson.

Bull in the Park

One child places himself in the centre of a circle of others. He then asks each of the circle in turn, "Where's the key of the park?" and is answered by every one, except the last, "Ask the next-door neighbour." The last one answers, "Get out the way you came in." The centre one then makes a dash at the hands of some of the circle, and continues to do so until he breaks through, when all the others chase him. Whoever catches him is then Bull.—Liphook, Hants (Miss Fowler).

"The Bull in the Barn" is apparently the same game. The players form a ring; one player in the middle called the Bull, one outside called the King.

Bull: "Where is the key of the barn-door?"

Chorus: "Go to the next-door neighbour."

King: "She left the key in the church-door."

Bull: "Steel or iron?"

He then forces his way out of the ring, and whoever catches him becomes Bull.—Berrington (Burne's *Shropshire Folk-lore*, pp. 519, 520).

Another version is that the child in the centre, whilst the others danced around him in a circle, saying, "Pig in the middle and can't get out," replies, "I've lost my key but I will get out," and throws the whole weight of his body suddenly on the clasped hands of a couple, to try and unlock them. When he had succeeded he changed the words to, "I've broken your locks, and I have got out." One of the pair whose hands he had opened took his place, and he joined the ring.—Cornwall (*Folk-lore Journal*, v. 50).

(*b*) Mr. S. O. Addy says the following lines are said or sung in a game called " T' Bull 's i' t' Barn," but he does not know how it is played :—

> As I was going o'er misty moor
> I spied three cats at a mill-door ;
> One was white and one was black,
> And one was like my granny's cat.
> I hopped o'er t' style and broke my heel,
> I flew to Ireland very weel,
> Spied an old woman sat by t' fire,
> Sowing silk, jinking keys ;
> Cat's i' t' cream-pot up to t' knees,
> Hen's i' t' hurdle crowing for day,
> Cock's i' t' barn threshing corn,
> I ne'er saw the like sin' I was born.

Bulliheisle

A play amongst boys, in which, all having joined hands in a line, a boy at one of the ends stands still, and the rest all wind round him. The sport especially consists in an attempt to heeze or throw the whole mass on the ground.—Jamieson.

See " Eller Tree," " Wind up Jack," " Wind up the Bush Faggot."

Bummers

A play of children. " Bummers—a thin piece of wood swung round by a cord" (*Blackwood's Magazine*, Aug. 1821, p. 35). Jamieson says the word is evidently denominated from the booming sound produced.

Bun-hole

A hole is scooped out in the ground with the heel in the shape of a small dish, and the game consists in throwing a marble as near to this hole as possible. Sometimes, when several holes are made, the game is called " Holy."—Addy's *Sheffield Glossary ; Notes and Queries*, xii. 344.

Bunch of Ivy

Played by children in pairs (one kneeling and one standing) in a ring. The inner child of each pair kneels. The following dialogue begins with the inner circle asking the first question, which is replied to by the outer circle.

"What time does the King come home?"

"One o'clock in the afternoon."

"What has he in his hand?"

"A bunch of ivy."

The rhyme is repeated for every hour up to six, the outer circle running round the inner as many times as the number named. The children then change places and repeat.—Monton, Lancashire (Miss Dendy).

Bung the Bucket

—London (J. P. Emslie).

A number of boys divide themselves into two sides. One side, the Buckets, stoop down, as for "Leap-frog," arranging themselves one in front of the other. The hindmost supports himself against the one in front of him, and the front one

supports himself against a wall (fig.). They thus make an even and solid row of their backs. The other side, the Bungs, leap on to the backs of the Buckets, the first one going as far up the row as possible, the second placing himself close behind the first, and so on. If they all succeed in getting a secure place, they cry out twice the two first lines—

Bung the Bucket,
One, two, three.
Off, off, off!

If no breakdown occurs, the Buckets count one in their favour, and the Bungs repeat the process. When a breakdown occurs the Bungs take the place of the Buckets.—Barnes, Surrey (A. B. Gomme).

(*b*) Mr. Emslie, to whom I am indebted for the tune to this game, gives me the words as—

> Jump a little nag-tail,
> One, two, three.

He says, "I once heard this sung three times, followed by 'Ha! ha! he!' to the tune of the last bar." Mr. W. R. Emslie says the game is known at Beddgelert as "Horses, Wild Horses," he believes, but is not quite certain.

Northall (*Rhymes*, p. 401) describes a game very similar to this under "Buck," in which the rhyme and method of play is the same as in that game. He continues, "This is closely allied to a game called in Warwickshire 'Jack upon the Mopstick.' But in this there is no guessing. The leaping party must maintain their position whilst their leader says—

> Jack upon the mopstick,
> One, two, three, four, five, six, seven, eight, nine, ten,
> Count 'em off again."

Bunting

Name for "Tip-cat."—Cole's *S. W. Lincolnshire Glossary*.

Burly Whush

A game played at with a ball. The ball is thrown up by one of the players on a house or wall, who cries on the instant it is thrown to another to catch or kep it before it falls to the ground. They all run off but this one to a little distance, and if he fails in kepping it he bawls out "Burly Whush;" then the party are arrested in their flight, and must run away no farther. He singles out one of them then, and throws the ball at him, which often is directed so fair as to strike; then this one at which the ball has been thrown is he who gives "Burly Whush" with the ball to any he chooses. If the corner of a house be at hand, as is mostly the case, and any of the players escape behind it, they must still show one of their hands past its edge to the Burly Whush man, who sometimes hits it such a whack with the ball as leaves it dirling for an hour afterwards.—Mactaggart's *Gallovidian Encyclopædia*.

See "Ball," "Keppy Ball," "Monday."

Buttons

Two or more boys take two buttons in their right hands, and try to throw them both into a small hole in the ground about two yards off. The boy who succeeds in getting both buttons in begins first next game, and takes a button as prize. [This seems merely a mild form of marbles.]—Lincolnshire (Rev. — Roberts).

There were several games played with buttons—some on level ground, in a ring or square; but the most approved was with a hole dug in the earth near a wall, or near the trunk of a large tree. The hole should be about the cavity of a small tea-cup, the players toeing a scratched line about four or five feet from the hole, after tossing for first innings. Each of the players (mostly two) contribute an equal number of buttons, say from two to ten, and of equal value or quality. The one having first turn takes the whole of them in his hand, and by an under-throw, or rather a pitch, endeavours to get the whole, or as many as possible, into the hole. If all go clean into the hole, he wins the game, and takes the whole of the buttons started with; but if one or more of the buttons are left outside the hole, the non-player has then the choice of selecting one which he considers difficult to be hit, and requesting the player to hit it with his *nicker*. This is made of solid lead, about the size of a florin, but twice its substance, and each player is provided with one of his own. Much judgment is required in making this selection, the object being to make it most difficult not only to hit it, but to prevent it being hit without being knocked into the hole, or sending the nicker in, or sending another button in, or even not striking one at all. In any one of these cases the player loses the game, and the non-player takes the whole of the stakes. In playing the next game, the previous non-player becomes the player.—London (C. A. T. M.).

The following was the value of the buttons :—

(1.) The plain metal 3 or 4-holed flat button, called a Sinkie, say, value 1 point.

(2.) The same kind of button, with letters or inscription on the rim, valued at 2 points.

(3.) The small metal shank button, called a Shankie, without any inscription, valued at 3 points; if with inscription, at 4 points; the large sizes and corresponding description were valued relatively 4 and 5 points.

(4.) The small Shankies, with a crest (livery waistcoat buttons), 6 points, and the large corresponding, 7 points.

(5.) The small Shankies, with coat of arms, value 8 points, and the large corresponding, 9 points.

(6.) Ornamental and various other buttons, such as regimental, official, mounted and engraved in flowers, and other designs according to arrangement, up to 20 points.

See " Banger," " Cots and Twisses."

Buzz and Bandy

A local name for " Hockey," which was formerly a very popular game among the young men of Shrewsbury and Much Wenlock. Called simply " Bandy " at Ludlow and Newport. —*Shropshire Folk-lore*, p. 525.

Cache-pole

The game of " Tennis."—Jamieson.

Caiche

The game of " Handball."

> Thocht I preich nocht I can play at the caiche.
> I wait thair is nocht ane among you all
> Mair ferilie can play at the fute ball.
> —Lyndsay's *S. P. Repr.*, ii. 243.

This language Lyndsay puts into the mouth of a Popish parson. The game seems to be that of ball played with the hand, as distinguished from " Football."—Jamieson.

See " Ball."

Call-the-Guse

This game is supposed by Jamieson to be equivalent to

" Drive the Goose," and the game seems to be the same with
one still played by young people in some parts of Angus,
in which one of the company, having something that excites
ridicule unknowingly pinned behind, is pursued by all the rest,
who still cry out, " Hunt the Goose ! "—Jamieson.

Camp

A game formerly much in use among schoolboys, and occasionally played by men in those parts of Suffolk on the sea
coast—more especially in the line of Hollesley Bay between
the Rivers Orwell and Alde, sometimes school against school,
or parish against parish.   It was thus played : Goals were
pitched at the distance of 150 or 200 yards from each other ;
these were generally formed of the thrown-off clothes of the
competitors.   Each party has two goals, ten or fifteen yards
apart.   The parties, ten or fifteen on a side, stand in line,
facing their own goals and each other, at about ten yards distance, midway between the goals, and nearest that of their
adversaries.   An indifferent spectator, agreed on by the parties,
throws up a ball, of the size of a common cricket-ball, midway between the confronted players, and makes his escape.
It is the object of the players to seize and convey the ball
between their own goals.   The rush is therefore very great :
as is sometimes the shock of the first onset, to catch the falling ball.   He who first can catch or seize it speeds therefore
home, pursued by his opponents (thro' whom he has to make
his way), aided by the jostlings and various assistances of his
own *sidesmen.*   If caught and held, or in imminent danger of
being caught, he *throws* the ball—but must in no case *give*
it—to a less beleaguered friend, who, if it be not arrested in
its course, or he jostled away by the eager and watchful adversaries, catches it ; and he hastens homeward, in like manner
pursued, annoyed, and aided, winning the notch (or snotch)
if he contrive to *carry*, not *throw*, it between his goals.   But
this in a well-matched game is no easy achievement, and often
requires much time, many doublings, detours, and exertions.
I should have noticed, that if the holder of the ball be caught
with the ball in his possession, he loses a *snotch ;* if, therefore,

he be hard pressed, he *throws* it to a convenient friend, more free and in breath than himself. At the loss (or gain) of a *snotch*, a recommence takes place, arranging which gives the parties time to take breath. Seven or nine notches are the game—and these it will sometimes take two or three hours to win. Sometimes a large football was used—and the game was then called "Kicking Camp"—and if played with the shoes on, "Savage Camp."—Moor's *Suffolk Words*.

(*b*) The sport and name are very old. The "Camping pightel" occurs in a deed of the 30 Henry VI.—about 1486; Cullum's *Hawstead*, p. 113, where Tusser is quoted in proof, that not only was the exercise manly and salutary, but good also for the *pightel* or meadow:

> In meadow or pasture (to grow the more fine)
> Let campers be camping in any of thine;
> Which if ye do suffer when low is the spring,
> You gain to yourself a commodious thing.—P. 65.

And he says, in p. 56:

> Get campers a ball,
> To camp therewithall.

Ray says that the game prevails in Norfolk, Suffolk, and Essex. The Rev. S. Arnot, in *Notes and Queries*, 8th series, vol. ii. p. 138, who was rector of Ilket's Hall, in the county of Suffolk, says the ball was about the size of a cricket-ball, and was driven through a narrow goal; and from the evidence of the parish clerk it seems certain that it was not "Football." See also Spurden's *East Anglian Words*, and *County Folk-lore*, *Suffolk*, pp. 57–59.

There are Upper Campfield and Lower Campfield at Norton Woodseats. They are also called Camping fields. This field was probably the place where football and other village games were played. These fields adjoin the Bocking fields. In Gosling's Map of Sheffield, 1736, Campo Lane is called *Camper Lane*. The same map shows the position of the old Latin school, or grammar school, and the writing school. These schools were at a very short distance from Campo Lane, and it seems probable that here the game of football was played (Addy's *Sheffield Glossary*). "The camping-land appropriated to this game occurs in several instances in authorities of the fifteenth century" (Way's Note in *Prompt. Parv.*, p. 60). In Brinsley's *Grammar Schoole*, cited by Mr. Furnivall in *Early English Meals and Manners*, p. lxii., is this passage: "By this meanes also the schollars may be kept euer in their places, and hard to their labours, without that running out to the Campo (as they tearme it) at school times, and the manifolde disorders thereof; as watching and striuing for the clubbe and loytering then in the fields."

See "Football."

Canlie

A very common game in Aberdeen, played by a number of boys, one of whom is by lot chosen to act the part of Canlie. A certain portion of a street or ground, as it may happen, is marked off as his territory, into which, if any of the other boys presume to enter, and be caught by Canlie before he can get off the ground, he is doomed to take the place of Canlie, who becomes free in consequence of the capture. The game is prevalent throughout Scotland, though differently denominated: in Lanarkshire and Renfrewshire it is called "Tig," and in Mearns "Tick."—Jamieson.

See "Tig."

Capie-Hole

A hole is made in the ground, and a certain line drawn, called a Strand, behind which the players must take their stations. The object is at this distance to throw the bowl into the hole. He who does this most frequently wins. It is now more generally called "The Hole," but the old designation is not quite extinct. It is otherwise played in Angus. Three holes are made at equal distances. He who can first strike his bowl into each of these holes thrice in succession wins the game (Jamieson). It is alluded to in *The Life of a Scotch Rogue*, 1722, p. 7.

See "Bun-hole."

Carrick

Old name for "Shinty" in Fife.—Jamieson.

Carry my Lady to London

I. Give me a pin to stick in my thumb
   To carry my lady to London.
   Give me another to stick in my other
   To carry her a little bit farther.
                    —Belfast (W. H. Patterson).

II. London Bridge is broken,
    And what shall I do for a token?
    Give me a pin to stick in my thumb
    And carry my lady to London.
                    —*Notes and Queries*, 4th series, xii. 479.

III. Give me a pin to stick in my chin (? cushion)
     To carry a lady to London;
     London Bridge is broken down
     And I must let my lady down.
                    —Northall's *English Folk Rhymes*, p. 353.

(*b*) In this game two children cross hands, grasping each other's wrists and their own as well: they thus form a seat on which a child can sit and be carried about. At the same time they sing the verse.

Carrying the Queen a Letter

The King and Queen have a throne formed by placing two chairs a little apart, with a shawl spread from chair to chair. A messenger is sent into the room with a letter to the Queen, who reads it, and joins the King in a courteous entreaty that the bearer of the missive will place himself between them. When he has seated himself on the shawl, up jumps the King and Queen, and down goes the messenger on the floor.— Bottesford and Anderly (Lincolnshire), and Nottinghamshire (Miss M. Peacock).

(*b*) This is virtually the same game as "Ambassador," described by Grose as played by sailors on some inexperienced fellow or landsman. Between the two chairs is placed a pail of water, into which the victim falls.

Cashhornie

A game played with clubs by two opposite parties of boys, the aim of each party being to drive a ball into a hole belonging to their antagonists, while the latter strain every nerve to prevent this.—Jamieson.

Castles

A game at marbles. Each boy makes a small pyramid of three as a base, and one on the top. The players aim at these from a distant stroke with balsers, winning such of the castles as they may in turn knock down (Lowsley's *Glossary of Berkshire Words*). In London, the marble alluded to as "balser" was called "bonsor" or "bouncer" (J. P. Emslie).

See "Cockly Jock," "Cogs."

Cat and Dog

An ancient game played in Angus and Lothian. Three play, and they are provided with clubs. These clubs are called "dogs." The players cut out two holes, each about a foot in diameter, and seven inches in depth. The distance between them is about twenty-six feet. One stands at each hole with a club. A piece of wood about four inches long and one inch in diameter, called a Cat, is thrown from the one hole towards the other by a third person. The object is to prevent the Cat from getting into the hole. Every time that it enters the hole, he who has the club at that hole loses the club, and he who threw the Cat gets possession both of the club and of the hole, while the former possessor is obliged to take charge of the Cat. If the Cat be struck, he who strikes it changes places with the person who holds the other club ; and as often as these positions are changed one is counted in the game by the two who hold the clubs, and who are viewed as partners.—Jamieson.

(*b*) This is not unlike the "Stool-Ball" described by Strutt (*Sports and Pastimes*, p. 76), but it more nearly resembles "Club-Ball," an ancient English game (ibid., p. 83). The game of "Cat," played with sticks and a small piece of wood, rising in the middle, so as to rebound when struck on either side, is alluded to in *Poor Robin's Almanack* for 1709, and by Brand. Leigh (*Cheshire Glossary*) gives "Scute" as another name for the game of "Cat," probably from *scute* (O.W.), for boat, which it resembles in shape.

See "Cudgel," "Kit-cat," "Tip-cat."

Cat-Beds

The name of a game played by young people in Perthshire. In this game, one, unobserved by all the rest, cuts with a knife the turf in very unequal angles. These are all covered, and each player puts his hand on what he supposes to be the smallest, as every one has to cut off the whole surface of his division. The rate of cutting is regulated by a throw of the knife, and the person who throws is obliged to cut as deep as the knife goes. He who is last in getting his bed cut up is bound to carry the whole of the clods, crawling on his hands and feet, to a certain distance measured by the one next to him, who throws the knife through his legs. If the bearer of the clods let any of them fall, the rest have a right to pelt him with them. They frequently lay them very loosely on, that they may have the pleasure of pelting.—Jamieson.

Cat's Cradle

One child holds a piece of string joined at the ends on his upheld palms, a single turn being taken over each, and by inserting the middle finger of each hand under the opposite turn, crosses the string from finger to finger in a peculiar form. Another child then takes off the string on his fingers in a rather different way, and it then assumes a second form. A repetition of this manœuvre produces a third form, and so on. Each of these forms has a particular name, from a fancied resemblance to the object—barn-doors, bowling-green, hour-glass, pound, net, fiddle, fish-pond, diamonds, and others.—*Notes and Queries*, vol. xi. p. 421.

The following forms are those known to me, with their names. They are produced seriatim.

1. The cradle.
2. The soldier's bed.
3. Candles.
4. The cradle inversed, or manger.
5. Soldier's bed again, or diamonds.
6. Diamonds, or cat's eyes.
7. Fish in dish.
8. Cradle as at first.

The different orders or arrangements must be taken from the hands of one player by another without disturbing the arrangement.—A. B. Gomme.

(*b*) Nares suggests that the proper name is "Cratch Cradle," and is derived from the archaic word *cratch*, meaning a manger. He gives several authorities for its use. The first-made form is not unlike a manger. Moor (*Suffolk Words*) gives the names as cat's cradle, barn-doors, bowling-green, hour-glass, pound,

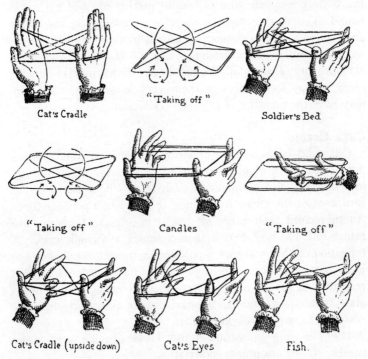

Cat's Cradle   "Taking off"   Soldier's Bed

"Taking off"   Candles   "Taking off"

Cat's Cradle (upside down)   Cat's Eyes   Fish.

net, diamonds, fish-pond, fiddle. A supposed resemblance originated them. Britton (*Beauties of Wiltshire*, Glossary) says the game in London schools is called "Scratch-scratch" or "Scratch-cradle."

The game is known to savage peoples. Professor Haddon noted it among the Torres Straits people, who start the game in the same manner as we do, but continue it differently (*Journ. Anthrop. Inst.*, xix. 361; and Dr. Taylor has pointed

out the significance of these string puzzles among savage
peoples in *Journ. Anthrop. Inst.*, ix. 26.

Cat-gallows

A child's game, consisting of jumping over a stick placed at
right angles to two others fixed in the ground.—Halliwell's
Dictionary.

(*b*) In Ross and Stead's *Holderness Glossary* this is called
"Cat-gallas," and is described as three sticks placed in the
form of a gallows for boys to jump over. So called in conse-
quence of being of sufficient height to hang cats from. Also
mentioned in Peacock's *Manley and Corringham Glossary* and
Elworthy's *West Somerset Words*, Brogden's *Provincial Words,
Lincs.*, Dickinson's *Cumberland Glossary*, Atkinson's *Cleveland
Glossary*, Brockett's *North Country Words*, Evans' *Leicestershire Glossary*, Baker's *Northants Glossary*, and Darlington's
South Cheshire Glossary. On one of the stalls in Worcester
Cathedral, figured in Wright's *Archæological Essays*, ii. 117,
is a carving which represents three rats busily engaged in
hanging a cat on a gallows of this kind.

Cat i' the Hole

A game well known in Fife, and perhaps in other counties.
If seven boys are to play, six holes are made at certain distances. Each of the six stands at a hole, with a short stick in
his hand; the seventh stands at a certain distance holding a
ball. When he gives the word, or makes the sign agreed
upon, all the six change holes, each running to his neighbour's
hole, and putting his stick in the hole which he has newly
seized. In making this change, the boy who has the ball tries
to put it into an empty hole. If he succeeds in this, the boy
who had not his stick (for the stick is the Cat) in the hole to
which he had run is put out, and must take the ball. There is
often a very keen contest whether the one shall get his stick,
or the other the ball, or Cat, first put into the hole. When the
Cat *is in the hole*, it is against the laws of the game to put the
ball into it.—Jamieson.

(*b*) Kelly, in his *Scottish Proverbs*, p. 325, says, "'Tine cat,

tine game;' an allusion to a play called 'Cat i' the Hole,' and
the English 'Kit-cat.' Spoken when men at law have lost
their principal evidence."

See "Cat and Dog," "Cudgel," "Kit-cat."

Cat after Mouse

This game, sometimes called "Threading the Needle," is
played by children forming a ring, with their arms extended
and hands clasped; one—the Mouse—goes outside the circle
and gently pulls the dress of one of the players, who thereupon
becomes the Cat, and is bound to follow wherever the Mouse
chooses to go—either in or out of the ring—until caught, when
he or she takes the place formerly occupied in the ring by
the Cat, who in turn becomes Mouse, and the game is recommenced.—Dorsetshire (*Folk-lore Journal*, vii. 214).

(*b*) Played at Monton, Lancashire (Miss Dendy); Clapham
Middle-Class School (Miss Richardson); and many other places.
It is practically the same game as "Drop Handkerchief," played
without words. It is described by Strutt, p. 381, who considers
"Kiss-in-the-Ring" is derived from this "Cat and Mouse."

Catchers

One bicken is required in this game, and at this a lad must
stand with a bat and ball in hand. He hits the ball away along
the sand. Another boy picks it up and asks the striker "How
many?" who replies—

> Two a good scat,
> Try for the bat.

The ball is then thrown to the bicken, and if it does not come
within the distance named—two bats—the striker again sends
the ball away, when the question is again asked—

> Three a good scat,
> Try for the bat.

And so on until the boy standing out throws the ball in to the
required distance.—Old newspaper cutting without date in my
possession (A. B. Gomme).

Chacke-Blyndman

Scotch name for "Blindman's Buff."—Jamieson.

Chance Bone

In Langley's abridgment of *Polydore Vergile*, f. l., we have a description of this game : " There is a game also that is played with the posterne bone in the hinder foote of a sheepe, oxe, gote, fallow, or redde dere, whiche in Latin is called *talus*. It hath foure chaunces : the ace point, that is named Canis, or Canicula, was one of the sides ; he that cast it leyed doune a peny, or so muche as the gamers were agreed on ; the other side was called Venus, that signifieth seven. He that cast the chaunce wan sixe and all that was layd doune for the castyng of Canis. The two other sides were called Chius and Senio. He that did throwe Chius wan three. And he that cast Senio gained four. This game (as I take it) *is used of children in Northfolke*, and they cal it the Chaunce Bone ; they playe with three or foure of those bones together ; it is either the same or very lyke to it."

See " Dibs," " Hucklebones."

Change Seats, the King's Come

In this game as many seats are placed round a room as will serve all the company save one. The want of a seat falls on an individual by a kind of lot, regulated, as in many other games, by the repetition of an old rhythm. All the rest being seated, he who has no seat stands in the middle, repeating the words " Change seats, change seats," &c., while all the rest are on the alert to observe when he adds, " the king's come," or, as it is sometimes expressed, change their seats. The sport lies in the bustle in consequence of every one's endeavouring to avoid the misfortune of being the unhappy individual who is left without a seat. The principal actor often slily says, " The king's *not* come," when, of course the company ought to keep their seats ; but from their anxious expectation of the usual summons, they generally start up, which affords a great deal of merriment.—Brand's *Pop. Antiq.*, ii. 409.

(*b*) Dr. Jamieson says this is a game well-known in Lothian and in the South of Scotland. Sir Walter Scott, in *Rob Roy*, iii. 153, says, " Here auld ordering and counter-ordering—but patience ! patience !—We may ae day play at *Change seats, the king's coming.*"

This game is supposed to ridicule the political scramble for places on occasion of a change of government, or in the succession.

See "Musical Chairs," "Turn the Trencher."

Checkstone

Easther's *Almondbury Glossary* thus describes this game. A set of checks consists of five cubes, each about half an inch at the edge, and a ball the size of a moderate bagatelle ball: all made of pot. They are called checkstones, and the game is played thus. You throw down the cubes all at once, then toss the ball, and during its being in the air gather up one stone in your right hand and catch the descending ball in the same. Put down the stone and repeat the operation, gathering two stones, then three, then four, till at last you have "summed up" all the five at once, and have suceeeded in catching the ball. In case of failure you have to begin all over again.

(*b*) In Nashe's *Lenten Stuff* (1599) occurs the following: "Yet towards cock-crowing she caught a little slumber, and then she dreamed that Leander and she were playing at checkstone with pearls in the bottom of the sea."

A game played by children with round small pebbles (Halliwell's *Dictionary*). It is also mentioned in the early play of *Apollo Shroving*, 1627, p. 49.

See "Chucks," "Fivestones."

Cherry Odds

A game of "Pitch and Toss" played with cherry-stones (Elworthy's *West Somerset Words*). Boys always speak of the stones as "ods."

Cherry-pit

"Cherry-pit" is a play wherein they pitch cherry-stones into a little hole. It is noticed in the *Pleasant Grove of New Fancies*, 1657, and in Herrick's *Hesperides*. Nares (*Glossary*) mentions it as still practised with leaden counters called Dumps, or with money.

Chicamy

> Chicamy, chickamy, chimey O,
> Down to the pond to wash their feet;
> Bring them back to have some meat,
> Chickamy, chickamy, chimey O.
>   —Crockham Hill, Kent (Miss Chase).

The children sing the first line as they go round and round. At the second line they move down the road a little, and turn round and round as they end the rhyme.

Chickidy Hand

> Chickidy hand,
> Chickidy hand,
> The Warner, my Cock,
> Crows at four in the morning.

Several boys, placing their clasped fists against a lamp-post, say these lines, after which they run out, hands still clasped. One in the middle tries to catch as many as possible, forming them in a long string, hand in hand, as they are caught. Those still free try to break through the line and rescue the prisoners. If they succeed in parting the line, they may carry one boy pig-a-back to the lamp-post, who becomes " safe." The boy caught last but one becomes " it " in the next game.—Deptford, Kent (Miss Chase).

See " Hunt the Staigie," " Stag Warning," " Whiddy."

Chinnup

A game played with hooked sticks and a ball, also called " Shinnup." Same as " Hockey."

Chinny-mumps

A school-boys' play, consisting in striking the chin with the knuckles; dexterously performed, a kind of time is produced. —Addy's *Sheffield Glossary*.

Chock or Chock-hole

A game at marbles played by " chocking " or pitching marbles in a hole made for the purpose, instead of shooting at a ring

(Northamptonshire, Baker's *Glossary*).   Clare mentions the
game in one of his poems.

Chow

A game played in Moray and Banffshire.   The ball is called
the Chow.   The game is the same as "Shinty."   The players
are equally divided.   After the Chow is struck off by one party,
the aim of the other is to strike it back, that it may not reach
the limit or goal on their side, because in this case they lose
the game, and as soon as it crosses the line the other party
cry Hail! or say that it is hail, as denoting that they have
gained the victory.   In the beginning of each game they are
allowed to raise the ball a little above the level of the ground,
that they may have the advantage of a surer stroke.   This is
called the "deil-chap," perhaps as a contraction of "devil," in
reference to the force expended on the stroke.   It may, however, be "dule-chap," the blow given at the "dule" or goal.—
Jamieson.

See "Hockey."

Chuck-farthing

Strutt says this game was played by boys at the commencement of the last century, and probably bore some analogy to
"Pitch and Hustle."   He saw the game thus denominated
played with halfpence, every one of the competitors having a
like number, either two or four; a hole being made in the
ground, with a mark at a given distance for the players to
stand, they pitch their halfpence singly in succession towards
the hole, and he whose halfpenny lies the nearest to it has the
privilege of coming first to a second mark much nearer than
the former, and all the halfpence are given to him; these he
pitches in a mass toward the hole, and as many of them as
remain therein are his due; if any fall short or jump out of it,
the second player—that is, he whose halfpenny in pitching lay
nearest to the first goer's—takes them and performs in like
manner; he is followed by the others as long as any of the
halfpence remain (*Sports*, pp. 386, 387).   There is a letter in
the *Spectator*, supposed to be from the father of a romp, who,
among other complaints of her conduct, says, "I have catched

her once at eleven years old at 'Chuck-farthing' among the boys."

Chuck-hole, Chuck-penny

Same game as "Chuck-farthing," with this difference, that if the pennies roll outside the ring it is a "dead heat," and each boy reclaims his penny.—Peacock's *Manley and Corringham Glossary;* and see Brogden's *Lincolnshire Words.*

Chucks

A game with marbles played by girls (Mactaggart's *Gallovidian Encyclopædia*). A writer in *Blackwood's Magazine,* August 1821, p. 36, says "Chucks" is played with a bowl and chucks—a species of shells (*Buccinum lapillus*) found on the sea-shore ["bowl" here probably means a marble]. Brockett (*North Country Words*) says this game is played by girls with five sea-shells called chucks, and sometimes with pebbles, called chuckie-stanes. Jamieson says a number of pebbles are spread on a flat stone; one of them is tossed up, and a certain number must be gathered and the falling one caught by the same hand.

See "Checkstones," "Fivestones."

Church and Mice

A game played in Fifeshire; said to be the same with the "Sow in the Kirk."—Jamieson.

Click

Two Homes opposite each other are selected, and a boy either volunteers to go Click, or the last one in a race between the Homes does so. The others then proceed to one of the Homes, and the boy takes up his position between them. The players then attempt to run between the Homes, and if the one in the middle holds any of them while he says "One, two, three, I catch thee; help me catch another," they have to stay and help him to collar the rest until only one is left. If this one succeeds in getting between the Homes three times after all the others have been caught, he is allowed to choose the one to go Click in the next game; if he fails, he has to go himself.—Marlborough, Wilts (H. S. May).

See " Cock."

Click, Clock, Cluck

A man called Click came west from Ireland,
A man called Click came west from Ireland,
A man called Click came west from Ireland,
    Courting my Aunt Judy.

A man called Clock came west from Ireland,
A man called Clock came west from Ireland,
A man called Clock came west from Ireland,
    Courting my Aunt Judy.

A man called Cluck came west from Ireland,
A man called Cluck came west from Ireland,
A man called Cluck came west from Ireland,
    Courting my Aunt Judy.

—Isle of Man (A. W. Moore).

These verses and the game are now quite forgotten, both in English and Manx. It was sung by children dancing round in a ring.

Clowt-clowt

" A kinde of playe called clowt-clowt, to beare about, or my hen hath layd."—*Nomenclator*, p. 299.

Clubby

A youthful game something like "Doddart."—Brockett's *North Country Words*.

Coal under Candlestick

A Christmas game mentioned in *Declaration of Popish Impostures*, p. 160.

Cob

A game at marbles played by two or three boys bowling a boss marble into holes made in the ground for the purpose, the number of which is generally four.—Baker's *Northamptonshire Glossary*.

Cobbin-match

A school game in which two boys are held by the legs and arms and bumped against a tree, he who holds out the longest being the victor.—Ross and Stead's *Holderness Glossary*.

Cobble

A name for " See-saw."—Jamieson.

Cobbler's Hornpipe

This was danced by a boy stooping till he was nearly in a sitting posture on the ground, drawing one leg under him until its toe rested on the ground, and steadying himself by thrusting forward the other leg so that the heel rested on the ground; the arms and head being thrown forwards as far as possible in order to maintain a balance. The thrust-out leg was drawn back and the drawn-in leg was shot out at the same time. This movement was repeated, each bringing down to the ground of the toe and heel causing a noise like that of hammering on a lap-stone. The arms were moved backwards and forwards at the same time to imitate the cobbler's sewing.—London (J. P. Emslie).

Cob-nut

The children in Yorkshire have a game which is probably an ancient English pastime. Numerous hazel-nuts are strung like the beads of a rosary. The game is played by two persons, each of whom has one of these strings, and consists in each party striking alternately, with one of the nuts on his own string, a nut of his adversary's. The field of combat is usually the crown of a hat. The object of each party is to crush the nuts of his opponent. A nut which has broken many of those of the adversary is a Cob-nut.—Brand, ii. 411; Hunter's *Hallamshire Glossary*.

(*b*) This game is played in London with chestnuts, and is called " Conquers." In Cornwall it is known as " Cock-haw."

The boys give the name of Victor-nut to the fruit of the common hazel, and play it to the words: "Cockhaw! First blaw! Up hat! Down cap! Victor!" The nut that cracks another is called a Cock-battler (*Folk-lore Journal,* v. 61). Halliwell describes this game differently. He says "it consists in pitching at a row of nuts piled up in heaps of four, three at the bottom and one at the top of each heap. The nut used for the pitching is called the Cob. All the nuts knocked down are the property of the pitcher." Alluding to the first described form, he says it "is probably a more modern game," and quotes Cotgrave *sub voce* "Chastelet" as authority for the earlier form in the way he describes it (*Dictionary*). Addy says the nuts were hardened for the purpose. When a nut was broken it was said to be "cobbered" or "cobbled" (*Sheffield Glossary*). Evans' *Leicestershire Glossary* also describes it. Darlington (*South Cheshire Words*) says this game only differs from "Cobblety-cuts" in the use of small nuts instead of chestnuts. George Eliot in *Adam Bede* has, "Gathering the large unripe nuts to play at 'Cob-nut' with" (p. 30). Britton's *Beauties of Wiltshire* gives the Isle of Wight and Hants as other places where the game is known.

See "Conquerors."

Cock

One boy is chosen Cock. The players arrange themselves in a line along one side of the playground. The Cock takes his stand in front of the players. When everything is ready, a rush across the playground is made by the players. The Cock tries to catch and "croon"—*i.e.,* put his hand upon the head of—as many of the players as he can when running from one side of the playground to the other. Those caught help the Cock in the rush back. The rush from side to side goes on till all are captured. To "croon" was the essential point in capturing. When a boy was being pursued to be taken prisoner, his great object was, when he came to close quarters with his pursuers, to save his head from being touched on the crown by one of them.—Nairn (Rev. W. Gregor).

At Duthil, Strathspey, this game goes by the name of

"Rexa-boxa-King." When the players have ranged themselves on one side of the playground, and the King has taken
his stand in front of them, he calls out "Rexa-boxa-King," or
simply "Rexa," when all the players rush to the other side.
The rush from side to side goes on till all are captured. The
one last captured becomes King in the next game.—Rev. W.
Gregor.

See "Click."

Cock-battler

Children, under the title of "Cock-battler," often in country
walks play with the hoary plantain, which they hold by the
tough stem about two inches from the head; each in turn tries
to knock off the head of his opponent's flower.—Cornwall (*Folk-
lore Journal*, v. 61).

In the North, and in Suffolk, it is called "Cocks," "a puerile
game with the tough tufted stems of the ribwort plantain"
(Brockett's *North Country Words*). Moor (*Suffolk Words*)
alludes to the game, and Holloway (*Dictionary of Provincialisms*) says in West Sussex boys play with the heads of rib
grass a similar game. Whichever loses the head first is conquered. It is called "Fighting-cocks."

Cock-fight

This is a boys' game. Two boys fold their arms, and then,
hopping on one leg, butt each other with their shoulders till one
lets down his leg. Any number of couples can join in this
game.—Nairn (Rev. W. Gregor).

Cock-haw.

See "Cob-nut."

Cock-stride

One boy is chosen as Cock. He is blindfolded, and stands
alone, with his legs as far apart as possible. The other boys
then throw their caps as far as they are able between the extended legs of the Cock (fig. 1). After the boys have thrown
their caps, and each boy has taken his stand beside his cap,
the Cock, still blindfolded, stoops down and crawls in search

of the caps (fig. 2). The boy whose cap he first finds has to run about twenty yards under the buffeting of the other boys, the

Fig. 1   Fig. 2

blows being directed chiefly to the head. He becomes Cock at the next turn of the game.—Rosehearty, Pitsligo (Rev. W. Gregor).

Cockertie-hooie

This game consists simply of one boy mounting on the neck of another, putting a leg over each shoulder and down his breast. The boy that carries takes firm hold of the legs of the one on his neck, and sets off at a trot, and runs hither and thither till he becomes tired of his burden. The bigger the one is who carries, the more is in the enjoyment to the one carried.—Keith (Rev. W. Gregor).

See "Cock's-headling."

Cockle-bread

Young wenches have a wanton sport, which they call moulding of Cocklebread; viz. they gett upon a Table-board, and then gather-up their knees and their coates with their hands as high as they can, and then they wabble to and fro with their Buttocks as if the[y] were kneading of Dowgh, and say these words, viz. :—

My Dame is sick and gonne to bed,
And I'le go mowld my cockle-bread.

In Oxfordshire the maids, when they have put themselves into the fit posture, say thus :—

My granny is sick, and now is dead,
And wee'l goe mould some cockle-bread.

Up with my heels, and down with my head,
And this is the way to mould cocklebread.
                              —Aubrey's *Remains*, pp. 43, 44.

To make "Barley bread" (in other districts, "Cockley bread")
this rhyme is used in West Cornwall:—

Mother has called, mother has said,
Make haste home, and make barley bread.
Up with your heels, down with your head,
That is the way to make barley bread.
                              —*Folk-lore Journal*, v. 58.

The Westmoreland version is given by Ellis in his edition
of Brand as follows:—

My grandy's seeke,
And like to dee,
And I'll make her
Some cockelty bread, cockelty bread,
And I'll make her
Some cockelty bread.

The term "Cockelty" is still heard among our children
at play.   One of them squats on its haunches with the hands
joined beneath the thighs, and being lifted by a couple of others
who have hold by the bowed arms, it is swung backwards and
forwards and bumped on the ground or against the wall, while
continuing the words, "This is the way we make cockelty
bread."—Robinson's *Whitby Glossary*, p. 40.

The moulding of "Cocklety-bread" is a sport amongst
hoydenish girls not quite extinct.   It consists in sitting on
the ground, raising the knees and clasping them with the hand,
and then using an undulatory motion, as if they were kneading
dough.

My granny is sick and now is dead,
And we'll go mould some cocklety bread;
Up with the heels and down with the head,
And that is the way to make cocklety bread.
                     —Hunter's MSS.; Addy's *Sheffield Glossary*.

(*b*) The *Times* of 1847 contains a curious notice of this
game.   A witness, whose conduct was impugned as light and

unbecoming, is desired to inform the court, in which an action for breach of promise was tried, the meaning of "mounting cockeldy-bread;" and she explains it as "a play among children," in which one lies down on the floor on her back, rolling backwards and forwards, and repeating the following lines:—

> Cockeldy bread, mistley cake,
> When you do that for our sake.

While one of the party so laid down, the rest sat around; and they laid down and rolled in this manner by turns.

These lines are still retained in the modern nursery-rhyme books, but their connection with the game of "Cockeldy-bread" is by no means generally understood. There was formerly some kind of bread called "cockle-bread," and *cocille-mele* is mentioned in a very early MS. quoted in Halliwell's *Dictionary*. In Peele's play of the *Old Wives Tale*, a voice thus speaks from the bottom of a well:—

> Gently dip, but not too deep,
> For fear you make the golden beard to weep.
> Fair maiden, white and red,
> Stroke me smooth and comb my head,
> And thou shalt have some *cockell-bread*.

Cockly-jock

A game among boys. Stones are loosely placed one upon another, at which other stones are thrown to knock the pile down.—Dickinson's *Cumberland Glossary*.

See "Castles."

Cock's-headling

A game where boys mount over each other's heads.—Halliwell's *Dictionary*.

See "Cockertie-hooie."

Cock-steddling

A boyish game mentioned but not described by Cope in his *Hampshire Glossary*. He gives as authority *Portsmouth Telegraph*, 27th September 1873.

Codlings

A game among youngsters similar to "Cricket," a short piece

of wood being struck up by a long stick instead of a ball by a
bat.   Also called "Tip and Go" or "Tip and Slash."—Robinson's *Whitby Glossary.*
    See "Cudgel."

Cogger

A striped snail shell.   It is a common boyish pastime to
hold one of these shells between the last joints of the bent
fingers, and forcibly press the apex against another held in a
similar manner by an opponent, until one of them, by dint of
persevering pressure, forces its way into the other; and the
one which in these contests has gained the most victories is
termed the Conqueror, and is highly valued (Northamptonshire,
Baker's *Glossary*).   The game is known as "Fighting Cocks"
in Evans' *Leicestershire Glossary.*   In London it was played
with walnut shells.

Cogs

The top stone of a pile is pelted by a stone flung from a
given distance, and the more hits, or "cogglings off," the greater
the player's score.—Robinson's *Whitby Glossary.*
    Apparently the same game as "Cockly-jock."

Common

A game played with a ball and crooked stick (cut from a tree
or hedge), with a crook at the end (same game as "Hurl").
—Dublin (Mrs. Lincoln).
    Mr. Patterson (*Antrim and Down Glossary*) mentions this
as "Hockey;" the same as "Shinney."   "Called in some
districts," he adds, "'Comun' and 'Kamman,' from the Irish
name for the game."

Conkers

The same game as "Cogger."   The game is more generally
called "playin at sneel-shells."—Ross and Stead's *Holderness
Glossary.*

Conquerors or Conkers

I.   Cobbly co !
    My first blow !

Put down your black hat,
And let me have first smack !
            —Burne's *Shropshire Folk-lore*, p. 531.

II. Obli, obli O, my first go ;
     And when the nut is struck,
     Obli, obli onker, my nut will conquer.
            —*Notes and Queries*, 5th series, x. 378.

III. Cobblety cuts,
     Put down your nuts.
            —Darlington's *Folk-speech of South Cheshire.*

IV. Obbly, obbly onkers, my first conquers ;
     Obbly, obbly O, my first go.
            —Lawson's *Upton-on-Severn Words and Phrases.*

V.   Hobley, hobley, honcor, my first conkor ;
     Hobbley, hobbley ho, my first go ;
     Hobley, hobley ack, my first crack.
            —Chamberlain's *West Worcestershire Glossary.*

(*b*) This game is played with horse chestnuts threaded on a string. Two boys sit face to face astride of a form or a log of timber. If a piece of turf can be procured so much the better. One boy lays his chestnut upon the turf, and the other strikes at it with his chestnut; and they go on striking alternately till one chestnut splits the other. The chestnut which remains unhurt is then "conqueror of one." A new chestnut is substituted for the broken one, and the game goes on. Whichever chestnut now proves victorious becomes "conqueror of two," and so on, the victorious chestnut adding to its score all the previous winnings. The chestnuts are often artificially hardened by placing them up the chimney or carrying them in a warm pocket; and a chestnut which has become conqueror of a considerable number acquires a value in schoolboys' eyes; and I have frequently known them to be sold, or exchanged for other toys (Holland's *Cheshire Glossary*). The game is more usually played by one boy striking his opponent's nut with his own, both boys standing and holding the string in their hands. It is considered bad play to strike the opponent's *string*. The nut only should be touched. Three tries are usually allowed.

(*c*) For information on various forms of this game, see *Notes and Queries*, 1878. See also Elworthy's *West Somerset Words*. The boy who first said the rhyme has first stroke at Oswestry. The game is elsewhere called "Cobbet" (Meole Brace) and "Cobbleticuts" (Burne's *Shropshire Folklore*, p. 531). In "Conquer-nuts" "obbly" was probably "nobbly" or "knobbly," expressing the appearance of the string of nuts; and "onkers" was probably invented as a rhyme to "conquers" (*Upton-on-Severn Words and Phrases*, by R. Lawson).

Contrary, Rules of

   I.   Here I go round the rules of contrary,
       Hopping about like a little canary.
       When I say " Hold fast," leave go ;
       When I say " Leave go," hold fast.
            —Cornwall (*Folk-lore Journal*, v. 52).

  II.   Here we go round the rules of contrary,
       When I say " Hold fast ! " let go, and when I say
       " Let go ! " hold fast.   —London (A. B. Gomme).

(*b*) A ring is formed by each child holding one end of a handkerchief. One child stands in the centre and acts as leader. The ring moves round slowly. The leader says the words as above while the ring is moving round, and then suddenly calls out whichever he chooses of the two sayings. If he says "Hold fast ! " every one must immediately let go the corner of the handkerchief he holds. They should all fall to the ground at once. When he says "Let go ! " every one should retain their hold of the handkerchief. Forfeits are demanded for every mistake.

This game, called " Hawld Hard," is commonly played about Christmas-time, where a number hold a piece of a handkerchief. One then moves his hand round the handkerchief, saying, " Here we go round by the rule of Contrairy ; when I say ' Hawld hard,' let go, and when I say ' Let go,' hawld hard." Forfeits are paid by those not complying with the order.— Lowsley's *Berkshire Glossary*.

Cop-halfpenny

The game of "Chuck-farthing."—Norfolk and Suffolk (Holloway's *Dict. of Provincialisms*).

Corsicrown

A square figure is divided by four lines, which cross each other in the crown or centre. Two of these lines connect the opposite angles, and two the sides at the point of bisection. Two players play; each has three men or flitchers. Now there are seven points for these men to move about on, six on the edges of the square and one at the centre. The men belonging to each player are not set together as at draughts, but mingled with each other. The one who has the first move may always have the game, which is won by getting the three men on a line.—Mactaggart's *Gallovidian Encyclopædia*.

See "Kit Cat Cannio," "Noughts and Crosses."

Cots and Twisses

A flat stone is obtained called a Hob, upon which those who are playing place equal shares of Cots and Twisses. Cots are brass buttons, and Twisses bits of brass—a Twiss of solid brass being worth many Cots. Each player provides himself with a nice flat [key] stone, and from an agreed pitch tosses it at the Hob. If he knocks off any of the Cots and Twisses nearer to the players than the Hob is, he claims them. The other players try to knock the Hob away with their key-stones from any Cots and Twisses that may not have been claimed; and if any key-stone touches Hob after all have thrown, the owner cannot claim any Cots and Twisses.—Earls Heaton (Herbert Hardy).

Each player selects a Cast or stone to pitch with; on another stone, called the Hob, the Cots and Twys are placed; at some distance Scops are set in the ground. First the players pitch from the Hob to the Scop, and the one who gets nearest goes first. He then pitches at the Hob, and if he knocks off the stakes he has them, provided his Cast is nearer to them than the Hob is; in failure of this, the other player tries. In pitching up, one Cast may rest on another, and if the boy

whose stone is underneath can lift it up to knock the other
Cast away, it has to remain at the place to which it has been
struck ; if he does not succeed in doing this, the second player
may lift off his Cast and place it by the side of the first.   Whoever knocks off the stakes, they go to the boy whose Cast is
nearest to them.   The Hob and Scop are usually three yards
apart.   The Cot was a button off the waistcoat or trousers,
the Twy one off the coat, and, as its name implies, was equal
to two Cots.   Formerly, when cash was much more rare than
now it is amongst boys, these formed their current coin.   The
game about 1820 seems to have been chiefly one of tossing,
and was played with buttons, then common enough.   Now,
metal buttons being rare, it is played with pieces of brass or
copper of any shape.   The expression, "I haven't a cot," is
sometimes used to signify that a person is without money.—
Easther's *Almondbury and Huddersfield Glossary.*

See "Banger," "Buttons."

Course o' Park

The game of "Course of the Park" has not been described,
but is referred to in the following verse :—

> "Buff" 's a fine sport,
> And so 's "Course o' Park."

—*The Slighted Maid,* 1663. p. 50.

Crab-sowl, Crab-sow

A game played with a bung or ball struck with sticks
(Brogden's *Provincial Words, Lincolnshire*).   This is played
on Barnes Common, and is apparently a form of "Hockey"
(A. B. Gomme).

Crates

The game of "Nine Holes."   This is the game described by
John Jones, M.D., in his book called *The Benefit of the Aun-
cient Bathes of Buckstones,* 1572, p. 12, as having been played
by ladies at Buxton for their amusement in wet weather.
See Pegge's *Anonymiana,* 1818, p. 126, and Addy's *Sheffield
Glossary.*

Cricket

A description of this game is not given here; its history and rules and regulations are well known, and many books have been devoted to its study. The word "Cricket" is given in Lawson's *Upton-on-Severn Words and Phrases* as a low wooden stool. He continues, "The game of 'Cricket' was probably a development of the older game of 'Stool-ball,' a dairymaid's stool being used for the wicket." Wedgwood (*Etym. Dict.*) suggests that the proper name for the bat was "cricket-staff," A.-S. *criec*, a staff.

See "Bittle-battle," "Stool-ball."

Crooky

An old game called "Crooky" was formerly played at Portarlington, Queen's co., and Kilkee, co. Clare. Fifty years ago it was played with wooden crooks and balls, but about twenty-five years ago, or a little more, mallets were introduced at Kilkee; while subsequently the name was changed to "Croquet." I have heard it stated that this game was introduced by the French refugees that settled at Portarlington. —G. H. Kinahan (*Folk-lore Journal*, ii. 265).

Cross and Pile

The game now called "Heads and Tails" (Halliwell's *Dictionary*). See *Nomenclator*, p. 299; Addy's *Sheffield Glossary*. Strutt points out that anciently the English coins were stamped on one side with a cross. See also Harland's *Lancashire Legends*, p. 139.

Cross-bars

A boys' game.—Halliwell's *Dictionary*.

Cross-questions

Nares (*Glossary*) mentions this game in a quotation from Wilson's *Inconstant Lady*, 1614. "Cross Questions and Crooked Answers" was a popular game at juvenile parties. The players sit in a circle, and each is asked in a whisper a question by the one on his left, and receives also in a whisper an answer to a question asked by himself of the person on his right. Each player must remember both the question he was asked and the answer he received, which have at the conclusion of the round to be stated aloud. Forfeits must be given if mistakes are made.—A. B. Gomme.

Cross Tig

One of the players is appointed to be Tig. He calls out the name of the one he intends to chase, and runs after him. Another player runs across between Tig and the fugitive, and then Tig runs after this cross-player until another player runs across between Tig and the fugitive; and so on. Each time a player crosses between Tig and the player he is following he leaves the original chase and follows the player who has crossed. When he captures, or, in some places, touches one of the players he is following, this player becomes Tig, and the game begins again.—Ireland (Miss Keane).

This game is known in and near London as "Cross Touch."

Cry Notchil

This is an old game where boys push one of their number into a circle they have made, and as he tries to escape push him back, crying, "No child of mine!" (Leigh's *Cheshire Glossary*). He adds, "This may be the origin of the husband's disclaimer of his wife when he 'notchils' her." To "cry notchil" is for a man to advertise that he will not be answerable for debts incurred by his wife.

Cuck-ball

A game at ball. The same as "Pize-ball." It is sometimes called "Tut-ball."—Addy's *Sheffield Glossary*.

See "Ball."

Cuckoo

A child hides and cries "Cuckoo." The seekers respond—
> Cuckoo cherry-tree,
> Catch a bird and bring it me.
> —Burne's *Shropshire Folk-lore*, p. 222.

Halliwell calls this a game at ball, and the rhyme runs—
> Cuckoo cherry tree,
> Catch a bird and bring it me;

> Let the tree be high or low,
> Let it hail, rain or snow.

See " Hide and Seek."

Cuddy and the Powks

Two boys join hands and feet over the back of a third, the which creeps away with them on hands and knees to a certain distance; and if able to do this, he, the Cuddy, must have a ride as one of the powks on some other's back.—Mactaggart's *Gallovidian Encyclopædia*.

Cudgel

Four or more boys can play this game, and sides are chosen. Two holes are made in the ground at a distance of about eight or ten feet apart. A ring about a foot in diameter is made round each hole. A boy stands at each hole with a stick, which he puts into the hole to guard it. Two other boys stand behind the holes, who act as bowlers. One of these throws a small piece of wood shaped like a Cat, and tries to pitch it into the hole. The boy guarding the hole tries to hit it with his

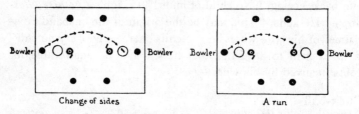

Change of sides   A run

stick. If he succeeds, he and the boy at the other hole run to each other's places. Should the boy who throws the piece of wood succeed in getting it into the hole, the batsmen are out. Should the Cat fall into the ring or a span beyond, one of the bowlers picks it up, and both run to a hiding-place. They then agree as to which of them should hold the Cat. This must be carried in such a way that it cannot be seen by the batsmen, both boys assuming the same attitude. Both boys then resume their previous places. They kneel down, still keeping the same attitudes. The batsmen, keeping their sticks in the holes, then agree which of the two holds the Cat. One batsman

runs across and puts his stick into the hole behind which the
boy kneels whom they consider has the Cat, the other then
running to his place. If they are right in their guess, the
holder of the Cat throws it across the ground for the opposite
bowler to put it in the hole before the second batsman reaches
it. If they guess wrongly, the holder of the Cat puts it into
the hole as soon as the batsman runs, and they then become the
batsmen for the next game. If the batsmen leave their holes
unguarded with the stick, the catsmen can at any time put
them " out," by putting the Cat in a hole. If more than two
boys on a side play, the others field as in " Cricket."—Barnes
(A. B. Gomme).

See " Cat and Dog."

Curcuddie

  I. Will ye gang to the lea, Curcuddie,
    And join your plack wi' me, Curcuddie ?
    I lookit about and I saw naebody,
    And linkit awa' my lane, Curcuddie.
        —Chambers' *Popular Rhymes*, p. 139.

  II. Will ye gang wi' me, Curcuddie,
    Gang wi' me o'er the lea ?
    I lookit roun', saw naebody ;
    Curcuddie, he left me.
        —Biggar (William Ballantyne).

(*b*) This is a grotesque kind of dance, performed in a shortened
posture, sitting on one's hams, with arms akimbo, the dancers
forming a circle of independent figures. It always excites a
hearty laugh among the senior bystanders ; but, ridiculous as
it is, it gives occasion for the display of some spirit and agility,
as well as skill, there being always an inclination to topple
over. Each performer sings the verse (Chambers ; Mactaggart's
Gallovidian Encyclopædia).

Mr. Ballantyne says that each one apart tried to dance by
throwing out their feet and jumping sideways.

(*c*) The first syllable of this word is, says Jamieson, undoubtedly the verb *curr*, to sit on the houghs or hams. The
second may be from Teut. *kudde*, a flock ; *kudd-en*, coire,

convenire, congregari, aggregari; *kudde wijs,* gregatim, cater-
vatim, q. to curr together.   The same game is called *Harry
Hurcheon* in the North of Scotland, either from the resemblance
of one in this position to a *hurcheon,* or hedge-hog, squatting
under a bush; or from the Belg. *hurk-en,* to squat, to *hurkle.*
—Jamieson.

See "Cobbler's Hornpipe," "Cutch-a-Cutchoo."

Curly Locks

I.   Curly locks, curly locks,
         Wilt thou be mine?
     Thou shalt not wash dishes
         Nor yet feed the swine;
     But sit on a fine cushion
         And sew a fine seam,
     And feed upon strawberries,
         Sugar and cream.
                     —Earls Heaton (Herbert Hardy).

II. Bonny lass, canny lass,
         Wilta be mine?
     Thou's nowder wesh dishes
         Nor sarra the swine:
     But sit on thy crippy, &c.
                     —Dickinson's *Cumberland Glossary.*

(*b*) Two children, a girl and a boy, separate from their
fellows, who are not particularly placed, the boy caressing the
girl's curls and singing the verses.

(*c*) This game is evidently a dramatic representation of

wooing, and probably the action of the game has never been quite completed in the nursery. The verses are given as "nursery rhymes" by Halliwell, Nos. cccclxxxiii. and ccccxciv. The tune is from Rimbault's *Nursery Rhymes*, p. 70. The words given by him are the same as the Earls Heaton version.

Currants and Raisins

> Currants and raisins a penny a pound,
> Three days holiday.

This is a game played "running under a handkerchief;" "something like 'Oranges and Lemons.'"—Lincoln (Miss M. Peacock).

Cushion Dance

This strain twice.   This once.

Play this as oft as is required.

—*Dancing Master*, 1686.

This music is exactly as it is printed in the book referred to.

(*b*) The following is an account of the dance as it was known in Derbyshire amongst the farmers' sons and daughters and the domestics, all of whom were on a pretty fair equality, very different from what prevails in farm-houses of to-day. The "Cushion Dance" was a famous old North-country amusement, and among the people of Northumberland it is still commonly observed. The dance was performed with boisterous fun, quite unlike the game as played in higher circles, where the conditions and rules of procedure were of a more refined order.

The company were seated round the room, a fiddler occupying a raised seat in a corner. When all were ready, two of the young men left the room, returning presently, one carrying a large square cushion, the other an ordinary drinking-horn, china bowl, or silver tankard, according to the possessions of the family. The one carrying the cushion locked the door, putting the key in his pocket. Both gentlemen then went to the fiddler's corner, and after the cushion-bearer had put a coin in the vessel carried by the other, the fiddler struck up a lively tune, to which the young men began to dance round the room, singing or reciting to the music :—

> Frinkum, frankum is a fine song,
> An' we will dance it all along;
> All along and round about,
> Till we find the pretty maid out.

After making the circuit of the room, they halted on reaching the fiddler's corner, and the cushion-bearer, still to the music of the fiddle, sang or recited :—

> Our song it will no further go!

The Fiddler : Pray, kind sir, why say you so?

The Cushion-bearer : Because Jane Sandars won't come to.

The Fiddler : She must come to, she shall come to,
> An' I'll make her whether she will or no.

The cushion-bearer and vessel-holder then proceeded with the dance, going as before round the room, singing " Frinkum, frankum," &c., till the cushion-bearer came to the lady of his choice, before whom he paused, placed the cushion on the floor at her feet, and knelt upon it. The vessel-bearer then offered the cup to the lady, who put money in it and knelt on the cushion in front of the kneeling gentleman. The pair kissed, arose, and the gentleman, first giving the cushion to the lady with a bow, placed himself behind her, taking hold of some portion of her dress. The cup-bearer fell in also, and they danced on to the fiddler's corner, and the ceremony was again gone through as at first, with the substitution of the name of " John " for " Jane," thus :—

The Lady :   Our song it will no further go!

The Fiddler : Pray, kind miss, why say you so?

The Lady :   Because John Sandars won't come to.

The Fiddler : He must come to, he shall come to,
> An' I'll make him whether he will or no!

The dancing then proceeded, and the lady, on reaching her choice (a gentleman, of necessity), placed the cushion at his feet. He put money in the horn and knelt. They kissed and rose, he taking the cushion and his place in front of the lady, heading the next dance round, the lady taking him by the coat-tails, the first gentleman behind the lady, with the horn-bearer in the rear. In this way the dance went on till all present, alternately a lady and gentleman, had taken part in the cere-mony. The dance concluded with a romp in file round the room to the quickening music of the fiddler, who at the close received the whole of the money collected by the horn-bearer.

At Charminster the dance is begun by a single person (either man or woman), who dances about the room with a cushion in his hand, and at the end of the tune stops and sings :—

Man :   This dance it will no further go.
Musician : I pray you, good sir, why say you so ?
Man :   Because Joan Sanderson will not come to.
Musician : She must come to, and she shall come to,
              And she must come whether she will or no.

Then the following words are sung as in the first example :—

Man : Welcome, Joan Sanderson, welcome, welcome.
Both : Prinkum-prankum is a fine dance,
          And shall we go dance it once again,
                And once again,
          And shall we go dance it once again ?
Woman : This dance it will no further go.
Musician : I pray you, madam, why say you so ?
Woman : Because John Sanderson will not come to.
Musician : He must come to, and he shall come to,
              And he must come whether he will or no.

And so she lays down the cushion before a man, who, kneeling upon it, salutes her, she singing—

          Welcome, John Sanderson, &c.

Then, he taking up the cushion, they take hands and dance round singing as before ; and this they do till the whole com-pany is taken into the ring. Then the cushion is laid down before the first man, the woman singing, " This dance," &c., as before, only instead of " come to," they sing " go fro," and in-stead of "Welcome, John Sanderson," &c., they sing "Farewell,

John Sanderson, farewell," &c., and so they go out one by one
as they came in.—Charminster (*Notes and Queries*, ii. 517, 518).

This description is almost the same as a seventeenth century
version. The dance is begun by a single person (either man
or woman), who, taking a cushion in his hand, dances about
the room, and at the end of the tune he stops and sings:—

> This dance it will no further go.

The Musician answers:

> I pray you, good sir, why say you so?

Man :   Because Joan Sanderson will not come to.

Musician : She must come to, and she shall come to,
> And she must come whether she will or no.

Then he lays down the cushion before a woman, on which
she kneels, and he kisses her, singing—

> Welcom, Joan Sanderson, welcom, welcom.

Then he rises, takes up the cushion, and both dance, singing—

> Prinkum-prankum is a fine dance,
> And shall we go dance it once again,
>> Once again, and once again,
> And shall we go dance it once again.

Then, making a stop, the wo(man) sings as before—

> This dance, &c.

Musician : I pray you, madam, &c.

Woman :   Because John Sanderson, &c.

Musician : He must, &c.

And so she lays down the cushion before a man, who,
kneeling upon it, salutes her, she singing—

> Welcom, John Sanderson, &c.

Then, he taking up the cushion, they take hands and dance
round, singing as before. And thus they do till the whole
company are taken into the ring. And then the cushion is
laid before the first man, the woman singing, "This dance," &c.
(as before), only instead of "come to," they sing "go fro," and
instead of "Welcom, John Sanderson," &c., they sing "Farewel,
John Sanderson, farewel, farewel;" and so they go out one by
one as they came in. *Note*, that the woman is kiss'd by all
the men in the ring at her coming in and going out, and the
like of the man by the woman.—*The Dancing Master:* London,

printed by J. P., and sold, by John Playford at his shop near
the Temple Church, 1686, 7th edition.

Another version gives the words as follows :—

> We've got a new sister in our degree,
> And she's welcome into our companee, companee.
> Mrs. Sargesson says she weänt come to,
> We'll make her whether she will or no,
> Will or no, will or no,
> We'll maäke her whether she will or no.

Children form a ring with one in the middle, who lays a
cushion on the ground. They sing the first two lines, and the
child in the centre points at one, and the others dance round
singing the other lines, the centre child dragging the imaginary
Mrs. Sargesson on to the cushion by force, kissing her, and
leaving her in the centre. Then Mrs. Sargesson points at one
in the ring, and the game begins again.—East Kirkby, Lincolnshire (Miss Maughan). The tune sung is the same as the
" Mulberry Bush."

Miss Baker (*Northamptonshire Glossary*) says the Cushion
Dance is still continued, with some variations, and generally
closes the evening's amusements. One of the young men
endeavours secretly to bring in a cushion, and locks the doors,
to prevent the escape of the young maidens ; then all the party
unite hands and dance round three times to the left and three
times to the right, after which the company all seat themselves,
except the young man who holds the cushion. He advances
to the fiddler, and says—

	This dance it will no further go.
Fiddler :	Why say you so ? why say you so ?
Cushion-holder :	Because the young women will not come to.
Fiddler :	They must come to, they shall come to,
	And tell them I say so.

The cushion-holder then goes to the girl he fancies most, and
drops the cushion at her feet. She kneels down with him on
the cushion, and he salutes her, and they then rise and dance
round and round to the fiddler. The girls then go through the
same thing, saying, "young men," and then "a young man," &c.,
until the whole company have gone through the same ceremony,

which concludes with all dancing round three times, as at the commencement.

The Norfolk and London versions are reduced to a simple "Kiss in the Ring" game, with the following verse:—

> Round the cushion we dance with glee,
> Singing songs so merrily;
> Round the cushion we dance with glee,
> Singing songs so merrily;
> Yet the punishment you must bear
> If you touch the cushion there.
>
> Sporle, Norfolk (Miss Matthews).

(c) Selden, in his *Table Talk*, thus refers to this game:— "The Court of England is much altered. At a solemn dancing first you have the grave measures, then the Cervantoes and the Golliards, and this is kept up with ceremony. At length to Trenchmore and the *Cushion Dance;* and then all the company dance, lord and groom, lady and kitchen-maid, no distinction. But in King Charles's time there has been nothing but Trenchmore and the Cushion Dance," &c. The "Whishin Dance" (an old-fashioned dance, in which a cushion is used to kneel upon), mentioned by Dickinson (*Cumberland Glossary*), is probably the same game or dance, "whishin" meaning cushion. Brockett (*North Country Words*) mentions "Peas Straw," the final dance at a rustic party; something similar to the ancient "Cushion Dance" at weddings. It is also recorded in Evans' *Leicestershire Glossary*, and by Burton in the following passage from the *Anatomy of Melancholy:* "A friend of his reprehended him for dancing beside his dignity, belike at some cushen dance." In the version from East Kirkby, Lincolnshire, the expression "in our degree" in the first line of the verse is apparently meaningless, and it is probably a corruption of "highdigees, highdegrees," a dialect word for roystering, high spirits, merriment, dancing, romping. Elworthy (*Somerset Words*) gives this word, and quotes the following line from Drayton:—

> Dance many a merry round and many a highdegy.
>
> —*Polyolbion*, Bk. xxv., l. 1162.

(d) The transition from a dance to a pure game is well

illustrated by the different versions, and the connection of the dance with the ceremony of marriage is obvious. A curious account of the merry-makings at marriages is given in Coverdale's *Christen State of Matrimony*, 1543: "After the banket and feast there beginneth a mad and unmannerly fashion ; for the bride must be brought into an open dauncing-place. Then is there such a running, leaping, and flinging among them that a man might think all these dauncers had cast all shame behinde them, and were become starke mad, and out of their wits, and that they were sworne to the devil's daunce. Then must the bride keep foote with all dauncers, and refuse none, how scabbed, foule, drunken, rude, and shameless soever he be. . . . After supper must they begin to pipe and daunce again of anew. And though the young persons come once towards their rest, yet can they have no quietness."—1575 edit., fol. 59, rev. 60. Edward L. Rimbault, writing in *Notes and Queries*, vi. 586, says it was formerly the custom at weddings, both of the rich as well as the poor, to dance after dinner and supper. In an old Court masque of James I.'s time, performed at the marriage ceremony of Philip Herbert and Lady Susan (MS. in the writer's possession), it is directed that, at the conclusion of the performance, "after supper" the company "dance a round dance." This was "dancing the bride to bed." William Chappell (*Notes and Queries*, ii. 442) says, "I have a tune called 'A round dance to dance the bride to bed.' It dates from about 1630, or earlier, and resembles that of 'The Hunt is up.'" Dancing was considered so essential at weddings (according to Grose) that if in a family the youngest daughter should chance to be married before her elder sisters, they must dance at her wedding without shoes. May not the custom of throwing of old and worn-out shoes after the bride have arisen from the practice of dancing? The danced-out shoes may have been the ones used. It is curious that the cushion is used in the marriage ceremonies of the Brahmins. Mr. Kearns, in his *Marriage Ceremonies of the Hindoos of the South of India*, p. 6, says that a stool or cushion is one of the preparations for the reception of the bridegroom, who on entering the apartment sits down on the stool which is presented to him. He says,

" I step on this for the sake of food and other benefits, on this variously splendid footstool." The bride's father then presents to him a cushion made of twenty leaves of cúsa grass, holding it up with both hands and exclaiming, " The cushion! the cushion! the cushion!" The bridegroom replies, " I accept the cushion," and taking it, places it on the ground under his feet, while he recites a prayer. It is probable that we may have in the " Cushion Dance" the last relics of a very ancient ceremony, as well as evidence of the origin of a game from custom.

Cutch-a-Cutchoo

Children clasp their hands under their knees in a sitting posture, and jump thus about the room. The one who keeps up longest wins the game.—Dublin (Mrs. Lincoln).

(b) In *Notes and Queries*, x. 17, " E. D." says this amusement was fashionable sixty years ago, and from the low dresses worn then by ladies he mentions its indecency. He gives extracts from a satire called *Cutchacutchoo, or the Jostling of the Innocents*, 2nd ed., Dublin, in which the game and position are mentioned—

> Now she with tone tremendous cries
> Cutchacutchoo.
> Let each squat down upon her ham,
> Jump like a goat, puck like a ram.

" Uneda," at same reference (x. 17), speaks of it as a known game in Philadelphia. The analogy which this game has to some savage dances is curious; a correspondent in *Notes and Queries*, ix. 304, draws attention to the illustration, in Richardson's *Expedition to Arctic Shores* (vol. i. p. 397), of a dance by the " Kutchin-Kutcha" Indians, a parallel to the name as well as the dance which needs some research in America.

See " Curcuddie," " Hop-frog."

Cutters and Trucklers

A remembrance of the old smuggling days. The boys divide into two parties; the Trucklers try to reach some given point before the Cutter catches them.—Cornwall (*Folk-lore Journal*, v. 60).

Dab

Dab a prin in my lottery book ;
Dab ane, dab twa, dab a' your prins awa'.

A game in which a pin is put at random in a school-book, between the leaves of which little pictures are placed. The successful adventurer is the person who puts the pin between two leaves including a picture which is the prize, and the pin itself is the forfeit (*Blackwood's Magazine*, Aug. 1821, p. 36). This was a general school game in West London in 1860–1866 (G. L. Gomme).

Dab-an-thricker

A game in which the *dab* (a wooden ball) is caused to spring upwards by a blow on the *thricker* (trigger), and is struck by a flat, bottle-shaped mallet fixed to the end of a flexible wand, the distance it goes counting so many for the striker.—Ross and Stead's *Holderness Glossary*.

This is the same as " Knur and Spell."

Dab-at-the-hole

A game at marbles (undescribed).—Patterson's *Antrim and Down Glossary*.

Dalies

A child's game, played with small bones or pieces of hard wood. The *dalies* were properly sheep's trotters.—Halliwell's *Dictionary*.

Evidently the same game as "Fivestones" and "Hucklebones."

Davie-drap

Children amuse themselves on the braesides i' the sun, playing at " Hide and Seek " with this little flower, accompanying always the hiding of it with this rhyme, marking out the circle in which it is hid with the forefinger :—

Athin the bounds o' this I hap,
My black and bonny davie-drap ;
Wha is here the cunning yin
My davie-drap to me will fin.

—Mactaggart's *Gallovidian Encyclopædia*.

The davie-drap is a little black-topped field-flower.

Deadily

A school game, not described.—Mactaggart's *Gallovidian Encyclopædia*.

Diamond Ring

My lady's lost her diamond ring;
I pitch upon you to find it!

Children sit in a ring or in a line, with their hands placed together palm to palm, and held straight, the little finger downmost between the knees. One of them is then chosen to represent a servant, who takes a ring, or some other small article as a substitute, between her two palms, which are pressed flat together like those of the rest, and goes round the circle or line placing her hands into the hands of every player, so that she is enabled to let the ring fall wherever she pleases without detection. After this she returns to the first child she touched, and with her hands behind her says the above words. The child who is thus addressed must guess who has the ring, and the servant performs the same ceremony with each of the party. They who guess right escape, but the rest forfeit. Should any one in the ring exclaim "I have it!" she also forfeits; nor must the servant make known who has the ring until all have guessed under the same penalty. The forfeits are afterwards cried as usual.—Halliwell's *Nursery Rhymes*, p. 223.

(*b*) This game was a general favourite at juvenile parties years ago. The hands were held in the posture described by Halliwell, but any child was pitched upon for the first finder, and afterwards the child in whose hands the ring was found had to be finder. There was no guessing; the closed hands were looked into (A. B. Gomme). Mr. Addy has collected a similar game called "My lady's lost a gold ring," and Mr. Newell (*Games and Songs of American Children*, p. 150) has another, "Hold fast my gold ring."

Dibbs

A game played with the small knuckle-bones taken from legs of mutton; these bones are themselves called "dibs" (Lowsley's

Glossary of Berkshire Words). Holloway's *Dictionary* says five of these bones are used by boys, with which they play a game called " Dibs " in West Sussex.

See " Check-stones," " Fivestones," " Hucklebones."

Dinah

No one in the house but Dinah, Dinah,
No one in the house I know, I know ;
No one in the house but Dinah, Dinah,
Playing on the old banjo.

A ring is formed, and a girl stands blindfolded inside. As the verse is sung and finished, Dinah goes to any one in the ring, and, if successful in guessing her name, takes her place, the other taking the place of Dinah, the game going on as before.—Earls Heaton (Herbert Hardy).

" Dinah " was a Christy Minstrel song in the " fifties." It is probable that the game, which resembles " Buff," has been played to the tune of the song. Singing a chorus would soon follow.

See " Buff," " Muffin Man."

Dip o' the Kit

A rustic game, undescribed and marked as obsolescent.—Peacock's *Manley and Corringham Glossary.*

Dish-a-loof

A singular rustic amusement. One lays his hand down on a table, another clashes his upon it, a third his on that, and so on (fig. 1). When all the players have done this, the one who has his hand on the board pulls it out and lays it on the one uppermost (fig. 2): they all follow in rotation, and so a continual clashing and dashing is kept up; hence the name " Dish." Those who win the game are those who stand out longest—viz., those who are best at enduring pain. Tender hands could not stand it a moment: one dash of a rustic "loof" would make the blood spurt from the tip of every finger. It is a piece of pastime to country lads of the same nature as "Hard Knuckles" (Mactaggart's *Gallovidian Encyclopædia*). This is a well-known game for small children in

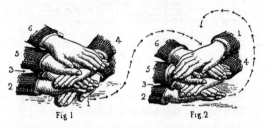

Fig 1   Fig. 2

London. After each child's hands have been withdrawn and replaced on top as many times as possible without deranging the order, a general scramble and knocking of hands together ends the game (A. B. Gomme). Jamieson (*Etymological Dict.*) gives this as a sport of children.

See "Dump," "Green Grass," "Hot Cockles."

Doddart

A game played in a large level field with a bent stick called "doddart." Two parties, headed by two captains, endeavour to drive a wooden ball to their respective boundaries (Halliwell's *Dictionary*). Brockett (*North Country Words*) adds to this that the captains are entitled to choose their followers by alternate votes. A piece of globular wood called an "orr" or "coit" is thrown down in the middle of the field and driven to one of two opposite hedges—the alley, hail-goal, or boundary. The same game as "Clubby," "Hockey," "Shinney," "Shinneyhaw."

Doncaster Cherries

One boy kneels, holding a long rope, the other end of which is held by another boy; the other players stand round about with handkerchiefs in hands, knotted. The one who holds the rope-end and standing cries out—

> Doncaster cherries, ripe and sound ;
> Touch 'em or taste 'em—
> Down, you dogs !
> —Earls Heaton, Yorkshire (H. Hardy).

This is evidently a version of " Badger the Bear," with a different and apparently degraded formula.

Dools

A school game.   The dools are places marked with stones, where the players always remain in safety—where they dare neither be caught by the hand nor struck with balls.   It is only when they leave these places of refuge that those out of the doons have any chance to gain the game and get in ; and leave the doons they frequently must—this is the nature of the game.   Now this game seems to have been often played in reality by our ancestors about their doon-hills.—Mactaggart's *Gallovidian Encyclopædia*.

Down in the Valley

I. Down in the valley where the green grass grows
Stands E—— H——, she blows like a rose.
She blows, she blows, she blows so sweet.
In came F—— S—— and gave her a kiss.
E—— made a pudding, she made it nice and sweet,
F—— took a knife and fork and cut a little piece.
Taste of it, taste of it, don't say nay,
For next Sunday morning is our wedding day.
First we'll buy a money box,
Then we'll buy a cradle ;
Rock, rock the bottom out,
Then we'll buy another.
Bread and cheese all the week, cork on Sunday,
Half a crown on Saturday night, and a jolly good dance on
Monday.   —Cowes, Isle of Wight (Miss E. Smith).

II. Down in the meadows where the green grass grows,
To see —— blow like a rose.
She blows, she blows, she blows so sweet.

Go out, ——; who shall he be ?
—— made a pudding,
She made it so sweet,
And never stuck a knife in
Till —— came to eat.
Taste, love, taste, love, don't say nay,
For next Monday morning is your wedding day.
He bought her a gown and a guinea gold ring,
And a fine cocked hat to be married in.

> —West Haddon, Northamptonshire ; Long Itchington,
> Warwickshire (*Northants Notes and Queries*, ii. 105).

III. Down in the valley the violets grow.
Dear little ——, she blows like a rose.
She blows, she blows, she blows so sweet.
   Come along in.
Buy a shawl, buy a new black shawl,
A bonnet trimmed with white and a new parasol.
Oh dear, oh dear, what can I do,
For next Monday morning is my wedding due.

> —Shipley, Horsham ; *Notes and Queries*,
> 8th series, i. 210 (Miss Busk).

(*b*) The children form a ring by joining hands, one child standing in the centre. They dance round. At the mention of the second name one from the ring goes into the centre. The two kiss at the end of the verse, and the first child takes the place in the ring, and the game begins again.

See "All the Boys," "Oliver, Oliver, follow the King."

Drab and Norr
A game similar to "Trippit and Coit."—Halliwell's *Dict.*

Draw a Pail of Water

> —Sporle, Norfolk (Miss Matthews).

I.   Draw a pail of water
     For my lady's daughter;
     My father's a king and my mother's a queen,
     My two little sisters are dressed in green,
     Stamping grass and parsley,
     Marigold leaves and daisies.
     One rush, two rush,
     Pray thee, fine lady, come under my bush.
             —Halliwell's *Nursery Rhymes*, Games, cclxxxvii.

II. Draw a pail of water,
     Send a lady a daughter;
     One o' my rush, two o' my rush,
     Please, young lady, creep under the briar bush.
                     —Liphook, Hants (Miss Fowler).

III. Draw, draw water,
     For my lady's daughter;
       One in a rush,
       Two in a bush,
     Pretty my lady, pop under the bush.
                 —Berrington and Ellesmere (*Shropshire
                         Folk-lore*, p. 521).

IV. Draw a bucket o' water
     For a lady's daughter;
     One and a hush, two and a rush,
     Please, young lady, come under my bush.
                     —Fochabers (Rev. W. Gregor).

V.   Draw a bucket of water
     For a lady's daughter;
       One in a bush,
       Two in a bush,
       Three in a bush,
       Four in a bush,
         And out you go.
                 Crockham Hill, Kent (Miss Chase).

VI. Drawing a bucket of water
     For my lady's daughter;

Put it in a chestnut tree,
And let it stay an hour.
One of you rush, two may rush,
Please, old woman, creep under the bush ;
The bush is too high, the bush is too low,
Please, old woman, creep under the bush.
                    —Hampshire (Miss Mendham).

VII. Draw a pail of water
      For a lady's daughter ;
      Give a silver pin for a golden ring—
      Oh pray, young lady, pop under.
                    —Northants (Rev. W. D. Sweeting).

VIII. Draw a bucket of water
       For my lady's daughter ;
       One go rush, and the other go hush,
       Pretty young lady, bop under my bush.
                    —Sporle, Norfolk (Miss Matthews).

IX.   Draw a bucket of water
      For the farmer's daughter ;
      Give a gold ring and a silver watch,
      Pray, young lady, pop under.
                    —Sporle, Norfolk (Miss Matthews).

X.   Draw a bucket of water
      For my lady's daughter ;
      A guinea gold ring
      And a silver pin,
      So pray, my young lady, pop under.
                    —Haydon (Herbert Hardy).

XI.   Draw a bucket of water
      To wash my lady's garter ;
      A guinea gold ring
      And a silver pin,
      Please, little girl, pop under.
                    —Earls Heaton (Herbert Hardy).

XII. See-saw, a bucket of water,
      To wash my lady's garter.

One in a rush, and two in a bush,
To see a fine lady pop under a bush.
> —Anderby, Lincolnshire, and Nottinghamshire
> near the Trent (Miss Peacock).

XIII.   One we go rush,
Two we go push;
Lady come under the corner bush.
> —Shepscombe, Gloucestershire
> (Miss Mendham).

XIV.   Sift the lady's oaten meal, sift it into flour,
Put it in a chest of drawers and let it lie an hour.
  One of my rush,
  Two of my rush,
Please, young lady, come under my bush.
My bush is too high, my bush is too low,
Please, young lady, come under my bow.
Stir up the dumpling, stir up the dumpling.
> —Belfast (W. H. Patterson).

XV.   Sieve my lady's oatmeal,
  Grind my lady's flour;
Put it in a chestnut,
  Let it stand an hour.
One may rush, two may rush;
Come, my girls, walk under the bush.
> —Halliwell's *Nursery Rhymes*, Games, cclxxxviii.

(*b*) The Berrington version of this game is played as
follows:—Two girls face each other, holding each other by
both hands. Two others face each other, holding both hands
across the other two. They see-saw backwards and forwards,
singing the lines (fig. 1). One girl gets inside the enclosing
hands (fig. 2, and they repeat till all four have "popped
under" (fig. 3, when they "jog" up and down till they fall on
the floor! (fig. 4). At Ellesmere only *two* girls join hands,
and as many "pop under" as they can encircle. The
Lincolnshire and Norfolk versions are played practically in
the same way. In the Liphook version the children stand
in two and two opposite to each other; the children on

one side of the square hold hands up at the third line,
and the other two children run under the hands of the first
two.   There is no pause, but the verse is sung time after time,
so that the four children are nearly always moving.   In the
other Hampshire version four girls stand in a square, each
holding the hands of the one opposite to her, pulling each
other's hands backwards and forwards singing the lines.   Two
arms are then raised, and one girl comes under; this is repeated till all four girls have come under the arms, then

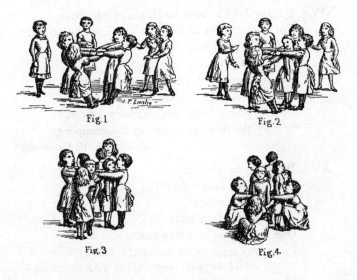

Fig. 1   Fig. 2

Fig. 3   Fig. 4

their arms encircle each other's waists and they dance round.
In the Scottish version there are only two girls who join hands
and pull each other backwards and forwards, repeating the
words.   Halliwell describes a different action to any of these.
A string of children, hand in hand, stand in a row.   A child
stands in front of them as leader; two other children form
an arch, each holding both of the hands of the other.   The
string of children pass under the arch, the last of whom is
taken captive by the two holding hands.   The verses are
repeated until all are taken.—Halliwell's *Nursery Rhymes*,
cclxxxvii.

   (c) The analysis of the game rhymes is as follows :—

No.	Halliwell's Version.	Liphook (Hants).	Shropshire.	Fochabers (Scotland).	Hampshire.	Northants.	Norfolk (1).	Norfolk (2).
1.	Draw a pail of water.	Draw a pail of water.	Draw, draw water.	Draw a bucket o water.	Drawing a bucket of water.	Draw a pail of water.	Draw a bucket of water.	Draw a bucket of water.
2.	—	—	—	—	—	—	—	—
3.								
4.	For my lady's daughter.	Send a lady a daughter.	For my lady's daughter.	For a lady's daughter.	For my lady's daughter.	For a lady's daughter.	For my lady's daughter.	For the farmer's daughter.
5.	—	—	—	—	Put it in a chestnut tree.	—	—	—
6.					Let it stay an hour.			
7.	My father's a king and my mother's a queen.							
8.		—	—	—	—	—	—	—
9.	My two little sisters are dressed in green.							
10.	Stamping grass and parsley.	—	—	—	—	—	—	—
11.	Marigold leaves and daisies.							
12.	One rush, two rush.	One o' my rush, two o' my rush.	One in a rush, two in a bush.	One and a hush, two and a rush.	One of you rush, two may rush.	—	One go rush and the other go hush.	—
13.	—	—	—	—		Give a silver pin for a golden ring.	—	Give a gold ring and a silver watch.
14.	Pray thee, fine lady, come under my bush.	Please, young lady, creep under the *briar* bush.	Pretty my lady, pop under the bush.	Please, young lady, come under my bush.	Please, old woman, creep under the bush.	Pray, young lady, pop under.	Pretty young lady, bop under my bush.	Pray, young lady, pop under.
15.					The bush is too high, the bush is too low.			
16.					Please, old woman, creep under the bush.			
17.	—	—	—	—		—	—	—
18.								

No.	Haydon.	Earls Heaton.	Lincolnshire and Nottinghamshire.	Gloucestershire.	Belfast.	Halliwell's Version (No. 2).	Crockham Hill.
1.	Draw a bucket of water.	Draw a bucket of water.	See saw, a bucket of water.	—	—	—	Draw a bucket of water.
2.	—	—	—	—	Sift the lady's oatmeal.	Sieve my lady's oatmeal.	—
3.	For my lady's daughter.	—	—	—	Sift it into flour.	Grind my lady's flour.	—
4.	—	—	—	—	—	—	For a lady's daughter.
5.	—	To wash my lady's garter.	To wash my lady's garter.	—	—	—	—
6.	—	—	—	—	Put it in a chest of drawers.	Put it in a chestnut.	—
7.	—	—	—	—	Let it lie an hour.	Let it stand an hour.	—
8.	—	—	One in a rush and two in a bush.	One we go rush, two we go push.	One of my rush, two of my rush.	One may rush, two may rush.	One in a bush,
9.	—	—	—	—	—	—	two in a bush,
10.	—	—	—	—	—	—	three in a bush,
11.	—	—	—	—	—	—	four in a bush.
12.	—	—	—	—	—	—	—
13.	A guinea gold ring and a silver pin. Pray, young lady, pop under.	A guinea gold ring and a silver pin. Please, little girl, pop under.	To see a fine lady pop under a bush.	Lady, come under the corner bush.	Please, young lady, come under my bush.	Come, my girls, walk under the bush.	—
14.	—	—	—	—	My bush is too high, my bush is too low.	—	—
15.	—	—	—	—	Please, young lady, come under my bow.	—	—
16.	—	—	—	—	Stir up the dumpling.	—	—
17.	—	—	—	—	—	—	—
18.	—	—	—	—	—	—	And out you go.

The analysis shows that the majority of the variants retain four principal incidents of what must have been the original form of the game, and the fact of the Gloucestershire version having come down with only two of the incidents, namely, the two most common to all the variants (12 and 14), shows that the game has been in a state of decadence. The four principal incidents, Nos. 1, 4, 12, and 14, point distinctly to some water ceremonial; and if it may be argued that the incidents which occur in only one or two of the variants may be considered to have belonged to the original type, we shall be able to suggest that this game presents a dramatic representation of ancient well-worship. The incidents which occur in one version only are those given by Mr. Halliwell, and unfortunately the locality from which he obtained this variant is unknown. Still it is an earlier version than those which are now printed for the first time, and may without doubt be looked upon as genuine. Taking all the incidents of the various versions as the means by which to restore the earliest version, it would appear that this might have consisted of the following lines :—

Draw a pail of water
For a lady's daughter ;
Her father's a king, her mother's a queen,
Her two little sisters are dressed in green,
Stamping grass and parsley, marigold leaves and daisies ;
Sift the lady's oatmeal, sift it into flour,
Put it in a chestnut tree, let it lie an hour ;
Give a silver pin and a gold ring,
One and a hush ! two and a rush !
Pray, young lady, pop under a bush ;
My bush is too high, my bush is too low,
Please, young lady, come under my bow !

(*d*) This restoration of the words, though it probably is far from complete, and does not make so good a game rhyme as the reduced versions, nevertheless shows clearly enough that the incidents belong to a ceremonial of primitive well-worship. The pulling of the hands backwards and forwards may be taken to indicate the raising of water from a well. If this is conceded, the incidents might be grouped as follows :—

(1.) Drawing of water from a well.

(2.) For a devotee at the well.

(3.) Collecting flowers for dressing the well.

(4.) Making of a cake for presentation.

(5.) Gifts to the well [the silver pin, gold ring, and probably the garter].

(6.) Command of silence.

(7.) The presence of the devotee at the sacred bush.

All these are incidents of primitive well-worship (see Gomme's *Ethnology and Folk-lore*, pp. 82–103). Garland dressing is very general; cakes were eaten at Rorrington well, Shropshire (Burne's *Shropshire Folk-lore*, p. 433); pins and portions of the dress are very general offerings; silence is strictly enforced in many instances, and a sacred tree or bush is very frequently found near the well.

The tune of the Hampshire game (Miss Mendham's version) is practically the same as that of the " Mulberry Bush."

Newell (*Games of American Children*, p. 90) gives a version of this game.

Drawing Dun out of the Mire

Brand, quoting from "an old collection of satires, epigrams, &c.," says this game is enumerated among other pastimes:

> At shove-groat, venter-point, or crosse and pile,
> At leaping o'er a Midsummer bone-fier,
> Or at *the drawing Dun out of the myer*.

So in the *Dutchesse of Suffolke*, 1631:

> Well done, my masters, lends your hands,
> *Draw Dun out of the ditch*;
> Draw, pull, helpe all, so, so, well done.
> [*They pull him out*.

They had shoved Bishop Bonner into a well, and were pulling him out.

We find this game noticed at least as early as Chaucer's time, in the *Manciple's Prologue*:

> Then gan our hoste to jape and to play,
> And sayd, sires, what? *Dun is in the mire*.

Nares (*Glossary*) says this game was a rural pastime, in

which *Dun* meant a dun horse, supposed to be stuck in the mire, and sometimes represented by one of the persons who played.

Gifford (*Ben Jonson*, vol. vii. p. 283), who remembered having played at the game (doubtless in his native county, Devonshire), thus describes it :—" A log of wood is brought into the midst of the room : this is Dun (the cart horse), and a cry is raised that he is stuck in the mire. Two of the company advance, either with or without ropes, to draw him out. After repeated attempts they find themselves unable to do it, and call for more assistance. The game continues till all the company take part in it, when Dun is extricated of course ; and the merriment arises from the awkward and affected efforts of the rustics to lift the log, and sundry arch contrivances to let the ends of it fall on one another's toes."

Drop Handkerchief

This is a game similar to Cat and Mouse, but takes its name from the use of the handkerchief to start the pursuit. Various rhyming formulæ are used in some places. In Monton, Lancashire (Miss Dendy), no rhyme is used.

The children stand in a ring. One runs round with a handkerchief and drops it ; the child behind whom it is dropped chases the dropper, the one who gets home first takes the vacant place, the other drops the handkerchief again.

In Shropshire the two players pursue one another in and out of the ring, running under the uplifted hands of the players who compose it : the pursuer carefully keeping on the track of the pursued (Burne's *Shropshire Folk-lore*, p. 512).

The Dorsetshire variant is accompanied by a rhyme :

I wrote a letter to my love ;
I carried water in my glove ;
And by the way I dropped it—
I dropped it, I dropped it, I dropped it, &c.

This is repeated until the handkerchief is stealthily dropped immediately behind one of the players, who should be on the alert to follow as quickly as possible the one who has dropped it, who at once increases her speed and endeavours to take the place left vacant by her pursuer.　Should she be caught before she can succeed in doing this she is compelled to take the handkerchief a second time.　But if, as it more usually happens, she is successful in accomplishing this, the pursuer in turn takes the handkerchief, and the game proceeds as before.— Symondsbury (*Folk-lore Journal*, vi. 212).

> Jack lost his supper last night,
> And the night before; if he does again to-night,
> He never will no more—more—more—more.

> I wrote a letter to my love,
> And on the way I dropt it;
> Some of you have picked it up,
> And got it in your pocket—pocket—pocket—pocket.

> I have a little dog, it won't bite you—
> It won't bite you—it won't bite you—
> It *will* bite you.
> 　　　　　　　　　　　—Leicestershire (Miss Ellis).

The Forest of Dean version is the same as the Dorsetshire, except that the child who is unsuccessful in gaining the vacant place has to stand in the middle of the ring until the same thing happens to another child.—Miss Matthews.

In Nottinghamshire the children form in a ring; one walks round outside the ring singing and carrying a handkerchief:

> I wrote a letter to my love, and on the way I dropt it;
> One of you has picked it up and put it in your pocket.
> It isn't you, it isn't you, &c. &c.; it is you.

The handkerchief is then dropped at some one's back, the one at whose back the handkerchief was dropped chasing the other.

Or they say:

> I lost my supper last night, I lost it the night before,
> And if I lose it again to-night, I'll knock at somebody's door.
> It isn't you, it isn't you, &c. &c.; it's you.
> 　　　　　　　　　　　　—Miss Winfield.

At Winterton and Lincoln the children form a circle, standing arms-length apart.　A child holding a handkerchief occupies the centre of the ring and sings:

Wiskit-a-waskit,
A green leather basket ;
I wrote a letter to my love,
And on the way I lost it ;
Some of you have picked it up,
And put it in your pocket.
I have a little dog at home,
And it shan't bite you,
(Here the singer points to each child in turn)
Nor you, nor you, nor you ;
But it shall bite *you*.

Then she drops the handkerchief before her chosen playmate, who chases her in and out of the ring under the arms of the other children until she is captured. The captor afterwards takes the place in the centre, and the original singer becomes a member of the circle.—Miss M. Peacock.

The Deptford version of the verse is as follows :—

I had a little dog whose name was Buff,
I sent him up the street for a penny'orth of snuff,
He broke my box and spilt my snuff,
I think my story is long enough—
'Tain't you, and 'tain't you, and 'tis you !
—Deptford, Kent (Miss Chase).

A Staffordshire and Sharleston version gives some altogether different formulæ :—

What colour's the sky ?
Blue.
Look up again.
Like a W.
Follow me through every little hole that I go through.
—Staffordshire (Rev. G. T. Royds, Rector of Haughton).

At Sharleston the centre child says, "What colour is t' sky ? " The other answers, "Blue." Centre child says, "Follow me true." Here the centre child runs in and out between the others until the one who was touched catches her, when they change places, the first joining the children in the ring.—Sharleston (Miss Fowler).

At Beddgelert, Wales (Mrs. Williams), this game is called Tartan Boeth.   It is played in precisely the same manner as the English game, but the words used are:

Tartan Boeth, Oh ma'en llosgi, Boeth iawn
Hot Tart.   Oh, it burns! very hot!

At the words, "Very hot!" the handkerchief is dropped.

(b) In this game no kissing takes place, and that this is no mere accidental omission may be shown by Mr. Udal's description of the Dorsetshire game.   He was assured by several persons who are interested in Dorset Children's Games that the indiscriminate kissing (that is, whether the girl pursued runs little or far, or, when overtaken, whether she objects or not) with which this game is ordinarily associated, as played now both in Dorset and in other counties, was not indigenous to this county, but was merely a pernicious after-growth or outcome of later days, which had its origin in the various excursion and holiday fêtes, which the facilities of railway travelling had instituted, by bringing large crowds from the neighbouring towns into the country.   He was told that thirty years ago such a thing was unknown in the country districts of Dorset, when the game then usually indulged in was known merely as "Drop the Handkerchief" (*Folk-lore Journal*, vii. 212).

In other cases the rhymes are used for a purely kissing game, for which see "Kiss in the Ring."

Dropping the Letter

An undescribed Suffolk boys' game.—Moor's *Suffolk Words*, p. 238.

Duck under the Water

Each child chooses a partner, and form in couples standing one before the other, till a long line is formed.   Each couple holds a handkerchief as high as they can to form an arch.   The couple standing at the end of the line run through the arch just beyond the last couple standing at the top, when they stand still and hold their handkerchief as high as possible, which is the beginning of the second arch; this is repeated by every last couple in succession, so that as many arches as are wanted can be formed.—East Kirkby, Lincolnshire (Miss K. Maughan).

Miss Baker (*Northamptonshire Glossary*) says the game is played in that county. Formerly in the northern part of the county even married women on May Day played at it under the May garland, which was extended from chimney to chimney across the village street.

Duck at the Table

A boys' game, played with round stones and a table-shaped block of stone.—Patterson's *Antrim and Down Glossary*.

Probably the same as Duckstone.

Duck Dance

Last verse only.

—London (A. B. Gomme).

> I saw a ship a sailin',
> A sailin' on the sea,
> And oh, it was laden
> With pretty things for me [thee].
>
> There were comfits in the cabin,
> And apples in the hold;
> The sails were made of silk,
> And the masts were made of gold.
>
> Four and twenty sailors
> That sat upon the deck,
> Were four and twenty white mice
> With chains about their necks.
>
> The captain was a duck,
> With a packet on his back;
> And when the ship began to move,
> The captain cried "Quack! quack!"
>
> —Northamptonshire, *Revue Celtique*, iv. 200;
> Halliwell's *Nursery Rhymes*, No. ccclxxvii.

(*b*) A number of little girls join hands and form a ring. They all jump round and sing the verses. The game ends by the girls following one of their number in a string, all quacking like ducks.—Northamptonshire.

(*c*) Halliwell does not include it among his games, but simply as a nursery paradox. The tune given is that to which I as a child was taught to sing the verses as a song. We did not know it as a game. The "Quack, quack!" was repeated as another line to the notes of the last bar given, the notes gradually dying away (A. B. Gomme).

Duck Friar
The game of "Leap-frog."—*Apollo Shroving*, 1627, p. 83.

Ducks and Drakes
A pastime in which flat stones or slates are thrown upon the surface of a piece of water, so that they may dip and emerge several times without sinking (Brockett's *North Country Words*). "Neither cross and pile nor ducks and drakes are quite so ancient as hand dandy" (Arbuthnot and Pope, quoted in Todd's *Johnson*).

Halliwell gives the words used in the game both formerly and at the present day. If the stone emerges only once it is a duck, and increasing in the following order :—

2. A duck and a drake,
3. And a halfpenny cake,
4. And a penny to pay the old baker,
5. A hop and a scotch is another notch,
6. Slitherum, slatherum, take her.

—Halliwell's *Dictionary*.

Hen-pen,
Duck and mallard,
Amen.

—Somersetshire (Holloway's *Dict. of Provincialisms*).

A duck and a drake
And a white penny cake.

—Hampshire (Holloway's *Dict. of Provincialisms*).

A duck and a drake
And a penny white cake,
And a skew ball.
—Peacock's *Manley and Corringham Glossary.*

Moor (*Suffolk Words and Phrases*) gives the names for the number of times the stone emerges, as (1) "a duck;" (2) "a duck an' a drake;" if thrice, "a duck an' a drake an' a fi'epenny cake;" four times is "a duck an' a drake an' a fi'epenny cake, an' a penny to pah the baker." If more than four, "a duck," "a duck an' a drake," &c., are added. These distinctions are iterated quickly to correspond in time as nearly as may be with the dips of the stone. A flattish stone is evidently the best for this sport.

(*b*) This game is also given by Mr. Addy in his *Sheffield Glossary*, and by Holland (*Cheshire Glossary*), Brogden (*Provincial Words, Lincolnshire*), Lowsley (*Berkshire Glossary*), Nares' *Glossary*, and Baker's *Northants Glossary.* Miss Courtenay gives "Scutter" and "Tic Tac Mollard" as Cornish names for the game (*West Cornwall Glossary*). See also Halliwell's *Nursery Rhymes*, p. 139, and Strutt's *Sports and Pastimes*, p. 326.

Butler, in his *Hudibras* (p. ii. canto iii. l. 302), makes it one of the important qualifications of his conjurer to tell—

What figur'd slates are best to make
On wat'ry surface *duck* or *drake.*

The following description of this sport is given by Minucius Felix, ed. 1712, p. 28, which evinces its high antiquity: "Pueros videmus certatim gestientes, testarum in mare jaculationibus ludere. Is lusus est, testam teretem, jactatione fluctuum lævigatam, legere de litore: eam testam plano situ digitis comprehensam, inclinem ipsum atque humilem, quantum potest, super undas irrorare: ut illud jaculum vel dorsum maris raderet, vel enataret, dum leni impetu labitur; vel summis fluctibus tonsis emicaret, emergeret, dum assiduo saltu sublevatur. Is se in pueris victorem ferebat, cujus testa et procurreret longius, et frequentius exsiliret."

"From this pastime," says Moor, "has probably arisen the application of the term to a spendthrift—of whose approaching ruin we should thus speak : 'Ah, he'ave made fine ducks and drakes of a's money, that a' have.'"—*Suffolk Words.*

Duckstone

A large stone called the Duckstone or Duck-table is placed on the ground, generally with a wall for a background, but this is of little consequence.   Several boys take a stone each, and a place pretty near the Duckstone is chosen for "home."   One of the boys puts his stone on the Duckstone, and he is called the Tenter.   He has to guard the home and catch the other boys if he can.   Each boy in turn throws his stone at the stone on the Duck-table and immediately runs home.   The Tenter tries to catch him before he can touch the wall or post or whatever is chosen for the home.   If the Tenter can catch him he becomes Tenter, and puts his stone on the Duckstone, and the original Tenter takes his turn in throwing.   One rule of the game is that the Tenter's stone must always be on the Duck-table when he is trying to catch a boy, so if it is knocked off it must be replaced before he can try to catch the boy running "home." The chance of getting home is increased for the boy who knocks it off.—North-West Lincolnshire (Rev. — Roberts and Miss Peacock).

(*b*) Similar versions are from Earls Heaton (Herbert Hardy), Ireland (*Folk-lore Journal,* ii. 265), Peacock (*Manley and Corringham Glossary*).   Addy (*Sheffield Glossary*) gives this game with the following addition : If a duck falls short of the Duckstone, and the one whose duck is on the stone sees that he can *wand* or *span* with his hand the distance between the duck thus thrown and the Duckstone, he shouts out "Wands," and if he can wand or span the distance he takes his duck off, and the duck thus thrown is put on.   Holland (*Cheshire Glossary*), Darlington (South Cheshire), Baker (*Northants Glossary*), and Brogden (*Provincial Words, Lincolnshire*), also give this game.   Elworthy (*West Somerset Words*) calls it "Duck," and "Ducks off" and "Cobbs off" in Dorsetshire.   In London the boy repeats the words, "Gully, gully, all round the hole, one duck on," while he is playing (*Strand Magazine,* November 1891).   Newell (*Games,* p. 188) calls it "Duck on a Rock."

Duffan Ring

Name for " Cat and Mouse " in Cornwall. — *Folk-lore Journal*, v. 57.

Dumb Crambo

An undescribed game mentioned in Moor's *Suffolk Words*, p. 238.

Dumb Motions

Two sides are chosen, which stand apart from each other inside the line of their den.   One side chooses a trade, and goes to the opposite side imitating working at the trade and giving the initial letters of it.   If the opposite side guesses the name of the trade, the players run to their own den, being chased by their opponents.   If any of the players are caught they must go to the opposite side.   In turn the opposite side chooses a trade, and imitates the actions practised.—Cork, Ireland (Miss Keane).

This is called " An Old Woman from the Wood " in Dorsetshire.   The children form themselves into two ranks.

The first rank says :

Here comes an old 'oman from the wood.

The second party answers :

What cans't thee do ?

First Party :   Do anythin'.

Second Party :   Work away.

This the children proceed to do, some by pretending to sew, some to wash, some to dig, some to knit, without any instruments to do it with.   If the opposite side guess what they are doing, they change sides.   This game, Miss Summers believes, is very old, and has been played by several generations in the village of Hazelbury Bryan.—Dorsetshire (*Folk-lore Journal*, vii. 230).

See " Trades."

Dump

A boys' amusement in Yorkshire, in vogue about half a century ago, but now believed to be nearly obsolete.   It is played in this manner. The lads crowd round and place their fists endways, the one on the other, till they form a high pile of hands. Then a boy, who has one hand free, knocks the piled fists off one by one, saying to every boy as he strikes his fist away, "What's there, Dump?" He continues this process till he comes to the last fist, when he exclaims:—

> What's there?
> Cheese and bread, and a mouldy halfpenny!
> Where's my share?
> I put it on the shelf, and the cat got it.
> Where's the cat?
> She's run nine miles through the wood.
> Where's the wood?
> T' fire burnt it.
> Where's the fire?
> T' waters sleekt (extinguished) it.
> Where's the water?
> T' oxen drank it.
> Where's the oxen?
> T' butcher killed 'em.
> Where's the butcher?

Upon the church tops cracking nuts, and you may go and eat the shells; and them as speaks first shall have nine nips, nine scratches, and nine boxes over the lug!

Every one then endeavours to refrain from speaking in spite of mutual nudges and grimaces, and he who first allows a word to escape is punished by the others in the various methods adopted by schoolboys. In some places the game is played differently. The children pile their fists in the manner described above; then one, or sometimes all of them, sing:

> I've built my house, I've built my wall;
> I don't care where my chimneys fall!

The merriment consists in the bustle and confusion occasioned by the rapid withdrawal of the hands (Halliwell's *Nursery Rhymes*, p. 225). Compare Burne's *Shropshire Folk-lore*, p. 529.

Northall (*Folk Rhymes*, p. 418) gives the following rhymes as said in Warwickshire while the fists are being piled on one another:—

> Here's one hammer on the block,
> My men, my men ;
> There's one hammer, &c., my man John.
> Dibble the can, blow bellows, blow,
> Fire away, lads, for an hour or so.

See " Dish-a-loof," " Sacks."

Dumps

A game at marbles or taw, played with holes scooped in the ground (Roxburgh, Jamieson). Grose gives *dump* as signifying " a deep hole of water " (*Provincial Glossary*).

Dust-point

A game in which boys placed their points in a heap, and threw at them with a stone. Weber and Nares give wrong explanations. It is alluded to in Cotton's Works, 1734, p. 184.

> I'll venter on their heads my brindled cow,
> With any boy at dust-point they shall play.
> —Peacham's *Thalia's Banquet*, 1620.

Nares (*Glossary*) suggests that this game and blow-point resembled the game of Push-pin. See also Halliwell's *Dictionary*.

Eller Tree

A number of young men and women stand in a line, a tall girl at one end of the line representing the tree. They then begin to wrap round her, saying, " The old eller tree grows thicker and thicker." When they have all got round her (the tree), they jump all together, calling out, " A bunch of rags, a bunch of rags," and try to tread on each other's toes.— Sheffield, Yorks (S. O. Addy).

(*b*) The tree is the alder. It abounds in the North of England more than in any other part of the kingdom, and seems always to have been there held in great respect and veneration. Many superstitions also attach to the tree. It is possible from these circumstances that the game descends from an old custom of encircling the tree as an act of worship, and the allusion to the " rags " bears at least a curious relationship to tree worship.

If this conclusion is correct, the particular form of the game preserved by Mr. Addy may be the parent form of all games

in which the act of winding is indicated.   There is more reason for this when we consider how easy the notion of clock-winding would creep in after the old veneration for the sacred alder tree had ceased to exist.

See "Bulliheisle," "Wind up the Bush Faggot," "Wind up the Watch."

Ezzeka

Old Ezzeka did one day stand
Upon a barrel top;
The bung flew out, and all at once
It went off with a pop. —Dronfield (S. O. Addy).

This game is usually played in a house or schoolroom, by boys and girls.   A boy or girl is chosen who is considered to be able to stand a joke.   He sits on a chair.   A stool is put behind, upon which a boy called "Ezzeka" stands.   Then the other boys and girls in the room sing the lines.   As they are finished, Ezzeka, who has a bottle of water in his hand, takes out the cork, and pours the water upon his victim's head. This game may be compared with the game of "King Arthur" mentioned by Brand (*Pop. Antiq.*, ii. 393).

Father's Fiddle

This is a boys' game.   One boy says to another, "Divv (do) ye ken (know) aboot my father's fiddle?"   On replying that he does not, the questioner takes hold of the other's right hand with his left, and stretches out the arm. With his right hand he touches the arm gently above the elbow, and says, " My father had a fiddle, an' he brook (broke) it here, an' he brook it here" (touching it below the elbow), "an' he brook it throw the middle," and comes down with a sharp stroke on the elbow-joint.—Keith, Fochabers (Rev. W. Gregor).

This is probably the same game as that printed by Halliwell, No. cccxxxv., to which the following rhyme applied :—

> My father was a Frenchman,
> He bought for me a fiddle ;
> He cut me here, he cut me here,
> He cut me right in the middle.

Feed the Dove

An undescribed game mentioned in an old poem called *Christmas* (i. 285), quoted in Ellis's Brand, i. 517: "Young men and maidens now at 'Feed the Dove' (with laurel leaf in mouth) play."

Find the Ring

> O the grand old Duke of York
> He had ten thousand men,
> He marched them up the hill ago
> And he marched them down again.
> And when they were up they were up,
> And when they were down they were down,
> And when they were half-way up the hill
> They were neither up nor down.
>
> —Sheffield (S. O. Addy).

A ring of chairs is formed, and the players sit on them. A piece of string long enough to go round the inner circumference of the chairs is procured. A small ring is put upon the string, the ends of which are then tied. Then one of the players gets up from his chair and stands in the centre. The players sitting on the chairs take the string into their hands and pass the ring round from one to another, singing the lines. If the person standing in the centre can find out in whose hand

the ring is, he sits down, and his place is taken by the one who
had the ring.   The game is sometimes played round a haycock
in the hayfield.

Miss Dendy sends a similar rhyme from Monton, Lancashire,
where it is known simply as a marching game.   For similar
rhymes, see Halliwell's *Nursery Rhymes*, p. 3.

See " Paddy from Home," " Tip it."

Fippeny Morrell

"Twice three stones, set in a crossed square, where he wins
the game that can set his three along in a row, and that is
fippeny morrell I trow."—*Apollo Shroving*, 1626.

See " Nine Men's Morice," " Noughts and Crosses."

Fire, Air, and Water

The players seat themselves in a circle.   One of the players
has a ball, to which a string is fastened.   He holds the string
that he may easily draw the ball back again after it is thrown.
The possessor of the ball then throws it to one in the circle,
calling out the name of either of the elements he pleases.   This
player must, before ten can be counted, give the name of an
inhabitant of that element.   When " Fire " is called, strict
silence must be observed or a forfeit paid.—Cork, Ireland
(Miss Keane).

The players were seated in a half-circle, and the possessor
of the ball faced the others.   There was no string attached
to the ball, but it was necessary that it should hit the child it
was thrown to.   When " Fire " was called, " Salamander " and
" Phœnix " were allowed to be said.   The third time " Fire "
was called, silence was observed, and every player bowed
the head.   We called it " Earth, Air, Fire, and Water."   A forfeit
had to be paid for every mistake.—London (A. B. Gomme).

It seems probable that a survival of fire-worship is shown
by this game.

Fivestones

This game was played by a newspaper boy at Richmond
Station for me as follows :—He had five square pieces of tile or

stone about the size of dice. He took all five pieces in the palm of the hand first, then threw them up and caught them on the back of the hand, and then from the back of the hand into the palm. Four of the stones were then thrown on the ground; the fifth was thrown up, one stone being picked up from the ground, and the descending fifth stone caught in the same hand; the other three pieces were next picked up in turn. Then two were picked up together in the same manner twice, then one, then three, then all four at once, the fifth stone being thrown up and caught with each movement. All five were then thrown up and caught on the back of the hand, and then thrown from the back and caught in the palm. When he dropped one, he picked it up between his outstretched fingers while the other stones remained on the back of the hand; then he tossed and caught it likewise. Then after throwing up the five stones and catching them on the back of the hand and the reverse, all five being kept in the palm, one was thrown up, and another deposited on the ground before the descending stone was caught. This was done to the three others in turn. Then with two at a time twice, then one and three, then all four together, then from the palm to the back of the hand, and again to the palm. This completed one game. If mistakes were made another player took the stones. Marks were taken for successful play. This boy called the game "Dabs."—A. B. Gomme.

In South Notts this game was called "Snobs." It was played with small stones or marbles. There were nine sets of tricks. First One-ers (of which there were five in the set), then Two-ers (two in set), Three-ers (three in set), Four-ers (four in set), Four Squares (four in set), Trotting Donkeys (eight in set, I believe), Fly-catchers (six or seven in set), Magic (five in set), and Magic Fly-catchers (five in set). One-ers is played thus:—The five stones are thrown into the air and caught on the back of the hand. If all are caught they are simply tossed up again and caught in the hollow of the hand, but if any are not caught they have to be picked up, one by one, another stone being at the same time thrown into the air and caught with the one picked up in the hand. Two-ers, Three-ers, and Four-ers, are played in the same way, except that the stones not caught on the back of the hand have to be arranged in twos, threes, and fours respectively by the hand on which the caught stones are lying meanwhile, and then each lot has to be picked up altogether. If the number that fall when the stones are first thrown up won't allow of this, the player has to drop the required number (but no more) from his hand. In Magic the play is just the same as in One-ers, except that instead of only throwing up a single stone and catching it as the others are in turn picked up, the whole number, except those remaining to be picked up, are thrown and caught. In Four Squares, four of the stones are arranged in a square, each of them is then picked up, whilst the remaining stone is flung upwards and caught; the one picked up is then tossed up, and the one originally tossed up is put down in the place of the other, which is caught as it descends, and the process repeated "all round the square." Trotting Donkeys is similarly played, except that the four stones are arranged in a line—not in a square—and I believe there is some other slight difference, but I forget what. Fly-catchers is played like One-ers, except that the stone thrown into the air while the others are being picked up, is not simply caught by being allowed to fall into the hand, but by an outward movement of the hand is *pounced on*, hawk-fashion, from above. Magic Fly-catchers is played in precisely the same way, except that as in simple Magic, not one stone, but all are thrown up and caught—that is, if there are four on the ground one only is thrown up for the first, two for the second, three for the third, and so on until they are all picked up. This is, of course, the most difficult part of all, and, in fact, only experts were expected to do it. Every failure means "out," and then your opponent has his turn. The winner is the one who gets through first. Such is the game as I remember it, but I have an uneasy suspicion that I have missed something out. I seem to remember one trick in which all the stones on the ground had to be picked up at once *where they lay*—scrambled up so to speak. Or it may be (and, in fact, I think it was) that sometimes, to add to the difficulty of the game, we picked up the groups of two, three, and four in Two-ers, Three-ers, and Four-ers in this fashion, instead of first placing them together.—Epworth, Doncaster (C. C. Bell).

In Wakefield the set of pot checks, which represents five hucklebones, now consists of four checks and a ball about the size of a large marble. The checks are something like dice, but only two opposite sides are plain, the other four being fluted. The table played on is generally a doorstep, and it is made ready by drawing a ring upon it with anything handy which will make a mark. There are twelve figures or movements to be gone through as follows. Some have special names, but I do not learn that all have.

1. The player, taking the checks and ball in the right hand, throws down the checks, keeping the ball in the hand. If any check fall outside the ring the player is "down." There is skill needed in the throwing of the checks in this and the following movements, so that they may be conveniently placed for taking up in the proper order. The checks being scattered, the player throws up the ball, takes up one check, and catches the ball as it comes down, or, as it is sometimes played, after it has bounced once from the step. This is repeated till all the checks are taken up.

2. As the last figure, but the checks are taken up two at a throw.

3. As the last, but at the first throw one check, called the Horse, is taken up, and at the second the remaining three checks at once, called the Cart.

4. As before, but all the checks taken up together.

5. Called Ups and Downs. The checks are taken up at one throw, and set down outside the ring at the next. This is done first with one, then with two, and so on.

6. Each check is touched in turn as the ball is thrown.

7. The checks are separately pushed out of the ring.

8. Each check in turn is taken up and knocked against the ground.

9. Each check is taken up and tapped upon another.

10. The checks are first arranged three in a line, touching each other, and the fourth placed at the top of that at one end of the row. This is called the Cradle. It has to be taken

down check by check, and if, in taking one, another is moved, the player is out.

11. Like the last, but the checks are put one above another to make a Chimney.

12. Called the Dish-clout—I know not why, unless it be that it wipes up the game. The movement used in taking up the checks is thus described :—" Take hold of the sleeve of the right hand with the left ; throw up the ball, and twist your right hand underneath and over your left, and catch the ball. With the hand still twisted throw up the ball and untwist and catch it." The checks are picked up in the course of the twisting.

These I am told are the orthodox movements ; and I do not doubt that in them there is much of very old tradition, although the tenth and eleventh must have been either added or modified since pot checks came into use, for the figures could not be built up with the natural bones. Some other movements are sometimes used according to fancy, as for example the clapping of the ground with the palm of the hand before taking up the checks and catching the ball.—J. T. Micklethwaite (*Arch. Journ.*, xlix. 327–28).

I am told that in the iron districts of Staffordshire, the round bits of iron punched out in making rivet holes in boiler plates are the modern representatives of hucklebones.—*Ibid.*

In Westminster four stones are held in the right hand, a marble is thrown up, and all four stones thrown down, and the marble allowed to bounce on the hearthstone or pavement, and then caught in the same hand after it has rebounded. The marble is then thrown up again, and one of the four stones picked up, and the marble caught again after it has rebounded. This is done separately to the other three, bringing all four stones into the hand. The marble is again bounced, and all four stones thrown down and the marble caught. Two stones are then picked up together, then the other two, then one, then three together, then all four together, the marble being tossed and caught with each throw. An arch is then formed by placing the left hand on the ground, and the four stones are again thrown down, the marble tossed, and the four stones put separately into the arch, the marble being caught after it has rebounded each time; or the four stones are separately put between the fingers of the left hand in as straight a row as possible. Then the left hand is taken away, and the four stones caught up in one sweep of the hand. Then all four stones are thrown down, and one is picked up before the marble is caught. This is retained in the hand, and when the second stone is picked up the first one is laid down before the marble is caught; the third is picked up and the second laid down, the fourth picked up and the third laid down, then the fourth laid down, the marble being tossed and caught again each time. The stones have different names or marks (which follow in rotation), and in picking them up they must be taken in their proper order, or it is counted as a mistake. The game is played throughout by the right hand, the left hand only being used when "arches" is made. The marble should be thrown up about the same height each toss, and there should be little or no interval between the different figures.—Annie Dicker.

I saw this game played in Endell Street, London, W.C., by two girls. Their game was not so long nor so complete as the above. They did not throw all four stones down as a preliminary stage, but began with the second figure, the four gobs being placed in a square ⁞ , nor were they particular as to which stones they picked up. They knew nothing of numbering or naming them. Their marble was called a "jack." They had places chalked on the pavement where they recorded their successful "goes," and the game was played in a ring.—A. B. Gomme.

An account sent me from Deptford (Miss Chase) is doubtless the same game. It begins with taking two "gobs" at once, and apparently there are eight stones or gobs to play with. The marble or round stone which is thrown up is called a "tally." The directions for playing are—

> We take twoses,
> We take threeses,
> We take fourses,
> We take sixes,
> We take eights.

Chain eggs—*i.e.*, to pick up one and drop it again until this has been done to each stone. Arches—*i.e.*, gobs in a row. This was described by the player as "while the tally is up to sweep the whole row or line off the ground into the arch of the finger and thumb before catching the tally."

(*b*) These games are variants of one common original. It is the same game as that described by F. H. Low in the *Strand Magazine*, ii. 514, as played in the London streets. The marble there is called a "buck." "Pegsy" was the name of the No. 5 stage of the Wakefield version, and this varies too, inasmuch as it was the same gob which is picked up and then laid down before catching the buck.

Mr. Kinahan says, "'Jackstones,' played with three or four small stones that are thrown up in the air and caught again, seems to have been a very ancient game, as the stones have been found in the *crannogs* or lake-dwellings in some hole near the fireplaces, similar to where they are found in a cabin at the present day. An old woman, or other player, at the present time puts them in a place near the hob when they stop their game and go to do something else" (*Folk-lore Journal*, ii. 266). In the Græco-Roman saloon, British Museum, is a statue originally composed of two boys quarrelling at the game of "Tali" (see *Townley Gallery*, i. 305; Smith's *Dict. Greek and Roman Antiq.*, s.v. *Talus*), and it is interesting to note that in the Deptford game the marble is called a "Tally."

Mr. Kinahan's note suggests that "Fivestones" may be an independent game, instead of a derivative from "Hucklebones." If this is so, we have interesting evidence of the spread or transmission of one game from at least two centres. Professor Attwell, in *Notes and Queries*, 8th ser., iv. 201, suggests that "Hucklebones" was introduced into Europe by the Romans, and was spread throughout the countries which formed the empire by means of Roman colonists and soldiers. Mr. Newell (*Games*, pp. 190–93) describes a similar game to "Fivestones" played in Boston under the name of "Otadama," or "Japanese Jacks." This game is of Japanese origin, "Tedama" (that is, "Handballs") being its proper name. He says there can be no doubt that the two forms of this amusement are branches of the same root; and we thus have an example of a game which, having preserved its essential characteristics for thousands of years, has fairly circumnavigated the globe, so that the two currents of tradition, westward and eastward, from Europe and Asia, have met in America.

See "Checkstones," "Dibs," "Hucklebones," "Jackstones."

Flowers

Sides are chosen; each side must have a "home" at the top and bottom of the ground where the children are playing. One side chooses a flower and goes over to the other side, the members of which stand in a row facing the first side. The first side states the initial letters of the flower it has chosen, and when the second side guesses the right flower they run and try to catch as many of the opposite side as they can before they reach their home. The captives then become members of the side which captured them.—Bitterne, Hants (Mrs. Byford).

Follow my Gable

—Earls Heaton, Yorkshire.

—Redhill, Surrey.

I.   Follow my gable 'oary man,
     Follow my gable 'oary man,
     I'll do all that ever I can
     To follow my gable 'oary man.

> We'll borrow a horse and steal a gig,
> And round the world we'll have a jig,
> And I'll do all that ever I can
> To follow my gable 'oary man.
>> —Earls Heaton, Yorks (Herbert Hardy).

II. Holy Gabriel, holy man,
> Rantum roarum reeden man,
> I'll do all as ever I can
> To follow my Gabriel, holy man.*
>> —Redhill, Surrey (Miss G. Hope).

III. I sell my bat, I sell my ball,
> I sell my spinning-wheel and all;
> And I'll do all that ever I can
> To follow the eyes of the drummer man.
>> —Luton, Bedfordshire (Mrs. Ashdown).

(*b*) In the Yorkshire version a ring is formed with one child in the middle as the 'Oary Man. Whatever he, or she, does, all in the ring must mimic, going round and singing at the same time. Any one found late in changing the action or idle in obeying the caperings of the central child becomes the 'Oary Man in place of the child taking that part. Both girls and boys play. In the Redhill version, Holy Gabriel kneels in the middle of the circle. He acts as leader, and always had the fiddle as his instrument, though he now usually plays the pianoforte as his first instrument. The other children choose any instrument they like. Holy Gabriel pretends to play the fiddle, and all the other children play their own instruments until Holy Gabriel changes his to one of theirs, when that one must immediately begin to play the fiddle, and continue until Holy Gabriel takes another instrument or returns to the fiddle. This is done in vigorous pantomime. In the Luton variant the children sit in a semicircle, the Drummer faces them. He plays the drum; all the other children play on any other instrument they like. If the other players do not at once change their instrument, or neglect to sing the lines, a forfeit is demanded.

* A variant of the second line is, "Ranting, roaring, heely man." "I suppose he was Irish," said my informant, "as he was named 'Healey'" (Miss G. Hope).

(*c*) Mr. Hardy says some sing this game, "Follow my game an holy man." Mr. Hardy once thought it was the remnant of a goblin story of a hoary man of the gable or house-roof, who presided over the destinies of poor cottagers, and he had begun to make out the folk tale. The fairy would sometimes come down, and, playing his antics, compel whomsoever observed him to follow him in a mimicking procession. Miss Hope writes of "Holy Gabriel" that the game is played at Mead Vale, a small village in Surrey, but is unknown at larger villages and towns a few miles off. Some of the women who played it in their youth say that it began in the Primitive Methodist school at Mead Vale. It is played at Outword, also a remote village, and was introduced there by a stonemason, who stated that he had learned it from a cousin who had been in America. Further inquiry by Miss Hope elicited the fact that the cousin had learned the game, when a boy, in his native place in Lancashire. He did not know whether it was a well-known game there. This information points perhaps to a modern origin, but in such cases it must be borne in mind that people are very fond of suggesting recent circumstances as the cause of the most ancient traditions or customs. The obvious analogy to the incident in the myth of the Pied Piper, and to the Welsh custom at St. Almedha Church, near Brecknock, recorded by Giraldus Cambrensis, where the imitation of a frenzied leader is carried out as a religious ceremony, rather suggests that in this game we may have a survival of a ceremonial so common among early or uncultured people, the chief incident of which is the frenzied dancing of a god-possessed devotee.

Follow my Leader

This is a boys' game. Any number can take part in it. It requires a good extent of country to play it well. The boy who is the swiftest runner and the best jumper is chosen as Leader. He sets out at a good speed over the fields, tries to jump as many ditches or burns, jumping such from one side to the other again and again, to scramble over dykes, through hedges, over palings, and run up braes. The others have to follow

him as they can. This steeplechase continues till the followers
are all tired out.—Keith (Rev. W. Gregor).

This is a very general game among schoolboys, but in Here-
ford it was a town custom occurring once in seven years on
11th October (*Folk-lore Journal*, v. 75).

Fool, Fool, come to School

This game is played under the name of " Foolie, Foolie " at
Duthil, Strathspey. The players are placed in a row, either
standing or sitting. Two are chosen, the one as Namer and
the other as Foolie. Foolie withdraws, if not out of sight, at
least out of range of hearing. The Namer then gives a name
secretly to each player. When this is done, he calls on
Foolie—Foolie, Foolie, come to your schoolie.

Foolie pays no attention to this call. It is again repeated,
but with the same results. This goes on for several times.
At last the Namer calls out—

Foolie, Foolie, come to your schoolie ;
Your bannocks are burnin' an' ready for turnin'.

Foolie always obeys this call, comes and stations himself
beside the Namer. A little chaffing generally goes on against
Foolie. The Namer says, "Come chise me oot, come chise
me in, tae " so and so, naming one by the assumed fancy name.
Foolie makes choice of one. If the choice falls right, the one
so chosen steps from the line and stands beside Foolie. If the
choice falls wrong, the one named remains in the line. All the
players' names are called out in this way. If any stand unchosen by Foolie, the Namer then goes up to each and asks if
he wants, *e.g.*, " an aipple," " an orange," " a kirk," " a cottage,"
&c. Each one whispers what he wants. The same question
is put to Foolie. If he answers, *e.g.*, " orange," the one so
named steps out and stands beside Foolie. All not first chosen
are gone over in this way. Those left unchosen take their
stand beside the Namer. There is then a tug-of-war, with the
Namer and Foolie as the leaders.—Keith (Rev. W. Gregor).

In Hants the children stand *vis-à-vis*, as in a country dance.
One of the number is sent out of earshot, and the others decide
with the Captain as to the name of the bird each wishes to

personate. The Captain then calls to the child who is out, "Tom Fool, Tom Fool, come home from school, and pick me out a blackbird," "cuckoo," or other bird. If Tom Fool is wrong in his guessing after three trials, he is condemned to run the gauntlet, being pelted with gloves or handkerchiefs not too mercifully.—Bitterne, Hants (Miss Byford).

In Sussex there is the same action with the following words, but there is no chasing or hitting—

> Of all the birds in the air,
> Of all the fishes in the sea,
> You can pick me out [   ].

If the children fail to do so, they say—

> Poor fool, been to school,
> Learn more in a week ;
> Been there seven years
> And hasn't learnt a bit.
>
> —Hurstmonceux, Sussex (Miss Chase).

The same game is played indoors in Cornwall, the reply being—

> Fool, fool, go back to school
> And learn your letters better.
>
> —Cornwall (*Folk-lore Journal*, v. 99-80).

See "Namers and Guessers."

Foot and Over

One boy out of a number stoops in the position for "Leap-frog" at an agreed fixed line. From the players he chooses a Leader and a Foot. The Leader first leaps over the stooping boy at a foot from the line ; the other players then leap in turn each at a foot further from the line, the stooping boy moving forward from the line for each player ; finally the Foot leaps as far as the distance leapt by the last boy. If this is accomplished, the Leader hops from the line and then leaps ; the followers hop and leap each a foot further than each other ; finally the Foot hops and leaps as far as the distance covered by the last boy. If this is accomplished, the Leader hops twice and then leaps ; the same process going on until one of the boys fails, who then takes the place of the stooping boy, and the game begins again. If the Foot covers any longer distance than the Leader, the Leader stoops down.—Earls Heaton, Yorks. (H. Hardy).

This game is general. Mr. Emslie describes the London version somewhat differently. After all the boys had jumped over the first boy's back, a cry of "Foot it" was raised, and the boy who had given the back placed one of his feet at a right

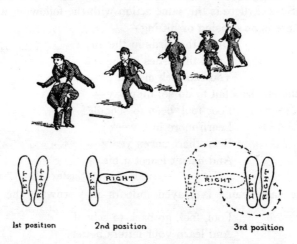

1st position   2nd position   3rd position

angle to the other, and in this way measured a "foot's length" from the starting-place. All the boys then "overed" his back from the original line, the last one crying "Foot it," and then the measuring ceremony was again gone through, and the game commenced again, and continued in the same manner until one of the boys failed to "over" the back, when he became Back.

Football

The modern game of "Football" is too well known to need description here, and, like "Cricket," it has become no longer a children's game. As to its origin, there are many ball games, such as "Camping," which have been suggested as the original form of "Football." Every school almost had some peculiarity in the method of playing, and Eton, Winchester, Uppingham, and Rugby are well-known examples. It is not a little interesting to note, now that "Football" has settled down into a national game organised by county committees, that one of the

forms of play officially recognised is the old Rugby game, the
other form, known as the "Association," being arrived at by
agreement of those interested in the game.

To illustrate the ancient origin of the game, and its serious
import as a local contest rather than a sport, some examples may
be given. It is still (1877) keenly contested at Workington on
Easter Tuesday on the banks of, and not unfrequently in, the river
Derwent (Dickinson's *Cumberland Glossary*). At Derby there
was a football contest between the parishes of All Saints' and
St. Peter's. The ball was thrown into the market-place from
the Town Hall. The moment it was thrown the "war cries"
of the rival parishes began, and the contest, nominally that of
a football match, was in reality a fight between the two sections
of the town; and the victors were announced by the joyful
ringing of their parish bells (Dyer's *Popular Customs*, p. 75).
At Chester-le-Street the game was played between what were
termed "up-streeters" and "down-streeters," one side endeavouring to get the ball to the top of the town, whilst their
opponents tried to keep it near the lower or north end. At one
o'clock the ball was thrown out from near the old commercial
hotel, the Queen's Head, in the centre of the town, and it has
often been received by over three and four hundred people, so
great was the interest taken in this ancient sport. At Asborne
the struggle was between the "up'ards" and "down'ards." At
Dorking the divisions were between the east and west ends of
the town, and there was first a perambulation of the streets by
the football retinue composed of grotesquely dressed persons.
At Alnwick the divisions were the parishes of St. Michael's and
St. Paul's. At Kirkwall the contest was on New Year's Day,
and was between "up the gates" and "down the gates," the ball
being thrown up at the Cross. At Scarborough, on the morning
of Shrove Tuesday, hawkers paraded the streets with parti-
coloured balls, which were purchased by all ranks of the community. With these, and armed with sticks, men, women, and
children repaired to the sands below the old town and indiscriminately commenced a contest. The following graphic
account of Welsh customs was printed in the *Oswestry Observer*
of March 2, 1887 : "In South Cardiganshire it seems that about

eighty years ago the population, rich and poor, male and female, of opposing parishes, turned out on Christmas Day and indulged in the game of 'Football' with such vigour that it became little short of a serious fight. The parishioners of Cellan and Pencarreg were particularly bitter in their conflicts; men threw off their coats and waistcoats and women their gowns, and sometimes their petticoats. At Llanwenog, an extensive parish below Lampeter, the inhabitants for football purposes were divided into the Bros and the Blaenaus. A man over eighty, an inmate of Lampeter Workhouse, gives the following particulars:—In North Wales the ball was called the Bêl Troed, and was made with a bladder covered with a Cwd Tarw. In South Wales it was called Bél Ddu, and was usually made by the shoemaker of the parish, who appeared on the ground on Christmas Day with the ball under his arm. The Bros, it should be stated, occupied the high ground of the parish. They were nicknamed 'Paddy Bros,' from a tradition that they were descendants from Irish people who settled on the hills in days long gone by. The Blaenaus occupied the lowlands, and, it may be presumed, were pure-bred Brythons. The more devout of the Bros and Blaenaus joined in the service at the parish church on Christmas morning. At any rate, the match did not begin until about mid-day, when the service was finished. Then the whole of the Bros and Blaenaus, rich and poor, male and female, assembled on the turnpike road which divided the highlands from the lowlands. The ball having been redeemed from the Crydd, it was thrown high in the air by a strong man, and when it fell Bros and Blaenaus scrambled for its possession, and a quarter of an hour frequently elapsed before the ball was got out from among the struggling heap of human beings. Then if the Bros, by hook or by crook, could succeed in taking the ball up the mountain to their hamlet of Rhyddlan they won the day; while the Blaenaus were successful if they got the ball to their end of the parish at New Court. The whole parish was the field of operations, and sometimes it would be dark before either party scored a victory. In the meantime many kicks would be given and taken, so that on the following day some of the competitors would be unable to walk, and sometimes a kick on the shins would lead the two men concerned to abandon the game until they had decided which was the better pugilist. There do not appear to have been any rules for the regulation of the game; and the art of football playing in the olden time seems to have been to reach the goal. When once the goal was reached, the victory was celebrated by loud hurrahs and the firing of guns, and was not disturbed until the following Christmas Day. Victory on Christmas Day, added the old man, was so highly esteemed by the whole countryside, that a Bro or Blaenau would as soon lose a cow from his cow-house as the football from his portion of the parish."

(*b*) In Gomme's *Village Community*, pp. 241–44, the position of football games as elements in the traditions of race is discussed, and their relationship to a still earlier form of tribal games, where the element of clan feuds is more decidedly preserved, is pointed out.

Forfeits

Forfeits are incurred in those games in which penalties are exacted from players for non-compliance with the rules of the game; "Buff," "Contrary," "Crosspurposes," "Fire, Air, and Water," "Follow my Gable," "Genteel Lady," "Jack's Alive," "Old Soldier," "Twelve Days of Christmas," "Turn the Trencher," "Wadds," and others. These games are described under their several titles, and the formula for forfeits is always the same. Small articles belonging to the players must be given by them every time a forfeit is incurred, and these must be redeemed at the close of the game. They are "cried" in the following manner:—One of the players sits on a chair having the forfeits in her lap. A child kneels on the ground and buries his face in his hands on the lap of the person who holds the forfeits. The "crier" then takes up indiscriminately one of the forfeits, and holding it up in the sight of all those who have been playing the games (without the kneeling child seeing it), says—

Here's a very pretty thing and a very pretty thing,
And what shall be done to [*or*, by] the owner of this very
    pretty thing?

The kneeling child then says what the penance is to be. The owner of the forfeit must then perform the penance before the other players, and then another forfeit is "cried."

The more general penances imposed upon the owners of the forfeits are as follows, but the list could be very much extended:—

Bite an inch off the poker.

Kneel to the prettiest, bow to the wittiest, and kiss the one you love best.

Stand in each corner of the room, sigh in one, cry in another, sing in another, and dance in the other.

Put yourself through the keyhole.

Place two chairs in the middle of the room, take off your shoes, and jump over them.

Measure so many yards of love ribbon.

Postman's knock.

Crawl up the chimney.

Spell Opportunity.

Miss Burne mentions one penance designed to make the victim ridiculous, as when he is made to lie on his back on the floor with his arms extended, and declare—

> Here I lie!
> The length of a looby,
> The breadth of a booby,
> And three parts of a jackass!
>
> *—Shropshire Folk-lore*, pp. 526-27.

(*c*) Halliwell gives, in his *Nursery Rhymes*, pp. 324–26, some curious verses, recorded for the first time by Dr. Kenrick in his Review of Dr. Johnson's Shakespeare, 1765, on "rules for seemly behaviour," in which the forfeits imposed by barbers as penalties for handling razors, &c., are set forth. Although "barbers' forfeits" are not of the same nature as the nursery forfeits, it is possible that this general custom among so important a class of the community in early times as barbers may have suggested the game. Both Forby in his *Vocabulary of East Anglia* and Moor in his *Suffolk Words* bear testimony to the general prevalence of barbers' forfeits, and it must be borne in mind that barbers were also surgeons in early days.

A curious custom is also recorded in another East Anglian word-list, which may throw light upon the origin of the game from popular custom. "A forfeit is incurred by using the word 'water' in a brew-house, where you must say 'liquor;' or by using the word 'grease' in a chandlery, where it is 'stuff' or 'metal.' The forfeit is to propitiate the offended *genius loci*" (Spurden's *East Anglian Vocabulary*). The element of divination in the custom is perhaps indicated by a curious note from Waldron, in his *Description of the Isle of Man* (*Works*, p. 55), "There is not a barn unoccupied the whole twelve days, every parish hiring fiddlers at the public charge. On Twelfth Day the fiddler lays his head on some of the wenches' laps, and a third person asks who such a maid or such a maid shall marry, naming the girls then present one after another; to which he answers according to his own whim, or agreeable to the intimacies he has taken notice of during this time of merriment. But whatever he says is as absolutely depended on as an oracle; and if he happen to couple two people who have an aversion to each other, tears and vexation succeed the mirth. This they call cutting off the fiddler's head; for after this he is dead for the whole year." Redeeming the forfeits is called "Crying the Weds," in Burne's *Shropshire Folk-lore*, p. 526. See "Wadds."

Fox

> Fox, a fox, a brummalary
> How many miles to Lummaflary? Lummabary?
> Eight and eight and a hundred and eight.
> How shall I get home to-night?
> Spin your legs and run fast.

Halliwell gives this rhyme as No. ccclvii. of his *Nursery Rhymes*, but without any description of the game beyond the words, "A game of the fox." It is probably the same game as "Fox and Goose."

Fox and Goose (1)

In Dorsetshire one of the party, called the Fox, takes one end of the room or corner of a field (for the game was equally played indoors or out); all the rest of the children arrange

themselves in a line or string, according to size, one behind the
other, the smallest last, behind the tallest one, called Mother
Goose, with their arms securely round the waist of the one in
front of them, or sometimes by grasping the dress.

The game commences by a parley between the Fox and
Goose to this effect, the Goose beginning.

"What are you after this fine morning?"

"Taking a walk."

"With what object?"

"To get an appetite for a meal."

"What does [will] your meal consist of?"

"A nice fat goose for my breakfast."

"Where will you get it?"

"Oh, I shall get a nice morsel somewhere; and as they are
so handy, I shall satisfy myself with one of yours."

"Catch one if you can."

A lively scene follows. The Fox and Mother Goose should
be pretty evenly matched; the Mother with extended arms
seeking to protect her Brood, while the Fox, who tries to dodge
under, right and left, is only allowed in case of a successful
foray or grasp to secure the last of the train. Vigorous efforts
are made to escape him, the Brood of course supplementing
the Mother's exertions to elude him as far as they are able,
but without breaking the link. The game may be continued
until all in turn are caught.—*Folk-lore Journal*, vii. 217-18.

In Lancashire the children stand in line behind each other,
holding each other by the waist. One stands facing them and
calls out—

> My mother sits on yonder chimney,
> And she says she *must* have a chicken.

The others answer—

> She *can't* have a chicken.

The one then endeavours to catch the last child of the tail,
who when caught comes behind the captor; repeat until all
have changed sides.—Monton, Lancashire (Miss Dendy).

A version of this game played at Eckington, Derbyshire,
is played as follows:—A den is chalked out or marked out for
the Fox. A larger den, opposite to this, is marked out for the

Geese. A boy or a girl represents the Fox, and a number of others the Geese. Then the Fox shouts, "Geese, Geese, gannio," and the Geese answer, "Fox, Fox, fannio." Then the Fox says, "How many Geese have you to-day?" The Geese reply, "More than you can catch and carry away." Then the Geese run out of the den, and the Fox tries to catch them. He puts as many as he catches into his den (S. O. Addy).

(b) This game is a very general one at Christmas time. It is practically the same as "Gled Wylie," and "Hen and Chickens," and the "Hawk and Chickens" of Mr. Newell's *Games and Songs of American Children*, pp. 155–56. By referring to these games it will be seen that the whole group are mimic representatives of farmyard episodes, though the animal characters are giving way to more domestic affairs, as shown in the Pins and Needles version of "Hen and Chickens." It is possible that the different animals which are victims to the Fox appearing in the different games may arise from local circumstances, and that in this case a real distinction exists between the various names by which this game is known. A game called "Wolf and Deer," similar to "Fox and Geese," is given in *Winter Evening Amusements*, by R. Revel. The last one at the end of the tail may, if she has no other chance of escape, try and place herself before the Deer or Hen. She is then no longer to be hunted; all the others must then follow her example until the deer becomes the last of the line. The game then terminates by exacting a forfeit for each lady whom the Wolf has suffered to escape his clutches (pp. 64, 65).

See "Gled Wylie," "Hen and Chickens," "Old Dame."

Fox and Geese (2)

A game known by this name is played with marbles or pegs on a board on which are thirty-three holes, or on the pavement, with holes scraped out of the stones. To play this game there are seventeen pieces called Geese, and another one either larger or distinguished from the Geese by its colour, which is called the Fox. The Fox occupies the centre hole, and the Geese occupy nine holes in front, and four on each side of him.

The vacant holes behind are for the Geese and Fox to move in. The game is for the Geese to shut up the Fox so that he cannot move. All the pieces can be moved from one spot to another in the direction of the lines, but cannot pass over two holes at once. The Geese are not permitted to take the Fox. The Fox's business is to take all, or as many of the Geese as will prevent him from being blockaded. The Fox can take the Geese whenever there is a vacant space behind them, which he passes to, then occupies.

This game has been very popular among schoolboys in all ages. Mr. Micklethwaite, in a paper on the Indoor Games of School Boys in the Middle Ages (*Arch. Journ.* xlix. 322), gives instances of finding figures of this game cut " in the cloister benches of Gloucester Cathedral and elsewhere, and there are several on the twelfth century tomb at Salisbury, miscalled Lord Stourton's," and also at Norwich Castle. For the date of these boards, Mr. Micklethwaite says for the last three centuries and a half cloisters everywhere in England have been open passages, and there have generally been schoolboys about. It is therefore not unlikely that they should have left behind them such traces as these play-boards. But if they are of later date they would not be found to be distributed in monastic cloisters with respect to the monastic arrangement, and we do find them so. Strutt describes the game (*Sports,* p. 319).

See " Nine Men's Morris," " Noughts and Crosses."

Fox in the Fold

" The Tod (Fox) i' the Faul (Fold)." This game is commonly played by boys. Any number of boys join hands and stand in a circle to form the Faul. The boy that represents the Tod is placed within the circle. His aim is to escape. To effect this he rushes with all his force, increased by a run, against the joint hands of any two of the players. If the rush does not unloose the grasp, he hangs on the two arms with all his weight, pressing and wriggling. If he fails he makes a rush at another two, always selecting those players he thinks weakest. When he does break through he rushes off at the top of his speed, with all the players in full cry, till he is caught and

brought back.   The game begins anew with another boy as
Tod.—Keith (Rev. W. Gregor).

See "Bull in the Park," "Frog in the Middle."

Fox in the Hole

All the players are armed with handkerchiefs.   One of the
players is chosen for Fox, who has his den marked out.   The
Fox hops out on one leg, with his handkerchief ready to strike.
The players gather round him and attack him.   If he can
strike one of his assailants without putting his foot to the
ground from his hopping position, the player so struck is
chased by the others into the den, and he then becomes the
Fox for another round of the game.—Cork (Miss Keane).

Halliwell (*Nursery Rhymes*, p. 228) describes the game in
practically the same manner, but adds that when the Fox is
coming out he says—

> The Fox gives warning
> It's a cold and frosty morning,

after which he is at liberty to hop out and use his handkerchief.

(*b*) This game is alluded to in *Soliman and Perseda*, 1599;
Florio, p. 480; *Herrick*, i. 176.   See Halliwell's *Dictionary*.
Professor Mayor communicated to the *Gentleman's Magazine*
of 1848 (ii.), p. 147, the following early allusions to the game
from old dictionaries :—

Gouldman, London, MDCLXIV. — "*Ascoliasmus*, Empusæ
ludus : a kind of play wherein boys lift up one leg and hop
with the other, where they beat one another with bladders tied
to the end of strings.   Fox to thy hole."

Holyoke, MDCLXXVII.—"*Empusa.* παρὰ τὸ ἑνὶ ποδίζειν,
quòd uno incedat pede.   Hence *empusam agere* is used for a
play, hopping on one leg ; with us, Fox to his hole."

Id. "*Ascoliasmus.*   A kind of play that children use when
they hop on one leg, called Fox to thy hole."

Cambridge Dict. MDCXCIII. — "*Ascol.*   A kind of play
wherein boys hopping on one leg beat one another with gloves
or pieces of leather, and is called Fox to thy hole."

Coles, 7th ed. 1711.—"*Ascol.*   The play called Fox to the

hole.— *Empus*.   Ludus Empusæ.   Scotch hoppers, or Fox in the hole."

A similar game to this is played at Earls Heaton, Yorkshire (Mr. Hardy), and called "Goose and Gander." Two players, the Goose and the Gander, stand in a ring, each on one leg. They hop out in turn, and try to catch one of the other players without letting their other leg touch the ground. If they fail in this they get "strapped" back to the ring. When either are successful, the player who is caught takes the place of either Goose or Gander in turn. The game is also mentioned in *Useful Transactions in Philosophy*, 1708–9.

French Jackie

This game is played either by boys or girls or by both together. One is chosen to stand alone; the other players join hands and form a circle. The one outside the circle goes round it and touches on the back one of the circle. He then runs off round the circle, and the one who was touched runs off in the opposite direction round the circle. The aim of each player is to reach the vacant place in the circle first. The one left out has to repeat the same action. The game may go on for any length of time.—Keith (Rev. W. Gregor).

At Barnes this game is called "Gap." It is known as "French Tag" in the Forest of Dean, Gloucestershire (Miss Matthews), and "Tap-back" at Bitterne, Hants (Mrs. Adam).

French and English

The children choose sides under a leader, and a boundary line is made in the middle of the ground dividing the French and English territory. A handkerchief is then placed in the back part of each territory to represent a flag. The object is to obtain as many flags from the opposite side as possible. If a person is captured before having seized a flag, he is taken prisoner, and must be rescued by one of his own side. Thus, for instance, an Englishman enters the French territory and tries to reach the flag. If he is seen by the French before he reaches the flag, he is taken prisoner and is placed near the flags, and the next Englishman rescues him instead of taking a flag. As soon as the flag is taken, one of the party must put another handkerchief in its place. A player cannot be taken prisoner after having obtained the handkerchief or flag. The winning side is decided by counting the flags and prisoners. —Bitterne, Hants (Mrs. Byford).

This is a very general game, and is known as "Scotch and English" in the north, where some interesting details occur, for which see "Scotch and English."

French Blindman's Buff

The children kneel in a circle, one standing blindfolded in the middle. The kneeling children shout, "Come point to me with your pointer."—Monton, Lancashire (Miss Dendy).

See "Buff," "Dinah," "Muffin Man."

Friar-rush

A Christmas game, mentioned in the *Declaration of Popish Impostures*, 1603.

Frincy-francy

A game played between the dances at balls in farm-houses. A chair was placed in the middle of the barn or room; the master of the ceremonies led to the chair a young woman, who sat down and named the young man whom she was willing should kiss her. This he did, and then took the seat which the lady vacated. He then called out the name of some favourite girl, who was led up to him; there was another kiss. The girl then took the seat, and so on (county of Down). The same game is called "Frimsey-framsey" in parts of the county of Antrim.—Patterson's *Antrim and Down Glossary*.

Compare "Cushion Dance."

Frog-lope

Name for "Leap-frog."—Addy's *Sheffield Glossary*.

Frog in the Middle

One child is seated on the ground with his legs under him; the other players form a ring round. They then pull or buffet the centre child or Frog, who tries to catch one of them without rising from the floor. The child who is caught takes the place of the centre child. Another method of playing the game is similar to "Bull in the Park." The child in the centre tries to break out of the ring, those forming it keeping the Frog in the ring by any means in their power, while still keeping their hands clasped. They sometimes sing or say—

Hey! hey! hi! Frog in the middle and there shall lie;
He can't get out and he shan't get out—hey! hey! hi!

They dance round when saying this, all keeping a watch on the

Frog, who suddenly makes a rush, and tries to break through the ring.—London (A. B. Gomme).

Strutt describes this game, and gives an illustration from a fourteenth century MS. which is here reproduced from the original (*Sports*, p. 303). Newell (*Games of American Children*, p. 171) also mentions it, and gives the rhyme as—

Frog in the sea, can't catch me!

Gap

The same as "French Jackie." This game is called "Tap-back" or "Tat-back" at Bitterne, Hants.

Garden Gate

Children join hands and form a ring. One child stands inside the ring; this child walks round and asks one of the circle, called the Keeper—

Have you the key of the garden gate?
Open and let me go through.

The Keeper replies—

> My next-door neighbour's got the key;
> Ask him and he'll give it to you.

This is repeated by each one in the circle. Then the inside child comes again to the Keeper and says—

> None of the neighbours have got the key,
> So you must let me go through.

The Keeper answers—

> I've lost the key of the garden gate,
> And cannot let you through.

Then all the ring say—

> You must stop all night within the gate,
> Unless you have strength to break through.

The child inside then attempts to break through, and if he succeeds in breaking any of the clasped hands the one who first gives way has to take the place in the centre.—Roxton, St. Neots (Miss Lumley).

See "Bull in the Park."

Gegg

"To smuggle the Gegg," a game played by boys in Glasgow, in which two parties are formed by lot, equal in number, the one being denominated the Outs, the other Ins. The Outs are those who go out from the den or goal, where those called the Ins remain for a time. The Outs get the Gegg, which is anything deposited, as a key, a penknife, &c. Having received this, they conceal themselves, and raise the cry, "Smugglers!" On this they are pursued by the Ins; and if the Gegg (for the name is transferred to the person who holds the deposit) be taken, they exchange situations—the Outs become Ins and the Ins Outs. This play is distinguished from "Hy-spy" only by the use of the Gegg. One of the Ins who is touched by one of the Outs is said to be taken, and henceforth loses his right to hold the Gegg. If he who holds the Gegg gets in the den, the Outs are winners, and have the privilege of getting out again. The Outs, before leaving the den, shuffle the Gegg, or smuggle it so between each other that the Ins do not know which person has it. He who is laid hold of, and put to the question, is supposed to deny that he has the Gegg: if he escapes with it, he gets out again.— Jamieson.

Genteel Lady

A player begins thus:—" I, a genteel lady (or gentleman) came from that genteel lady (or gentleman) to say that she (or he) owned a tree." The other players repeat the words in turn, and then the leader goes over them again, adding, " with bronze bark." The sentence goes round once more, and on the next repetition the leader continues, " with golden branches." He afterwards adds, " and silver leaves," " and purple fruit," " and on the top a milk-white dove," and, finally, " mourning for the loss of his lady-love."

If a player should fail in repeating the rigmarole, there is a fine to pay. A " pipe-lighter " is stuck in her hair, and she must say " one-horned lady " instead of " genteel lady." When a second horn is added, of course she says " two-horned," and so forth. Some players wear half-a-dozen before the conclusion of the game. The game is called " The Wonderful Tree." —Anderby, Lincolnshire (Miss M. Peacock).

In some parts of Yorkshire it is customary to say " no-horned lady " instead of " genteel lady " at the beginning of the game.

When we played this game we said " always genteel " after " genteel lady," and varied the formula. For instance, the first player would say, " I, a genteel lady, always genteel, come from a genteel lady, always genteel, to say she lives in a house with twelve windows," or words were used beginning with the letter A. Each player must repeat this, and add something else in keeping with a house; or sentences had to be made in which words beginning with the letter A must be said, the other players doing the same alphabetically.—London (A. B. Gomme).

Mr. Newell, in writing of this game, says that the " lamp-lighter " or " spill " was lighted when placed in the hair of the players who made mistakes. He does not mention forfeits being exacted.—*Games*, p. 139.

Ghost at the Well

One of the party is chosen for Ghost (if dressed in white so much the better); she hides in a corner; the other children are a mother and daughters. The eldest daughter says:—

"Mother, mother, please give me a piece of bread and butter."

M. "Let me (or 'leave me') look at your hands, child. Why, they are very dirty."

E. D. "I will go to the well and wash them."

She goes to the corner, the Ghost peeps up, and she rushes back, crying out—

"Mother! mother! I have seen a Ghost."

M. "Nonsense, child! it was only your father's nightshirt I have washed and hung out to dry. Go again."

The child goes, and the same thing happens. She returns, saying—

"Yes! mother! I have seen a ghost."

M. "Nonsense, child! we will take a candle, and all go together to search for it."

The mother picks up a twig for a candle, and they set off. When they come near to the Ghost, she appears from her hiding-place, mother and children rush away in different directions, the Ghost chases them until she has caught one, who in her turn becomes Ghost.—West Cornwall (Miss Courtney, *Folk-lore Journal*, v. 55).

This game was "Ghost in the Copper" in London. It was played in the same way as above. Chairs formed the copper, and the ghost crouched down behind. The "Mother" was "washing" at a tub, also formed with two chairs. The eldest daughter was told she could not go to school to-day; she must stop at home and help hang up the clothes. The other children go to play. The Mother said, "Here, Jane, take this (pretending to give her a garment out of the wash-tub) and put it in the copper, and push it down well with the stick." Jane goes to the copper and pretends to take off the lid. When she puts the washed garment in, and pokes down with the stick, the Ghost jumps up. She cries out as above, the Mother saying, "Nonsense, child! it's only some of the boiling clothes."

The child goes again, and the game proceeds as above. It is generally played now as "Ghost."—A. B. Gomme. It is mentioned by Newell (*Games*, p. 223).

Giants

A Giant is chosen, and he must be provided with a cave. A summer-house will do, if there is no window for the Giant to see out of. The others then have to knock at the door with their knuckles separately. The Giant rushes when he thinks all the children have knocked, and if he succeeds in catching one before they reach a place of safety (appointed beforehand) the captured one becomes Giant.—Bitterne, Hants (Mrs. Byford). See "Wolf."

Giddy

> Giddy, giddy, gander,
> Who stands yonder ?
> Little Bessy Baker,
> Pick her up and shake her ;
> Give her a bit of bread and cheese,
> And throw her over the water.
> —Warwickshire.

(*b*) A girl being blindfolded, her companions join hands and form a ring round her. At the word "Yonder" the blindfolded girl points in any direction she pleases, and at line three names one of the girls. If the one pointed at and the one named be the same, she is the next to be blinded; but, curiously enough, if they be not the same, the one named is the one. Meanwhile, at line four, she is not "picked up," but is shaken by the shoulders by the still blindfolded girl; and at line five she is given by the same "bread and cheese," *i.e.*, the buds or young leaves of what later is called "May" (*Cratægus oxyacantha*) ; and at line six she is taken up under the blinded girl's arm and swung round. — Warwickshire (*Notes and Queries*, 6th Ser., viii. 451).

Gilty-galty (or gaulty)

A boy's game. One boy is chosen, who says :—

> Gilty-galty four-and-forty,
> Two tens make twenty.

He then counts one, two, three, four, &c., up to forty, having his eyes covered by his hands, and the others hide while he is saying the "nominy." At the conclusion he uncovers his eyes, and if he sees any boys not yet hidden they have to stand still. He seeks the rest, but if he moves far away from his place, called the "stooil" (stool), one of the hidden boys may rush out and take it, provided he can get there first. Should he fail in this he also has to stand aside; but if any one succeeds, then all run out as before, and the same boy has to say the "nominy" again. On the other hand, if he finds all the boys without loosing his "stooil," the boy first caught has to take his place and say the "nominy." The game was thus played in 1810, and is so still, both here and at Lepton.—Easther's *Almondbury and Huddersfield Glossary.*

Gipsy

> I charge my children, every one,
> To keep good house while I am gone.
> You, and you [points], but specially you
> [or sometimes, but specially Sue],
> Or else I'll beat you black and blue.

One child is selected for Gipsy, one for Mother, and one for Daughter Sue. The Mother says the lines, and points to several children to emphasise her words. During her absence the Gipsy comes in, entices a child away, and hides her. This process is repeated till all the children are hidden, when the mother has to find them.—Halliwell (*Nursery Rhymes,* p. 228).

See "Mother, Mother, the Pot Boils Over," "Witch."

Gled-wylie

The name of a singular game played at country schools. One of the largest of the boys steals away from his comrades, in an angry-like mood, to some dykeside or sequestered nook, and there begins to work as if putting a pot on a fire. The others seem alarmed at his manner, and gather round him, when the following dialogue takes place:—

They say first to him—

> What are ye for wi' the pot, gudeman?
> Say what are ye for wi' the pot?

We dinna like to see ye, gudeman,
    Sae thrang about this spot.

We dinna like ye ava, gudeman,
    We dinna like ye ava.
Are ye gaun to grow a gled, gudeman ?
    And our necks draw and thraw ?

He answers—
    Your minnie, burdies, ye maun lae ;
    Ten to my nocket I maun hae ;
    Ten to my e'enshanks, and or I gae lye,
    In my wame I'll lay twa dizzen o' ye by.

The mother of them, as it were, returns—
  Try't than, try't than, do what ye can,
  Maybe ye maun toomer sleep the night, gudeman ;
  Try't than, try't than, Gled-wylie frae the heugh,
  Am no sae saft, Gled-wylie, ye'll fin' me bauld and teugh.

After these rhymes are said the chickens cling to the mother
all in a string. She fronts the flock, and does all she can to
keep the kite from her brood, but often he breaks the row and
catches his prey.—Mactaggart's *Gallovidian Encyclopedia*.

Evidently denominated from the common mode of designat-
ing the kite among the vulgar (Jamieson). "The Greedy
Gled's seeking ye," is one of the lines of a rhyme used in
"Hide and Seek" in Edinburgh. Glead, or Gled, is also a
Yorkshire and Cheshire name for a kite. "As hungry as a
Glead" (*Glossary*, by an Old Inhabitant).—Leigh (*Cheshire
Glossary*).

See "Fox and Goose," "Hen and Chickens," "Hide and
Seek."

Glim-glam
The play of "Blind Man's Buff."—Banffshire, Aberdeen
(Jamieson).

Gobs
A London name for the game of "Hucklebones."
See "Fivestones."

Green Grass

"Will you come?" "No!"

"Will you come?" "Yes!"

—Middlesex (Miss Collyer).

"Will you come?" "No!"
"Will you come?" "Yes!"

—London (A. B. Gomme).

—Congleton (Miss A. E. Twemlow).

I.   A dis, a dis, a green grass,
      A dis, a dis, a dis;
   Come all you pretty fair maids
      And dance along with us.

   For we are going roving,
      A roving in this land;
   We'll take this pretty fair maid,
      We'll take her by the hand.

   Ye shall get a duke, my dear,
      And ye shall get a drake;
   And ye shall get a young prince,
      A young prince for your sake.

   And if this young prince chance to die,
      Ye shall get another;
   The bells will ring, and the birds will sing,
      And we'll clap hands together.
          —Chamber's *Popular Rhymes*, pp. 137–38.

II.   A-diss, a-diss, a-green grass,
      A-diss, a-diss, a-dass;
   Come, my pretty fair maid,
      And walk along with us.

   For you shall have a dik-ma-day,
      You shall have a drāgon;
   You shall have a nice young man
      With princes for his thēgan (or sēgan).
          —Lanarkshire (W. G. Black).

III.   A dish, a dish, a green grass,
      A dish, a dish, a dish,
   Come all you pretty maidens
      And dance along wi' us.

For we are lads a roving,
 A roving through the land,
We'll take this pretty fair maid
 By her lily white hand.

Ye sall get a duke, my dear,
 An ye sall get a drake,
An ye sall get a bonny prince
 For your ain dear sake.

And if they all should die,
 Ye sall get anither;
The bells will ring, the birds will sing,
 And we'll clap our hands together.
     —Biggar (W. Ballantyne).

IV. Dissy, dissy, green grass,
  Dissy, dissy, duss,
Come all ye pretty fair maids
 And dance along with us.

You shall have a duck, my dear,
 And you shall have a drake,
And you shall have a nice young man
 To love you for your sake.

If this young man should chance to die
 And leave the girl a widow,
The birds shall sing, the bells shall ring,
 Clap all your hands together.
   —Yorkshire (Henderson's *Folk-lore, Northern
     Counties*, p. 27).

V. Dossy, dossy green grass,
  Dossy, dossy, doss,
Come all ye pretty fair maids
 And dance upon the grass.

I will give you pots and pans,
 I will give you brass,
I will give you anything
 For a pretty lass.

I will give you gold and silver,
   I will give you pearl,
I will give you anything
   For a pretty girl.

Take one, take one, the fairest you can see.

You shall have a duck, my dear,
   You shall have a drake,
You shall have a young man
   Apprentice for your sake.

If this young man shall wealthy grow
   And give his wife a feather,
The bells shall ring and birds shall sing
   And we'll all clap hands together.
           —Roxton, St. Neots (Miss Lumley).

VI.   Walking up the green grass,
     A dust, a dust, a dust!
  We want a pretty maiden
     To walk along with us.

  We'll take this pretty maiden,
     We'll take her by the hand,
  She shall go to Derby,
     And Derby is the land!

  She shall have a duck, my dear,
     She shall have a drake,
  She shall have a nice young man
     A-fighting for her sake!

  Suppose this young man was to die,
     And leave the poor girl a widow;
  The bells would ring and we should sing,
     And all clap hands together!
          —Berrington (*Shropshire Folk-lore*, p. 511).

VII. Tripping up the green grass,
     Dusty, dusty, day,
  Come all ye pretty fair maids,
     Come and with me play.

You shall have a duck, my dear,
　And you shall have a swan,
And you shall have a nice young man
　A waiting for to come.

Suppose he were to die
　And leave his wife a widow,
Come all ye pretty fair maids,
　Come clap your hands together!

　　　Will you come?
　　　No!

Naughty man, he won't come out,
　He won't come out, he won't come out,
Naughty man, he won't come out,
　To help us in our dancing.

　　　Will you come?
　　　Yes!

Now we've got our bonny lad,
　Our bonny lad, our bonny lad,
Now we've got our bonny lad,
　To help us in our dancing.
　　　　　　　　　—Middlesex (Miss Collyer).

VIII.　Stepping on the green grass
　　　　Thus, and thus, and thus;
　　Please may we have a pretty lass
　　　　To come and play with us?
　　We will give you pots and pans,
　　　　We will give you brass,

　　　　　No!

　　We will give you anything
　　　　For a bonny lass.

　　　　　No!

　　We will give you gold and silver,
　　　　We will give you pearl,
　　We will give you anything
　　　　For a pretty girl.

Yes!

You shall have a goose for dinner,
   You shall have a darling,
You shall have a nice young man
   To take you up the garden.

But suppose this young man was to die
   And leave this girl a widow?
The bells would ring, the cats would sing,
   So we'll all clap together.
                    —Frodingham and Nottinghamshire (Miss
                              M. Peacock).

IX.   Stepping up the green grass,
         Thus, and thus, and thus;
      Will you let one of your fair maids
         Come and play with us?
      We will give you pots and pans,
         We will give you brass,
      We will give you anything
         For a pretty lass.

         No!
      We won't take your pots and pans,
         We won't take your brass,
      We won't take your anything
         For a pretty lass.

      Stepping up the green grass,
         Thus, and thus, and thus;
      Will you let one of your fair maids
         Come and play with us?
      We will give you gold and silver,
         We will give you pearl,
      We will give you anything
         For a pretty girl.

         Yes!

      Come, my dearest [Mary],
         Come and play with us,

You shall have a young man
　　Born for your sake.
And the bells shall ring
　　And the cats shall sing,
And we'll all clap hands together.
　　　　　　　—Addy's *Sheffield Glossary.*

X.　Up and down the green grass,
　　　This, and that, and thus;
　　Come all you fair maids
　　　And walk along with us.

　　Some will give you silver,
　　　Some will give you gold,
　　Some will give you anything
　　　For a pretty lass.

　　Don't you think [*boy's name*]
　　　Is a handsome young man?
　　Don't you think Miss [*child who has been choosing*]
　　　Is as handsome as he?

　　Then off with the glove
　　　And on with the ring;
　　You shall be married
　　　When you can agree.

　　Take hold of my little finger,
　　　Maycanameecan,
　　Pray tell me the name
　　　Of your young man.
　　　　　　　—Hurstmonceux, Sussex (Miss Chase).

XI.　Here we come up the green grass,
　　　Green grass, green grass,
　　Here we come up the green grass,
　　　Dusty, dusty, day.

　　Fair maid, pretty maid,
　　　Give your hand to me,
　　I'll show you a blackbird,
　　　A blackbird on the tree.

We'll all go roving,
  Roving side by side,
I'll take my fairest ——,
  I'll take her for my bride.

          Will you come ?
No !

Naughty miss, she won't come out,
  Won't come out, won't come out,
Naughty miss, she won't come out,
  To help us with our dancing.

          Will you come ?
Yes !

Now we've got our bonny lass,
  Bonny lass, bonny lass,
Now we've got our bonny lass,
  To help us with our dancing.
                    —London (A. B. Gomme).

XII. Here we go up the green grass,
      The green grass, the green grass ;
      Here we go up the green grass,
      So early in the morning.

          Fair maid, pretty maid,
      Give your hand to me,
          And you shall see a blackbird,
      A blackbird on the tree ;
          All sorts of colours
      Lying by his side,
          Take me, dearest [——],
      For to be my bride—

          Will you come ?
No !

Naughty old maid, she won't come out,
She won't come out,
To help us with our dancing—

          Will you come ?
Yes !

Now we've got the bonny lass,
Now we've got the bonny lass,
To help us with our dancing.
　　　　　　　　—Liphook, Hants (Miss Fowler).

XIII. Trip trap over the grass,
If you please, will you let one of your [eldest] daughters come,
Come and dance with me?
I will give you pots and pans,
I will give you brass,
I will give you anything
　　For a pretty lass—
No!
I will give you gold and silver,
I will give you pearl,
I will give you anything
　　For a pretty girl.

Take one, take one, the fairest you may see.

The fairest one that I can see
Is pretty [Nancy], come to me;

You shall have a duck, my dear,
And you shall have a drake,
And you shall have a young man,
Apprentice for your sake.

If this young man should happen to die,
And leave this poor woman a widow,
The bells shall all ring and the birds shall all sing,
And we'll clap hands together.
　　　　　　—Halliwell's *Popular Nursery Rhymes*, cccxxxii.

XIV. Will you take gold and silver, or will you take brass,
Will you take anything for a pretty lass?

No! we'll not take gold and silver, no! we'll not take brass;
We'll not take anything for a pretty lass.

Will you take the keys of school, or will you take brass?
Will you take anything for a pretty lass?

Yes! we'll take the keys of school; yes! we will take brass;
We will take anything for a pretty lass.

Come, my dear [Mary Anne], and give me your right hand,
And you shall have a duck, my dear,
You shall have a drake;
You shall have a nice young man
To fiddle for your sake.

The birds will sing, the bells will ring,
And we'll all clap hands together.
—Congleton Workhouse School (Miss A. E. Tremlow).

(c) The popular version of this game is played by the greater number of the children forming a line on one side with joined hands, and one child (sometimes two or more) facing them, advancing and retiring while singing the verses. When he asks the question, "Will you come?" one girl on the opposite side answers "No!" and afterwards "Yes!" When this is said, she goes to the opposite side, and the two dance round together while singing the next verse. The game begins again by the two singing the verses, and thus getting a third child to join them, when the game proceeds for a fourth, and so on.

The Congleton and London versions are played by two lines of children of about equal numbers. In the Lincolnshire version the above description answers, except that when the last line is sung every one claps hands. In the Sussex version the child at the end of the line is taken over by the child who sings the verses, and they lock their little fingers together while singing the remainder.

Addy (*Sheffield Glossary*) says :—"Two children advance and retire on one side. When the opposite side says 'Yes!' the two take the first child in the row and dance round with her, singing the remaining verse. This is called ' the wedding.'"

The Lanarkshire version is quite a different one, and contains rather remarkable features. Mr. Black says that the game was played entirely by girls, never by boys, and generally in the months of May or June, about forty years ago. The children sang with rather mincing and refined voices, evidently making an effort in this direction. They walked, with their hands clasped behind their backs, up and down the road. Each child was crowned with rushes, and also had sashes or girdles of rushes.

Mr. Ballantyne says in his boyhood it was played by a row of boys on one side and another of girls opposite. The boys selected a girl when singing the third verse.

In the Roxton version, one child at the end of the line of children acts as "mother." One child advances as "suitor," and says the three first verses. The "mother" replies with the next line. The "suitor" chooses a girl and says the next verse, and then all the children sing the last verse. This is the same action as in Halliwell's version.

(*d*) The analysis of the game-rhymes is on pp. 164–67. This analysis presents us with a very good example of the changes caused by the game-rhymes being handed down by tradition among people who have forgotten the original meaning of the game. The first line in the Scotch version contains the word "dis," which is not known to the ordinary vocabulary. Another word, of similar import, is "dik-ma-day" in the Lanarkshire version. Two other words occur, namely, "the-gan" in the Lanarkshire, and "maycanameecan" in the Sussex versions, which are also not to be found in ordinary vocabularies. The two last words appear only once, and cannot, therefore, be used for the purpose of tracing out an original form of the game-rhyme, because on the system of analysis adopted they may be arbitrary introductions and totally unconnected with the original rhymes. This, however, is not the case with the two first-mentioned words, and I am inclined to consider them as forming part of the earliest version. The word "dis" is carried through no less than ten out of the fourteen variants, the gradation in the forms being as follows :—

                    dis
                    dass
                    dish
                    diss[y]—duss
                    dossy
                    this—thus
                       —dust
                       —dust[y]

No.	Scotland (Chambers).	Lanarkshire.	Biggar.	Yorkshire.	Roxton.	Shropshire.
1.	A-dis, a-dis, a green grass.	A-dis, a-dis, a green gass.	A dish, a dish, a green grass.	Dissy, dissy, green grass.	Dossy, dossy, green grass.	—
2.	—	—	—	—	—	Walking up the green grass.
3.	A-dis, a-dis, a-das.	A-dis, a-dis, a-dass.	A dish, a dish, a dish.	Dissy, dissy, duss.	Dossy, dossy, doss.	A dust, a dust, a dust.
4.	—	—	—	—	—	—
5.	—	—	—	—	—	We want a pretty maiden.
6.	Come all ye pretty maids,	Come my pretty fair maid.	Come 'all ye pretty maids,	Come all ye pretty maids.	Come all ye pretty maids.	To walk along with us.
7.	And dance along with us.	And walk along with us.	And dance along with us.	And dance along with us.	Dance upon the grass.	—
8.	For we are going a-roving.	—	For we are lads a roving.	—	—	—
9.	We'll take this maid by the hand.	—	We'll take this pretty fair maid by the hand.	—	—	We'll take her by the hand.
10.	—	—	—	—	—	—
11.	—	—	—	—	—	She shall go to Derby,
12.	You shall have a duke, my dear.	You shall have a dik-ma-day.	Ye sall get a duke.	You shall have a duck.	You shall have a duck (after No. 19)	She shall have a duck, my dear.
13.	—	—	—	—	I will give pots and pans.	—
14.	—	—	—	—	...... brass.	—
15.	—	—	—	—	...... gold and silver.	—
16.	—	—	—	—	...... pearl,	—
17.	—	—	—	—	...... anything.	—
18.	—	—	—	—		—
19.	—	—	—	—	For a pretty lass,	—
20.	You shall have a drake.	You shall have a dragon.	Ye sall get a drake.	You shall have a drake.	You shall have a drake.	She snall have a drake.
21.	—	—	—	—	—	—
22.	—	—	—	—	—	—

	I	II	III	IV	V	VI
23. [8.]						
24.	And ye shall get a young prince,	You shall have a nice young man.	Ye sall get a bonny prince.	You shall have a nice young man.	You shall have a young man.	She shall have a nice young man.
25.						
26.	A young prince for your sake.		For your ain sake.	To love you for your sake.	Apprentice for your sake.	A fighting for her sake.
27.						
28.	If this young prince should die.		If they all should die.			
29.				If this young man should chance to die.	If this young man should wealthy grow.	Suppose this young man was to die.
30.						
31.	Ye shall get another.					
32.			Ye sall get anither.	And leave the girl a widow.		And leave the girl a widow.
33.					And give his wife a feather.	
34.		With princes for his thegan.				
35.	Bells will ring and birds shall sing.		The bells will ring, birds will sing.	Birds shall sing and bells ring.	Bells shall ring and birds sing.	Bells ring and we shall sing.
36.						
37.	We'll all clap hands together.		We'll all clap hands together.	Clap all your hands together.	We'll all clap hands together.	And all clap hands together.
38.						
39.						
40.						
41.						
42.						
43.						
44.						
45.						
46.						

No.	Lincolnshire, Frodingham.	Sussex, Hurstmonceux.	Middlesex.	London.	Hants, Liphook.	Halliwell.	Sheffield.
1.	—	—	—	—	—	—	—
2.	Stepping up the green grass,	Up and down the green grass,	Tripping up the green grass.	Here we come up the green grass.	Here we go up the green grass,	Trip, trap, over the grass,	Stepping up the green grass,
3.	Thus, and thus, and thus.	Thus, and that, and thus.	—	—	—	—	Thus, and thus, and thus.
4.	—	—	Dusty, dusty day.	On a dusty, dusty day.	So early in the morning.	—	—
5.	Please may we have a pretty lass.	Come all ye fair maids.	Come all ye pretty maids.	Fair maid, pretty maid, —	Fair maid, pretty maid,	Please let one of your daughters come.	Will you let one of your fair maids.
6.	—	And walk along with us,	Come and with us play.	—	—	Come and dance with me.	Come and play with us.
7.	To come and play with us,	—	—	[See below.] Give your hand to me.	Give your hand to me.	—	—
8.	—	—	—	—	—	Take one, take the fairest you can see.	—
9.	—	—	—	—	—	Pretty [ ] come to me.	—
10.	—	—	—	—	—	—	—
11.	—	—	—	—	—	—	—
12.	—	—	You shall have a duck.	—	—	You shall have a duck, my dear.	—
13.	We will give you pots and pans.	—	—	—	—	I will give you pots and pans.	We will give you pots and pans.
14.	...... brass.	Some will give us silver ...... gold.	—	—	—	...... brass.	...... brass.
15.	...... gold and silver.	—	—	—	—	...... gold and silver.	...... gold and silver.
16.	...... pearl.	—	—	—	—	...... pearl.	...... pearl.
17.	...... anything.	—	—	I'll show you a blackbird.	You shall see a blackbird.	...... anything.	...... anything.
18.	—	—	—	—	—	—	—
19.	For a pretty lass.	—	—	—	—	For a pretty girl.	For a pretty lass.
20.	You shall have a goose for dinner.	—	You shall have a swan.	—	—	You shall have a drake,	—
21.	—	Take hold of my finger. Maycanameecan.	—	—	—	—	—
22.	—	—	—	We'll all go roving.	All sorts of colours lying by his side.	—	—
23.	—	—	—	—	—	—	—
[8.]	—	—	—	—	—	—	—
24.	You shall have a nice young man.	—	You shall have a nice young man.	—	—	You shall have a young man.	You shall have a nice young man.

	Col 1	Col 2	Col 3	Col 4	Col 5	Col 6	Col 7
25.	—	Pray tell me the name	—	I'll take [ ] for my	Take [ ]] for my	—	—
26.	—	of your young man.	—	my bride.	bride.	—	—
27.	To take you up the garden.	—	A waiting for to come.	—	—	—	—
28.	—	—	—	—	—	Apprentice for your sake.	Born for your sake.
29.	Suppose this young man was to die.	—	—	—	—	—	—
30.	—	—	Suppose he were to die.	—	—	If this young man should happen to die.	—
31.	And leave the girl a widow.	—	—	—	—	—	—
32.		—	And leave his wife a widow.	—	—	And leave the poor woman a widow.	—
33.	—	—		—	—		—
34.	Bells would ring, cats would sing.	—	—	—	—	Bells shall ring, birds shall sing.	Bells shall ring, cats shall sing.
35.		—	—	—	—		
36.	—	—	Come all ye pretty fair maids.	—	—	—	—
37.	So we'll all clap hands together.	—	Come clap your hands together.	—	—	We'll all clap hands together.	We'll all clap hands together.
38.	—	Don't you think [ ] a nice young man?	—	—	—	—	—
39.	—	Don't you think [ ] as handsome as he?	—	—	—	—	—
40.	—	Then off with the glove, on with the ring.	—	—	—	—	—
41.	—	You shall be mar-	—	—	—	—	—
42.	—	ried when you can agree.	—	—	—	—	—
43.	—	—	—	Naughty miss, she won't come out.	Naughty old maid, she won't come out.	—	—
44.	—	—	—	To help us with our dancing.	To help us with our dancing.	—	—
45.	—	—	—	Now we've got our bonny lass.	Now we'll get our bonny lass.	—	—
46.	—	—	—	To help us with our dancing.	To help us with our dancing.	—	—

What the meaning of this word is it may be impossible to ascertain, though probably Mr. Newell may be correct in his suggestion that it represents the old English word "adist," the opposite of "ayont," meaning "this way," "come hither" (*Games of American Children*, p. 51). But the point really is, that the version which contains the oldest word-forms would probably be the purest in other respects. The analysis of the whole game confirms this view, as the Scottish and Yorkshire versions are nearly parallel, while the discrepancies begin to creep in with the Shropshire version, reaching their last stage in the versions recorded by Halliwell and from Congleton. Following this line of argument, "dik-ma-day" becomes first "duke, my dear," and then "duck, my dear." Turning next to the import of the rhymes, apart from special words used, it is curious to note that "dis" is only converted into "dusty," and hence into "dusty day," in two versions out of the fourteen. The Lincolnshire version agrees with Halliwell's version in making some curious offers for a pretty lass, but these rhymes are probably an innovation. In the same way the incidents numbered 39–40, occurring in the Sussex version, and 43–46 occurring in the London and Hants versions, are borrowings from other games, and not original portions of this. The Congleton version is evidently incomplete.

(*e*) Henderson, in describing the curious rites accompanying the saining or blessing of a corpse in the Scottish Lowlands, states that empty dishes are arranged on the hearth as near as possible to the fire, and after certain ceremonies in connection therewith have been performed, the company join hands and dance round the dishes, singing this burden :—

> A dis, a dis, a dis,
> A green griss ;
> A dis, a dis, a dis.
> —*Folk-lore of Northern Counties*, p. 54.

This rhyme is, it will be seen, the same as the first two lines of the game, the word "griss" in the burial-rhyme becoming "grass" in the game-rhyme, "grisse" being the old form for "grass" or herb (Halliwell, *Provincial Glossary*, quotes a MS. authority for this). This identification of the game-rhyme would suggest that the game originally was a child's dramatic imitation of an old burial ceremony, and it remains to be seen whether the signification of the words would carry out this idea.

In the first place, the idea of death is a prominent incident in the game, appearing in seven out of the fourteen versions. In all these cases the death is followed by the clapping of hands and bell-ringing, and in five cases by the singing of birds. Clapping of hands occurs in two other cases, and bell-ringing in one other case, not accompanied by the death incident. Now it is singular that the burial-rite which has just been quoted is called Dish-a-loof; and a reference to the game of "Dish-a-loof" [under that title], will show that it derives its name from the clapping of hands. In the ceremony, as described by Henderson, although songs and games are part of the burial-ceremony, there is no specific mention of hand-clapping; but it is conceivable that the action at one time formed part of the ceremony, and hence the name "Dish-a-loof." This would not account for the promise of a duck, drake, &c., as in incidents Nos. 12 and 20; nor for the promise of a young prince or young man; but these incidents might very well be variants of some earlier forms which are not now discoverable, especially as love-games were played at funerals, and as the tendency, in the less complete forms of the game as they have come down to us, is in the direction of transposing the game into a complete love-game. The use of rushes in the Lanarkshire game might indicate the funeral garland (Aubrey's *Remaines*, pp. 109, 139). For clapping of hands to indicate bell-tolling or bell-ringing at times of death see Napier's *Folklore*, p. 66. Henderson (p. 63) says the "passing bell" was supposed in former times to serve two purposes: it called on all good Christians within hearing to pray for the departing spirit, and it scared away the evil spirits who were watching to seize it, or at least to scare and terrify it.

On the whole evidence from the rhymes, therefore, I should be disposed to class this game as originally belonging to burial, and not love, rites.

Green Gravel

—Madeley, Shropshire (Miss Burne).

—Earls Heaton (H. Hardy).

—Sporle, Norfolk (Miss Matthews).

—Redhill, Surrey (Miss G. Hope).

—Lancashire (Mrs. Harley).

—Derbyshire (Mrs. Harley).

I. Green gravel, green gravel, your grass is so green,
   The fairest young damsel that ever was seen;
   We washed her, we dried her, we rolled her in silk,
   And we wrote down her name with a glass pen and ink.
   Dear Annie, dear Annie, your true love is dead,
   And we send you a letter to turn round your head.
                         —Belfast (W. H. Patterson).

II. Green gravel, green gravel, the grass is so green,
    The fairest young lady that ever was seen;
    I'll wash you in milk,
    And I'll clothe you with silk,
    And I'll write down your name with a gold pen and ink.
    O Sally, O Sally, your true love is dead,
    He sent you a letter to turn round your head.
              —Berrington, Oswestry (*Shropshire Folk-lore*, p. 510).

III. Around the green gravel the grass is so green,
     All the pretty fair maids are plain to be seen;

Wash them in milk, and clothe them in silk,
Write their names down with a gold pen and ink.
All but Miss " Jenny," her sweetheart is dead ;
She's left off her wedding to turn back her head.

O mother, O mother, do you think it is true ?
O yes, child ! O yes, child !
Then what shall I do ?
We'll wash you in milk, and dress you in silk,
And write down your name with a gold pen and ink.
                    —Derbyshire and Worcestershire (Mrs. Harley).

IV.   Green gravel, green gravel,
      The grass is so green,
      Such beautiful flowers
      As never were seen.
      O Annie [or any name], O Annie,
      Your sweetheart is dead !
      He has sent you a letter
      To turn back your head.
                          —Earls Heaton, Yorkshire (H. Hardy).

V.   Green gravel, green gravel,
      The grass is so green,
      The fairest young damsels
      As ever were seen.
      O ——, O ——, your true love is dead ;
      He sent you a letter
      To turn round your head.

      Green gravel, green gravel,
      The grass is so green,
      The dismalest damsels
      As ever were seen.
      O ——, O ——, your true love's not dead ;
      He sends you a letter
      To turn back your head.
                          —Lincoln, Winterton, and Wakefield
                               (Miss Fowler and Miss Peacock).

VI. Green gravel, green gravel, the grass is so green,
     The fairest young lady [damsel] that ever was seen.

O ——, O ——, your true love is dead;
He's sent you a letter to turn round your head.
—Redhill, Surrey (Miss G. Hope);
Lancashire (Mrs. Harley).

VII. Green meadows, green meadows, your grass is so green,
The fairest young damsel that ever was seen;
O Mary, O Mary, your sweetheart is dead;
We've sent you a letter to turn back your head.

Or, Green gravel, green gravel, the grass is so green,
and following on as above.
—Sporle, Norfolk (Miss Matthews).

VIII. Green grover, green grover, your grass is so green,
The prettiest young lady that ever was seen.
O ——, O ——, your true love is dead;
I send you this letter, so turn round your head.
—Gainford, Durham (Miss Eddleston).

IX. Green gravels, green gravels,
The grass is so green,
And all the pretty maidens
Are not to be seen,
Except —— (said twice),
And she's not [?] to be seen,
So I send you a letter to turn round your head.
—Hampshire (Miss E. Mendham).

X. Green gravels, green gravels, the grass is so green,
Fine pencils, fine pencils, as ever were seen.
O Mary! O Mary! your true love is dead,
And he's sent you a letter to turn round your head.
—Wales (*Byegones,* 1890).

XI. Yellow gravel, yellow gravel,
The grass is so green,
The fairest young lady
That ever was seen.
O ——, O ——,
Your true love is dead;
I send you a letter to turn round your head.
—Cowes, Isle of Wight (Miss E. Smith).

XII. Green gravel, green gravel, the grass is so green,
Said the fairest young damsel that ever I've seen.
O mother, O mother, my true-love is dead,
He sent me this letter to turn round my head.
O mother, O mother, do you think this is true?
O yes, love! O yes, love!
And what shall I do?
I'll wash you in butter-milk, I'll dress you in silk,
I'll write down your name with my gold pen and ink.
—Isle of Man (A. W. Moore).

XIII. Green gravel, green gravel, the grass is so green,
The flowers are all faded and none to be seen.
O [Dolly], O [Dolly], your sweetheart is dead,
He's sent you a letter to turn back your head.

Wallflowers, wallflowers, growing up so high,
We are but little, and we shall have to die!
Excepting [Dolly Turner], she's the youngest girl.
O for shame, and fie for shame, and turn your back to
home again.   —Madeley, Shropshire (Miss Burne).

XIV. Green gravel, green gravel, the grass is so green,
The fairest young lady that ever was seen.
As I went up Miss Betsey's stairs to buy a frying-pan,
There sat Miss Betsey a-kissing her young man.

She pulled off her glove and showed me her ring,
And the very next morning the bells did ring.
Dear Betsey, dear Betsey, your true love is dead,
He's sent you a letter to turn back your head.
—Summertown, Oxford (A. H. Franklin,
Midland Garner, vol. ii. p. 32).

XV. Round the green gravel the grass grows green,
All pretty fair maids are fit to be seen;
Wash them in milk, and clothe them in silk,
And write down their names with pen and black ink—
Choose one, choose two, choose the fairest daughter.

Now, my daughter, married to-day,
Like father and mother they should be,

To love one another like sister and brother—
I pray you now to kiss one another.

Now my daughter Mary's gone,
With her pockets all lined with gold;
On my finger a gay gold ring—
Good-bye, Mary, good-bye.

Now this poor widow is left alone,
Nobody could marry a better one;
Choose one, choose two—
Choose the fairest daughter.   —Sheffield (S. O. Addy).

XVI.   Round the green gravel the grass is so green,
And all the fine ladies that ever were seen;
Washed in milk and dressed in silk,
The last that stoops down shall be married.

[Johnnie Smith] is a nice young man,
And so is [Bessie Jones] as nice as he;
He came to the door with his hat in his hand,
Inquiring for [Miss Jones].

She is neither within, she is neither without,
She is up in the garret a-walking about.
Down she came, as white as milk,
With a rose in her bosom as soft as silk.

Silks and satins be ever so dear,
You shall have a kiss [gown?], my dear,
So off with the glove and on with the ring—
To-morrow, to-morrow, the wedding begins.
          —Forest of Dean, Gloucestershire (Miss Matthews).

XVII.   Around a green gravill
The grass is so green,
And all the fine ladies
Ashamed to be seen.
They wash 'em in milk
And dress 'em in silk—
We'll all cou' don' together.

My elbow, my elbow,
My pitcher and my can ;
Isn't ——
A nice young gell ?
Isn't ——
As nice as her—
They shall be married with a guinea-gold ring.

I peep'd through the window,
I peep'd through the door,
I seed pretty ——
A-dancin on the floor ;
I cuddled her an' fo'dled her,
I set her on my knee ;
I says pretty ——
Won't [ëe ?] you marry me.

A new-swept parlour,
An' a new-made bed,
A new cup and saucer
Again we get wed.
If it be a boy, he shall have a hat,
To follow with his mammy to her na', na', na' ;
If he be a gell, she shall have a ring,
To follow with her mammy to her ding, ding, ding.
                              —Wakefield (Miss Fowler).

(c) The more general way of playing this game is to form a
ring of children simply. The children walk round singing the
verse as in the Belfast version, and when the last line is sung, the
child whose name is mentioned turns round, facing the outside
of the ring and having her back to the centre. She continues to
hold hands with the others, and dances round with them in that
position. This is repeated until all the children have "turned"
their backs to the inside of the ring. Here the game ends in
many cases, but another verse is sung in the Lincoln, Winterton, and Wakefield versions from Miss Peacock, and this was
sung also in the London version. The second verse thus terminates the game, with the players one by one reversing their
position and facing the centre of ring as at first. In the

Forest of Dean and Wakefield versions the action of the game is somewhat different. A child stands in the centre of the ring of children, without apparently taking much part in the game, except to name the children in turn. In the Wakefield version, however (Miss Fowler, No. xvii.), a little boy stands in the middle of a circle of girls who sing the first verse. At "We'll all cou' don' together," all crouch down, as if in profound respect, then rising slowly, sing the next verse. After "My pitcher and my can," each child mentions her own name. At "Isn't —— as nice as her?" each mentions her sweetheart's name, and the child thus chosen goes into the circle. At the end of the fourth verse they all clap hands, and the one that is sweetheart to him in the middle kisses him. The "crouching down" is also done in the Forest of Dean version when singing the fourth line. The last one to stoop has to name her sweetheart. When this is done, the children all dance round and sing the other lines.

(d) The analysis of the game-rhymes is on pp. 178–181. The most constant formulæ of this game-rhyme are shown by this analysis to be Nos. 1, 6, 7, 13, 15, 18, 23, and the variants, though important, are not sufficient to detract from the significance of the normal version. It is evidently a funeral game. The green gravel and the green grass indicate the locality of the scene; "green," as applied to gravel, may mean freshly disturbed, just as green grave means a freshly made grave. The tenant of the new grave is the well-loved lady of a disconsolate lover, and probably the incidents of washing and dressing the corpse, and putting an inscription on the place where it is laid, are indicated by Nos. 13 and 15. The dirge, or singing to the dead, is indicated by Nos. 18, 23, and 26, and the beauty of the first line is in complete accord with the mournful music. That No. 26 occurs in only two variants, Derbyshire and the Isle of Man, is curious, as the pathos of this appeal is very apparent in the movement of the game. The communion with the dead which is indicated by No. 23 is by no means considered impossible by the peasantry. In confirmation of this being a representation of an old funeral ceremony, it may be pointed out that the action

No.	Belfast.	Shropshire.	Derbyshire.	Earls Heaton, Yorks.	Lincolnshire.	Redhill, Surrey.	Sporle, Norfolk.	Gainford, Durham.	Hants.
1.	Green gravel.	Green gravel.	Around the green gravel.	Green gravel.	Green gravel.	Green gravel.	—	—	Green gravels.
2.	—	—	—	—	—	—	—	—	—
3.	—	—	—	—	—	—	Green meadows.	Green grover.	—
4.	—	—	—	—	—	—	—	—	The grass is so green.
5.	Your grass is so green.	The grass is so green.	The grass is so green.	The grass is so green.	The grass is so green.	The grass is so green.	Your grass is so green.	Your grass is so green.	—
6.	The fairest damsel ever seen.	—	—	—	Fairest damsel ever seen.	Fairest damsel ever seen.	Fairest damsel ever seen.	—	—
7.	—	—	—	—	—	—	—	—	—
8.	—	The fairest young lady ever seen.	—	—	—	—	—	Prettiest young lady ever seen.	—
9.	—	—	All pretty maids are plain to be seen.	—	—	—	—	—	—
10.	—	—	—	Such beautiful flowers ever seen.	—	—	—	—	—
11.	—	—	—	—	—	—	—	—	All pretty maidens are *not* to be seen.
12.	—	Wash you in milk, clothe in silk.	Wash them in milk, clothe in silk.	—	—	—	—	—	—
13.	Washed her, dried her, rolled her in silk.	—	—	—	—	—	—	—	—
14.	—	—	—	—	—	—	—	—	—

	A	B	C	D	E	F	G	H	I
15.	Wrote name in glass pen and ink.	—	—	—	—	—	—	—	—
16.	—	Write name in gold pen and ink.	Write names in gold pen and ink.	—	—	—	—	—	—
17.	Your true love is dead.	True love is dead.	Hersweetheart is dead.	Sweetheart is dead.	True love is dead.	True love is dead.	Sweetheart is dead.	True love is dead.	—
18.									
19.									Except —— she's not to be seen.
20.	—	—	—	—	—	—	—	—	—
21.	—	—	—	—	—	—	—	—	—
22.	—	—	—	—	—	—	—	—	—
23.	He sent letter to turn your head.	He sent letter to turn your head.	—	He sent letter to turn your head.	He sent letter to turn your head.	He sent letter to turn your head.	We sent letter to turn your head.	I send letter to turn your head.	I send letter to turn round your head.
24.			She's left off her wedding to turn back her head.						
25.	—	—	Mother, is it true; What shall I do? [Then repeat Nos. 14 & 16.]	—	—	—	—	—	—
26.	—	—		—	—	—	—	—	—
27.	—	—	—	—	True love not dead, he sends letter to turn your head.	—	—	—	—
28.	—	—	—	—	—	—	—	—	—
29.	—	—	—	—	—	—	—	—	—
30.	—	—	—	—	—	—	—	—	—
31.	—	—	—	—	—	—	—	—	—

No.	Wales.	Isle of Wight.	Isle of Man.	Madeley.	Oxfordshire.	Sheffield.	Forest of Dean.	Wakefield.
1.	Green gravel.	—	Green gravel,	Green gravel.	Green gravel.	—	—	—
2.	—	—	—	—	—	Round the green gravel.	Round the green gravel.	Around the green gravill.
3.	—	—	—	—	—	—	—	—
4.	—	—	—	—	—	—	—	—
5.	The grass is so green.	Yellow gravel. The grass is so green.	The grass is so green, Fairest damsel ever I've seen.	The grass is so green.	The grass is so green.	The grass grows green.	The grass is so green.	The grass is so green.
6.	—	—	—	—	—	—	—	—
7.	—	Fairest young lady ever seen.	—	—	Fairest young lady ever seen.	—	—	—
8.	—	—	—	—	—	—	All fine ladies ever were seen.	—
9.	—	—	—	—	—	All pretty fair maids are fit to be seen,	—	—
10.	—	—	—	Flowers all faded, none to be seen.	—	—	—	—
11.	—	—	—	—	—	—	—	All fine ladies ashamed to be seen.
12.	Fine pencil as ever was seen.	—	—	—	—	—	—	—
13.	—	—	[Wash you in butter-milk, dress in silk.] (After No. 26.)	—	—	Wash them in milk, clothe in silk.	Washed in milk, dressed in silk.	Wash 'em in milk, dress in silk.
14.	—	—	—	—	—	—	—	—
15.	—	—	Write name with my gold pen and ink.] (After No. 26.)	—	—	—	—	—
16.	—	—	—	—	—	—	—	—
17.	—	—	—	—	—	Write names with pen and black ink.	—	—

No.	1	2	3	4	5	6	7	8
18.	True love is dead.	True love is dead.	True love is dead.	Sweetheart is dead.	[True love is dead.] (After No. 25.)	—	—	We'll all cow down together.
19.	| |	| |	| |	| |	—	—	—	—
20.	|	|	|	|	Betsy kissing her young man.	—	—	—
21.	|	|	|	|	—	Choose the fairest daughter.	—	—
22.							Last to stoop down shall be married.	We'll all cow down together.
23.	He's sent letter to turn head.	I send you letter to turn round your head.	He sent this letter to turn my head.	I've sent letter to turn your head.	[He sent letter to turn back your head.] (After No. 25.)	—	He came to inquire, down she came, so off with glove and on with ring, to-morrow the wedding begins.	They shall be married with gold ring.
24.	| |	| |	| |		She showed her ring and bells did ring.	Married to-day, so kiss one another.	—	—
25.								
26.			Mother, is it true? What shall I do?			—	—	—
27.	| | |	| | |	| | |	[Wallflowers verses follow.]	—	—	—	—
28.								
29.	|	|	|	|	—	Poor widow left alone, and choose the fairest daughter.	—	—
30.	|	|	|	|	—	—	—	[Dancing, cuddling, asking to marry.] [Furnishing.] [If a boy, he's to have a hat; if a girl, a ring.]
31.	| |	| |	| |	| |	—	—	—	—
32.								

of turning backwards during the singing of the dirge is also represented in the curious funeral ceremony called "Dish-a-loof," which is described in Henderson's *Folk-lore of the Northern Counties*, p. 53. Henderson's words are: "All the attendants, going out of the room, return into it backwards, repeating this rhyme of 'saining.'" The additional ceremony of marriage in four of the games is clearly an interpolation, which may have arisen from the custom of playing love and marriage games at funerals and during the watching with the corpse, or may be a mere transition to the more pleasant task of love-making as the basis of a game. The Derbyshire incident (No. 24) may indicate indeed that the funeral is that of a young bride, and in that case the tendency to make the game wholly a marriage game is accounted for. The decay which has set in is apparent by the evident attempt to alter from "green gravel" to "green grover" and "yellow gravel" (Nos. 4 and 5), and to introduce pen and black ink (No. 17). The addition of the incongruous elements from other games (Nos. 27–31) is a frequent occurrence in modern games, and is the natural result of decadence in the original form of the game. Altogether this game-rhyme affords a very good example of the condition of traditional games among the present generation of children.

(*e*) Other versions, actually or practically identical with the Redhill (Surrey) version, have been sent by Miss Blair (South Shields); Mr. H. S. May, Ogbourne and Manton (Wilts); Mrs. Haddon (Cambridge); Mrs. Harley (Lancashire); and Miss Burne, Platt, near Wrotham (Kent). There are also similar printed versions in *Folk-lore Journal*, vi. 214 (Dorsetshire); *Folk-lore Record*, v. 84 (Hersham, Surrey). Northall prints a version in his *Folk Rhymes*, 362–3, identical with No. 17. The tune of the Platt version sent by Miss Burne, and the Ogbourne and Manton (H. S. May), are almost identical, except the termination. This seems to be the most general tune for the game. The Lancashire tune is the same as the London version.

Miss Burne says of the Madeley version: "I never knew 'Green Gravel' and 'Wallflowers' played together as in this way elsewhere (I had not got this variant when I wrote *Shrop-*

shire Folk-lore), except at Much Wenlock, where they reverse the two verses, and only sing *one line* (the last) of 'Green Gravel.' But I feel sure they must have been *meant* to go together (see my note in *Shropshire Folk-lore*, p. 510), and I can explain them, I think. The ring of girls are dancing on the green grass plot in the middle of an old-fashioned sixteenth-century walled garden: each gets the news of her lover's death, and 'turns her face to the wall,' the old token of hopeless sorrow. Then they apostrophise the wallflowers in the border surrounding the grass plot against the old high wall; and here another variant explains the lament (second line)—

Wallflowers, wallflowers, growing up so high,
We shall all be maidens [and so], we shall all die;

Except the youngest (who will meet with another lover), whether as an instance of the proverbial luck of the 'youngest born,' or as a piece of juvenile giddiness and inconstancy, I cannot say; but considering the value set on true love and hopeless constancy in the ballad-lore, and the special garland which distinguished the funerals of bereaved but constant maidens, and the solemnity of betrothal in old days, the latter seems probable, especially considering the 'for shame.' "

The incidents of *washing* a corpse in milk and *dressing* it in silk occur in "Burd Ellen," Jamieson's *Ballads*, p. 125.

"Tak up, tak up my bonny young son,
Gar *wash* him wi' the *milk*;
Tak up, tak up my fair lady,
Gar row her in the *silk*."

Green Grow the Leaves (1)

—Earls Heaton (Mr. Hardy).

I.   Green grow the leaves (or grows the ivy)
round the old oak tree,
Green grow the leaves round the old oak tree,

Green grow the leaves round the old oak tree,
    As we go marching on.

Bless my life I hardly knew you,
Bless my life I hardly knew you,
Bless my life I hardly knew you,
    As we go marching on.
                    —Lincolnshire and Nottinghamshire
                            (Miss Peacock).

II.   Green grow the leaves on the old oak tree,
      I love the boys and the boys love me,
          As we go marching on.
                          —Sharleston (Miss Fowler).

III. I love the boys and the boys love me,
      I love the boys and the boys love me,
      I love the boys and the boys love me,
          As we go marching home.

      Glory, glory, hallelujah!
      Glory, glory, hallelujah!
      Glory, glory, hallelujah!
          As we go marching home.

      The old whiskey bottle lies empty on the shelf,
      The old whiskey bottle lies empty on the shelf,
      The old whiskey bottle lies empty on the shelf,
          As we go marching home.
                    —Earls Heaton, Yorkshire (Herbert).

(*b*) In Lincolnshire and Nottinghamshire the game is played by the children forming a circle and dancing round, singing. The first and third lines are sung three times. Partners are chosen during the singing of the last line. Miss Peacock adds, "The rest wanting, as my informant had forgotten the game." In the Sharleston version the children march round two by two, in a double circle, with one child in the centre, singing the verse. At the conclusion, the children who are marching on the inner side of the circle leave their partners and take the place of one in front of them, while the centre child endeavours to get one of the vacant places, the child turned out taking the place of the one in the centre, when the game begins again.

In the Earls Heaton version there is the circle of children, with one child in the centre, who chooses a partner after the lines have been sung.

(*c*) From this it would seem that while the Lincolnshire and Nottinghamshire words appear to be the most complete, the action has been preserved best at Sharleston. The acting of this version is the same as that of "The Jolly Miller." The third variant is evidently an imitation of the song, "John Brown."

Green Grow the Leaves (2)

—Northants (R. S. Baker).

Green grow the leaves on the hawthorn tree,
Green grow the leaves on the hawthorn tree,
We jangle and we wrangle and we never can agree,
But the tenor of our song goes merrily, merrily, merrily,
The tenor of our song goes merrily.

—R. S. Baker (*Northants Notes and Queries*, ii. 161).

(*b*) One couple is chosen to lead, and they go off, whither they will, followed by a long train of youths and maidens, all singing the refrain. Sometimes the leaders part company, and branch off to the right or left; the others have to do the same, and not until the leaders meet can they join again. They march arm in arm.

(*c*) Mr. R. S. Baker, who records this, says a Wellingborough lady sent him the tune and words, and told him the game was

more like a country dance than anything else, being a sort of
dancing " Follow My Leader."

Gully

A sink, or, failing that, a particular stone in the pavement
was the " Gully." Some boy chosen by lot, or one who volun-
teered in order to start the game, laid his top on the ground at
some distance from the " Gully." The first player then spun
his top, pegging at the recumbent top, so as to draw it towards
the " Gully." If he missed the top, he stooped down and took
up his own top by pushing his hand against it in such a
manner that the space between his first and second finger
caught against the peg and forced the top into the palm of his
hand. He then had " a go " at the recumbent top (I forget
what this was called), and sent his own top against it so as to
push it towards the " Gully." If he missed, he tried again and
again, until his own top could spin no longer. If he did not
hit the top with his own while it was spinning, his top had to
be laid down and the other one taken up, and its owner took
his turn at pegging. When a spinning-top showed signs of
exhaustion, and the taking it up might kill it, and it was not
very far from the down-lying top, its owner would gently push
it with his finger, so as to make it touch the other top, and so
avoid putting it into the other's place. This was called " kissing," and was not allowed by some players. When one player
succeeded in sending the top into the " Gully," he took it up
and fixed it by its peg into a post, mortar of a wall, or the best
place where it could be tolerably steady. Holding it by one
hand, he drove the peg of his own top as far as he could into
the crown of the victim top. This was called " taking a grudge."
He then held either his own or the victim top and knocked the
other against the wall, the object being to split the victim. He
was allowed three " grudges." If the top did not give way,
the other players tried in turn. If the top did not split, it was
returned to its owner, but any boy who succeeded in splitting
it through the middle, so that the peg fell out, took possession
of the peg. I have seen a top split at the side in such a way
as to be quite useless as a top, though no peg was gained. I

remember, too, a schoolfellow of mine drawing from his pocket some seven or eight pegs, the trophied memorials of as many tops.—London (J. P. Emslie).

See "Hoatie," "Hoges," "Peg-top."

Hairry my Bossie

This is a game of chance. The players are two, and may be boys or girls, or a boy and a girl. The stakes may be pins, buttons, marbles, or anything for which children gamble. One player puts a number, one, two, three or more, of the articles to be gambled for into the hollow of the closed hand, and says, "Hairry my bossie;" the other answers, "Knock 'im down," upon which he puts his closed hands down with a blow on his knees, and continues to strike them upwards and downwards on the knee, so as to give the opponent in play an idea of the number of objects concealed by the sound given forth. He then says, "How many blows?" and gets the reply, "As many's goes." A guess is then made. If the guess is correct the guesser gets the objects. If the guess is incorrect the guesser has to make up the difference between the number guessed and the real number. The players play alternately. This game was played for the most part at Christmas.—Keith (Rev. W. Gregor).

(b) Hairry = "rob," Bossie = "a wooden bowl," commonly used for making the leaven in baking oat-cakes, and for making "brose."

This is a very general game amongst schoolboys.

Half-Hammer

The game of "Hop-step-and-jump," Norfolk. This game is played in the west of Sussex, but not in the east. It is played thus by two or more boys. Each boy in his turn stands first on one leg and makes a hop, then strides or steps, and lastly, putting both feet together, jumps. The boy who covers the most ground is the victor.—Halliwell's *Dictionary*.

Han'-and-Hail

A game common in Dumfries, thus described by Jamieson. Two goals called hails, or dules, are fixed on at about a distance of four hundred yards. The two parties then place themselves in the middle between the goals or dules, and one of the players, taking a soft elastic ball, about the size of a man's fist, tosses it into the air, and, as it falls, strikes it with his palm towards his antagonists. The object of the game is for either party to drive the ball beyond the goal which lies before them, while their opponents do all in their power to prevent this. As soon as the ball is gowf't, that is, struck away, the opposite party endeavour to intercept it in its fall. This is called keppan' the ba'. If they succeed in this attempt, the player who does so is entitled to throw the ball with all his might towards his antagonists. If he kep it in the first bound which it makes off the ground, called a stot, he is allowed to haunch, that is, to throw the ball by bringing his hand with a sweep past his thigh, to which he gives a stroke as his hand passes, and discharging the ball at the moment when the stroke is given. If the ball be caught in the second bounce, the catcher may hoch the ball, that is, throw it through below one of his houghs. If none of the party catch the ball, it must be gowf't in the manner before described. As soon as either of the parties succeed in driving the ball, or, as it is called, hailin' the dules, the game then begins by one of the party which was successful throwing the ball towards the opposing goal and the other party striving to drive it back.

Hand in and Hand out

A game played by a company of young people who are drawn up in a circle, when one of them, pitched upon by lot, walks round the band, and, if a boy, hits a girl, or, if a girl, she strikes a boy whom she chooses, on which the party striking and the party struck run in pursuit of each other till the latter is caught, whose lot it then becomes to perform the same part. A game so called was forbidden by statute of Edward IV.—Halliwell's *Dictionary*.

See " Drop Handkerchief."

Handy-Croopen

A game in which one of the players turns his face to the wall, his hand resting upon his back. He must continue in position until he guesses who struck his hand, when the striker takes his place.—Orkney and Shetland (Jamieson's *Dictionary*.

See " Hot Cockles."

Handy Dandy

I.   Handy dandy,
    Sugary candy—
    Top or bottom ?

    Handy spandy,
    Jack a dandy—
    Which good hand will you have ?
    —Halliwell's *Dictionary: Nursery Rhymes*, p. 216.

II.   Handy dandy riddledy ro—
    Which will you have, high or low ?
        —Halliwell's *Nursery Rhymes*, p. 216.

III.   Handy pandy,
    Sugary candy,
    Which will you have—
    Top or bottom ?   —London (A. B. Gomme).

IV.   Handy pandy, Jack a dandy,
    Which hand will you have ?
       —Burne's *Shropshire Folk-lore*, p. 530.

(*b*) The hands are closed, some small article is put in one of them behind the back of the player. The closed fists are then turned rapidly round one another while the rhyme is being said, and they are then placed one on top of the other. A guess is then made by any one of the players as to which hand the object is in. If correct, the guesser obtains the object; if incorrect, the player who performs " Handy dandy" keeps it.

(*c*) This game is mentioned in *Piers Plowman*, p. 69 ot Wright's edition. Douce quotes an ancient MS. which curiously mentions the game as "men play with little children at 'handye-dandye,' which hand will you have" (ii. 167). Johnson says: "' Handy dandy,' a play in which children change hands and places: ' See how yon justice rails upon yon simple thief! Hark, in thine ear: change places, and, handy dandy,

which is the justice, which is the thief?" (*King Lear*, iv. 6).
Malone says, "'Handy dandy' is, I believe, a play among
children, in which something is shaken between two hands,
and then a guess is made in which hand it is retained." See
Florio's *Italian Dictionary*, 1598: "Bazzicchiare, to shake
between the hands; to play 'Handy dandy.'" Pope, in his
Memoirs of Cornelius Scriblerus, in forbidding certain sports
to his son Martin till he is better informed of their antiquity,
says: "Neither cross and pile, nor ducks and drakes, are quite
so ancient as 'Handy dandy,' though Macrobius and St. Augus-
tine take notice of the first, and Minutius Foelix describes the
latter; but 'Handy dandy' is mentioned by Aristotle, Plato,
and Aristophanes." Browne, in *Britannia's Pastorals* (i. 5),
also alludes to the game.

See "Neiveie-nick-nack."

Hap the Beds

A singular game, gone through by hopping on one foot, and
with that foot sliding a little flat stone out of an oblong bed,
rudely drawn on a smooth piece of ground. This bed is
divided into eight parts, the two of which at the farther end
of it are called the Kail-pots. If the player then stands at one
end, and pitches the smooth stone into all the divisions one
after the other, following the same on a foot (at every throw),
and bringing it out of the figure, this player wins not only the
game, but is considered a first-rate daub at it; failing, however, to go through all the parts so, without missing either a
throw or a hop, yet keeping before the other gamblers (for
many play at one bed), still wins the curious rustic game.—
Mactaggart's *Gallovidian Encyclopædia*.

A game called "The Beds," mentioned by a writer in *Blackwood's Magazine*, August 1821, p. 36, as played in Edinburgh
when he was a boy by girls only, is described as a game
where a pitcher is kicked into chalked divisions of the pavement, the performer being on one leg and hopping.

See "Hop-scotch."

Hard Buttons

Several boys place one button each close together on a line.

The game consists in hitting a particular button out of this line with the nicker without touching the others.   This is generally played in London streets, and is mentioned in the *Strand Magazine*, ii. 515.

See "Banger," "Buttons."

Hare and Hounds

A boys' game.   One boy is chosen as the Hare.   He carries with him a bag filled with strips of paper.   The rest of the boys are the Hounds.   The Hare has a certain time (say fifteen minutes) allowed him for a start, and he goes across country, scattering some paper on his way in order to indicate his track.   He may employ any manœuvre in order to deceive his pursuers, but must keep up the continuity of his paper track-signs.   The Hounds follow him and try to catch him before he gets home, which is a place agreed upon beforehand. —London (G. L. Gomme).

In Cornwall the leader, when at fault, says—

> Uppa, uppa, holye ! If you don't speak
> My dogs shan't folly.
> > —Courtney (*Folk-lore Journal*, v. 73).

Other versions of this holloa are—

> Whoop, whoop, and hollow !
> Good dogs won't follow
> Without the hare cries, Peewit.
> > —Halliwell's *Nursery Rhymes*, p. 66.

> Sound your holler,
> Or my little dog shan't foller.
> > —Northall's *English Folk Rhymes*, p. 357.

This game is played in Wales under the name of " Hunt the Fox."   The Fox has a certain time given him for a start, the other players then go after him.—Beddgelert (Mrs. Williams).

Harie Hutcheon

A game among children, in which they hop round in a ring, sitting on their hams.—Jamieson.

See " Curcuddie," " Cutch-a-cutchoo," " Hirtschin Hairy."

Hark the Robbers

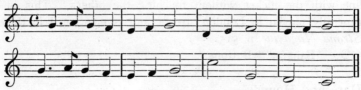

—Tong, Shropshire (Miss R. Harley).

I.   Hark the robbers coming through,
    Coming through,
  Hark the robbers coming through,
    My fair lady.

  What have the robbers done to you,
    Done to you,
  What have the robbers done to you,
    My fair lady?

  You have stole my watch and chain,
    Watch and chain,
  You have stole my watch and chain,
    My fair lady.

  Half-a-crown you must pay,
    You must pay,
  Half-a-crown you must pay,
    My fair lady.

  Half-a-crown we cannot pay,
    Cannot pay,
  Half-a-crown we cannot pay,
    My fair lady.

  Off to prison you must go,
    You must go,
  Off to prison you must go,
    My fair lady.   —Deptford, Kent (Miss Chase).

II.   Here are the robbers coming through,
    Coming through, coming through,
  Here are the robbers coming through,
    My fair lady.

What will the robbers do to you,
   Do to you, do to you,
What will the robbers do to you,
    My fair lady?

Steal your watch and break your chain,
   Break your chain, break your chain,
Steal your watch and break your chain,
    My fair lady.

Then they must go to jail,
   Go to jail, go to jail,
Then they must go to jail,
    My fair lady.   —Belfast (W. H. Patterson).

III.   Hark the robbers
      Coming through, coming through,
        My fair lady.

They have stolen my watch and chain,
    Watch and chain, watch and chain.

Off to prison they shall go,
   They shall go, they shall go,
    My fair lady.
    —Wolstanton, Stoke-on-Trent (Miss A. A. Keary).

IV.   Hark the robbers coming through,
      Coming through, coming through,
    Hark the robbers coming through,
      My fair lady.

What's the robbers done to you,
   Done to you, done to you,
What's the robbers done to you,
    My fair lady?

They have stole my watch and chain,
   Watch and chain, watch and chain,
They have stole my watch and chain,
    My fair lady.

What's the price will set you free,
   Set you free, set you free,
What's the price will set you free,
    My fair lady?

Half-a-guinea will set me free,
   Will set me free, will set me free,
Half-a-guinea will set me free,
    My fair lady.

Half-a-guinea you shall not have,
   Shall not have, shall not have,
Half-a-guinea you shall not have,
    My fair lady.

Let's join hands, it is too late,
   'Tis too late, 'tis too late,
Let's join hands, it is too late,
    My fair lady.
             —Tong, Shropshire (Miss R. Harley).

V. Hark at the robbers going through,
    Through, through, through; through, through, through;
  Hark at the robbers going through,
    My fair lady.

What have the robbers done to you,
   You, you, you; you, you, you?
What have the robbers done to you,
    My fair lady?

Stole my gold watch and chain,
   Chain, chain, chain; chain, chain, chain;
Stole my gold watch and chain,
    My fair lady.

How many pounds will set us free,
   Free, free, free; free, free, free?
How many pounds will set us free,
    My fair lady?

A hundred pounds will set you free,
   Free, free, free; free, free, free;
A hundred pounds will set you free,
   My fair lady.

We have not a hundred pounds,
   Pounds, pounds, pounds; pounds, pounds, pounds;
We have not a hundred pounds,
   My fair lady.

Then to prison you must go,
   Go, go, go; go, go, go;
Then to prison you must go,
   My fair lady.

To prison we will not go,
   Go, go, go; go, go, go;
To prison we will not go,
   My fair lady.

                    —Shipley, Horsham (*Notes and Queries*,
                          8th Series, i. 210, Miss Busk).

VI.   See the robbers coming through,
         Coming through, coming through,
      See the robbers coming through,
         A nice young lady.

Here's a prisoner we have got,
   We have got, we have got,
Here's a prisoner we have got,
   A nice young lady.

How many pounds to set her free,
   Set her free, set her free,
How many pounds to set her free,
   A nice young lady?

A hundred pounds to set her free,
   Set her free, set her free,
A hundred pounds to set her free,
   A nice young lady.

A hundred pounds we cannot give,
   We cannot give, we cannot give,
A hundred pounds we cannot give,
   A nice young lady.

Then to prison she must go,
   She must go, she must go,
Then to prison she must go,
   A nice young lady.

If she goes we'll go too,
   We'll go too, we'll go too,
If she goes we'll go too,
   A nice young lady.

Round the meadows we will go,
   We will go, we will go,
Round the meadows we will go,
   A nice young lady.
            —Settle, Yorks. (Rev. W. S. Sykes).

VII.   O what has this poor prisoner done,
     Poor prisoner done, poor prisoner done?
   O what has this poor prisoner done,
     So early in the morning?

She stole my watch and lost my key,
   Lost my key, lost my key,
She stole my watch and lost my key,
   So early in the morning.

How many pounds to set her free,
   Set her free, set her free?
How many pounds to set her free,
   So early in the morning?

Five hundred pounds to set her free,
   Set her free, set her free,
Five hundred pounds to set her free,
   So early in the morning.

Five hundred pounds we have not got,
  Have not got, have not got,
Five hundred pounds we have not got,
  So early in the morning.

So off to prison she must go,
  She must go, she must go,
So off to prison she must go,
  So early in the morning.

If she go then I'll go too,
  I'll go too, I'll go too,
If she go then I'll go too,
  So early in the morning.

So round the meadows we must go,
  We must go, we must go,
So round the meadows we must go,
  So early in the morning.
        —Sporle, Norfolk (Miss Matthews).

(*b*) In the Deptford version two girls join hands, holding them up as an arch for the other players to tramp through. The first two verses are sung first by one and then by the other of the two girls. At the finish of these the girl then going through the arch is stopped, and the third, fourth, and fifth verses are sung by the two girls alternately. Then finally both girls sing the last verse, and the child is sent as prisoner behind one or other of the two girls. The verses are then begun again, and repeated afresh for each of the troop marching through the arch until all of them are placed behind one or other of the two girls. The two sides thus formed then proceed to tug against each other, and the strongest side wins the game.

The Belfast version is practically the same, except that the verses are not sung as a dialogue, but by all the players together, and the prisoner, when caught, has the choice of sides, by being asked, "Which will you have, a golden apple or golden pear?" and according to the answer given is sent behind one of the leaders. The Norfolk and Shropshire games are different. Miss Matthews thus describes the Norfolk game: "Two girls take hold of hands, and another, the prisoner, stands between them.   The rest form themselves into a line opposite, and advance and retreat while singing the first verse, the gaolers singing the next verse, and so on alternately. [At the end of the last verse but one] the children break the line, form themselves into a ring, and dance round the prisoner, singing the final verse."   Miss Harley describes the Shropshire version as follows: "The first six verses are sung by the alternate parties, who advance and retire, tramping their feet, at first, to imitate the robbers.   The last verse is sung altogether going round in a ring."   In the Shipley version, Miss Busk says: "The children form themselves into two lines, while two or three, representing the robbers, swagger along between them.   When the robbers sing the last verse they should have attained the end of the lines [of children], as during the parley they were safe; having pronounced the defiance they run away.   The children in the lines rush after them, and should catch them and put them in prison."

(c) The analysis of this game is easy.   The Deptford, Belfast, and Wolstanton versions are clearly enough dramatic representations of the capture of a robber, and probably the game dates from the period of the prevalence of highway robbery.   The Wolstanton version shows us that the game is breaking up from its earlier form, while the Norfolk and Shropshire versions show a fresh development into the mere game for children, apart from its original significance.   The action of the game confirms this view.   The Norfolk action seems to be the most nearly perfect in its dramatic significance, and the Shropshire action comes next.   The action of the other games seems to have been grafted on to the superior form of "Oranges and Lemons."   It is probable that this fact has preserved the words more completely than in the other cases, where the force of the robber action would become less and less as actual experience of robbers and robbery died out.   Altogether, this game supplies a very good example of the change produced in games by changes in the actual life which gave rise to them. It is singular that the verses of this game also enter into the composition of "London Bridge is broken down."   It is probable, therefore, that it may be an altered form of the game of "London Bridge." The refrain, "My fair lady," occurs in both games.

See "London Bridge."

Hats in Holes

A boys' game. The players range their hats in a row against the wall, and each boy in turn pitches a ball from a line at some twenty-five feet distance into one of the hats. The boy into whose hat it falls has to seize it and throw it at one or other of the others, who all scamper off when the ball is "packed in." If he fails to hit he is out, and takes his cap up. The boy whose cap is left at the last has to "cork" the others, that is, to throw the ball at their bent backs, each in turn stooping down to take his punishment.—Somerset (Elworthy's *Dialect*).

See "Balls and Bonnets."

Hattie

A game with preens, pins, on the crown of a hat. Two or more may play. Each lays on a pin, then with the hand they strike the side of the hat time about, and whoever makes the pins by a stroke cross each other, lifts those so crossed.—Mactaggart's *Gallovidian Encyclopædia*.

Hawkey

A game played by several boys on each side with sticks called "hawkey bats," and a ball. A line is drawn across the middle of the ground from one side to the other ; one party stands on one side of the line and the opposite party on the other, and neither must overstep this boundary, but are allowed to reach over as far as their bats will permit to strike the ball. The object is to strike the ball to the farther end to touch the fence of the opposing party's side, when the party so striking the ball scores one, and, supposing nine to be the game, the party obtaining that number first of course wins the game.— West Sussex (Holloway's *Dict. of Provincialisms*).

See "Bandy," "Doddart," "Hockey."

Headicks and Pinticks

This game was played only at Christmas. The number of

players was two. The stakes were pins. One player laid in the hollow of the hand, or on one of the forefingers, a pin, and then placed the other forefinger over it so as to conceal it. He then held up his hand to his opponent and said, "Headicks or pinticks ? " His opponent made a guess by pointing with his finger and saying "Headicks," or "Pinticks." If the guess was correct he gained the pin, but if it was incorrect he forfeited one. The players played alternately.—Keith (Rev. W. Gregor).

Another version seems to be " Headim and Corsim." Pins are hid with fingers in the palms of the hands ; the same number is laid alongside them, and either " Headim" or "Corsim" called out by those who do so. When the fingers are lifted, if the heads of the pins hid and those beside them be lying one way when the crier cried "Headim," then that player wins ; but if "Corsim," the one who hid the pins wins. This is the king of all the games at the preens.—Mactaggart's *Gallovidian Encyclopædia.*

The editors of Jamieson's *Dictionary* say that the name should be " Headum and Corsum."

Heads and Tails

That plan for deciding matters by the "birl o' a bawbee." The one side cries " Heads " (when the piece is whirling in the air) and the other "Tails," so whichever is uppermost when the piece alights that gains or settles the matter, heads standing for the King's head and tails for the figure who represents Britannia.—Mactaggart's *Gallovidian Encyclopædia.* This is a general form of determining sides or beginning a game all over the country.

Hecklebirnie

A play among children in Aberdeenshire. Thirty or forty children in two rows, joining opposite hands, strike smartly with their hands thus joined on the head or shoulders of their companion as he runs the gauntlet through them. This is called "passing through the mires of Hecklebirnie."—Jamieson.

The editors of Jamieson append a lengthy note connecting

the name of this game with the northern belief that the wicked
were condemned to suffer eternal punishment in Hecla, the
volcanic mountain in Iceland.

See "Namers and Guessers."

Hen and Chicken

> Chickery, chickery, cranny crow,
> I went to the well to wash my toe,
> When I got back a chicken was dead.

This verse is said by the Hen to her Chickens, after which
they all go with the Hen to search for the dead Chicken.   On
their way they meet the Fox.   The following dialogue between
the Fox and Hen ensues, the Hen beginning :—

> What are you doing ?
> Picking up sticks.
> What for ?
> To make a fire.
> What's the fire for ?
> To boil some water.
> What's the water for ?
> To boil some chickens in.
> Where do you get them from ?
> Out of your flock.
> That I'm sure you won't.
>   —Derbyshire (*Folk-lore Journal*, i. 386).

The game is played in the usual manner of "Fox and
Goose" games.   One is chosen to be the Hen, and one to be
the Fox.   The rest are the Chickens.   The Chickens take hold
of each other's waists, the first one holding the Hen's waist.
At the end of the dialogue the Fox tries to get hold of one of
the chickens.   If he succeeds in catching them, they all with
the Fox try to dodge the Hen, who makes an effort to regain
them.

It is known at Winterton under the name of "Pins and
Needles."   The players stand in a row, one behind another,
with one of the party as their Leader.   Another player, called
"Outsider," pretends to scratch the ground.   The Leader asks
the questions, and the Outsider replies—

What are you scratching for ?
Pins and needles.
What do you want your pins and needles for ?
To mend my poke.
What do you want your poke for ?
To put some sand in.
What do you want your sand for ?
To sharpen knives with.
What do you want your knives for ?
To cut all the little chickens' heads off with.

Here the Outsider tries to dodge past the Leader to catch one of the children at the further end of the row, the Leader meanwhile attempting to bar her progress. When at last she succeeds, the child caught takes her place, and the game is recommenced.—Winterton (Miss M. Peacock).

See " Fox and Goose," " Gled-wylie."

Here comes a Lusty Wooer

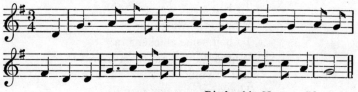

—Rimbault's *Nursery Rhymes.*

Here comes a lusty wooer,
My a dildin, my a daldin ;
Here comes a lusty wooer,
Lily bright and shine a'.

Pray who do you woo ?
My a dildin, my a daldin ;
Pray who do you woo ?
Lily bright and shine a'.

For your fairest daughter,
My a dildin, my a daldin ;
For your fairest daughter,
Lily bright and shine a'.

> Then there she is for you,
> My a dildin, my a daldin ;
> Then there she is for you,
> Lily bright and shine a'.
>
> —Ritson (*Gammer Gurton's Garland*, 1783).

Northall says this game is played after the manner of the "Three Dukes" (*Folk Rhymes*, p. 383). Halliwell (*Nursery Rhymes*, p. 98) has a version, and Rimbault (*Nursery Rhymes*) gives both words and tune. It is also contained in *The Merrie Heart* (p. 47). See "Jolly Hooper," "Jolly Rover."

Here comes One Virgin

> Here comes one Virgin on her knee,
> On her knee, on her knee,
> Here comes one Virgin on her knee,
> Pray what will you give her ?
>
> When did you come ?
>
> I came by night and I came by day,
> I came to steal poor Edie away.
>
> She is too old, she is too young,
> She hasn't learnt her virgin tongue.
>
> Let her be old or let her be young,
> For her beauty she must come.
>
> In her pocket a thousand pounds,
> On her finger a gay gold ring.
>
> Good-bye, good-bye, my dear.
>
> —Hurstmonceux, Sussex (Miss Chase).

One child stands by herself, and the rest of the players range themselves in line. The child sings the first verse and the line replies, the four succeeding verses being alternately sung. After the last line the girl tries to pull one whom she has chosen from the line toward her. If not successful, she must try again. If she is, they both stand in the middle, and commence singing the words again with—

> Here come *two* virgins on their knees, &c.

Probably a degraded version of "Three Lords from Spain."

Here I sit on a Cold Green Bank

Here I sit on a cold green bank
On a cold and frosty morning.

We'll send a young man [*or* woman] to take you away,
To take you away,
We'll send a young man to take you away,
On a cold and frosty morning.

Pray tell me what his name shall be? [*or*]
Pray, whom will you send to take me away?

We'll send Mr. —— to take you away.

The children form a ring around one of the party, who sits in the middle, and says the two first lines. Then those in the circle dance round her, singing the next four lines. This is repeated three times, with the refrain, "On a cold," &c., after which the dancing and singing cease, and the child is asked, "Sugar, sweet, or vinegar, sour?" Her answer is always taken in a contrary sense, and sung, as before, three times, whilst the children circle round. The one in the middle then rises to her feet. The boy (or girl) named advances and kisses her, they change places, and the game begins again.—Cornwall (*Folk-lore Journal*, v. 56–57).

Here stands a Young Man

I. Here stands a young man who wants a sweetheart,
    With all his merry maids round him;

He may choose from east, he may choose from west,
He may choose the prettiest girl that he loves best.

Now this young couple is married together,
We propose they kiss each other.
—Glapthorn (*Northants Notes and Queries*,
i. 214, A. Palmer).

II. Here stands a young lady [lass] who wants a sweetheart,
    Wants a sweetheart, wants a sweetheart,
    And don't know where to find one, find one, find one.
    Choose the prettiest that you loves best.

Now you're married I wish you joy,
First a girl and then a boy,
Seven years after son and daughter,
Pray you come to kiss together.
—Longcot, Berkshire (Miss I. Barclay).

(*b*) A ring is formed by the players joining hands, one child standing in the centre. The ring dance round singing the first four lines. At the fourth line the child in the centre chooses one from the ring, who goes into the centre with her. The marriage formula or chorus is then sung, the two kiss, and the one who was first in the centre joins the ring, the second one choosing another in her turn. Played by both boys and girls.

See " Sally Water," " Silly Old Man."

Here we go around, around

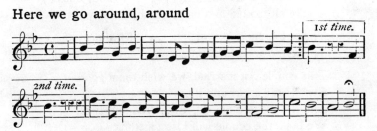

Our shoes are made of leather,
Our stockings are made of silk,
Our pinafores are made of calico,
As white as any milk.

Here we go around, around, around,
And we shall touch the ground.
—Barnes and London Streets (A. B. Gomme).

A ring is formed by the children joining hands. They walk round singing the first four lines. They then dance round quickly and sit down suddenly, or touch the ground with their clothes.

A version of this game from Liphook, Hants, almost identical in words, has been sent by Miss Fowler, and another from Crockham Hill, Kent, by Miss Chase.

Here's a Soldier

Here's a soldier left his lone [*qy.* alone],
Wants a wife and can't get none.

Merrily go round and choose your own,
Choose a good one or else choose none;
Choose the worst or choose the best,
Or choose the very one you like best.

What's your will, my dilcy dulcy officer?
What's your will, my dilcy dulcy dee?

My will is to marry, my dilcy dulcy officer;
My will is to marry, my dilcy dulcy dee.

Come marry one of us, my dilcy dulcy officer;
Come marry one of us, my dilcy dulcy dee.

You're all too old and ugly, my dilcy dulcy officer;
You're all too old and ugly, my dilcy dulcy dee.

Thrice too good for you, sir, my dilcy dulcy officer;
Thrice too good for you, sir, my dilcy dulcy dee.

This couple got married, we wish them good joy,
Every year a girl and a boy,
And if that does not do, a hundred and two,
We hope the couple will kiss together.
        —Annaverna, co. Louth (Miss R. Stephen).

(*b*) One child stands in the middle, the others dance round singing. The one in the middle chooses another before the four last lines are sung. Then the rest dance round singing these lines, and kiss each other.

(*c*) It is evident that these words comprise two distinct games, which have become mixed in some inexplicable fashion. The first six lines and the last four are one game, a ring form, with the marriage formula and blessing. The other portion of the game is a dialogue game, evidently having had two lines of players, questions being asked and answers given. It is, in fact, a part of the "Three Dukes" game. The first part is a kiss-in-the-ring game, a version of "Here stands a Young Man," "Silly Old Man," and "Sally Water."

Hewley Puley   Take this! What's this?
Hewley Puley.
Where's my share?
About the kite's neck.
Where's the kite?
Flown to the wood.
Where's the wood?
The fire has burned it.
Where's the fire?
The water's quenched it.
Where's the water?
The ox has drunk it.
Where's the ox?
The butcher has killed it.
Where's the butcher?
The rope has hanged him.
Where's the rope?
The rat has gnawed it.
Where's the rat?
The cat has killed it.
Where's the cat?

Behind the door, cracking pebble-stones and marrow-bones for
yours and my supper, and the one who speaks first shall
have a box on the ear. —Halliwell's *Nursery Rhymes*, p. 222.

The children are seated, and the questions are put by one of
the party who holds a twisted handkerchief or something of
the sort in the hand. The handkerchief was called "hewley
puley," and the questions are asked by the child who holds it.
If one answers wrongly, a box on the ear with the handkerchief
was the consequence; but if they all replied correctly, the one
who broke silence first had that punishment.

For similar rhymes see "Dump," "Mother, may I go out?"

Hey Wullie Wine

I.   Hey Wully wine, and How Wully wine,
     I hope for hame ye'll no incline;
     Ye'll better light, and stay a' night,
     And I'll gie thee a lady fine.

Wha will ye gie, if I wi' ye bide,
To be my bonny blooming bride,
And lie down lovely by my side?

I'll gie thee Kate o' Dinglebell,
A bonny body like yersell.

I'll stick her up in the pear-tree
Sweet and meek, and sae is she:
I lo'ed her ance, but she's no for me,
Yet I thank ye for your courtesy.

I'll gie thee Rozie o' the Cleugh,
I'm sure she'll please thee weel eneugh.

Up wi' her on the bane dyke,
She'll be rotten or I'll be ripe:
She's made for some ither, and no me,
Yet I thank ye for your courtesy.

Then I'll gie ye Nell o' sweet Sprinkell,
Owre Galloway she bears the bell.

I'll set her up in my bed-head,
And feed her wi' milk and bread;
She's for nae ither, but jist for me,
Sae I thank ye for your courtesy.
　　　　　—Mactaggart's *Gallovidian Encyclopædia.*

II.　I maun ride hame, I maun gang hame,
　　　And bide nae langer here;
　　The road is lang, the mirk soon on,
　　　And howlets mak' me fear.

　　Light doon and bide wi' us a' night,
　　　We'll choose ye a bonnie lass;
　　Ye'll get your wull and pick o' them a',
　　　And the time it soon wull pass.

　　Which ane will ye choose,
　　　If I with you will bide?

　　The fairest and rarest
　　　In a' the kintra side.

A girl's name was then mentioned.   If the lad was pleased with the choice made, he replied—

> I'll set her up on a bonnie pear-tree,
> It's tall and straight, and sae is she ;
> I'd keep wauken a' night her love to be.

If he was not pleased, he replied in one or other of the next three verses—

> I'll set her up ayont the dike,
> She'll be rotten ere I be ripe,
> The corbies her auld banes wull pike.

> I'll set her up on a high crab-tree,
> It's sour and dour, and so is she ;
> She may gang to the mools unkissed by me.

> Though she be good and fair to see,
> She's for another, and no for me ;
> But I thank you for your courtesie.

When a girl took the place of the lad, she replied in one or other of the three following, according as she was angry or pleased—

> I'll put him in a riddle
> And riddle him o'er the sea,
> And sell to Johnny Groat's
> For a Scotch bawbee.

> I'll set him up on my lum-head [chimney],
> And blaw him up wi' pouther and lead ;
> He'll never be kissed though he be dead.

> I'll set him up at my table head,
> Feed him wi' sweet milk and bread,
> If he likes gang hame on his fine steed.
> > —Biggar (Wm. Ballantyne).

(*b*) In Biggar, all the players were seated round the hearth-stone, lads on one side, lassies the other; one lad rising up said the first verse, then one acting as "maister" said the next verse.   The young man then said the next two lines, to which the other replied in the two following, and naming at the close any girl he thought would be acceptable.   If the lad was pleased he sang the next verse. If he was not pleased with the girl offered him he replied in either of the three following verses. The first of the three was generally said if the girl was thought to be too old ; if bad-tempered, the second. If the lad found no fault, but wished to politely refuse, he sang the last verse. The girl then was asked in her turn, and the same formula gone through, she saying either of the three last verses given. Forfeits were demanded for every refusal, and were cried at the end of the game.

(*c*) Mr. Ballantyne writes : "This game was a great favourite in my father's house. This was a forfeit game, forfeits being called 'wadds.'" Chambers, *Popular Rhymes*, p. 124, gives a version of this game. It is practically the same as Mr. Ballantyne's version, with only a few verbal differences. Mactaggart says, "The chief drift of this singular game seemed to be to discover the sweethearts of one another," and such discoveries are thought valuable, but not so much as they were anciently. In any case, it appears to me that the game is an early one, or, at all events, a reflection of early custom.

Hickety, Bickety

> Hickety, bickety, pease-scone,
> Where shall this poor Scotchman gang ?
> Will he gang east, or will he gang west,
> Or will he gang to the craw's nest ?
> —Chambers (*Popular Rhymes*, p. 122).

One boy stands with his eyes bandaged and his hands against a wall, with his head resting on them. Another stands beside him repeating the rhyme, whilst the others come one by one and lay their hands upon his back, or jump upon it. When he has sent them all to different places he turns round and calls, "Hickety, bickety!" till they have all rushed back to the place, the last in returning being obliged to take his place, when the game goes on as before.

Chambers adds, "The 'craw's nest' is close beside the eye-bandaged boy, and is therefore an envied position." Newell, *Games*, p. 165, refers to this game.

See "Hot Cockles."

Hickety-hackety

The game of Hop-scotch, played with a piece of tile, which has to be kicked by the player with the foot on which he hops over lines into various squares marked on the ground.—Somersetshire (Elworthy's *Dialect*).

See "Hop-scotch."

Hick, Step, and Jump

The game of "Hop, step, and jump."—Somerset (Holloway's *Dict. of Provincialisms*).

See "Half-Hammer."

Hide and Seek (1)

A writer in *Blackwood's Magazine*, August 1821, p. 36, mentions this as a summer game. It was called "Ho, spy!" the words which are called out by those boys who have hidden. He says the watchword of "Hide and seek" was "hidee," and gives as the rhyme used when playing—

> Keep in, keep in, wherever you be,
> The greedy gled's seeking ye.

This rhyme is also given by Chambers (*Popular Rhymes*, p. 122). Halliwell gives the rhyme as—

> Hitty titty indoors,
> Hitty titty out,
> You touch Hitty titty,
> And Hitty titty will bite you.
> —*Nursery Rhymes*, p. 213.

At Ashford-in-the-Water the words used were—

> One a bin, two a bin, three a bin, four,
> Five a bin, six a bin, seven, gie o'er;
> A bunch of pins, come prick my shins,
> A loaf brown bread, come knock me down.
> I'm coming!   —*Reliquary*, viii. 57.

The words are said by the one who has to find the person hidden.

In Scotland the game is called "Hospy," and is played by boys only, and it can be played only in a village or hamlet in which there is the means of hiding. A Spy is chosen, and a spot, called Parley, is fixed upon at which the Spy stands till all the other players are hid, and to which he can run when pursued. When the players are hid, the cry, "Hospy," *i.e.*, "Ho! spy!" is raised by them. The Spy then sets out to find them. The moment he detects one he turns and runs with all his might to the Parley, pursued by the one he has discovered. If he is overtaken, he must carry on his back the pursuer to the Parley. The same thing is gone through till all the players are discovered.—Keith (Rev. W. Gregor).

Jamieson says, "'Hy Spy,' a game resembling 'Hide and Seek,' but played in a different manner. The station, which in England is called Home, is here the Den, and those who keep it are the Seekers, and are called the Ins. Those who hide themselves, instead of crying 'Hoop,' as in England, cry 'Hy spy;' and they are denominated the Outs. The business of the Ins is, after the signal is given, to lay hold of the Outs before they can reach the den. The captive then becomes one of the Ins; for the honour of the game consists in the privilege of hiding oneself." Jamieson adds, "Hy is still used in calling after a person, to excite attention, or when it is wished to warn him to get out of the way." Strutt describes it as "Harry-Racket," or "Hide and Seek" (*Sports*, p. 381).

At Cork two sides are chosen for Spy; one side hides while the other side hunts. When the hunters see one of the hidden players, they call out, "I spy ——," and the child's name. The player called must run after the Spy and try to catch him before he reaches his Den; if he succeeds, the one caught must go to the opposite side of players, then next time the spies hide, and those who have been hiding, spy (Miss Keane). A more general form of the game is for one child to hide, and to make a noise in a disguised voice to give notice of his whereabouts, or to call out "Whoop!" or "Coo!" Until this noise or call is made, the searchers may not seek him. If when spied or discovered the hider cannot reach home before being caught, he again has to hide (A. B. Gomme).

(*b*) In the parish church of Bawdrip is a monument to Edward Lovell, his wife Eleanor (*née* Bradford), and their two daughters Maria and Eleanor. The inscription touching the latter is :—

"Eleanora . . . obiit Jun. 14, 1681. Hanc, subito et immaturo (ipsos pene inter hymenæos) fato correptam, mœstissimus luxit maritus, et in gratam piamq. parentum sororis et dilectissimæ conjugis memoriam, monumentum hoc erigi voluit." Tradition connects. this sudden death—"ipsos pene inter hymenæos"—with the story of the bride playing at "Hide and Seek." It is curious that, in Haynes Bayly's song, the bridegroom's name should be Lovell. There is no mention on the monument of the name of the bereaved husband. The father, Edward Lovell, was fourteen years rector of Bawdrip and fellow of Jesus College, Cambridge, and died in 1675, and so could not have been present at the wedding, as represented in the song. He came from Batcombe, near Castle-Cary; at which latter place the Lovells were seated in very early days.— *Notes and Queries*, 4th Ser., ix. 477.

Cope (*Hampshire Glossary*) calls the game "I spy I." Lowsley (*Berkshire Glossary*) says, "In playing this game, the seeker has to call out 'I spy!' to the one he finds before he may start for home." It is called "Hy Spy" in Patterson's *Antrim and Down Glossary*; Evans' *Leicestershire Glossary*, "Hide and Wink;" Barnes' *Dorset Glossary*, "Hidy Buck."

In Pegge's *Alphabet of Kenticisms* the game is given as "Hide and Fox." *Cf.* "Hide Fox, and all after," *i.e.*, let the fox hide and the others go to seek him; Hamlet, iv. 2, 32. In Stead's *Holderness Glossary*, "Hed-o." In the North Riding it is "Lam-pie-sote-it," also called "Felto" in Robinson's *Whitby Glossary*. He also mentions that the hidden child cries "How-ly" to the finder. Apparently the same as the south country "Whoop," a signal to the finder to begin the search. Addy (*Sheffield Glossary*) says this game is called "Felt and Laite." Holland (*Cheshire Glossary*) speaks of it as "I Spy."

See "Davie Drap."

Hide and Seek (2)

—London.

 I. Beans and butter,
   Come home to supper,
   'Tis all ready done.
       —Hampshire (Miss Mendham).

 II. Little pigs come to supper,
   Hot boiled beans and ready butter.
       —Northall's *Folk Rhymes*, p. 409.

 III. Hot beans and butter!
   Please to come to supper!
      —Much Wenlock (*Shropshire Folk-
       lore*, p. 525).

 IV. Hot boiled beans, and very good butter,
   Ladies and gentlemen, come to supper.
       —London (A. B. Gomme).

 V. Vesey vasey vum,
   Buck aboo has come!
   Find it if you can and take it home,
   Vesey vasey vum.
      —Newlyn West, near Penzance
      (*Folk-lore Journal*, v. 49).

One child hides an article, while those who are to search
for it go in another room (or out of the way somewhere). When
it is hidden, they are called to find it by one of the above
rhymes being sung or said. The searchers are enabled more
readily to find the hidden article by being told "hot," "very
hot," "scorching," "burning," or "cold," "very cold," and
"freezing," when near to or far from the hidden article.
Sometimes several may agree to hide the article, and only one
to be the finder. In the Penzance game one child is blindfolded,
other children hide something, then shout the words. Search
is then made for the hidden object: when found, the finder in
his turn is blindfolded. There appears to be some mistake in
the description of this game.

Hinch-Pinch

The name of an old Christmas game mentioned in *Declaration of Popish Impostures*, 1603.

Hinmost o' Three

A game played on village greens.—Dickinson's *Cumberland Glossary, Supplement.*

Hirtschin Hairy

The players (boy or girl) cower down on their haunches, "sit doon curriehunkers," and hop round and round the floor like a frog, clapping the hands first in front and then behind, and crying out, "Hirtschin Hairy." It is sometimes called "Hairy Hirtschin." In Lothian the players try to knock each other over by hustling against one another.—Rev. W. Gregor.

Same game as "Harie Hutcheon."

See "Curcuddie," "Cutch-a-cutchoo," "Hop-frog."

Hiry-hag

A boys' game, in which several, joining hands, endeavour to catch another, who, when caught, is beaten with caps, the captors crying out—

> Hiry-hiry-hag,
> Put him in a bag, &c.
>
> —Ross and Stead's *Holderness Glossary.*

Hiss and Clap

All the boys are requested to leave the room, when the girls take their seats, leaving a vacant place on the right side of each girl for the gentleman of her choice. Each boy in turn is then summoned by another who acts as doorkeeper, and asked to guess which lady he imagines has chosen him for her partner. Should he guess rightly he is allowed to take his seat by the lady who has chosen him, while the other girls loudly clap hands. Should he guess wrongly he is hissed, and sent out of the room by the doorkeeper.—Cork, Ireland (Miss Keane).

At Long Eaton in Nottinghamshire Miss Youngman records a similar game to this, with a rhyme that is probably taken from a popular song or ballad. The successful candidate for the girl's choice claims a kiss, but if unsuccessful he is beaten out of the room with knotted handkerchiefs.

Hitch Jamie; Hitch Jamie, Stride and Loup

The boyish play of "Hop, Step, and Jump."—Atkinson's *Cleveland Glossary*.

Brockett (*North Country Words*) calls this "Hitch."

See "Half-Hammer," "Hick, Step, and Jump."

Hitchapagy

An undescribed Suffolk game.—Halliwell's *Dictionary*.

Hitchy Cock Ho

An undescribed Suffolk game.—Moor's *Suffolk Words*.

Hity Tity

The Somerset name for "See-Saw."

Hoatie, Hots

When a number of boys agree to have a game at the Pearie or peg-top, a circle is drawn on the ground, within which all the tops must strike and spin. If any of them bounce out of the circle without spinning, it is called a Hoatie. The punishment to which the Hoatie is subjected consists in being placed in the ring, while all the boys whose tops ran fairly have the privilege of striking—or, as it is called, "deggin"—it till it is either split or struck out of the circle. If either of these take place, the boy to whom the Hoatie belonged has the privilege of playing again.—Upper Lanarkshire (Jamieson).

See "Gully," "Hoges."

Hob-in-the-Hall

An old game mentioned by Wycherley (*Plain Dealer*, 1677).

Hockerty Cokerty

The same game as "Cockerty-hooie."

Hockey

This game is played with a solid indiarubber ball from two to two and a half inches in diameter. The players each have a bent or hooked stick or "hockey." They take opposite sides. The object of the game is for each side to drive the ball through their opponents' goal. The goals are each marked by two poles standing about eight to ten feet apart, and boundaries are marked at the sides. The ball is placed in the middle of the ground. It is started by two players who stand opposite each other, the ball lying between their two sticks. They first touch the ground with their hockey-sticks, then they touch or strike their opponents' stick. This is repeated three times. At the third stroke they both try to hit the ball away. The ball may only be played by a hockey-stick, and a goal is gained when the ball is played between the posts by the opposing party.— Barnes (A. B. Gomme).

(b) In Ross and Stead's *Holderness Glossary* this game is described under the name of "Shinnup." Robinson (*Mid Yorkshire Glossary*) gives it under "Shinnops," a youth's game with a ball and stick, heavy at the striking end, the player manœuvring to get as many strokes as possible and to drive the ball distances. "Shinnoping" is also used for the game in operation. "Jowling," or "Jowls," is given in Robinson's *Whitby Glossary*, as a game played much the same as "Hockey." "Baddin" is the name given to it in Holland's *Cheshire Glossary*. Another name is "Doddart" (Brockett, *North Country Words*).

(c) An old custom in vogue in bygone days was Rotherham Fair, or what was called "Whipping Toms," which took place in the Newarkes every Shrove Tuesday. So soon as the pancake bell rang men and boys assembled with sticks having a knob or hook at the end. A wooden ball was thrown down, and two parties engaged in striving which could get the ball by striking it with their sticks to one end of the Newarke first—those who did so were the victors. This game was called "Shinney," or "Hockey." About one o'clock the Whipping Toms appeared on the scene of action. These were three men clad in blue smock frocks, with very long waggon whips, who were accompanied by three men with small bells. They commenced driving the men and boys out of the Newarkes. It was very dangerous sometimes; they would lash the whip in such a manner round the legs of those they were pursuing as to throw them down, which produced laughter and shouting. Some would stop, and turn to the whipper and say, "Let's have a pennyworth," and he would guard and parry off the lashes with his shinney stick. When the whipper was successful in lashing him he demanded his penny, and continued lashing until he paid. This was continued until five o'clock, then the game terminated. This was suppressed, I believe, in 1847. At that period it was a prevalent idea that it could not be abolished, as it was connected with an "old charter." It is believed in the town that this custom was to commemorate the driving out of the Danes from the Newarkes at the time they besieged Leicester.—Leicester (Robert Hazlewood).

See "Bandy," "Camp," "Football," "Hood," "Hurling."

Hoges

"The hoges," a boy's game played with "peeries" (peg-tops). The victor is entitled to give a certain number of blows with the spike of his peerie to the wood part of his opponent's.—Patterson's *Antrim and Down Glossary*.

See "Gully," "Hoatie."

Ho-go

A game played with marbles. The first player holds up a number in his closed hand and says, "Ho-go;" the second says, "Handfull;" the first then says, "How many?" The other guesses. If he should guess correctly he is entitled to take them all; but otherwise he must give the difference between the number he guessed and the number actually held up to make.—Lowsley's *Berkshire Words*. It is also called "How many eggs in a basket?"—London (J. P. Emslie).

See "Hairry my Bossie."

Hoilakes

The name of a game of marbles which are cast into a hole in the ground.—Easther's *Almondbury and Huddersfield Glossary*.

Holy Bang

A game with marbles, which consists in placing a marble in a hole and making it act as a target for the rest. The marble which can hit it three times in succession, and finally be shot into the hole, is the winning ball, and its owner gets all the other marbles which have missed before he played.—London (*Strand Magazine*, ii. 519).

See "Bridgeboard," "Capie Hole," "Hundreds."

Honey Pots

—London (J. P. Emslie).

A number of children stoop down in a row, clasping their hands under their legs. One child stands in front of them, and acts as owner or seller; another acts as purchaser (fig. 1). The purchaser inquires—

Have you any honey pots for sale?

Yes, plenty; will you walk round and taste them?

The purchaser goes round, pretending to taste each one in turn, inquiring the price and weight; finds fault with several, one being too sweet and the other not fresh enough, and so on. When one honey pot is discovered to the purchaser's taste, she

Fig 1   Fig. 2

is lifted by the purchaser and owner, or by two children who act as weights or scales, and then swung by her arms backwards and forwards to estimate her weight and price (fig. 2). As long as the child can keep her hands clasped, so long is the swinging kept up; and as many times as they count, so many

is the number of pounds she weighs. The seller sometimes
said, when each one was bought—

> Take her and bake her,
> And into pies make her,
> And bring her back
> When she is done.

They were not brought back, and the "owner" had to catch
and bring back each one. When sold, the honey pot is taken
to the other side, or "home" of the purchaser. The game
goes on till all the honey pots are sold. — London (A. B.
Gomme).

In Sporle, a girl clasps her hands under her legs to form a
seat, and two others swing her by the arms, saying—

> Honey pot, honey pot, over the river ;
> When the old cat dies you shall have the liver.
>
> —Miss Matthews.

In a version sent by Miss Chase, and told her by a London
maidservant, the children sit as in "Hunt the Slipper." One
steps in a corner out of earshot ; the rest are named "Gooseberry Tart," "Cherry Tart," &c., by another, who recalls the
child in the corner with—

> Fool, fool, come to school,
> Pick me out a [cherry tart, as the case may be].

If he chooses the wrong one he is told—

> Go back and learn your A, B, C.

If rightly—

> Take him and bake him,
> And give me a piece
> When he's done.

The child is then led off in a squatting position. Later the one
who named them pretends tasting, and says, "Very nice," or
"You must be baked longer," when another squatting walk
and wait takes place.

A version sent by Mr. J. P. Emslie is similar to the other
London versions—

> "Buy my fine honey to-day.
> Which shall I buy ?
> Taste 'em and try.

The child would then go round, pretending to taste, saying,

'Don't like that one,' till one was approved. That one was
then swung round to the tune given, the words being—

> An apple for the king and a pear for the queen,
> And a good jump over the bowling green.

At the last bar they swung the child higher and higher, and at
the last note they swung it as high as they could. I believe
the last note in the music should be G, but it was raised to
give effect."

In Scotland the game is called " Hinnie Pigs," and is played
as follows. The boys sit down in rows, hands locked beneath
their hams. Round comes one of them, the honey merchant,
who feels those who are sweet and sour, by lifting them by the
arm-pits and giving them three shakes. If they stand these
without the hands unlocking below they are then sweet and
saleable, fit for being office-bearers of other ploys.—Mactaggart's *Gallovidian Encyclopædia*.

In Ross and Stead's *Holderness Glossary* this is described as
a girls' game, in which two carry a third as a pot of honey to
market. It is mentioned by Addy (*Sheffield Glossary*) and
by Holland (*Cheshire Glossary*). Mr. Holland adds, "If the
hands give way before twenty is reached it is counted a bad
honey pot; if not, it is a good one."

In Dublin the seller sings out—

> Honey pots, honey pots, all in a row,
> Twenty-five shillings wherever you go—
> Who'll buy my honey pots ?   —Mrs. Lincoln.

The game is mentioned by a writer in *Blackwood's Magazine*,
August 1821, p. 36, as being played in Edinburgh when he was
a boy.

Hood

A game played at Haxey, in the Isle of Axholme, on the
6th of January. The Hood is a piece of sacking, rolled tightly
up and well corded, and which weighs about six pounds. This
is taken into an open field on the north side of the church, to
be contended for by the youths assembled for that purpose.
When the Hood is about to be thrown up, the Plough-bullocks
or Boggins, as they are called, dressed in scarlet jackets, are

placed amongst the crowd at certain distances. Their persons are sacred, and if amidst the general row the Hood falls into the hands of one of them, the sport begins again. The object of the person who seizes the Hood is to carry off the prize to some public-house in the town, where he is rewarded with such liquor as he chooses to call for. This pastime is said to have been instituted by the Mowbrays, and that the person who furnished the Hood did so as a tenure by which he held some land under the lord. How far this tradition may be founded on fact I do not know, but no person now acknowledges to hold any land by that tenure.—Stonehouse's *Isle of Axholme*, p. 291.

W. J. Woolhouse (*Notes and Queries*, 2nd series, v. 95) says when the Hood is thrown up by the Chief of the Boggons or by the officials, it becomes the object of the villagers to get the Hood to their own village, the other eleven men, called Boggons, being stationed at the corners and sides of the field, to prevent, if possible, its being thrown out of the field; and should it chance to fall into any of their hands, it is "boggoned," and forthwith returned to the chief, who again throws it up, as at the commencement of the game. The next day is occupied by the Boggons going round the villages singing as waits, and they are regaled with hot furmenty; from some they get coppers given them, and from others a small measure of wheat. The day after that they assume the character of Plough-bullocks, and at a certain part of Westwood-side they "smoke the Fool"—that is, straw is brought by those who like, and piled in a heap, a rope being tied or slung over the branches of the tree next to the pile of straw; the other end of the rope is fastened round the waist of the Fool, and he is drawn up and fire is put to the straw, the Fool being swung to and fro through the smoke until he is well-nigh choked, after which he goes round and collects whatever the spectators choose to give him. The sport is then at an end till the next year. The land left by Lady Mowbray was forty acres, which are known by the name of "Hoodlands," and the Boggons' dresses and the Hood are made from its proceeds.

In the contiguous parish of Epworth a similar game is played under the same name, but with some variations. The Hood is not here carried away from the field, but to certain goals, against which it is struck three times and then declared free. This is called "wyking" the Hood, which is afterwards thrown up again for a fresh game.—*Notes and Queries*, 6th series, vii. 148.

See "Football," "Hockey."

Hoodle-cum-blind

Name for "Blind Man's Buff."—Baker's *Northamptonshire Glossary*.

Hoodman Blind

Name for "Blind Man's Buff." Mentioned in *Hamlet*, iii. 4; *Merry Devil of Edmonton;* and *Wise Women of Hogsden*.

Hooper's Hide

Name for "Blind Man's Buff."—Nares' *Glossary*.

Hop-crease

The game of "Hop-scotch."—Halliwell's *Dictionary*.

Hop-frog

The players bend as though about to sit on a *very low* stool, then spring about with their hands resting on their knees.—Dorsetshire (*Folk-lore Journal*, vii. 234).

Miss Peacock says that a game called "Hop-frog over the Dog" is played at Stixwould, Lincolnshire, in the same way as "Leap-frog."

See "Curcuddie," "Cutch-a-cutchoo," "Harie Hutcheon," "Hirtschin Hairy."

Hop-score

Game of "Hop-scotch."—Hunter's *Glossary of Hallamshire*.

Hop-scotch

A game, the object of which is to eject a stone, slate, or "dump" out of a form linearly marked on the ground in different directions, by hopping without touching any of the lines.—Halliwell's *Dictionary*.

In the plan (fig. 8) the players first lay the stone on the back
of the hand, and *walk* through the plan, stepping into each
division, throw it up and catch it.   Then the stone is *thrown*
back from No. 7 outside No. 1.   Now it is placed on the toe,
and the child walks through again, throwing up the foot when
out, to catch the stone in the hand.   Another way, done on the
same plan, is for the player to place the stone in No. 1, leave
it there, and hop into each division and back, then place it
in No. 2, and repeat the hopping, and so on through all the
figures.   There is no *kicking* of the stone, as is usual in
London.—Roxton, St. Neots (Miss Lumley).

From Crockham Hill, Kent, Miss Chase sends four versions.

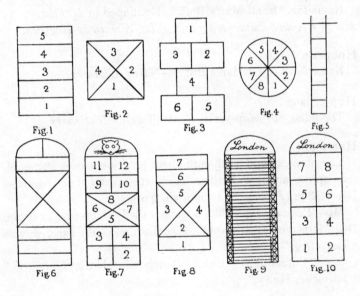

Fig. 1   Fig. 2   Fig. 3   Fig. 4   Fig. 5

Fig 6   Fig. 7   Fig. 8   Fig. 9   Fig. 10

In the first plan (fig. 1) the game is :—Throw stone into No. 1.
Hop from No. 1 to No. 5 and back.   Then pick it up.   So on
successively.   After having thrown it into No. 5, begin to reverse
by throwing stone into No. 1 while standing at No. 5—return
with it on your thumb.   Throw into No. 2—return with stone
on your eye.   Throw into No. 3—return with stone in your
palm.   Throw into No. 4—return with stone on your head.
Throw into No. 5—return with stone on your back.   In each

case, upon reaching the goal without dropping it, throw up and catch it as it falls.

In the second plan (fig. 2) the game is :—Throw stone into No. 1. Pick it up. Hop, not touching lines, from No. 1 to No. 4, and "out." Throw stone into No. 2. Do as before. And so successively into Nos. 3 and 4. Next balance stone on shoe, then on the palm of hand, then on the back of hand, then on the head, then on the shoulder, then on the eye (tilt head back to keep it from falling). In each case walk round once with it so balanced and catch at end.

In the third plan (fig. 3) the game is :—Put pebble in No. 1. Pick up. Hop, having one foot in No. 2 and the other in No. 3. Step into No. 4. Hop, having one foot in No. 5 and the other in No. 6. Jump round. Go back as you came. Then with stone on shoe, walk through the figure, kick it up and catch at the close. Place stone on eyelid; walk through the same figure, dropping it off into hand at close. This is called "jumping."

In the fourth plan (fig. 4) the game is :—Throw stone into No. 1. Pick it up. Hop from No. 1 to No. 8, not touching lines. So successively into Nos. 2, 3, 4, &c. Walk into No. 1 with stone on foot, and out at No. 8. Kick it up and catch it. The same with stone on thumb. Toss it up and catch. Again with stone on your back. Straighten up, let it slide into your hand.

In Stead's *Holderness Glossary*, this is described as a boys' or girls' game, in which the pavement is chalked with numbered crossed lines, and a pebble or piece of crockery is propelled onward by the foot, the performer hopping on one leg, the number reached on the chalk-line being scored to him or her. At Whitby it is called "Pally-ully," and played with rounded pieces of pot the size of a penny. Divisions are chalked on the pavement, and the "pally-ullies" are impelled within the lines by a hop on one leg, and a side shuffle with the same foot (*Whitby Glossary*). It is sometimes called "Tray-Trip." Atkinson describes the figure as oblong, with many angular compartments (*Cleveland Glossary*). Jamieson defines "Beds" as "Hop-scotch," a game denominated from the form, sometimes by strangers called squares. In Aberdeen the spaces marked out are sometimes circular.

Mrs. Lincoln sends a diagram of the game from Dublin (fig. 6). Addy (*Sheffield Glossary*) under the name of "Hop-score" says it is a game in which certain squares are drawn or *scored* on the ground. The piece of stone which is pushed with the foot is called the "scotch." Elworthy (*West Somerset Words*) says a piece of tile is kicked over lines and into squares marked on the ground. It is called "Hickety-Hackety," also "Huckety." Cope (*Hampshire Glossary*) says it is played in Hants. Moor (*Suffolk Words and Phrases*) describes this game under the name of "Scotch-hob," by hopping and kicking a bit of tile from bed to bed of a diagram which he gives (fig. 5, here printed). Brockett (*North Country Words*) calls it "Beds." Barnes (*Dorset Glossary*) only says "hopping over a parallelogram of scotches or chalk-lines on the ground." F. H. Low, in *Strand Magazine*, ii. 516, says the divisions are respectively named onesie, twosie, threesie, foursie, and puddings. It is called "Hop-bed" at Stixwold in Lincolnshire (Miss Peacock), "Hop-score" in Yorkshire (Halliwell, *l.c.*), and "Hitchibed" in Cleveland, Yorks. (*Glossary of Cleveland Words*). Strutt describes it (*Sports*, p. 383); and Wood's *Modern Playmate*, p. 32, gives a diagram similar to one seen on a London pavement by A. B. Gomme (see fig. 7). Mr. Emslie has sent me figs. 9 and 10, also from London streets. Newell (*Games*, p. 188) speaks of it as a well-known game in America.

Mr. Elworthy (*West Somerset Words*) says, "Several of these (diagrams marked on the ground) are still to be seen, scratched on the ancient pavement of the Roman Forum." Mr. J. W. Crombie says, "The game of 'Hop-scotch' was one of considerable antiquity, having been known in England for more than two centuries, and it was played all over Europe under different names. Signor Pitré's solar explanation of its origin appeared improbable to him, for not only was the evidence in its favour extremely weak, but it would require the original number of divisions in the figure to have been twelve instead of seven, which was the number indicated by a considerable body of evidence. It would seem more probable that the game at one time represented the progress of the soul from earth to heaven through various intermediate states, the name given to the last court being most frequently paradise or an equivalent, such as crown or glory, while the names of the other courts corresponded with the eschatological ideas prevalent in the early days of Christianity." Some such game existed before Christianity, and Mr. Crombie considered that it had been derived from several ancient games. Possibly the strange myths of the labyrinths might have had something to do with "Hop-scotch," and a variety of the game played in England, under the name of "Round Hop-scotch," was almost identical with a game described by Pliny as being played by the boys of his day. Mr. Crombie also said he "believed that the early Christians adopted the general idea of the ancient game, but they not only converted it into an allegory of heaven, with Christian beliefs and Christian names; they Christianised the figure also; they abandoned the heathen labyrinth and replaced it by the form of the Basilicon, the early Christian church, dividing it into seven parts, as they believed heaven to be divided, and placing paradise, the inner sanctum of heaven, in the position of the altar, the inner sanctum of their earthly church."

See "Hap the Beds."

Hop, Step, and Jump
See "Half-Hammer."

Hornie

A game among children in which one of the company runs after the rest having his hands clasped and his thumbs pushed out before him in resemblance of horns. The first person whom he touches with his thumbs becomes his property, joins hands with him, and aids in attempting to catch the rest: and so on until they are all made captives. Those who are at liberty still cry out, "Hornie, Hornie."—Lothian (Jamieson).

Jamieson says: "Whether this play be a vestige of the very ancient custom of assuming the appearance and skins of animals, especially in the sports of Yule, or might be meant to symbolise the exertions made by the devil (often called 'Hornie') in making sinful man his prey, and employing fellow-men as his coadjutors in this work, I cannot pretend to determine."

See " Hunt the Staigie," " Whiddy."

Hornie Holes

A game in which four play, a principal and an assistant on each side. A. stands with his assistant at one hole, and throws what is called a Cat (a piece of stick, and frequently a sheep's horn), with the design of making it alight in another hole at some distance, at which B. and his assistant stand ready to drive it aside. The bat or driver is a rod resembling a walking-stick.

The following unintelligible rhyme is repeated by a player on the one side, while they on the other are gathering in the Cats, and is attested by old people as of great antiquity:—

> Jock, Speak, and Sandy,
> W' a' their lousy train
> Round about by Errinborra,
> We'll never meet again.
> Gae head 'im, gae hang 'im,
> Gae lay 'im in the sea;
> A' the birds o' the air
> Will bear him companee.
> With a nig-nag, widdy- [*or* worry-] bag,
> And an e'endown trail, trail;
> Quoth he.
> —Jamieson.

The game is also called " Kittie-cat."

See " Cat and Dog," " Cudgel," " Tip-cat."

Horns

" A' Horns to the Lift," a game of young people. A circle is formed round a table, and all placing their forefingers on the table, one cries, " A' horns to the lift! Cat's horns upmost!" If on this any one lift his finger, he owes a wad, as cats have no horns. In the same manner, the person who does not raise his fingers when a horned animal is named is subjected to a forfeit.—Jamieson.

Hot Cockles

At Sheffield a boy is chosen for a Stump, and stands with his
back against a wall. Another boy bends his back as in "Leap-
frog," and puts his head against the Stump. The cap of the
boy who bends down is then taken off, and put upon his back
upside down. Then each of the other boys who are playing
puts the first finger of his right hand into the cap. When all
the fingers are put into the cap, these lines are sung—

> The wind blows east, the wind blows west,
> The wind blows o'er the cuckoo's nest.
> Where is this poor man to go?
> Over yond cuckoo's hill I O.

Then the boy whose back is bent jumps up, and the others
run away crying out, "Hot cockles." The boy who is caught
by the one whose back was first bent has to bend his back
next time, and so on.—S. O. Addy.

At Cork a handkerchief is tied over the eyes of one of the
company, who then lays his head on a chair, and places his
hand on his back with the palm uppermost. Any of the party
come behind him and give him a slap on his hand, he in the
meantime trying to discover whose hand it is that strikes.—
Miss Keane.

"Hot Cockles" is an old game, practised especially at
Christmas. One boy sits down, and another, who is blindfolded, kneels and lays his head on his knee, placing at the
same time his open hand on his own back. He then cries,
"Hot cockles, hot!" Another then strikes his open hand,
and the sitting boy asks who strikes. If the boy guessed
wrongly, he made a forfeit; but if rightly, he was released.—
Notes and Queries, 4th series, ix. 262.

The sport is noticed by Gay—

> As at hot-cockles once I laid me down,
> I felt the weighty hand of many a clown;
> Buxoma gave a gentle tap, and I
> Quick rose and read soft mischief in her eye.

Halliwell describes it rather differently. The blindfolded
boy lies down on his face, and, being struck, must guess who
it is that hit him. A good part of the fun consisted in the

hardness of the slaps, which were generally given on the throne
of honour. He quotes from a MS. play as follows—

> It is edicted that every Grobian shall play at Bamberye hott
> cockles at the four festivals.
> Indeed a verye usefull sport, but lately much neglected to
> the mollefieinge of the flesh.   —Halliwell's *Dictionary*.

Nares' *Glossary* also contains quotations from works of 1639,
1653, and 1697 which illustrate the game. Mr. Addy says " that
this game as played in Sheffield is quite different from that described under the same title in Halliwell's *Dictionary*. Aubrey
(p. 30) speaks of ' Hot Cockles ' as a game played at funerals
in Yorkshire, and the lines here given show that this was the
game. The lines—

> Where is this poor man to go ?
> Over yond cuckoo's hill I O,

embodies the popular belief that the soul winged its way like a
bird, and they remind one of the passing of the soul over
Whinny Moor (see funeral dirge in Aubrey's *Remains of Gen-*

tilisme, p. 31). Grimm mentions the cuckoo hill (Gauchsberg).
He says, ' Originally in Gauchsberg the bird himself may very
well have been meant in a mystic sense which has fallen dark
to us now ' (*Teut. Myth.*, ii. 681). We know, too, the old
belief that the cuckoo tells children how many years they have
to live. These lines are also sometimes said, in addition to
those given above—

Elder belder, limber lock,
Three wives in a clock ;
Sit and sing, and call a spring,
O-u-t spells out.

The boy who bends down is supposed to be undergoing a great penalty." Strutt (*Sports*, p. 394) describes this game, and gives an illustration which is here reproduced from the original MSS. in the Bodleian.

This game may have originated from a custom at funerals of practising spells for the safe and speedy passage of the departing spirit to its destination, or from divination mysteries to foretell who would be the next among the mourners to follow the dead body to the grave. The spirit of prophecy was believed to exist in a dying person. See " Handy Croopen."

How many Miles to Babylon

I.   King and Queen of Cantelon,
     How many miles to Babylon ?
     Eight and eight and other eight.
     Will I get there by candle-light ?
     If your horse be good and your spurs be bright.
     How mony men have ye ?
     Mae nae ye daur come and see.
     —Chambers' *Popular Rhymes*, p. 124 ;
          Mactaggart's *Gallovidian Encyclopædia.*

II. How many miles to Babylon ?
     Three score and ten.
     Will we be there by candle-light ?
     Yes, and back again.
     Open your gates and let us go through.
     Not without a beck and a boo.
     There's a beck, and there's a boo,
     Open your gates and let us go through.
     —Nairn, Scotland (Rev. W. Gregor).

III. How far to Banbury Cross ?
     Four score and ten.
     Can I get there by candle-light ?
     Yes, if your legs are long and light.

Please to let me go ?
Not without you bend and bow [pronounced bo].
Here's my bend [curtseys],
And here's my bow [touches forehead],
Now will you let me go ?
                    —Fernham and Longcot (Miss I. Barclay).

IV.   How many miles to Babylon ?
Three score and ten.
Can we get there by candle-light ?
Yes, and back again.
Open your gates as wide as you can,
And let King George and his family go through.
Not without a back, not without a bow,
Not without a curtsey, and then I'll let you through.
                    —South Shields (Miss Blair).

V.   How many miles to Babylon ?
Three score and ten.
Can I get there o' candle-light ?
There and back again.
Here's my black [raising one foot],
And here's my blue [raising the other],
Open the gates and let me through.
                    —Annaverna, Ravendale, co. Louth, Ireland
                        (Miss R. Stephen).

VI.   How many miles to Barney Bridge ?
Three score and ten.
Will I be there by candle-light ?
Yes, if your legs are long.
A curtsey to you, another to you,
If you please will you let the king's horses go through ?
Yes, but take care of your hindmost man.
                    —Belfast (W. H. Patterson).

VII.   How many miles to Gandigo ?
Eighty-eight almost, or quite.
Can I [we] get there by candle-light ?
Yes, if your legs are long and light.

Open the gate as high as the sky,
And let the king and his queen go by.
—Dorsetshire (*Folk-lore Journal*, vii. 230, 231).

VIII.   How many miles to Banbury ?
Three score and ten.
Can I get there by candle-light ?
Yes, and back again.
But mind the old witch doesn't catch you.
—London (Miss Dendy).

IX.   How many miles to Barley Bridge ?
Three score and ten.
Can I get there by candle-light ?
Yes, if your legs be long.
A courtesy to you, and a courtesy to you,
If you please will you let the king's horses through ?
Through and through shall they go,
For the king's sake ;
But the one that is the hindmost
Will meet with a great mistake.
—Halliwell's *Popular Rhymes*, p. 217.

X.   How many miles to Barney Bridge ?
Three score and ten.
Will I be there by Candlemass ?
Yes, and back again.
A curtsey to you, another to you,
And pray, fair maids, will you let us through ?
Thro' and thro' shall you go for the king's sake,
But take care the last man does not meet a mistake.
—Dublin (Mrs. Lincoln).

XI.   How many miles to Burslem ?
Three score and ten.
Can we get there by candle-light ?
Yes, and back again.
Open the gates so wide, so wide,
And let King George aside, aside ;
The night is so dark we cannot see,
Thread the needle and go through.
—Isle of Man (A. W. Moore).

XII.   How many miles to Banbury Cross?
        Three score and ten.
        Shall we get there by midnight?
        Yes, if you run well.
        Then open your gates as wide as the sky,
        And let King George and his men pass by.
        It is so dark we cannot see, so thread the needle Nancy,
        Thread the needle **Nancy**.
        One, two, three.
                —Warwick (from a little girl living near Warwick,
                        through Mr. C. C. Bell).

XIII.   How many miles to London?
        Three score ten.
        Can I get there by candle-light?
        Yes, and back again.
        Open the gate and let me through.
        Not unless you're black and blue.
        Here's my black and here's my blue,
        Open the gates and let me through.
        Dan, Dan, thread the needle; Dan, Dan, sew.
                —*Suffolk County Folk-lore*, p. 63.

XIV.   How many miles to Babylon?
        Three score and ten.
        Shall I be there by candle-light?
        Yes, there and back again.
        Open the gates as wide as high,
        And let King George and his family pass by.
                —Wales (*Folk-lore Record*, v. 88).

XV.   How many miles to ⎰ Barley Bridge?
                            ⎱ Banbury?
                            ⎰ London?
        Four score and ten [*or*, Fifty miles and more].
        Shall we be there by candle-light?
        Oh, yes, and back again.
                [*Or, at Market Drayton.*
        Shift your feet with nimble light,
        And you'll be there by candle-light.]

Open the gates as wide as the sky,
And let King George and his lady go by.
            —Market Drayton, Ellesmere, Whitchurch,
                 (Burne's *Shropshire Folk-lore*, p. 522).

XVI.   How many miles to Bethlehem ?
        Three score and ten.
        Shall we get there by candle-light ?
        Yes, there and back again.
        So open the gates and let King George and his family
            go through.   —Hayton, near York (H. Hardy).

XVII.   How far is it to Babylon ?
        Three score miles and ten.
        Can I get there by candle-light ?
        Yes, there and back again.
                        —Sporle, Norfolk (Miss Matthews).

XVIII. How many miles to Babylon ?
        Three score and ten.
        Can you get there by candle-light ?
        O yes, and back again.
                        —Hanbury, Staffordshire (Miss E. Hollis).

XIX.   Open the gates as wide as high,
        And let King George and I go by ;
        It is so dark I cannot see
        To thread my grandmother's needle.
                        —Surrey (*Folk-lore Record*, v. 88).

(*b*) There are two methods of playing this game, one in which a King and Queen are represented, and the other in which gates of a city are represented. Of the first Chambers and Mactaggart practically give the same account. The latter says, " Two of the swiftest boys are placed between two ' doons ' or places of safety; these, perhaps, are two hundred yards distant. All the other boys stand in one of these places or doons, when the two fleet youths come forward and address them with the rhyme. When out, they run in hopes to get to Babylon or the other doon, but many get not near that place before they are caught by the runners, who ' taens ' them, that is, lay their hands upon their heads, when they are not allowed to run any more in that game, that is, until they all be taened or taken."

The Norfolk game seems to resemble the Scotch, though in a much less complete form. Miss Matthews describes it as follows:—"A line of children is formed, and the two standing opposite it sing the questions, to which the line reply; then the two start off running in any direction they please, and the others try to catch them."

The second method of playing is best described by the Rev. Walter Gregor, from the Nairn game, which is known as "The Gates of Babylon." Mr. Gregor writes as follows:—"This game may be played either by boys or girls. Two of the players join hands, and stand face to face, with their hands in front as if forming a gate. Each of these has a secret name. The other players form themselves into a line by clasping each

Fig 1   Fig 2

other round the waist from behind. They go up to the two that form the gate, and the leader asks the first question, as in version No. 2. The dialogue then proceeds to the end. The two then lift their arms as high as they can, still joined, and the line of players passes through. All at once the two bring their arms down on one and make him (or her) prisoner. The prisoner is asked in a whisper, so as not to disclose the secret name, which of the two is to be chosen. The one so captured takes his (or her) stand behind the one chosen. The same process is gone through till all the players are taken captive, and have stationed themselves behind the one or the other of the two forming the gate. The last one of the line goes through three times. The first time the word 'breakfast' is pronounced; the second time 'dinner;' and the third time 'supper.' The player then chooses a side. The two sides

have then a tug of war. The game ends at this point with girls.
With boys the conquered have to run the gauntlet.   The
victors range themselves in two lines, each boy with his cap
or handkerchief tightly plaited in his hand, and pelt with all
their might the vanquished as they run between the lines.
The boys of Nairn call this running of the gauntlet, 'through
fire an' watter.'"

The method of playing the Warwick, Fernham, and Louth versions is practically the same. The children stand in half-circle
beginning with the two tallest at either end. All clasp hands.
The two at one end question those at the other end alternately
(fig. 1). At the last line the two that have been answering
hold their hands up to form a bridge, and all the others thread
through, still holding hands (the bridge advancing slowly) (fig. 2).
The Louth version is also sometimes played as "Oranges
and Lemons." This is also the case with the Belfast, South
Shields, Ellesmere, and Dublin versions.   Miss Burne also
gives a second method of playing this game at Ellesmere : she
says, " The whole number of players stand in two rows facing
each other, each player joining hands with the one opposite.
The pair at the lower end parley with the pair at the top, and
then run under the extended arms of the others, receiving
thumps on the back as they go, till they reach the upper end,
and become the top couple in their turn."   The Hanbury version is played in a similar way. Two lines stand close together
holding handkerchiefs across. The questions are asked and
answered by the top and bottom players.   Then two children
run under the line of handkerchiefs. The Dorset version is
played by as many as like standing, two and two, opposite
each other, each of them taking with the right hand the right
hand of the other ; then the two that are the King and Queen
say or sing the first question, to which the others reply,
and the dialogue ends in this manner. Then all the other
pairs hold up their hands as high as they can, and the King
and Queen run through the archway and back again, and so on
with the next pair, and other pairs in turn. The Isle of Man
version is played, Mr. Moore says, the same as other "Thread
the Needle " games.

(c) The game is evidently dramatic in form, and perhaps is illustrative of some fact of history, such as the toll upon merchandise entering a walled town. The changes in the words of the different versions are not very great, but they show the influence of modern history upon the game. The appearance of King George evidently points to the date when it was frequently played, though the older versions are doubtless those in which his Majesty does not do duty. Mactaggart has the following quaint note which perhaps may supply the origin, though it seems a far cry to the Crusaders:—"This sport has something methinks of antiquity in it; it seemeth to be a pantomime of some scenes played off in the time of the Crusades. 'King and Queen o' Cantilon' evidently must be King and Queen of Caledon, but slightly changed by time. Then Babylon in the rhyme, the way they had to wander and hazard being caught by the infidels, all speak as to the foundation of the game" (Mactaggart's *Gallovidian Encyclopædia*).

In the *Gentleman's Magazine* for December 1849, in a review of the *Life of Shirley*, it is stated that in many parts of England the old game of "Thread the Needle" is played to the following words, which refer to the gate of the city of Hebron, known as the "needle's eye."

> How many miles to Hebron?
> Three score and ten.
> Shall I be there by midnight?
> Yes, and back again.
> Then thread the needle, &c.

The game is also described in *Notes and Queries*, iv. 141, as played in the same way as above, and the writer adds there are subsequent evolutions by which each couple becomes in succession the eye of the needle.

Howly

A street game played by boys in a town, one of them hiding behind a wall or house-end, and crying "Howly" to the seekers.—Atkinson's *Cleveland Glossary*.

See "Hide and Seek."

Huckie-buckie down the Brae

Children in Lothian have a sport in which they slide down a hill, sitting on their hunkers (Jamieson). The well-known custom at Greenwich is probably the same game, and there are examples at Tumbling Hill, a few miles from Exeter, at May Pole Hill, near Gloucester, and other places.

Huckle-bones

Holloway (*Dict. of Provincialisms*) says that the game is called "Huckle-bones" in East Sussex and "Dibs" in West Sussex. Parish (*Dict. of Sussex Dialect*) mentions that huckle-bones, the small bone found in the joint of the knee of a sheep, are used by children for playing the game of "Dibs;" also Peacock's *Manley and Corringham Glossary*. Barnes (*Dorset Glossary*) says, "A game of toss and catch, played mostly by two with five dibs or huckle-bones of a leg of mutton, or round pieces of tile or slate." Halliwell's description is clearly wrong. He says it was a game formerly played by throwing up the hip-bone of some animal, on one side of which was a head of Venus and on the other that of a dog. He who turned up the former was the winner (*Dictionary*). Miss J. Barker writes that "Huckle-bones" is played in Hexham; and Professor Attwell (Barnes) played the game as a boy, and is still a proficient in it; he played it recently for my benefit with his set of real huckle-bones (A. B. Gomme); and see *Notes and Queries*, 9th ser., iv. 378, 379.

The figures or sets are practically the same as those described under "Fivestones." The game is very ancient. In the *Sanctuarie of Salvation*, &c., translated from the Latin of Levinus Lemnius by Henry Kinder (8vo, London, printed by H. Singleton), p. 144, we read, "These bones are called 'huckle-bones' or 'coytes.'" For further information relating to this game, as played by the ancients, the reader may consult *Joannis Meursii Ludibunda, sive de Ludis Græcorum, Liber singularis* (8vo, Lugd. Bat. 1625), p. 7, and *Dan. Souterii Palamedes*, p. 81; but more particularly, *I Tali ed altri Strumenti lusori degli antichi Romani, discritti da Francesco de 'Ficoroni*, 4to, Rom. 1734. Against the suggestion that the modern game is derived directly from the Romans, is the fact that it is known in countries never traversed or occupied by the Romans. Thus Dr. Clarke, in his *Travels in Russia*, 1810, p. 106, says: "In all the villages and towns from Moscow to Woronetz, as in other parts of Russia, are seen boys, girls, and sometimes even old men, playing with the joint-bones of sheep. This game is called 'Dibbs' by the English. It is of very remote antiquity; for I have seen it very beautifully represented on Grecian vases; particularly on a vase in the collection of the late Sir William Hamilton, where a female figure appeared most gracefully delineated kneeling upon one knee, with her right arm extended, the palm downwards, and the bones ranged along the back of her hand and arm. In this manner the Russians play the game."

See "Dalies," "Fivestones."

Hummie

The game otherwise called "Shinty." The shinty or hummie is played by a set of boys in two divisions who attempt to drive with curved sticks a ball, or what is more common, part of the vertebral bone of a sheep, in opposite directions (*Blackwood's Magazine*, August 1821, p. 36). If one of the adverse party happens to stand or run among his opponents, they call out "Hummie, keep on your own side."—Jamieson.

Hundreds

A game at marbles, which is carried on until one of the players scores 100 or some other high number agreed upon. Any number can play, but it is best described for two players, A. and B. First the players taw up to a hole; if both get in, they repeat the process until one is left out, say B.; then A. counts 10. Should both fail, the nearest goes first. He may now lay his taw about the hole or fire at the other, on hitting which he counts another 10. He now goes for the hole again, and failing, lies where he happens to stop. If he misses, B. from his present position tries to get into the hole, and failing, lies still; but if he reaches the hole, he counts 10, and proceeds as A. had done. The one who first gets the 100 (or other number) now goes in for his "pizings," which performance takes place thus :—The loser, so far, is lying about, and the winner goes back to "drakes," and again tries to lodge in the hole; and if he succeeds, the game is up. If not, he lies still, and the loser tries for the hole; if he gets in he counts another 10, or if he should succeed in hitting the winner he scores his adversary's 100 to his own number, and then goes on for his "pizings" as the other had done. In failure of either securing the game thus, the process is repeated at "drakes." When, however, the one who is on for his "pizings" manages to taw into the hole, the game is concluded.—Easther's *Almondbury and Huddersfield Glossary.*

Hunt the Hare

A game among children, played on the ice as well as in the fields (Brockett's *North Country Words*). Strutt (*Sports*, p. 381) says "Hunt the Hare" is the same game as "Hunt the Fox." In this game one boy is permitted to run out, and having law given to him—that is, being permitted to go to a certain distance from his comrades before they pursue him—their object is to take him, if possible, before he can return home.

See "Hare and Hounds."

Hunt the Slipper

—Lancashire (Mrs. Harley).

All the players but one sit on the floor in a circle with their legs crossed (Turkish fashion), one acting as Chief, all pretending to work at making or mending shoes. The other player brings a slipper to the Chief Cobbler, and desires it to be mended, saying—

> Cobbler, cobbler, mend my shoe,
> Get it done by half-past two.

The child walks away, and returns in a few moments and asks whether the shoe is ready. The Cobbler says, "Not quite; call again in an hour's time," or makes any other excuse which occurs to him. When the child calls again, she is told it has been sent home. After several pretences the child declares an intention to search for it. The Cobblers in the ring then all place their hands under their knees, and pass the slipper secretly from one to another in such a way as to prevent the owner of the shoe getting it for some time. The Cobbler from whom the slipper is taken becomes the owner next time (Barnes, A. B. Gomme). In the Nottinghamshire version (Miss Peacock) the rhyme is—

> Cobbler, cobbler, mend my shoe,
> Give it a stitch and that will do.

Versions from Wakefield, Liphook, Ellesmere, and other places are practically the same as the Barnes game, but Mr. Udal gives an elaboration of the Dorsetshire game in the *Folk-lore Journal*, vii. 238. One Lancashire version (Miss Dendy) reverses the characters by making the Cobbler run round the ring, and the children requiring the shoe to be mended, call out, " Blackie, come mend my slipper." Mrs. Harley, in another Lancashire version, gives the words sung to the tune printed as—

Pass on, pass on, passy on the slipper ;
The best fun we ever had was passing on the slipper.

Holloway (*Dict. of Provincialisms*) says this game was well known in Somerset, Hants, Sussex, but now is almost out of fashion. He describes it as being played without words. The child who has to find the shoe stands in the centre of the circle. The chief amusement arises from the one in the circle who has the slipper striking the one who stands up (the searcher) while he or she is steadily looking for it in an opposite direction. Strutt (*Sports*, p. 387) also describes this game.

Hunt the Staigie

A boys' game. One is chosen to be the Staigie (little stallion). The other players scatter themselves over the playground. The Staigie locks his fingers into each other. He then repeats the words—

> Hunt the Staigie,
> Huntie, untie, staige,
> Ailleman, ailleman, aigie,

and rushes off with his hands locked, and tries to touch one of the players. He must not unlock his hands till he has caught one. When he has captured one, the two join hands and hunt

for another. When another is caught, he joins the two. This goes on till all are hunted down.—Keith (Rev. W. Gregor).

See "Chickidy Hand," "Whiddy."

Hunting

—Earls Heaton (Herbert Hardy).

—Epworth (C. C. Bell).

I. Oh, a-hunting we will go, a-hunting we will go;
    We'll catch a little fox and put him in a box,
            And never let him go.   —Bath (Miss Large).

        II. Hunting we will go, brave boys,
             Hunting we will go;

We'll catch an old fox
And put him in a box,
For a-hunting we will go.
Halt! shoulder arms! fire!
—Horncastle, North Kelsey, Lincoln (Miss Peacock).

III.   O have you seen the Shah,
       O have you seen the Shah?
       He lights his pipe on a star-light night,
       O have you seen the Shah?
       For a-hunting we will go,
       A-hunting we will go;
       We'll catch a fox and put him in a box,
       A-hunting we will go.
                                   —Epworth, Doncaster (C. C. Bell).

(*b*) The players march two by two, all singing. The first pair let go hands, separate, and skip widely apart, still singing. Gradually, in this manner, two separate lines are formed, until, following each other and singing, the pairs come together again, join hands, and march and sing in couplets linked.

The Bath game is played by the children standing in two rows facing each other, and clapping hands and singing the verse. At the same time the two children facing each other at the top of the lines join hands and trip down and up between the lines. Their hands are unclasped, and the two children run down the outside of the lines, one running on each side, and meet at the bottom of the lines, where they stand. The two children now standing at the top proceed in the same way: this is continued until all the children have done the same. A ring is then formed, when the children again clap and sing. Any number can play at this game.

In the Epworth version the children range themselves in double rank at one end of the room or playground, and march down to the other end hand in hand. At the bottom they loose hands and divide, the first rank turning right, the second left, and march back in two single files to the other end again, where they re-form as at first, and repeat their manœuvre, singing the verses alternately.

The Lincolnshire game is played by the children walking two and two in a circle round one of their companions, singing. The players then stand facing the child in the centre, and place their hands on their partners' shoulders. After the lines are sung the centre child cries out, " Halt! Shoulder arms! Fire!" at which words each child kisses his partner. If the commander sees any one hesitate, or avoid kissing, he runs forward and takes the defaulter's place, leaving him to fill the middle position.

Similar versions are played at Earls Heaton (Mr. Hardy), Forest of Dean (Miss Matthews), Ellesmere (Burne, *Shropshire Folk-lore*, p. 574), Derbyshire (*Folk-lore Journal*, i. 386).

Hurling

A game played with a ball. The players are divided into two equal parties, each of which tries to secure and keep the ball in their possession. The prize is a ball made of cork, covered with silver.—Courtney's *West Cornwall Glossary*.

In Taylor's *Antiquitates Curiosæ*, p. 144, it is stated:—" The game of hurling consisted in throwing or hurling a ball of wood about three inches in diameter, and covered with plated silver, sometimes gilt. On the ball was frequently a Cornish motto allusive to the game, and signifying that fair play was best. Success depended on catching the ball dexterously when dealt, and conveying it away through all the opposition of the adverse party, or, if that was impossible, to throw it into the hands of a partner, who, in his turn, was to exert his utmost efforts to convey it to his own goal, which was often three or four miles distant from that of his adversaries."

T. Durfey's *Collin's Walk through London*, 1690, p. 192, says : " Hurling is an ancient sport us'd to this day in the countys of Cornwall and Devon, when once a year the hardy young fellows of each county meet; and a cork ball thinly plated with silver being thrown up between 'em, they run, bustle, and fight for it, to the witty dislocating of many a shrew'd neck, or for the sport of telling how bravely their arms or legs came to

be broke, when they got home." It is fully described by
Carew in his *Survey of Cornwall*, 1602, p. 73.

It is also a very ancient Irish game, and Mr. Kinahan says :
"Many places are called after it : such as, Killahurla, the hurlers'
church ; Gortnahurla, the field of the hurlers ; Greenanahurla,
the sunny place of the hurlers ; this, however, is now generally
corrupted into hurling-green. The hurling-green where the
famous match was played by the people of Wexford against
those of Cather (now divided into the counties of Carlow and
Wicklow), and where the former got the name of yellow bellies,
from the colour of the scarfs they wore round their waist, is a
sunny flat on the western side of North Wicklow Gap, on the
road from Gorey to Trinnahely. There are also many other different names that record the game."—*Folk-lore Journal*, ii. 266.

See "Bandy," "Camp," "Football," "Hockey," "Hood,"
"Shinty."

Hurly-burly

An undescribed boys' game. In it the following rhyme is
used—

Hurly-burly, trumpy trace,
The cow stands in the market-place ;
Some goes far, and some goes near,
Where shall this poor sinner steer ?
—*Patterson s Antrim and Down Glossary.*

For a similar rhyme see "Hot Cockles."

Huss

Children play a game which is accompanied by a song beginning—

Hussing and bussing will not do,
But go to the gate, knock, and ring—
Please, Mrs. Brown, is Nellie within ?
—*Parish's Dictionary of the Sussex Dialect.*

Hustle Cap

A boys' game, played by tossing up halfpence. It is mentioned in *Peregrine Pickle*, cap. xvi. Cope (*Hampshire Glossary*) says, "Halfpence are placed in a cap and thrown up, a
sort of 'pitch-and-toss.'"

Hynny-pynny

A peculiar game at marbles, sometimes called " Hyssy-pyssy,"
played in some parts of Devon and Somerset.   A hole of some
extent was made in an uneven piece of ground, and the game
was to shoot the marbles at some object beyond the hole without letting them tumble into it.   The game occasionally commenced by a ceremony of no very delicate description, which
sufficed to render the fallen marble still more ignominious.—
Halliwell's *Dictionary*.

Isabella

—Ogbourne, Wilts (H. S. May).

—Earls Heaton (H. Hardy).

—London (A. B. Gomme).

I. Isabella, Isabella, Isabella, Farewell!
    Last night when we parted
    I left you broken-hearted,
    And on a green mountain,
    There stands a young man.

    Could you love him?
    Could you love him?
    Could you love him?   Farewell!

    Choose one, love,
    Choose one, love,
    Choose one, love, Farewell!

    Take a walk, love,
    Take a walk, love,
    Take a walk, love, Farewell!

    In the ring, love,
    In the ring, love,
    In the ring, love, Farewell!

    Put the ring on,
    Put the ring on,
    Put the ring on, Farewell!

    Go to church, love,
    Go to church, love,
    Go to church, love, Farewell!

    Take a kiss, love,
    Take a kiss, love,
    Take a kiss, love, Farewell!

Shake hands, love,
Shake hands, love,
Shake hands, love, Farewell!
                    —Enborne, Newbury (M. Kimber).

II.   Isabella, Isabella, Isabella, Farewell!
      Last night when I departed
      I left her broken-hearted;
      Upon the steep mountain
      There stands a young man.

      Who'll you choose, love?
      Who'll you choose, love?
      Who'll you choose, love?   Farewell!

      Go to church, love,
      Go to church, love,
      Go to church, love, Farewell!

      Say your prayers, love,
      Say your prayers, love,
      Say your prayers, love, Farewell!

      Put your ring on,
      Put your ring on,
      Put your ring on, Farewell!

      Come back, love,
      Come back, love,
      Come back, love, Farewell!

      Roast beef and plum pudding,
      Roast beef and plum pudding,
      Roast beef and plum pudding,
      For our dinner to-day.

      Kiss together, love,
      Kiss together, love,
      Kiss together, love, Farewell!
                    —Ogbourne, Wilts (H. S. May).

III.   Isabella, Isabella, Isabella, Farewell!
      Last night when I departed
      I left you broken-hearted
      Broken-hearted on the mountain,
      On the mountain, Farewell!

      Choose your loved one, choose your loved one,
      Choose your loved one, Farewell!

      Kiss your hand, love, kiss your hand, love,
      Kiss your hand, love, Farewell!

      Go to church, love, go to church, love,
      Go to church, love, Farewell!

      Say your prayers, love, say your prayers, love,
      Say your prayers, love, Farewell!

      Come to dinner, love, come to dinner, love,
      Come to dinner, love, Farewell!

      What have you for dinner, for dinner, for dinner,
      What have you for dinner, for dinner to-day?

      Roast beef and plum pudding, plum pudding, plum
          pudding,
      Roast beef and plum pudding, plum pudding to-day.
                    —Southampton (Mrs. W. R. Carse).

IV.   Isabella, Isabella, Isabella, Farewell!
      Last night I met you downhearted and sad,
      And down by the river I met your young man.

      Choose a lover, choose a lover,
      Choose a lover, Farewell!

      Walk to church, love, walk to church, love,
      Walk to church, love, Farewell!

      Come to the ring, love, come to the ring, love,
      Come to the ring, love, Farewell!

      Give a kiss, love, give a kiss, love,
      Give a kiss, love, Farewell!
               —West Grinstead, Sussex (*Notes and Queries*,
                    8th Series, i. 249, Miss Busk).

V. Arabella!
    Arabella!
    Arabella!   Farewell!

    Last night when we parted
    I left you broken-hearted
    Down by the mill-side.

    Who'll you have, love?
    Who'll you have, love?
    Who'll you have, love?   Farewell!

    Go to church, love,
    Go to church, love,
    Go to church, love, Farewell!

    Come back, love,
    Come back, love,
    Come back, love, Farewell!

    Shake hands, love,
    Shake hands, love,
    Shake hands, love, Farewell!

    Take a kiss, love,
    Take a kiss, love,
    Take a kiss, love, Farewell!
        —Platt School, near Wrotham, Kent (Miss Burne).

VI. Isabella, Isabella, Isabella, Farewell!
     Last night when we parted
     I left you broken-hearted,
     And on the green meadow
     You was standing alone.

     Choose a sweetheart, choose a sweetheart,
     Choose a sweetheart, fair maid.

     Take her hand, love, take her hand, love,
     Take her hand, love, fair maid.

     Kneel down, love, kneel down, love,
     Kneel down, love, fair maid.

Take a kiss, love, take a kiss, love,
Take a kiss, love, fair maid.

Now you're married I wish you joy,
First a girl and then a boy,
Seven years after son and daughter;
Pray, young couple, come kiss together.

Kiss her once, kiss her twice, kiss her three times over.
—From a London nursemaid, 1878 (A. B. Gomme).

VII. Isabella, Isabella, Isabella, Farewell!
Last night when we parted
I believed you broken-hearted,
As on the green mountain
You stands [*qy.* sang] like a lark.

Go to church, love, go to church, love,
Go to church, love, Farewell!

In the ring, love, in the ring, love,
In the ring, love, Farewell!

Give a kiss, love, give a kiss, love,
Give a kiss, love, Farewell!

Isabella, Isabella, Isabella, Farewell!
—Fernham and Longcot (Miss I. Barclay).

VIII. Isabella, Isabella, Isabella, Farewell!
Last night when I departed I left her broken-hearted;
On the hill yonder there stands your young man.

Fetch him here, love, fetch him here, love,
Fetch him here, love, Farewell!

Shut the gates, love, shut the gates, love,
Shut the gates, love, Farewell!

Open the gates, love, open the gates, love,
Open the gates, love, Farewell!

Go to church, love, go to church, love,
Go to church, love, Farewell!

Show your ring, love, show your ring, love,
Show your ring, love, Farewell!
                    —Hanbury, Staffs. (Miss E. Hollis).

IX.   The trees are uncovered, uncovered, uncovered,
      The trees are uncovered, Isabella, for me!

      Last night when we parted we were all broken-hearted,
      Isabella, Isabella, Isabella, for me!

      Then give me your hand, love, your hand, love, your
          hand, love,
      Then give me your hand, love, and a sweet kiss from you.
                    —Earls Heaton (Herbert Hardy).

X.   When the trees are uncovered, Isabellow, for me.
      Last night when we parted
      She was nigh broken-hearted,
      Isabellow, Isabellow, Isabellow, for me.

      Your hand, love, your hand, love,
      Then give me your hand, love,
      Take a sweet kiss from me.
      —Winterton, Nottinghamshire and Yorkshire (Miss Peacock).

XI.   Isabella, Isabella, Isabella, Farewell!
      Last night when we parted I left you broken-hearted,
      And down by the river you saw your young man.

      In the stream, love, in the stream, love,
      In the stream, love, Farewell!

      Go to church, love, go to church, love,
      Go to church, love, Farewell.

      In the ring, love, in the ring, love,
      In the ring, love, Farewell!
                    —Long Eaton, Nottinghamshire (Miss Youngman).

      XII.   Elizabella, Farewell!
             Last night as we parted
             She left me broken-hearted,
             And on a green mountain
             She looked like a dove.

Choose your loved one,
Choose your loved one,
Choose your loved one, Farewell!

Go to church, love, Farewell!
Say your prayers, love, Farewell!
In the ring, love, Farewell!

Shake hands, loves,
Shake hands, loves, Farewell!

Give a kiss, loves,
Give a kiss, loves, Farewell!

—Liphook, Hants (Miss Fowler).

XIII. Last night when we parted
She was nigh broken-hearted,
To-morrow we gather
And a bright welcome be.
Then give me your hand, love,
Your hand, love, your hand, love,
Then give me your hand, love,
    Isabella for me.
    Isabella, Isabella,
    Isabella for me.

—North Derbyshire (S. O. Addy).

(*b*) In the Enborne, Newbury, version (Miss Kimber) a ring is formed by the children (boys and girls) joining hands. Another child stands in the centre. The ring of children walk round while singing the verses. The singing is confined to the ring. When the centre child is told to "choose," she selects a boy from the ring, who goes into the centre and they stand together. At the next verse these two children walk out of the ring arm-in-arm. When the next verse is sung they return, and again stand in the centre. At the next verse the boy pretends to put a ring on the girl's finger. They walk out of the ring when told to go to church (two children in the ring unclasping hands to let them walk out, and again clasping hands after they return), and kiss each other and shake hands when the two next verses are sung.

The child who was first in the centre then joins the ring, and the game proceeds in the same way with the second child, who chooses in his turn. All the other versions follow the same rules, suiting their actions to the words, except Ogbourne, Wilts, in which the two children in the centre sing the verse, "roast beef and plum pudding." They stand face to face, take hold of each other's hands, and sway their arms from side to side. The ring then sing the concluding verse. In those versions where "say your prayers" and "kneel down" occur, the two centre children kneel, and hold their open hands together in front of them to imitate a book. In the London version (A. B. Gomme) a handkerchief was laid on the ground, and the two children stood on each side of it and clasped hands across it. In the Fernham and Longcot version the one child leads the other out of the ring at "go to church," with a graceful half-dancing motion, and back again in the same way. The first child joins the ring while the refrain is sung. In the Hanbury version the centre child pretends to be weeping; another child stands outside the ring and goes into it; when the two meet they kiss. In the North Derbyshire version (Mr. S. O. Addy) a ring is formed of young men and women, a young man being in the centre. He chooses a young woman at the singing of the fifth line, and then joins the ring, the girl remaining in the centre.

(c) The tunes of all versions are very similar. The tune of the Newbury game (Miss Kimber) is the same as the *first* part of the Ogbourne tune printed (Mr. H. S. May); that from Nottingham (Miss Youngman) is the same as the first part of the London version. This is also the case with the Hanbury, Staffs. (Miss E. Hollis) and Fernham and Longcot game. What difference there is is very slight. The Platt, Kent, game (Miss Burne), is sung to the same tune as "Green Gravel," given *ante*, p. 170. The *first* portion only of the tune is repeated for all verses sung after the first verse. The Barnes game is sung to the same tune as the Earls Heaton (Mr. Hardy), which is printed *ante*. A version played at Barnes is almost identical with the Southampton version, and another collected by Miss Thoyts in Berkshire (*Antiquary*, vol. xxvii. p. 193) is similar

to the Hanbury version. The first lines run—Choose your
lover; Open the gates; Go to church, love; Kneel down, love;
Say your prayers, love; Put on the ring; Stand up, love; In
the ring, love; Kiss together, love.

(d) The words of all the versions are sufficiently similar to
analyse without a special form. The game appears to be
purely a love and marriage game, and has probably had its
origin in a ballad, and this idea is strengthened by the fact
that only one version (London) has the marriage formula sung
at the end, and this is probably an arbitrary addition. The
lover is represented as lonely and disconsolate, and the remedy
suggested is to choose a sweetheart. The marriage ceremony
is of the simplest description—the clasping of hands and the
kissing within the circle probably implying the betrothal at a
spot sacred to such functions, similar to the Standing Stones
of Stenness. Whatever may have been the original intention
of these stones, they came in more recent times to be the
resort of lovers, who joined their right hands through the
hole in the altar stones in the belief that this ceremony
would add additional solemnity to the betrothal. Miss
Gordon Cumming, in her *Tour in the Hebrides*, mentions the
fact of the marriage ceremony being of the simplest—a man
and woman standing facing each other and clasping hands
over a particular stone. Walking arm-in-arm is a sign in
Dorsetshire that a couple are married. The mention of the
"roast beef and plum pudding" for dinner has probably had
its origin in the wedding dinner or breakfast, and the inviting
of friends to assemble for the wedding dinner. The word
"Isabella" may have been originally something quite different
from the name of a girl. I am inclined to think the word
was not the name of a person at all; possibly it was something addressed to a particular person in words the sense of
which are now lost, and the nearest idea to it was this name.
The same thing may also apply to the word "farewell," and
hence the incongruity of the first few lines in nearly all versions.

Jack's Alive.

A number of people sit in a row, or on chairs round a

parlour. A lighted wooden spill or taper is handed to the first, who says—

> Jack's alive, and likely to live;
> If he dies in your hand you've a forfeit to give.

The one in whose hand the light expires has to pay a forfeit. As the spill is getting burnt out the lines are said very quickly, as everybody is anxious not to have to pay the forfeit.—Addy's *Sheffield Glossary.*

At Egan, in Derbyshire, a number of persons sit round a fire; one of them lights a stick, twirls it round, and says—

> Little Nanny Cockerthaw,
> What if I should let her fa'?

The others reply—

> Nine sticks and nine stones
> Shall be laid on thy bare back bones
> If thou shouldst let fa'
> Little Nanny Cockerthaw.

If the ember or lighted stick goes out whilst any one is twirling it round, and whilst the lines are being said, he has to lie on the floor, when stones, chairs, or other articles of furniture are piled upon him.—S. O. Addy.

Mactaggart calls it " Preest Cat," and says that it is an ingleside game. A piece of stick is made red in the fire; one hands it to another, saying—

> About wi' that, about wi' that,
> Keep alive the preest cat.

Then round is handed the stick, and whomsoever's hand it goes out in, that one is in a wad, and must kiss the crook, the cleps, and what not, ere he gets out of it.

> Lilly cuckoo, lilly cuckoo,
> Sticks and stanes lie at thy weary banes
> If thou fa', for a' I blaw,
> Lilly cuckoo, lilly cuckoo.

This rhyme is common in the " Preest Cat" sport toward the border. Anciently, when the priest's cat departed this life, wailing began in the country side, as it was thought it became some supernatural being—a witch, perhaps, of hideous form—

so to keep it alive was a great matter.—Mactaggart's *Gallo-vidian Encyclopædia.*

He also refers to a game called "Robin-a-Ree," much like "Preest Cat," only in passing the burnt stick round the ring the following rhyme is said—

> Robin-a-Ree, ye'll no dee wi' me,
> Tho' I birl ye roun' three times and three;
> O Robin-a-Ree, O Robin-a-Ree,
> O dinna let Robin-a-Reerie dee.

Robin-a-Ree occurs in an old song.—Mactaggart's *Gallovidian Encyclopædia.*

In Cornwall it is known as "Robin's a-light," and is played around the fire. A piece of stick is set on fire and whirled around rapidly in the hand of the first player, who says, "Robin's a-light, and if he go out I will saddle your back." It is then passed to the next, who says the same thing, and so on. The person who lets the spark die out has to pay a forfeit.—Scilly (Courtney's *West Cornwall Glossary*). A rhyme at Lostwithiel is known as follows—

> Jack's alive, and likely to live;
> If he die in my hand a pawn (forfeit) I'll give.
>
> —(J. W.)

Jamieson (*Dictionary*) says, "To do 'Dingle-dousie,' a stick is ignited at one end and given as a plaything to a child." Elworthy (*West Somerset Words*) does not give this as a game, but says a burning stick was whirled round and round very quickly, so as to keep up the appearance of a ribbon of fire. Miss Burne (*Shropshire Folk-lore*, p. 530), says, "Children wave a burning stick in the air, saying—

> A girdle o' gold, a saddle o' silk,
> A horse for me as white as milk,

an evident relic of divinations or incantations practised with bonfires." Halliwell (*Nursery Rhymes*, p. 213) gives the rhyme as—   Jack's alive, and in very good health,

> If he dies in your hand you must look to yourself;

the game being played in the same way as the Sheffield version (see also Halliwell's *Dictionary* and Moor's *Suffolk Words*).

(*b*) This is a very significant game, and its similarity in miniature to the old tribal custom of carrying the fiery cross to rouse the clans at once suggests the possible origin of it.   The detention of the fiery cross through neglect or other impediment was regarded with much dread by the inhabitants of the place in which it should occur.   This subject is discussed in Gomme's *Primitive Folkmoots*, p. 279 *et seq.*

Jack, Jack, the Bread's a-burning

> Jack, Jack, the bread's a-burning,
> All to a cinder;
> If you don't come and fetch it out
> We'll throw it through the winder.

These lines are chanted by players that stand thus.   One places his back against a wall, tree, &c., grasping another, whose back is toward him, round the waist; the second grasps a third, and so on.   The player called Jack walks apart until the conclusion of the lines.   Then he goes to the others and pokes at or pats them, saying, " I don't think you're done yet," and walks away again.   The chant is repeated, and when he is satisfied that the bread is " done" he endeavours to pull the foremost from the grasp of the others, &c.—Warwickshire (Northall's *Folk Rhymes*, p. 390).

See " Mother Mop."

Jack upon the Mopstick

See " Bung the Bucket."

Jackysteauns

A game among school-girls, played with small pebbles, and sometimes with plum or cherry stones (Dickinson's *Cumberland Glossary*).   " A children's game, played with five white pebbles called Jackstones," says Mr. Patterson (*Antrim and Down Glossary*).   The game is called " Jack."

See " Fivestones," " Hucklebones."

Jauping Paste-eggs

A youthful amusement in Newcastle and the neighbourhood at Easter.   One boy, holding an egg in his hand, challenges another to give blow for blow.   One of the eggs is sure to be fractured in the conflict, and its shattered remains become the spoil of the conqueror.

See "Conkers."

Jenny Jones

—Platt, near Wrotham, Kent (Miss Burne).

—Northants (Rev. W. D. Sweeting).

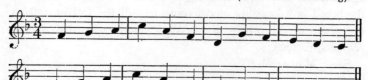

—Belfast (W. H. Patterson).

I.   I'm come to court Janet jo,
     Janet jo, Janet jo,
     I'm come to court Janet jo,
     How's she the day?

     She's up the stair washin',
     Washin', washin',
     She's up the stair washin',
     Ye canna see her the day.

[Then follow verses, the words of which are not given by Chambers, representing Jenny as bleaching, drying, and ironing clothes. At last they say—]

Janet jo's dead and gane,
Dead and gane, dead and gane;
Janet jo's dead and gane,
She'll never come hame!
—Chambers' *Popular Rhymes*, pp. 140–41.

II.   I'm come to court Janet jo, Janet jo, Janet jo,
Come to court Janet jo,
How is she the day?

She's butt the house washing, washing, washing
She's butt the house washing,
You can't see her to-day.

Fare ye well, ladies, ladies, ladies,
Fare ye well, ladies,
For I must away.
—West Scotland (*Folk-lore Record*, iv. 474).

III.   We've come to court Jinny jo,
Jinny jo, Jinny jo,
We've come to court Jinny jo,
Is she within?

Jinny jo's washing clothes,
Washing clothes, washing clothes,
Jinny jo's washing clothes,
You can't see her to-day.

So fare ye well, ladies,
O ladies, O ladies,
So fare ye well, ladies
And gentlemen too.

[These verses are repeated for—

(1) drying clothes,
(2) starching,
(3) ironing,
(4) ill,
(5) dying.

Then—]   Jinny jo's lying dead,
            Lying dead, lying dead,
            Jinny jo's lying dead,
            You can't see her to-day.

            So turn again, ladies,
            Ladies, ladies, ladies,
            So turn again, ladies,
            And gentlemen too.

            What shall we dress her in ?
            Dress her in, dress her in ?
            What shall we dress her in ?
            Shall it be red ?

            Red's for the soldiers,
            The soldiers, the soldiers,
            Red's for the soldiers,
            And that will not do.

[Various other colours are suggested in the same way, but
are found unsuitable—black because " black's for the mourners,"
green because " green's for the croppies," and so on till at last
white is named.]

            White's for the dead people,
            Dead people, the dead people,
            White's for the dead people,
            And that will just do.
                        —Belfast (*Notes and Queries*, 7th series,
                            xii. 492, W. H. Patterson).

IV.   I came to see Jenny jo, Jenny jo, Jenny jo,
        I came to see Jenny jo, is she within ?

        Jenny jo's washing clothes, washing clothes, washing
            clothes,
        Jenny jo's washing clothes, and ye can't see her to-day.

        Oh but I'm sorry, I'm sorry, I'm sorry,
        Oh but I'm sorry, I can't see her to-day.

        Farewell ladies, O ladies, O ladies,
        Farewell ladies, and gentlemen too.

[Then the same verses are repeated for—
           (1) starching clothes,
           (2) smoothing clothes,
           (3) dead,
the four lines above being repeated after each, and the verses proceed with—]

What shall we dress her in, dress her in, dress her in ?
What shall we dress her in ?   Shall it be black ?

Black for the sweeps, the sweeps, the sweeps,
Black for the sweeps, and that shall not do.

What shall we dress her in, dress her in, dress her in ?
What shall we dress her in ?   Shall it be blue ?

Blue for the sailors, sailors, sailors,
Blue for the sailors, and that shall not do.

What shall we dress her in, dress her in, dress her in ?
What shall we dress her in ?   Shall it be red ?

Red for the soldiers, soldiers, soldiers,
Red for the soldiers, and that shall not do.

What shall we dress her in, dress her in, dress her in ?
What shall we dress her in ?   Shall it be orange ?

Orange for the Orange-men, Orange-men, Orange-men,
Orange for the Orange-men, and that shall not do.

What shall we dress her in, dress her in, dress her in ?
What shall we dress her in ?   Shall it be white ?

White for the corpse, the corpse, the corpse,
White for the corpse, and that will just do.

We have lost a soldier, soldier, soldier,
We have lost a soldier, and the Queen has lost a man.
We will bury him in the bed of glory, glory, glory,
We will bury him in the bed of glory, and we'll never
    see him any more.
          —Holywood, co. Down (Miss C. N. Patterson).

V. I've come to see Jenny jo, Jenny jo, Jenny jo,
      I've come to see Jenny jo,
        How is she now ?

Jenny jo is washing clothes, washing clothes, washing
    clothes,
    Jenny jo is washing clothes,
      You can't see her now.

I've come to see Jenny jo, Jenny jo, Jenny jo,
    I've come to see Jenny jo,
      How is she now ?

Jenny jo is ironing clothes, ironing clothes, ironing clothes,
    Jenny jo is ironing clothes,
      You can't see her now.

I've come to see Jenny jo, Jenny jo, Jenny jo,
    I've come to see Jenny jo,
      How is she now ?

Jenny jo is sick, my dear, sick, my dear, sick, my dear,
    Jenny jo is sick, my dear,
      You can't see her now.

I've come to see Jenny jo, Jenny jo, Jenny jo,
    I've come to see Jenny jo,
      How is she now ?

Jenny jo is underboard, underboard, underboard,
    Jenny jo is underboard,
      You can't see her now.
             —Lismore (Miss F. Keane, collected from Miss
                Ward, National Schoolmistress).

VI. We've come to see Jenny Jones,
      Jenny Jones, Jenny Jones,
      We've come to see Jenny Jones,
      And how is she now ?

O Jenny is washing,
O washing, O washing,
O Jenny is washing,
And you can't see her now.

Very well, ladies, ladies, ladies,
Very well, ladies, and gentlemen too.

We've come to see Jenny Jones,
Jenny Jones, Jenny Jones,
We've come to see Jenny Jones,
And how is she now?

O Jenny is starching,
O starching, O starching,
O Jenny is starching,
And you can't see her now.

Very well, ladies, ladies, ladies,
Very well, ladies, and gentlemen too.

We've come to see Jenny Jones,
Jenny Jones, Jenny Jones,
We've come to see Jenny Jones,
And how is she now?

O Jenny is ironing,
O ironing, O ironing,
O Jenny is ironing,
And you can't see her now.

Very well, ladies, ladies, ladies,
Very well, ladies, and·gentlemen too.

We've come to see Jenny Jones,
Jenny Jones, Jenny Jones,
We've come to see Jenny Jones,
And how is she now?

O Jenny is ill,
O ill, O ill,
O Jenny is ill,
And you can't see her now.

Very well, ladies, ladies, ladies,
Very well, ladies, and gentlemen too.

We've come to see Jenny Jones,
Jenny Jones, Jenny Jones,
We've come to see Jenny Jones,
And how is she now?

O Jenny is dying,
O dying, O dying,
O Jenny is dying,
And you can't see her now.

Very well, ladies, ladies, ladies,
Very well, ladies, and gentlemen too.

We've come to see Jenny Jones,
Jenny Jones, Jenny Jones,
We've come to see Jenny Jones,
And how is she now?

O Jenny is dead,
Is dead, is dead,
O Jenny is dead,
And you can't see her now.

Very well, ladies, ladies, ladies,
Very well, ladies, and gentlemen too.

What shall we lay her in, lay her in, lay her in?
What shall we lay her in?   Shall it be red?

Red is for soldiers, soldiers, soldiers,
Red is for soldiers, and that won't do.

Very well, ladies, ladies, ladies,
Very well, ladies, and gentlemen too.

What shall we lay her in, lay her in, lay her in?
What shall we lay her in?   Shall it be blue?

Blue is for sailors, sailors, sailors,
Blue is for sailors, and that won't do.

Very well, ladies, ladies, ladies,
Very well, ladies, and gentlemen too.

What shall we lay her in, lay her in, lay her in ?
What shall we lay her in ?   Shall it be black ?

Black is for mourners, mourners, mourners,
Black is for mourners, and that won't do.

Very well, ladies, ladies, ladies,
Very well, ladies, and gentlemen too.

What shall we lay her in, lay her in, lay her in ?
What shall we lay her in ?   Shall it be white ?

White's what the dead wear, dead wear, dead wear,
White's what the dead wear, and that will just do.
                    —Hanwell, Middlesex, 1878 (A. B. Gomme).

VII.   We've come to see poor Jenny Jones, poor Jenny Jones,
          poor Jenny Jones,
       We've come to see poor Jenny Jones, how is she to-day ?

Poor Jenny is washing, washing, washing,
Poor Jenny is washing, washing hard to-day.

What time can we see her ?
At one o'clock.   (Clock strikes one.)

We've come to see poor Jenny Jones, poor Jenny Jones,
          poor Jenny Jones,
We've come to see poor Jenny Jones, how is she to-day ?

Poor Jenny is starching, starching, starching,
Poor Jenny is starching, you can't see her to-day.

When can we see her ?
At two o'clock.   (Clock strikes two.)

We've come to see poor Jenny Jones, poor Jenny Jones,
          poor Jenny Jones,
We've come to see poor Jenny Jones, how is she to-day ?

Poor Jenny is folding, folding, folding,
Poor Jenny is folding, you can't see her to-day.

When can we see her ?
At three o'clock.   (Clock strikes three.)

We've come to see poor Jenny Jones, poor Jenny Jones,
poor Jenny Jones,
We've come to see poor Jenny Jones, how is she to-day ?

Poor Jenny is ironing, ironing, ironing,
Poor Jenny is ironing, you can't see her to-day.

When can we see her ?
At four o'clock.   (Clock strikes four.)

We've come to see poor Jenny Jones, poor Jenny Jones,
poor Jenny Jones,
We've come to see poor Jenny Jones, how is she to-day ?

Poor Jenny is poorly, poorly, poorly,
Poor Jenny is poorly, you can't see her to-day.

When can we see her ?
At five o'clock.   (Clock strikes five.)

We've come to see poor Jenny Jones, poor Jenny Jones,
poor Jenny Jones,
We've come to see poor Jenny Jones, how is she to-day ?

Poor Jenny is dying, dying, dying,
Poor Jenny is dying, you can't see her to-day.

When shall we see her ?
(Come) at six o'clock.   (Clock strikes six.)

We've come to see poor Jenny Jones, poor Jenny Jones,
poor Jenny Jones,
We've come to see poor Jenny Jones, how is she to-day ?

Poor Jenny is dead, dead, dead,
Poor Jenny is dead, you can't see her to-day.

What colour will you have for the funeral for poor
Jenny Jones ?

Red ?

Red is for the soldiers, soldiers, soldiers,
Red is for the soldiers, and that won't do.

Blue ?

Blue is for the sailors, sailors, sailors,
Blue is for the sailors, and that won't do.

Pink ?

Pink is for the babies, babies, babies,
Pink is for the babies, and that won't do.

White ?

White is for a wedding, a wedding, a wedding,
White is for a wedding, and that won't do.

Black ?

Black is for the mourners, mourners, mourners,
Black is for the mourners, and that will do.

Poor Jenny Jones is dead, dead, dead,
Poor Jenny Jones is dead, and lies in her grave.
              —Southampton (from nursemaid of Mrs. W. R. Carse).

VIII. We've come to see Jenny Jones, Jenny Jones, Jenny
          Jones,
          We've come to see Jenny Jones, is she at home ?

          Jenny Jones is scrubbing, scrubbing, scrubbing,
          Jenny Jones is scrubbing, you can't see her now.

[Then follow verses asking alternately " Is she at home ? "
in the same words as the first verse, and answering that she is

                         (1) washing,
                         (2) ill,
                         (3) dying,
                         (4) dead ;

all of them in the same form as the second verse.   Then the
verses continue with—]

          Jenny Jones is dead, she is dead, she is dead,
          Jenny Jones is dead, you can't see her now.

          We'll come to the funeral, funeral, funeral,
          We'll come to the funeral, and how shall we dress ?

          You can come in yellow, in yellow, in yellow,
          You can come in yellow, that's how you can dress.

Yellow's for jealousy, jealousy, jealousy,
Yellow's for jealousy, so *that* won't do.

You can come in green, in green, in green,
You can come in green, that's how you can dress.

Green's forsaken, forsaken, forsaken,
Green's forsaken, so *that* won't do.

You can come in white, in white, in white,
You can come in white, that's how you can dress.

White's for weddings, weddings, weddings,
White's for weddings, so that won't do.

You can come in black, in black, in black,
You can come in black, that's how you can dress.

Black is for funerals, funerals, funerals,
Black is for funerals, so black will do.
                    —Colchester (from Miss G. M. Frances, Colchester,
                              through Miss Morris).

IX.   We've come to see Jenny Jones, Jenny Jones,
      We've come to see Jenny Jones.   How is she now?

Jenny is washing, washing, washing,
Jenny is washing, you can't see her now.

[Then follow the alternate question and answer; the questions in the same words as the first verse, and the answers in the same form as the second verse, stating that Jenny is

> (1) folding,
> (2) starching,
> (3) ironing,
> (4) ill,
> (5) dying,
> (6) dead;

then the verses proceed with—]

May we come to the funeral?
Yes.

May we come in red?
Red is for soldiers, you can't come in red.

May we come in blue ?
Blue is for sailors, you can't come in blue.

May we come in white ?
White is for weddings, you can't come in white.

May we come in black ?
Black is for funerals, so you can come in that.
                    —Bocking, Essex (*Folk-lore Record*, iii. 471).

X.   I come to see poor Jenny Joe,
         Jenny Joe, Jenny Joe,
         I come to see poor Jenny Joe,
         And how is she now ?

         She's washing, she's washing,
         And you can't see her now.

         Very well, ladies, ladies, ladies,
         Very well, ladies, and gentlemen too.

         I come to see poor Jenny Joe,
         Jenny Joe, Jenny Joe,
         I come to see poor Jenny Joe,
         And how is she now ?

         She's folding, she's folding,
         And you can't see her now.

         Very well, ladies, ladies, ladies,
         Very well, ladies, and gentlemen too.

         I come to see poor Jenny Joe,
         Jenny Joe, Jenny Joe,
         I come to see poor Jenny Joe,
         And how is she now ?

         She's ironing, she's ironing,
         And you can't see her now.

         Very well, ladies, ladies, ladies,
         Very well, ladies, and gentlemen too.

[Then follow alternate questions and answers in the same
manner for—   (1) dying,
                              (2) dead.

Then—]

> I come in my white dress, white dress, white dress,
> I come in my white dress, and how will that do?

> White is for wedding, wedding, wedding,
> White is for wedding, and that won't do.

> Very well, ladies, ladies, ladies,
> Very well, ladies, and gentlemen too.

> I come in my blue dress, blue dress, blue dress,
> I come in my blue dress, and how will that do?

> Blue is for sailors, sailors, sailors,
> Blue is for sailors, and that won't do.

[Then follow verses as before, beginning—
> Very well, ladies.
> I come in my red dress.
> Red is for soldiers,
> Very well, ladies.

Then—]

> I come in my black dress, black dress, black dress,
> I come in my black dress, and how will that do?

> Black is for funeral,
> And that will do
> To carry poor Jenny to the grave.
> —Sporle, Norfolk (Miss Matthews).

XI. We're come to see Jenny Jones, Jenny Jones, Jenny Jones,
Come to see Jenny Jones, how is she now?

> Jenny is a-washing, a-washing, a-washing,
> Jenny is a-washing, you can't see her now.

> Very well, ladies, very well, ladies,
> Very well, ladies, we can't see her now.

[Then follow the same verses for—
> (1) ironing,
> (2) badly,
> (3) dead;

And the singing proceeds with—]
>   Please, will white do, white do, white do ?
>   Please, will white do, please, will it do ?
>
>   White's for the weddingers, the weddingers,
>   White's for the weddingers, that won't do.
>
>   Please, will blue do, blue do, blue do ?
>   Please, will blue do, please will it do ?

[Then follow verses as before, beginning—
>   Blue's for the sailors, the sailors, the sailors.
>   Please, will red do, red do ?
>   Red's for the soldiers.

Then—]
>   Please, will black do, black do, black do ?
>   Black's for the funeral, black will do.
>> —Northamptonshire (Rev. W. D. Sweeting).

XII.   I've come to see how Jenny Jones is to-day.
>   You can't see her, she's washing.
>   I've come to see how Jenny Jones is to-day.
>   You can't see her, she's ironing [she's starching, she's
>   brewing, she's baking, *successively*].
>   I've come to see how Jenny Jones is to-day.
>   You can't see her, she's ill [then she's worse].
>   I've come to see how Jenny Jones is to-day.
>   You can't see her, she's dead !

Chorus.   There's red for the soldiers,
>   Blue for the sailors,
>   White for the angels [for the *baby*, Chirbury],
>   And black for the mourners [of poor Jenny Jones].
>> —Berrington, Chirbury (*Shropshire Folk-lore*, p. 577).

XIII.   We've come to see poor Jenny Jones.
>   Poor Jenny Jones is washing, you can't see her.
>   We've come to see poor Jenny Jones.
>   Poor Jenny Jones is drying, you can't see her.
>   We've come to see poor Jenny Jones.
>   Poor Jenny Jones is starching, you can't see her.

We've come to see poor Jenny Jones.
Poor Jenny Jones is ironing, you can't see her.
We've come to see poor Jenny Jones.
Poor Jenny Jones is dead, you can't see her.
What shall we follow, in red, blue, or black?
Red's for the soldier, blue for the sailor,
Black for the dead.

—Enborne School, Berks (Miss M. Kimber).

XIV.   Come to see Miss Jenny Jones,
         Miss Jenny Jones, Miss Jenny Jones;
         Come to see Miss Jenny Jones,
         And how is she to-day?

         Miss Jenny Jones is washing, washing, washing,
         Miss Jenny Jones is washing,
         You can't see her to-day.

         Farewell, ladies, ladies, ladies, and gentlemen too.

[Miss Jenny Jones is drying, starching, ironing, ill, worse, dying, and dead in turn. Then—]

         What shall we dress her in,
         Dress her in, dress her in?
         What shall we dress her in,
         Dress her in red?

         Red's what the soldiers wear,
         The soldiers wear, the soldiers wear,
         Red's what the soldiers wear,
         And that won't do.

         What shall we dress her in,
         Dress her in, dress her in?
         What shall we dress her in,
         Dress her in blue?

         Blue's what the sailors wear,
         Sailors wear, sailors wear;
         Blue's what the sailors wear,
         And that won't do.

What shall we dress her in,
Dress her in, dress her in ?
What shall we dress her in,
Dress her in black ?

Black's what the mourners wear,
The mourners wear, the mourners wear ;
Black's what the mourners wear,
And that won't do.

What shall we dress her in,
Dress her in, dress her in ?
What shall we dress her in,
Dress her in white ?

White's what the dead wear,
The dead wear, the dead wear ;
White's what the dead wear,
And that will do.   —Liphook, Hants (Miss Fowler).

XV.   Come to see Jinny Jones, Jinny Jones,
      Come to see Jinny Jones,
          And where is she now ?

      Jinny is washing, is washing,
      Jinny is washing,
          And you can't see her now.

      Very well, very well, lady, lady,
      Very well, lady,
          That will do.

[Then follow—   (1) starching,
                     (2) ironing,
                     (3) dying,
                     (4) dead.]

      What shall we follow in, follow in ?
      What shall we follow in ?
          We'll follow in blue.

Blue is for sailors, for sailors,
Blue is for sailors,
    And that won't do.
    [*or*, You can't follow her so.]

[Then follow—Red is for soldiers,
White is for weddings,
Yellow is for babies.]

Black is not deep enough, deep enough,
    That won't do.

What shall we follow in, follow in ?

We'll follow her in crape, crape [pronounced
    cray-ape].

You may follow her in crape, crape,
You may follow her in crape,
    That will do.   —Deptford (Miss E. Chase).

XVI. I've come to see Georgina, Georgina, Georgina,
I've come to see Georgina, how's she to-day ?

She's upstairs washing, washing, washing,
She's upstairs washing, and can't get away.

O very well, ladies, ladies, ladies,
We'll come another day.

We've come to see Georgina, Georgina, Georgina,
We've come to see Georgina, how's she to-day ?

She's upstairs ironing, ironing, ironing,
She's upstairs ironing, and can't get away.

[Then the two verses are repeated—
O very well, ladies.
We've come to see Georgina.
Then follows—]

She was coming downstairs with a basin of water, and
    she fell down and broke her toe, and she's dead.

And what shall we dress her in, dress her in, dress
    her in ?

And what shall we dress her in ? Dress her in red.

Red for the soldiers, soldiers, soldiers,
Red for the soldiers, and that shan't do.

[Then follow blue for the sailors, black for the mourners, and finally—]

What shall we dress her in, dress her in, dress her in?
What shall we dress her in?   Dress her in white.

White for the dead people, dead people, dead people,
White for the dead people, and that will do.
                    —Auchencairn, Kirkcudbright (A. C. Haddon).

XVII.   How's poor Jenny jo, Jenny jo, Jenny jo?
        He's very ill.
        Oh, very good, very good, very good.
        How's poor Jenny jo, Jenny jo, Jenny jo?
        He's fallen downstairs and broken his neck.
        Oh, very good, very good, very good.
        How's poor Jenny jo, Jenny jo, Jenny jo?
        He's dead.
        Oh, very good, very good, very good.
                    —Annaverna, Louth, Ireland (Miss R. Stephen).

(b) Two children stand apart; one, who personates the Mother, stands still and holds out her skirts with both hands; the other personates Jenny Jones, and kneels or stoops down in a crouching position behind her companion's outstretched skirts. The other players form a line by joining hands. They sing the first, third, and every alternate verse, advancing and retiring in line while doing so. The Mother sings the answers to their questions, standing still and hiding Jenny Jones all the time from view. When the verses are finished, Jenny Jones lies down as if she were dead, and the Mother stands aside. Two of the other players then take up Jenny Jones, one by the shoulders and the other by the feet, and carry her a little distance off, where they lay her on the ground. All the players follow, generally two by two, with their handkerchiefs at their eyes and heads lowered, pretending to grieve.

This is the more general way of playing the game. In those versions where the reply, "Very well, ladies," occurs, this is

sung by the line of children just before they sing, " We've come
to see Jenny Jones." Sometimes, as in the Berrington and
Chirbury game, two lines of children facing each other advance
and retire, singing the verses. They then carry Jenny Jones to
a corner, lay her down, stand in a circle round, and sing to her
the last verse. In the Hants versions sent by Miss Mendham, six or eight children carry Jenny stretched out and flat,
lay her down, cover her over, and then sing the last lines.
The rest of the children follow them. In the Irish (Belfast)
version the game is played in the same way; the funeral is
arranged, when Jenny suddenly comes to life again (W. H.
Patterson). In the Southampton version, after the carrying of
Jenny by her head and feet to the grave, and the other children
following and standing round, Jenny Jones rises up and pursues the children. She is called the Ghost. The children run
away in affected terror, calling out, " The Ghost !" Whoever
she catches becomes Jenny Jones in the next game. This
incident is also played in the Barnes, Northants, Annaverna,
co. Louth, Enborne and Liphook versions.

(c) This game is played very generally throughout the
country, and I have other versions collected from Earls Heaton
(Mr. H. Hardy), Barnes (A. B. Gomme), Cambridge (Mrs.
Haddon), Hampshire (Miss Mendham), Frodingham (Miss Peacock), Cowes, Isle of Wight (Miss E. Smith), Sulhampstead,
Berks (Miss Thoyts), and Platt, Kent (Miss Burne). These
versions are so similar to the Hanwell version, with the exception of the " Very well, ladies," that it is needless to print
them in full; special differences are noted hereafter. In some
places the game is said in a sing-song manner.

Some of the versions differ from the general type in two
ways—first, in the method of playing; secondly, in the wording
of the verses. The differences in the method of playing direct
attention to the connection of the game with ancient custom.
The game is always played by the players taking sides; but
one method is for one side to consist of only two children
(Mother and Jenny Jones), and the other side to consist of all
the other players; while the other method is for the players to
be divided into two sides of about equal numbers, each side

advancing and retiring in line when singing their part. Jenny Jones in some cases walks with the girls in her line until the funeral, when she is carried to the grave, and in others she stands alone behind the line. The way of performing the funeral also differs. Generally two of the players carry Jenny to the grave, the rest following two by two; but in one Hampshire version six or eight children carry Jenny, stretched out and flat, to the grave, and cover her over; in Holywood, co. Down, she is carried sitting on the crossed hands of two players; while in some versions no funeral is apparently performed, the words only being sung. Another significant incident is the Ghost. An additional incident occurs in the Liphook version, which represents her being "swung to life again" by two of the players.

These differences may perhaps be immaterial to the meaning and origin of the game, but they are sufficiently indicative of early custom to suggest the divergence of the game in modern times towards modern custom. Thus the players divided line-by-line follow the general form for children playing singing games, and it would therefore suggest itself as the earlier form for this game. The change of the game from the line-by-line action to the mother-and-line action would indicate a corresponding change in the prevailing custom which influenced the game. This custom was the wooing by a band of suitors of girls surrounded by their fellow-villagers, which became obsolete in favour of ordinary marriage custom. The dropping out of this custom would cause the game to change from a representation of both wooing and burial to one of burial only. As burial only the mother-and-line action is sufficient, but the presence of a wooing incident in the earlier form of the game is plainly revealed by the verse which sings, "Fare ye well, ladies," or, as it has become in the English variant, "Very well, ladies."

The difference in the wording of the versions is slight, and does not need formal analysis. Domestic occupation is shown throughout, washing and its attendants, drying, folding, starching and ironing being by far the most numerous, brewing, and baking only occurring in one. Illness, dying, and death are the usual forms for the later verses, but illness and dying are lost in several versions. The choosing of colours is in some versions not for the mourners but for the dead maiden, and in these cases (six) white is the colour chosen, for " white's what the dead wear."

This question of colours for the dead is a very important one. The dressing of the dead body of a maiden in white by her girl companions, and the carrying of the body by them to the grave, are known village customs, the whole village being invited to the funeral. The rising of the dead lover, and the belief that excessive mourning over a loved one disturbs his or her rest in the grave, thus causing the dead to rise and speak, are shown in old ballads; the belief that spirits of the dead haunt churchyards and places of their former abode may also be adduced in illustration of the ghost incident.

(d) The methods of playing, and the incidents revealed by the verses sung, show that this is perhaps the most realistic of all the singing games, the daily occupation, the illness, death, and burial being portrayed, first, in the words of the rhymes, and secondly, by the accompanying action. The Scottish versions make the opening incident that of a lover coming to the house of the loved one, then proceed to the domestic occupation, and finally to the death incident; while the English versions give the idea of village friends calling upon a favourite companion, and subsequently attending her funeral. That the former is the older of the two versions is confirmed by the great probability of the name "Jenny Jones" being a degraded form of "Janet jo." There is some evidence for this. The Sporle version gives it as "Jenny Joe," which is clearly a misunderstood rendering of "Jenny jo.' The corruption of this into "Jenny Jones" is exactly what might be expected from modern English ignorance of the pretty meaning of the word jo, "dear;" and to what lengths this corruption may proceed under such influences may be seen by versions from Earls Heaton, where we have " Jingy Jog;" Leeds, where we get "Jilly Jog;" and the Edinburgh version, where we have " Georgina."

This would be an argument for the Scottish home of the

rhymes, and for the direct borrowing of the name from Scotland by the English villagers. In furtherance of this view the following passage from Chambers may be quoted :—

In the Stewartry of Kirkcudbright, "Janet Jo" is a dramatic entertainment amongst young rustics. Suppose a party has met in a harvest or winter evening round a good peat fire, and it is resolved to have "Janet Jo" performed. Two undertake to personate a goodman and a goodwife; the rest a family of marriageable daughters. One of the lads, the best singer of the party, retires, and equips himself in a dress proper for representing an old bachelor in search of a wife. He comes in, bonnet in hand, bowing, and sings—

> Guid e'en to ye, maidens a',
> Maidens a', maidens a',
> Guid e'en to ye, maidens a',
> Be ye or no.

> I'm come to court Janet jo,
> Janet jo, Janet jo,
> I'm come to court Janet jo,
> Janet, my jo.

Goodwife sings—What'll ye gie for Janet jo,
> Janet jo, Janet jo ?
> What'll ye gie for Janet jo,
> Janet, my jo ?

Wooer—I'll gie ye a peck o' siller,
> A peck o' siller, peck o' siller,
> I'll gie ye a peck o' siller,
> For Janet, my jo.

Goodwife says—Gae awa', ye auld carle !

Then sings—Ye'se never get Janet jo,
> Janet jo, Janet jo,
> Ye'se never get Janet jo,
> Janet, my jo.

The wooer hereupon retires, singing a verse expressive of mortification, but soon re-enters with a reassured air, singing—

> I'll gie ye a peck o' gowd,
> A peck. o' gowd, a peck o' gowd,
> I'll gie ye a peck o' gowd,
>   For Janet, my jo.

The matron gives him a rebuff as before, and he again retires discomfited, and again enters, singing an offer of "twa pecks o' gowd," which, however, is also refused. At his next entry he offers "three pecks o' gowd," at which the good wife brightens up and sings—

> Come ben. beside Janet jo,
> Janet jo, Janet jo,
> Ye're welcome to Janet jo,
>   Janet, my jo.

The suitor then advances gaily to his sweetheart, and the affair ends in a scramble for kisses.—*Popular Rhymes*, pp. 141, 142.

On the other hand, it must not be overlooked that this game-drama and the game of "Janet Jo" have no connection beyond the name of the heroine and the wooing incident; so that the borrowing, if borrowing there be, might have been by Scotland, who improved the commonplace "Jenny Jones" into the pretty sweetness of her Scottish namesake. The Scottish version of the game leaves out the question of the colours for mourning, but, on the other hand, it contains the very important incident of the restoration of the dead. Chambers (*Popular Rhymes*, p. 141) suggests that this incident was introduced for the purpose of beginning the game again, but this seems extremely doubtful, in consideration of the Liphook variant, in which Miss Fowler says, "It is no uncommon thing for 'Jenny Jones' to be swung into life again;" and the still more significant Southampton version, where "'Jenny Jones' appears in the character of the Ghost, and scatters and pursues the surrounding mourners." This detail is also used by the Northants and Barnes children, the version of whose game is very like the Southampton one. On the whole, the analysis would suggest that there has been a game played by the children of both England and Scotland, the leading incidents of which have been varied in accordance with the conditions of life. Mr. Napier (*Folk-lore Record,* iv. 474), in his description of the West Scotland example, evidently considered the game to be thoroughly representative of Scottish life, and this, indeed, seems to be the most striking feature of the game in all the variants. The domestic economy which they reveal is in no case out of keeping with the known facts of everyday peasant life, and many a mother has denied to her child's friends the companionship they desired because of the work to be done.

In most cases the burden of the song rests upon the question of health, but in two cases, namely, Colchester and Deptford, the question is put as to where "Jenny Jones" is at the time of the visit. It is curious that the refrain of "Farewell, ladies," should appear in such widely separated districts as Scotland, Northamptonshire, Norfolk, Middlesex, Hants, Lincoln, and Barnes.

With reference to the colours for mourning, there is an obvious addition of crape introduced into the Deptford version which is very suggestive of the decadence going on. The four colours used in most versions are red, blue, white, and black, colours which have been known to the people from ancient times. Black is accepted as the correct colour in all versions except five, where white is declared to be the colour which the dead wear. The method of question and answer is adopted for all the rhyme-movements. The tune of the game, with but slight variation, in all the versions is the same as that given from Platt, near Wrotham, except the two which are printed from Northants and Belfast.

Jenny Mac

> Jenny Mac, Jenny Mac, Jenny Macghie,
> Turn your back about to me ;
> And if you find an ill baubee,
> Lift it up and gie't to me.

Two girls cross their arms behind their backs, and thus taking hold of each other's hands, parade along together, by daylight or moonlight, occasionally turning upon their arms,

as indicated in the rhyme.   Another rhyme for this amusement is—

> A basket, a basket, a bonny penny basket,
> A penny to you, and a penny to me,
> Turn about the basket.
>
> —Chambers's *Popular Rhymes*, p. 123.

See " Basket."

Jib-Job-Jeremiah

An undescribed Suffolk game.—Moor's *Suffolk Words*,
p. 238.

Jiddy-cum-jiddy

A northern name for " See Saw."

Jingle-the-bonnet

A game in which two or more put a halfpenny each, or any
piece of coin, into a cap or bonnet.   After jingling or shaking
them together, they are thrown on the ground; and he who
has most heads when it is his turn to jingle, gains the stakes
which were put into the bonnet.—Jamieson.

Halliwell (*Dictionary*) says this is a northern name for the
game of "Shake Cap," and Brockett (*North Country Words*)
speaks of it as a game much practised among the young pitmen
and keelmen.

Jingo-ring

> Here we go by jingo-ring, jingo-ring, jingo-ring,
> Here we go by jingo-ring, and round by merry-ma-tansy.
>
> —Sporle, Norfolk (Miss Matthews).

Sung to the " Mulberry or " Ivy bush " tune.

The children form a ring and dance round singing.   At the
last word they all fall down.

See " Merry-ma-tansa.

Jinkie

A game among children, in which they run round a table
trying to catch one whose business is by quick turns to elude
them.—Jamieson.

Jock and Jock's Man

A juvenile sport in which the *bon camarada* is to repeat all the pranks which the leader can perform.—Brockett's *North Country Words.*

See "Follow my Gable," "Follow my Leader."

Jockie Blind-man

Scotch name for "Blind Man's Buff."—Jamieson.
See "Blind Man's Buff."

Joggle along

I. Come all you young men
        In your youthful ways,
    And sow your wild oats
        In your youthful days.
    Then you'll be happy,
    Then you'll be happy,
        As you grow old.
    For the day's far spent,
        And the night's coming on,
    So give us your arm, and
        We'll joggle along.
                —Penzance, Cornwall (Mrs. Mabbott).

II. Come all ye young men, with your wicked ways,
    Sow all your wild oats in your youthful days,
    That we may live happy, that we may live happy,
    That we may live happy when we grow old.
    The day is far spent, the night's coming on,
    Give us your arm, and we'll joggle along,
    That we may live happy, &c., &c.
                —Cornwall (*Folk-lore Journal*, v. 57).

(*b*) There must be an odd number of players at this game. They form into couples, each standing behind the other, making a ring, the girls inside, one boy standing alone in the middle. As they go round they sing the verse. At the end each boy leaves hold of his partner's arm and catches the arm of the girl in front, the one who is standing in the centre trying in

the confusion to get into a place.   If he succeeds, the child left
out has to be the one in the centre the next time.

(*c*) Mr. Newell (*Games*, p. 101) says this game was called
the "Baptist Game" in Virginia, where it is said to be enjoyed
by pious people who will not dance.   The American game is
played in the same way as the English one.   Mr. Newell gives
the tune to which the game was sung.   The words are almost
identical.   This game is played in the same way as "Jolly
Miller," which see.

Johnny Rover

One boy is chosen to be Johnny Rover.   The other players
stand near him.   Rover cries out—

> A [I] warn ye ance, A warn you twice;
> A warn ye three times over;
> A warn ye a' t' be witty an' wise
> An flee fae Johnny Rover.

While the words are being repeated all the players are putting
themselves on the alert, and when they are finished they run
off in all directions, with Rover in full pursuit.   If a player
is hard pressed he has the privilege of running to "Parley,"
the place from which the players started, and which in all
games is an asylum.   If he is caught before he reaches it, he
becomes Johnny Rover for the next game.   The one first
captured becomes Rover.—Keith (Rev. W. Gregor).

Jolly Fishermen

—Tean, North Staffs. (Miss Burne).

I.   They were two jolly fishermen,
    They were two jolly fishermen,

They were two jolly fishermen,
And just come from the sea,
And just come from the sea.
They cast their nets into the sea,
And jolly fish caught we,
And jolly fish caught we,
And jolly fish caught we,
They cast their nets into the sea,
And jolly fish caught we.
        —Tean and Cheadle, North Staffs. (Miss Burne).

II.   There was three jolly fishermen,
        And they all put out to sea.
    They cast their nets into the sea,
        And the [three ?] jolly fish caught we.
            —North Staffs. Potteries (Mrs. Thomas Lawton).

(*b*) A circle is formed by joining hands, and two children stand in the centre. They walk round. At the seventh line the two in the centre each choose one child from the ring, thus making four in the centre. They then sing the remaining four lines. The two who were first in the centre then go out, and the game begins again, with the other two players in the centre.

(*c*) Miss Burne says this game is more often played as "Three Jolly Fishermen." At Cheadle, North Staffs., a few miles distant from Tean, this game is played by grown-up men and women.

Jolly Hooper

I.   Here comes a [or one] jolly hooper,
        Ring ding di do do,
        Ring ding di do do.

    And who are you looking for,
    In a ring ding di do do,
    In a ring ding di do do ?

    I am looking for one of your daughters,
    In a ring ding di do do,
    In a ring ding di do do.

What shall her name be,
In a ring ding di do do,
In a ring ding di do do ?

Her name shall be [Sarah],
In a ring ding di do do,
In a ring ding di do do.

Sarah shall ramble,
In a ring ding di do do,
In a ring ding di do do,
All around the chimney [jubilee] pot in 1881.
—Deptford, Kent (Miss Chase).

II.   I've come for one of your daughters,
With a ring a ding a my dolly;
I've come for one of your daughters
On this bright shining night.

Pray, which have you come for,
With a ring a ding a my dolly?
Pray which have you come for
On this bright shining night?

I've come for your daughter Mary,
With a ring a ding a my dolly;
I've come for your daughter Mary
On this bright shining night.

Then take her, and welcome,
With a ring a ding a my dolly;
Then take her, and welcome,
On this bright shining night [incomplete].
—Sheffield (S. O. Addy).

(*b*) A number of children stand against a wall, and a row of other children face them. They walk backwards and forwards, singing the first and third verses. Then the children who are standing still (against the wall) answer by singing the second and fourth verses. When these are sung the moving line of children take Mary and dance round, singing " some lines which my informant," says Mr. Addy, " has forgotten."

(c) I have no description of the way Miss Chase's game is played. It, too, is probably an incomplete version. The words "Ring ding di do do" show a possible connection between this and games of the "Three Dukes a-riding" type. They may or may not be variants of the same game.

See "Here comes a Lusty Wooer," "Here comes a Virgin," "Jolly Rover," "Three Dukes."

Jolly Miller

—Epworth, Doncaster (C. C. Bell).

—Earls Heaton (H. Hardy).

—Derbyshire (Mrs. Harley).

I.   There was a jolly miller, and he lived by himself,
     As the wheel went round he made his pelf;
     One hand in the hopper, and the other in the bag,
     As the wheel went round he took his grab.
                                  —Leicester (Miss Ellis).

II. There was a jolly miller, he lived by himself,
     As the mill went round he made his wealth;
     One hand in the hopper, another in his bag,
     As the wheel went round he made his grab.
                              —Liphook, Hants (Miss Fowler).

III. There was a jolly miller, and he lived by himself,
     As the wheel goes round he makes his wealth;
     One hand in his hopper, and the other in his bag,
     As we go round he makes his grab.
                          —Monton, Lancashire (Miss Dendy).

IV. There was a jolly miller, and he lived by himself,
     As the mill went round he gained his wealth;
     One hand in the hopper, and the other in the bag,
     As the mill went round he made his grab.

     Sandy he belongs to the mill,
     And the mill belongs to Sandy still,
     And the mill belongs to Sandy.
                              —Addy's *Sheffield Glossary*.

V.   There was a jolly miller, and he lived by himself,
     As the wheel went round he made his wealth;
     One hand in the upper and the other in the bank,
     As the wheel went round he made his wealth.
                          —Earls Heaton, Yorks. (Herbert Hardy).

VI. There was a jolly miller, and he lived by himself,
     As the wheel went round he made his grab;
     One hand in the other, and the other in the bag,
     As the wheel went round he made his grab.
                          —Nottinghamshire (Miss Winfield).

VII. There was a jolly miller, and he lived by himself (or by
the Dee),
The sails went round, he made his ground;
One hand in his pocket, the other in his bag.
—North Staffs. Potteries (Miss A. A. Keary).

(*b*) This game requires an uneven number of players. All
the children except one stand in couples arm in arm, each
couple closely following the other. This forms a double ring or
wheel (fig. 1). The odd child stands in the centre. The children
forming the wheel walk round in a circle and sing the verse.
When they come to the word "grab," those children standing
on the *inside* of the wheel leave hold of their partners' arms,
and try to catch hold of the one standing immediately in front
of their previous partners. The child in the centre (or Miller)

Fig. 1

Fig 2

tries (while they are changing places) to secure a partner and
place (fig. 2). If he succeeds in doing this, the one then left out
becomes the Miller. At Leicester the "odd" child, or "miller,"
stands *outside* the wheel or ring, instead of being in the centre,
and it is the outside children who change places. Mr. Addy,
in the Sheffield version, says, "The young men stand in the
outer ring, and the young women in the inner. A man stands
within the inner circle, quite near to it. The men try and grasp
the arm of the girl in front of them, and the man in the centre
also tries to grasp one; the man he displaces taking his place
as Miller. Then the three last lines are sung."

(*c*) Versions of this game, almost identical with the Leicester
version given here (with the exception that the word "wealth"
ends the second line instead of "pelf"), have been sent me
from East Kirkby, Lincolnshire (Miss K. Maughan); Epworth,

Doncaster (Mr. C. C. Bell); Settle, Yorks. (Rev. W. S. Sykes); Derbyshire (Mrs. Harley); Redhill, Surrey (Miss G. Hope); Ordsall, Nottinghamshire (Miss Matthews); Brigg, Lincolnshire (Miss J. Barker); and there are other versions from Hersham, Surrey (*Folk-lore Record*, v. 86); Cornwall (*Folklore Journal*, v. 57); Derbyshire (*Folk-lore Journal*, i. 385); Oswestry, Ellesmere (*Shropshire Folk-lore*, p. 512). Miss Peacock sends a version which obtains at Lincoln, Horncastle, Winterton, and Anderby, Lincolnshire, and in Nottinghamshire; it is identical with the Liphook version. Two versions from Sporle, Norfolk, which vary slightly from the Leicester, have been sent by Miss Matthews. The versions given from Lancashire, Yorks., Nottingham, and North Staffs. have been selected to show the process of decadence in the game. "Hopper" has first become "upper," and then "other." Of the North Staffs. Potteries version Miss Keary says, "How it ends I have never been able to make out; no one about here seems to know either." With the exception of these few variants, it is singular how stereotyped the words of the rhyme have become in this game.

(*d*) This game may owe its origin to the fact of the miller in olden times paying himself in kind from the corn brought to him to be ground. The miller is a well-known object of satire in old ballads and mediæval writers. It is, however, probable that the custom which formerly prevailed at some of the public festivals, of catching or "grabbing" for sweethearts and wives, is shown in this game. For instance, to account for a Scottish custom it is said that St. Cowie, patron saint of two parishes of Campbeltown, proposed that all who did not find themselves happy and contented in the marriage state, should be indulged with an opportunity of parting and making a second choice. For that purpose he instituted an annual solemnity, at which all the unhappy couples in his parish were to assemble at his church; and at midnight all present were blindfolded and ordered to run round the church at full speed, with a view of mixing the lots in the urn. The moment the ceremony was over, without allowing an instant for the people present to recover from their confusion, the word

" Cabbay (seize quickly) was pronounced, upon which every man laid hold of the first female he met with. Whether old or young, handsome or ugly, good or bad, she was his wife till the next anniversary of this custom (Guthrie's *Scottish Customs*, p. 168). Another old wedding superstition is alluded to by Longfellow :—

" While the bride with roguish eyes,
Sporting with them, now escapes and cries,
' Those who catch me, married verily this year will be.' "

See " Joggle Along."

Jolly Rover

—Derbyshire (Mrs. Harley).

Here comes one jolly rover, jolly rover, jolly rover,
Here comes one jolly rover, jolly rover, jolly rover,
A roving all day.

And what do you rove for, rove for, rove for ?
And what do you rove for ?
Lily white and shining.

I rove for my pleasure, my pleasure, my pleasure,
I rove for my pleasure, my pleasure, my pleasure,
Lily white and shining.

And what is your pleasure, your pleasure, your pleasure ?
What is your pleasure ?
Lily white and shining.

My pleasure's for to marry you, to marry you, to marry
you,
My pleasure's for to marry you,
Lily white and shining.

So through the kitchen and through the hall,
I choose the fairest of them all,
The fairest one that I can see
Is —, so come to me.
—Derbyshire (Mrs. Harley).

(*b*) A long row of children walk to and fro. One child, facing them on the opposite side, represents the Rover. He sings the first, third, and fifth verses. The row of children sing the second and fourth in response. After the fifth verse is sung the Rover skips round the long row, singing the sixth verse to the tune of "Nancy Dawson," or "Round the Mulberry bush." He chooses one of them, who goes to the opposite side with him, and the game goes on until all are rovers like himself.

See "Here comes a Lusty Wooer," "Jolly Hooper."

Jolly Sailors

I.	Here comes one [some] jolly, jolly sailor boy,
Who lately came on shore;
He [they] spent his time in drinking wine
As we have done before.

We are the Pam-a-ram-a-ram,
We are the Pam-a-ram-a-ram,
And those who want a pretty, pretty girl,
Must kiss her on the shore,
Must kiss her on the shore.
—Warwick (from a little girl, through Mr. C. C. Bell).

II.	He was a jolly, jolly sailor boy,
Who had lately come ashore;
He spent his time in drinking wine
As he had done before.

Then we will have a jolly, jolly whirl,
Then we will have a jolly, jolly whirl,
And he who wants a pretty little girl
Must kiss her on the shore.
—Forest of Dean, Gloucestershire (Miss Matthews).

III. Here comes one jolly sailor,
      Just arrived from shore,
      We'll spend our money like jolly, jolly joes,
      And then we'll work for more.

      We'll all around, around and around,
      And if we meet a pretty little girl
      We'll call her to the shore.
                          —Northants (Rev. W. D. Sweeting).

IV. Here comes four jolly sailor boys,
     Just lately come ashore;
     They spend their days in many merry ways,
     As they have done before.

     Round, round the ring we go,
     Round, round the ring,
     And he that choose his bonny, bonny lass
     Must kiss her on the floor.
                   —Raunds (*Northants Notes and Queries*, i. 232).

 V. Here come three jolly, jolly, jolly boys
     As lately come from shore;
     We will spend our time on a moonlight night
     As we have done before.

     We will have a round, a round, a round,
     We will have a round, a round, a round;
     Let the lad that delights in a bonny, bonny lass,
     Let him kiss her on the ground.
                          —Earls Heaton, Yorks. (Herbert Hardy).

VI. Here comes three jolly, jolly sailors,
     Just arrived on shore;
     We'll spend our money like merry, merry men,
     And then we'll work for more.

     Hurrah for the round, round ring,
     Hurrah for the round, round ring;
     And he that loves a pretty, pretty girl,
     Let him call her from the ring.
                          —Shipley, Horsham (*Notes and Queries*,
                             8th series, i. 210, Miss Busk).

(*b*) This game is played at Warwick as follows :—The children form a large ring, clasping hands and standing still. One child walks round inside the ring, singing the verses. This child then chooses another from the ring, bending on one knee and kissing her hand. The lines are then repeated, the two walking arm in arm round the inside of the ring. Another child is chosen out of the ring by the one who was chosen previously. This goes on until all are chosen out of the ring, walking two by two round inside. When the ring will no longer hold them, the two walk round outside. At Northants the ring walks round, and the child is *outside* the ring. Partners are chosen, and the two walk round outside the ring. The first two walk together till there is a third, then the three walk together till there is a fourth, then they go in couples. In the Northants version, from Raunds, four boys stand in the centre of the ring. When the verses are sung they choose four girls, and then take their places in the ring. The four girls then choose four lads, and so on. At Earls Heaton the children stand against a wall in a line. Another child walks up and down singing the verses, and chooses a partner. He spreads a handkerchief on the ground, and they kneel and kiss.

(*c*) The Shipley version is a "Kiss in the Ring" game. A version sent by the Rev. W. Slater Sykes from Settle, Yorkshire, is almost identical with the Earls Heaton version. Northall (*Folk Rhymes*, p. 369) says "to kiss on the floor" —*i.e.*, not in secret. He gives the words of a sort of musical catch, sung in the Midlands, similar in character to this game, which may once have been used in some courting game. Mr. Newell (*Games*, p. 124) gives a version sung in the streets of New York, and considers it to be a relic of antiquity, a similar round being given in *Deuteromelia*, 1609.

Jowls

A game played by boys, much the same as "Hockey," and taking its name, no doubt, from the mode of playing, which consists in striking a wooden ball or knorr from the ground in any given direction with a sufficiently heavy stick, duly curved at the striking end.—Atkinson's *Cleveland Glossary*.

It is also given in *Yorkshire Glossary* (Whitby).

See "Bandy," "Doddart," "Hockey."

Jud

A game played with a hazel nut bored and run upon a string.—Dickinson's *Cumberland Glossary*.

Probably the same game as "Conkers."

See "Conkers."

Keeling the Pot

Brockett mentions that a friend informed him that he had seen a game played amongst children in Northumberland the subject of which was "Keeling the Pot." A girl comes in exclaiming, "Mother, mother, the pot's boiling ower." The answer is, "Then get the ladle and keel it." The difficulty is to get the ladle, which is "up a height," and the "steul" wants a leg, and the joiner is either sick or dead (*Glossary North Country Words*). A sentence from *Love's Labour's Lost*, "While greasy Joan doth keel the pot," illustrates the use of the term "keel."

See "Mother, Mother, the Pot Boils over."

Keppy Ball

In former times it was customary every year, at Easter and Whitsuntide, for the mayor, aldermen, and sheriff of Newcastle, attended by the burgesses, to go in state to a place called the Forth, a sort of mall, to countenance, if not to join in the play of "Keppy ba" and other sports. This diversion is still in part kept up by the young people of the town (Brockett's *North Country Words*). It is also mentioned in Peacock's *Manley and Corringham Glossary*, and in Ross and Stead's *Holderness Glossary*.

Mr. Tate (*History of Alnwick*) says that a favourite pastime of girls, "Keppy ball," deserves a passing notice, because accompanied by a peculiar local song. The name indicates the character of the game; "kep" is from *cepan*, Anglo-Saxon, "kappan," Teut., "to catch or capture;" for when the game was played at by several, the ball was thrown into the air and "kepped," or intercepted, in its descent by one or other of the girls, and it was then thrown up again to be caught by some other.   But when the song was sung it was played out by one girl, who sent the ball against a tree and drove it back again as often as she could, saying the following rhymes, in order to divine her matrimonial future :—

> Keppy ball, keppy ball, Coban tree,
> Come down the long loanin' and tell to me,
> The form and the features, the speech and degree
> Of the man that is my true love to be.

> Keppy ball, keppy ball, Coban tree,
> Come down the long loanin' and tell to me
> How many years old I am to be.

> One a maiden, two a wife,
> Three a maiden, four a wife, &c.

The numbers being continued as long as the ball could be kept rebounding against the tree.

The following from Halliwell's *Nursery Rhymes*, p. 298, is also used for ball divination.   To "cook" is to toss or throw.

> Cook a ball, cherry tree;
> Good ball, tell me
> How many years I shall be
> Before my true love I do see?
> One and two, and that makes three;
> Thankee, good ball, for telling of me.

See "Ball," "Cuckoo," "Monday."

Kibel and Nerspel

This game was played at Stixwold seventy years ago.   It resembled "Trap, Bat, and Ball."   *Kibel* = bat, *ner* = ball of maplewood, *spel* = trap, with a limock (pliant) stick fastened to it.   The score was made by hitting the *ner* a certain distance, but not by the striker running, as in "Rounders."—Miss M. Peacock.

See "Nur and Spell."

King by your leave

"A playe that children have, where one sytting blyndefolde in the midle, bydeth so tyll the rest have hydden themselves, and then he going to seeke them, if any get his place in the meane space, that same is kynge in his roome."—Huloet, 1572.

See "Hide and Seek."

King Cæsar

One player is chosen to be King Cæsar by lot or naming. All the others stand in two rows, one row at each end of the ground. A line is drawn on the ground in front of them to mark "dens." All the players must keep within this line. King Cæsar stands in the middle of the ground. Any number of the players can then rush across the ground from one den to another. King Cæsar tries to catch one as they run. When he catches a boy he must count from one to ten in succession before he leaves hold of the boy, that boy in the meantime trying to get away. If King Cæsar succeeds in holding a boy, this boy stays in the centre with him and assists in catching the other players (always counting ten before a captive is secured). The dens must always be occupied by some players. If all the players get into one den, King Cæsar can go into the empty den and say, "Crown the base, one, two, three," three times before any of the other players get across to that den. If he succeeds in doing this, he can select a boy to run across from one den to the other, which that boy must do, King Cæsar trying to catch him. Other and bigger boys can help this one to get across, to save him from being captured, either by carrying him or running across with him. The game ends when all have been captured and are in the centre. King Cæsar and the other captured boys can leave the centre if they each successively catch three players.—Barnes (A. B. Gomme).

This game is called "King-sealing" in Dorsetshire.

See "King of Cantland," "Lamploo."

King Come-a-lay

A game played by boys. Two sets of boys, or sides, strive which can secure most prisoners for the King. — Shetland (Jamieson).

King of Cantland

A game of children, in which one of a company, being chosen King o' Cantland, and two goals appointed at a considerable distance from each other, all the rest endeavoured to run from one goal to the other; and those whom the King can seize in their course, so as to lay his hand upon their heads (which operation is called winning them), become his subjects, and assist him in catching the remainder.—Dumfries (Jamieson). Jamieson adds: "This game is called 'King's Covenanter' in Roxburgh." He also refers to the game of "King and Queen of Cantelon," recorded by Mactaggart. He considers the origin of this game to be representative of the contentions about the "Debatable Lands" on the border. This game was played at University Coll. School, London, under the name of "Kings" (A. Nutt).

See "How many miles to Barley Bridge?" "King Cæsar."

King o' the Castle

One boy is chosen as King. He mounts on any convenient height, a knoll, or dyke, or big stone, and shouts—

A'm King o' the Castle,
An' fah (who) 'll ding (knock) me doon?

The players make a rush at the King, and try to pull him down. A tussle goes on for a longer or a shorter time, according to the strength of the King and his skill in driving off his assailants. The boy that displaces the King becomes King, and is in his turn assaulted in the same way. The game may go on for any length of time. Another form of words is—

I'm the King o' the Castle,
An' nane can ding me doon.
                                   —Keith (Rev. W. Gregor).

Other words sung by the Scotch children are—

I, Willy Wastle,
Stand on my castle,
And a' the dogs o' your toon
Will no drive Willie Wastle doon.

Chambers (*Popular Rhymes*, p. 114) records the tradition that when Oliver Cromwell lay at Haddington he sent to require the governor of Home Castle, in Berwickshire, to surrender;

the governor is said to have replied in the above quatrain of juvenile celebrity.

The London version is for the boys to run up a hillock, when one of them declares as follows—

I'm the King of the Castle ;
Get down, you dirty rascal,

whereupon he pushes down his companions. If another boy succeeds in getting his place he becomes King, and repeats the doggerel (G. L. Gomme). This is a very popular boys' game. Newell (*Games*, 164) mentions it as prevalent in Pennsylvania. See "Tom Tiddler's Ground."

King Plaster Palacey

The players are a King and his three sons named White Cap, Red Cap, Brown Cap. Red Cap says, " Plaster Palacey had a son, whose name was old daddy White Cap." White Cap, in an injured voice, says, "Me, sir ? " The King says, "Yes, sir." White Cap answers, "You're a liar, sir." The King then says, "Who then, sir ? " White Cap answers, "Old daddy Red Cap."—Deptford, Kent (Miss Chase).

The game as given above is obviously incomplete, and no description as to how the game was played was sent me. Newell (*Games*, p. 145), describes a game, " The Cardinal's Hat," which is probably a variant of the original game, of which the above is only a fragment. I remember once witnessing a game in which a ball was passed from player to player, and in which the dialogue was similar. When one player was told that the ball was in his possession, the answer was, " What, me, sir ? " " Yes, you, sir." " Not I, sir." " Who then, sir ? " " White Cap, sir ; " the questions and answers were again repeated for Red Cap, and Blue Cap. When it was Black Cap's turn, I think the ball was thrown by this player to some one else ; whoever was hit by the ball had to chase and capture one, who became questioner ; but my recollection of the game is too slight for me to be certain either of the dialogue or the way the game terminated (A. B. Gomme). A game described in *Suffolk County Folk-lore*, p. 62, is apparently a version of this. It is there described as a forfeit game.

King William

—Earls Heaton, Yorks. (H. Hardy).

I.   King William was King David's son,
     And all the royal race is run ;
     Choose from the east, choose from the west,
     Choose the one you love the best.

     Down on this carpet you shall kneel
     While the grass grows in yonder field ;
     Salute your bride and kiss her sweet,
     Rise again upon your feet.
                    —Hanging Heaton, Yorks. (H. Hardy).

II. King William was King David's son,
     All the royal race is run ;
     Choose from the east, choose from the west,
     Choose the one that you love best ;
     If she's not here to take her part,
     Choose another with all your heart.
                              —Sheffield (S. O. Addy).

(*b*) In Sheffield a ring of young men and women is formed.
A man goes inside the ring and walks round within it, whilst the
others sing the verse.   The young man then chooses a sweetheart, and the two walk round arm-in-arm within the ring,
whilst the same verses are sung.   When the singing is ended,
the girl picks a young man, and so they all pair off.

(*c*) Mr. Addy entitles this game "Kiss in the Ring."   It
appears, however, from this description to lack the two
principal elements of most "kiss-in-the-ring" games—the
chase between pursued and pursuer, and the kissing in the
ring when the capture is made.   In the Hanging Heaton
version two children kneel and kiss in the middle of the ring.
Mr. Newell (*Games*, p. 73), in describing a game with a similar
rhyme, mentions a version which had been sent him from

Waterford, Ireland. He says, "We learn from an informant that in her town it was formerly played in this peculiar manner. Over the head of a girl who stood in the centre of a ring was held a shawl, sustained by four others grasping the corners." The game then proceeded as follows—

> King William was King George's son,
> From the Bay of Biscay O!
> Upon his breast he wore a star—
> Find your way to English schools.
> Down on the carpet you must kneel ;
> As the grass grows in the field,
> Salute your bride and kiss her sweet,
> And rise again upon your feet.

Then followed the game-rhyme, repeated with each stanza—

> Go choose you east, go choose you west,

apparently the same as last four lines of Sheffield version. King William is then supposed to enter—

> The first girl that I loved so dear,
> Can it be she's gone from me ?
> If she's not here when the night comes on,
> Will none of you tell me where she's gone ?

He then recognises the disguised girl—

> There's heart beneath the willow tree,
> There's no one here but my love and me.

"He had gone to the war, and promised to marry her when he came back. She wrapped a shawl about her head to see if he would recognise her." This was all the reciter could recollect; the lines of the ballad were sung by an old woman, the ring answering with the game-rhyme.

This version seems to indicate clearly that in this game we have preserved one of the ceremonies of a now obsolete marriage-custom—namely, the disguising of the bride and placing her among her bridesmaids and other young girls, all having veils or other coverings alike over their heads and bodies. The bridegroom has to select from among these maidens the girl whom he wished to marry, or whom he had already married, for until this was done he was not allowed to depart with his bride. This custom was continued in sport as one of the ceremonies to be gone through after the marriage was over, long after the custom itself was discontinued. For an instance of this see a "Rural Marriage in Lorraine," in *Folk-lore Record*, iii. 267–268. This ordeal occurs in more than one folk-tale, and it usually accompanies the incident of a youth having travelled for adventures, sometimes in quest of a bride. He succeeds in finding the whereabouts of the coveted girl, but before he is allowed by the father to take his bride away he is required to perform tasks, a final one being the choosing of the girl with whom he is in love from among others, all dressed alike and disguised. Our bridal veil may probably originate in this custom.

In the ballad from which Mr. Newell thinks the game may have originated, a maid has been given in marriage to another than her chosen lover. He rides to the ceremony with a troop of followers; the bride, seeing him approach, calls on her maidens to "take off her gold crown and coif her in linen white," to test her bridegroom's affection. This incident, I think, is not to test "affection," but the ordeal of recognising his bride, however disguised, and the fact that "the hero at once recognises his love, mounts with her on horseback, and flees to Norway," may be considered to support my view.

See also Brand, vol. ii. p. 141, under "Care Cloth."

King's Chair

Two children join hands, by crossing their arms, so as to form a seat. A third mounts on the crossed arms, and clasps the carriers round their necks, while they move on saying—

> King, King Cairy (carry)
> London lairy,
> Milk an bread,
> In the King's chairie.

This game is played at Keith, without the words. The words are used at Fochabers.—Rev. W. Gregor.

Jamieson says, "Lothian children, while carrying one of their number in this manner, repeat the following rhyme—

> Lend me a pin to stick i' my thumb,
> To carry the lady to London town."

He says this method of carrying is often used as a substitute for a chair in conveying adult persons from one place to another, especially when infirm. In other counties it is called " Queen's Cushion" and " Queen's Chair," also " Cat's Carriage."

Brockett (*North Country Words*) says, "' King's Cushion,' a sort of seat made by two persons crossing their hands, in which to place a third. The thrones on the reverses of the early Royal Seals of England and Scotland consist of swords, spears, snakes, &c., placed in the manner of a ' King's Cushion.'"

The method used is for both children to grasp the wrist of his left hand with the right, while he lays hold of the right wrist of his companion with his left hand. This way of hoisting or carrying is still used by schoolboys when they desire to honour a boy who has distinguished himself in the playground or schoolroom.

See " Carry my Lady to London."

Kirk the Gussie

A sort of play. The Gussie is a large ball, which one party endeavours to beat with clubs into a hole, while another party strives to drive it away. When the ball is lodged in the hole it is said to be " Kirkit."—Jamieson.

Kiss in the Ring

—Nottingham (Miss Youngman).

—Lancashire (Mrs. Harley).

—Earls Heaton, Yorks. (H. Hardy).

  I.   I sent a letter to my love,
        And on the way I dropped it ;
        And one of you have picked it up
        And put it in your pocket.
                   —Dorsetshire (*Folk-lore Journal*, vii. 213) ;
                   Penzance (Mrs. Mabbott).

  II.   I wrote a letter to my love, and on the way I lost it.
        Some one has picked it up.   Not you, not you (&c.),
          but you ! —Much Wenlock (*Shropshire Folk-lore*, p. 512).

  III.   I lost my supper last night, and the night before,
        And if I lose it this night, I shall never have it no more.
                —Berrington (*Shropshire Folk-lore*, p. 512).

  IV.   I've come to borrow the riddle (= sieve),
        There's a big hole in the middle.
        I've come to borrow the hatchet,
        Come after me and catch it.
                  —Chirbury (*Shropshire Folk-lore*, p. 512).

  V.   Down by the greenwood, down by the greenwood,
        Down by the greenwood tree,
        One can follow, one can follow,
        One can follow me.

        Where must I follow ? where must I follow?
        Follow, follow me.
        Where must I follow ? where must I follow ?
        Follow, follow me.   —Earls Heaton (H. Hardy).

  VI.   Mr. Monday was a good man,
        He whipped his children now and then ;
        When he whipped them he made them dance,
        Out of Scotland into France ;

Out of France into Spain,
Back to dear old England again.
O-u-t spells "out,"
If you please stand out.
I had a little dog and his name was Buff,
I sent him after a penn'orth of snuff,
He broke the paper and smelled the snuff,
And that's the end of my dog Buff.
He shan't bite you—he shan't bite you—he shan't bite
    you, &c., &c.—he *shall* bite you all over.
               —Dorsetshire (*Folk-lore Journal*, vii. 213).

VII.   I sent a letter to my love,
       I carried water in my glove,
       And by the way I dropped it.
           I did so!   I did so!

       I had a little dog that said "Bow! wow!"
       I had a little cat that said "Meow! meow!"
       Shan't bite you—shan't bite you—
       Shall bite you.   —Cornwall (*Folk-lore Journal*, v. 52).

VIII. I sent a letter to my love,
       I carried water in my glove,
       I dript it, I dropped it, and by the way I lost it.
           —Hersham, Surrey (*Folk-lore Record*, v. 87).

IX.   I have a pigeon in my pocket,
       If I have not lost it ;
          Peeps in, peeps out,
       By the way I've lost it ;
          Drip, drop,
       By the way I've lost it.   —Earls Heaton (H. Hardy).

X.   I have a pigeon in my pocket,
       It peeps out and in,
       And every time that I go round
       I give it a drop of gin.
       Drip it, drop it, drip it, drop it.
           —Settle, Yorkshire (Rev W. S. Sykes).

XI.   I sent a letter to my love,
      I thought I put it in my glove,
      But by the way I dropped it.
      I had a little dog said "Bow, wow, wow!"
      I had a little cat said "Mew, mew, mew!"
      It shan't bite you,
      It *shall* bite *you*.   —Bexley Heath (Miss Morris).

XII. I sent a letter to my love,
      And by the way I droppt it;
      I dee, I dee, I dee, I droppt it,
      And by the way I droppt it.   —Keith (Rev. W. Gregor).

XIII. I had a little dog, it shan't bite you,
      Shan't bite you, shan't bite you,
      Nor you, nor you, nor you.
      I had a little cat, it shan't scratch you,
      Shan't scratch you, nor you, nor you.

      I wrote a letter to my love, and on the way I dropped it.
      And one of you have picked it up and put it in your
            pocket.
      It wasn't you, it wasn't you, nor you, nor you, but it
            was *you*.   —London (A. B. Gomme).

XIV. I have a little dog and it lives in my pocket.
      It shan't bite you, &c.

      Now you're married I hope you'll enjoy
      First a girl and then a boy;
      Seven years gone, and two to come,
      So take her and kiss her and
      Send her off home.   —Wolstanton, North Staffs. Potteries
                                (Miss A. A. Keary).

(*b*) In Dorsetshire a ring is formed by all the players joining
hands except one. The odd player, carrying a handkerchief,
commences to walk slowly round the outside of the ring,
repeating the words; then, touching each one with her hand-

kerchief as she passes, she says, " Not you," "not you," "not you," &c., &c., till the favoured individual is reached, when it is changed to " But you ! " and his or her shoulder lightly touched at the same time. The first player then runs round the ring as fast as he can, pursued by the other, who, if a capture is effected (as is nearly always the case), is entitled to lead the first player back into the centre of the ring and claim a kiss. The first player then takes the other's place in the ring, and in turn walks round the outside repeating the same formula.—*Folk-lore Journal*, vii. 212 ; Penzance (Mrs. Mabbott).

In Shropshire, as soon as the player going round the ring has dropped the handkerchief on the shoulder of the girl he chooses, both players run *opposite ways* outside the ring, each trying to be the first to regain the starting-point. If the one who was chosen gets there first, no kiss can be claimed. It is often called " Drop-handkerchief," from the signal for the chase. The more general way of playing (either with or without words), as seen by me on village greens round London, is, when the handkerchief has been dropped, for the player to dart through the ring and in and out again under the clasped hands ; the pursuer must follow in and out through the same places, and must bring the one he catches into the ring before he can legally claim the kiss.

Elworthy (*West Country Words*), in describing this game, says : " The person behind whom the handkerchief is dropped is entitled to kiss the person who dropped it, if he or she can catch him or her, before the person can get round the ring to the vacant place. Of course, when a girl drops it she selects a favoured swain, and the chase is severe up to a point, but when a girl is the pursuer there often is a kind of donkey race lest she should have to give the kiss which the lad takes no pains to avoid." Mr. Elworthy does not mention any words being used, and it is therefore probable that this is the " Drop-hand-kerchief" game, which generally has no kissing. It also, in the way it is played, resembles " French Jackie." In the Wolstanton game, Miss Keary says : " If the owner of the handkerchief overtakes the one who is bitten as they run round, they shake hands and go into the middle of the ring, while the others sing the marriage formula. In Berkshire (*Antiq.* xxvii. 255) the game is played without words, and apparently no handkerchief or other sign is used. Miss Thoyts says the young man raises his hat when he embraces the young woman of his choice. To "throw (or fling) the handkerchief" is a common expression for an expected proposal of marriage which is more of a condescension than a complimentary or flattering one to the girl. "Kiss in the Ring" is probably a relic of the earliest form of marriage by choice or selection. The custom of dropping or sending a glove as the signal of a challenge may have been succeeded by the handkerchief in this game. Halliwell, p. 227, gives the game of "Drop Glove," in which a glove is used. For the use of handkerchiefs as love-tokens see Brand, ii. 92.

See " Drop Handkerchief," " French Jackie."

Kit-Cat

A game played by boys. Three small holes are made in the ground, triangularly about twenty feet apart, to mark the position of as many boys, each of whom holds a small stick, about two feet long. Three other boys of the adverse side pitch successively a piece of stick, a little bigger than one's thumb, called Cat, to be struck by those holding the sticks. On its being struck, the boys run from hole to hole, dipping the ends of their sticks in as they pass, and counting one, two, three, &c., as they do so, up to thirty-one, which is game. Or the greater number of holes gained in the innings may indicate the winners, as at cricket. If the Cat be struck and caught, the striking party is out, and another of his sidesmen takes his place, if the set be strong enough to admit of it. If there be only six players, it may be previously agreed that three *put outs* shall end the innings. Another mode of putting out is to throw the Cat home, after being struck, and placing or pitching it into an unoccupied hole, while the in-party are running. A certain number of misses (not striking the Cat) may be agreed on to be equivalent to a put out. The game may be played by two, placed as at cricket, or by four, or I believe more.—Moor's *Suffolk Words*; Holloway's *Dict. of Provincialisms*.

Brockett (*North Country Words*, p. 115) calls this "'Kitty-Cat,' a puerile game.

> Then in his hand he takes a thick bat,
> With which he used to play at 'Kit-Cat.'"
>
> —Cotton's *Works*, 1734, p. 88.

See "Cat and Do ;," "Cudgel," "Munshets," "Tip-Cat."

Kit-Cat-Cannio

A sedentary game, played by two, with slate and pencil, or pencil and paper. It is won by the party who can first get three marks (o's or x's) in a line; the marks being made alternately by the players o or x in one of the nine spots equidistant in three rows, when complete. He who begins has the advantage, as he can contrive to get his mark in the middle.—Moor's *Suffolk Words*.

The same game as "Nought and Crosses," which see.

Kittlie-cout

A game mentioned but not described by a writer in *Blackwood's Magazine*, August 1821, as played in Edinburgh. He mentions that the terms "hot" and "cold" are used in the game. The game of "Hide and Seek."—Jamieson.

Knapsack

One boy takes another by the feet, one foot over each shoulder, with his head downwards and his face to his back, and sets off running as fast as he can. He runs hither and thither till one or other of the two gets tired.—Keith (Rev. W. Gregor).

Knights

Two big boys take two smaller ones on their shoulders. The big boys act as horses, while the younger ones seated on their shoulders try to pull each other over. The "horses" may push and strike each other with their shoulders, but must not kick or trip up with their feet, or use their hands or elbows. The game is usually won by the Horse and Knight who throw their opponents twice out of three times (G. L. Gomme).

Strutt (*Sports*, p. 84) describes this, and says, "A sport of this kind was in practice with us at the commencement of the fourteenth century." He considers it to bear more analogy to wrestling than to any other sport. He gives illustrations, one

of which is here reproduced from the original MS. in the British Museum. The game is also described in the Rev. J. G. Wood's *Modern Playmate*, p. 12.

Knocked at the Rapper

The girl who spoke of this game, says Miss Peacock, could only remember its details imperfectly, but as far as she recollects it is played as follows :—The players dance round a centre child, leaving one of their number outside the circle. The dancers sing to the one in their midst—

Here comes ——,
He knocked at the rapper, and he pulled at the string,
Pray, Mrs. ——, is —— within ?

At "is —— within," the child outside the circle is named. The centre child says—

O no, she has gone into the town :
Pray take the arm-chair and sit yourself down.

The ring of children then sing—

> O no, not until my dearest I see,
> And then one chair will do for we.

Then all sing—

> My elbow, my elbow,
> My pitcher, and my can :
> Isn't —— —— a nice young girl ?

Mentioning the supposed sweetheart.

> Isn't —— —— as nice as she ?

Mentioning the outside child.

> They shall be married when they can agree.

Then the inside and outside children each choose a companion from the circle, and the rest repeat :—

> My elbow, my elbow, &c.

When the words have been sung a second time, the four children kiss, and the two from the circle take the places of the other, after which change the game begins again.—North Kelsey, Lincolnshire (Miss M. Peacock).

Knor and Spell

See " Nur and Spell."

Lab

A game of marbles (undescribed).—Patterson's *Antrim and Down Glossary*.

See " Lag."

Lady of the Land

Tong, Shropshire (Miss R. Harley).

I.   Here comes the lady of the land,
With sons and daughters in her hand ;
Pray, do you want a servant to-day ?

What can she do ?

She can brew, she can bake,
She can make a wedding cake
Fit for you or any lady in the land.

Pray leave her.

I leave my daughter safe and sound,
And in her pocket a thousand pound,
And on her finger a gay ring,
And I hope to find her so again.

—*Somerset and Dorset Notes and Queries*, i. 133.

II.   There camed a lady from other land,
      With all her children in her hand—
      Please, do you want a sarvant, marm?

      Leave her.

      I leaves my daughter zafe and zound,
      And in her pocket a thousan pound,
      And on her finger a goulden ring,
      And in her busum a silver pin.
      I hopes when I return,
      To see her here with you.
      Don't'e let her ramble; don't'e let her trot;
      Don't'e let her car' the mustard pot.

The Mistress says softly—
      She shall ramble, she shall trot,
      She shall carry the mustard pot.

—*Dorset County Chronicle*, April 1889;
Folk-lore Journal, vii. 228.

III. Here comes an old woman from Baby-land,
      With all her children in her hand.
      Pray take one of my children in.

[Spoken] What can your children do?

[Sung] One can bake, one can brew,
        And one can bake a lily-white cake.
        One can sit in the parlour and sing,
        And this one can do everything.

—Tong, Shropshire (Miss R. Harley).

IV.   Here comes a poor woman from Baby-land
      With three small children in her hand.
      One can brew, the other can bake,
      The other can make a pretty round cake.
      One can sit in the garden and spin,
      Another can make a fine bed for the king;
      Pray, ma'am, will you take one in?
                          —Halliwell's *Nursery Rhymes*, p. 72.

 V.   Here is a poor widow from Sandy Row,
      With all her children behind her.
      One can knit and one can sew,
      And one can make the winder go.
      Please take one in.

      Now poor Nellie she is gone
      Without a farthing in her hand,
      Nothing but a guinea gold ring.
      Good-bye, Nellie, good-bye!
                          —Belfast (W. H. Patterson).

VI.   Here comes an old woman from Baby-land,
      With six poor children by the hand.
      One can brew, one can bake,
      And one can make a lily-white cake;
      One can knit, one can spin,
      And one can make a bed for a king.
      Please will you take one in? [choose out one]

      Now poor —— she is gone
      Without a farthing in her hand,
      Nothing but a gay gold ring.
      Good-bye!   Good-bye!
      Good-bye, mother, good-bye!
                          —Isle of Man (A. W. Moore)

VII. Here comes a poor widow from Sandalam,
      With all her children at her hand;
      The one can bake, the other can brew,
      The other can make a lily-white shoe;
      Another can sit by the fire and spin,
      So pray take one of my daughters in.

The fairest one that I can see
Is pretty [Mary] come to me.

And now poor [Mary] she is gone
Without a guinea in her hand,
And not so much as a farthing.   Good-bye!
Good-bye, my love, good-bye!
                    —Forest of Dean, Gloucester (Miss Matthews).

VIII.   Here comes an old woman from Cumberland,
        With seven poor children in her hand;
        One can sing, the other can sew;
        One can sit up in the corner and cry, Alleluia!
        Choose the fairest you can see.
        The fairest one that I can see is ——, come to me.
        Now my daughter —— gone,
        A thousand pound in her pocket and a gold ring on her
            finger.
        Good-bye, mother, good-bye!
                    —Berkshire (Miss Thoyts, *Antiquary*, xxvii. 254).

IX.   There was an old woman from Sandyland
      With all her children in her hand.
      One can knit and one can sow [sew],
      One can make a lily-white bow.
      Please take one in.

When all the children have been taken in, the Old Woman
says—   There was an old woman from Sandiland
          With no children by the hand.
          Will you give me one?
                    —Ballynascaw School, co. Down (Miss C. N. Patterson).

(*b*) The first Dorsetshire game is played as follows:—Two
girls are chosen, the one to represent a lady and the other a
mother, who is supposed to be taking her children out to service.
She has one or more of them in each hand, and leads them up
to the lady, saying or singing the first verse.   The dialogue
then proceeds, and the verse is repeated until all the children
are similarly disposed of.   A few days are supposed to pass,
after which the mother calls to see her children, when the lady

tells her she cannot see them. At last she insists upon seeing them, and the children are all "sat down" behind the lady, and the mother asks one child what the lady has done to her; and she tells her "that the lady has cut off her nose, and made a nose-pie, and never give her a bit of it." Each one says she has done something to her and made a pie, and when all have told their tale "they all turn on her and put her to prison."

The second Dorsetshire game somewhat differs. One child takes seven or eight others whom she pretends are her children. Another child, presumably a mistress in want of servants, stands at a distance. The first child advances, holding the hand of her children, saying the first verse. The dialogue is concluded, and as the woman and her children are supposed to be out of hearing, the last couplet is said or sung. This process is gone through again until the mistress has engaged all the children as her servants, when she is supposed to let them all out to play with the mustard pots, which are represented by sticks or stones, in their hands.

The other versions are played as follows:—The children form a line, the one in the middle being the mother, or widow; they advance and retire, the mother alone singing the first verse. One child, who is standing alone on the opposite side, who has been addressed by the widow, then asks [not sings] the question. The mother, or widow, sings the reply, and points to one child when singing the last line, who thereupon crosses over to the other side, joining the one who is standing alone. This is continued till all have been selected. The Bally-nascaw version (Miss Patterson) is played in a similar way. One child sits on a bank, and the others come up to her in a long line. The "old woman" says the first five lines. No question is asked by the "lady," she simply takes one child. The "old woman" shakes hands with this child, and says good-bye to her. When all the children have been "taken in" by the one who personates the "lady," the "old woman" says the other three lines, and so one by one gets all the children back again. The Berkshire version (Miss Thoyts) is said, not sung, and is played with two leaders, "old woman" and "lover." As the lover chooses a child, that one is sent behind him, holding round his waist. Each child as she goes says, "Good-bye, mother, good-bye," and pretends to cry. Finally they all cry, and the game ends in a tug of war. This tug is clearly out of place unless only half the children are selected by one side. Miss Thoyts does not say how this is done.

(c) This game is called "School-teacher" in Belfast. The corruption of "Lady of the Land," to "Babyland," "Babylon," and "Sandiland," is manifest. It appears to be only fragmentary in its present form, but the versions undoubtedly indicate that the origin of the game arises from the practice of hiring servants. Mr. Halliwell has preserved another fragmentary rhyme, which he thinks may belong to this game.

> I can make diet bread
> Thick and thin,
> I can make diet bread
> Fit for the king ; (No. cccxliv.)

which may be compared with the rhyme given by Chambers (*Popular Rhymes*, p. 136), and another version given by Halliwell, p. 229.

If these rhymes belong to this game it would have probably been played by each child singing a verse descriptive of her own qualifications, and I have some recollection, although not perfect, of having played a game like this in London, where each child stated her ability to either brew, bake, or churn. It is worth noting that the Forest of Dean and Berkshire versions have absorbed one of the "selection" verses of the love-games. Mr. Halliwell, in recording the *Nursery Rhymes*, Nos. cccxliii. and cccxliv., as quoted above, says, "They are fragments of a game called 'The Lady of the Land,' a complete version of which has not fallen in my way." Mr. Udal's versions from Dorsetshire are not only called "The Lady of the Land," but are fuller than all the other versions, though probably these are not complete. Mr. Newell (*Games*, pp. 56–58) gives some versions of this game. He considers the original to have been a European game (he had not found an English example) in which there were two mothers, a rich and a poor one ; one mother begging away, one by one, all the daughters of the other.

(*d*) This game no doubt originates from the country practice of hiring servants at fairs, or from a dramatic " Hirings " being acted at Harvest Homes. The " Good-bye " of mother and daughters belongs, no doubt, to the original game and early versions, and is consistent with the departure of a servant to her new home. The " lover " incident is an interpolation, but there may have been a request on the part of the "mother" to the "lady" not to allow the girl followers or sweethearts too soon. As to the old practice of hiring servants, Miss Burne has noted how distinctly it stamps itself upon local custom (*Shropshire Folk-lore*, pp. 461, 464). That the practice forms the groundwork of this game is well illustrated by the following descriptive passage. " They stay usually two or three dayes with theire friends, and then aboute the fifth or sixth day after Martynmasse will they come to theire newe masters ; they will depart from theire olde services any day in the weeke, but theire desire (hereaboutes) is to goe to theire newe masters eyther on a Tewsday or on a Thursday ; for on a Sunday they will seldome remoove, and as for Monday, they account it ominous, for they say—

> Monday flitte,
> Neaver sitte ;

but as for the other dayes in the weeke they make no greate matter. I heard a servant asked what hee could doe, whoe made this answeare—

> I can sowe,
> I can mowe,
> And I can stacke ;
> And I can doe,
> My master too,
> When my master turnes his backe."
> —Best's *Rural Economy of Yorks.*, 1641 ;
> *Surtees Society*, pp. 135-136.

In *Long Ago*, ii. 130, Mr. Scarlett Potter mentions that in South Warwickshire it was customary at harvest-homes to give a kind of dramatic performance. One piece, called "The Hiring," represents a farmer engaging a man, in which work done by the man, the terms of service, and food to be supplied, are stated in rhymes similar to the above. See " Lammas."

Lady on the Mountain

—Barnes, Surrey (A. B. Gomme).

I.   There stands a lady on the mountain,
     Who she is I do not know;
     All she wants is gold and silver,
     All she wants is a nice young man.
     Choose one, choose two, choose the fairest one of the two.
     The fairest one that I can see,
     Is pretty ——, walk with me.
                              —Barnes, Surrey (A. B. Gomme).

II. There lives a lady on the mountain,
     Who she is I do not know;
     All she wants is gold and silver,
     All she wants is a nice young man.

     Choose one, choose two,
     Choose the fairest of the few.

     Now you're married I wish you joy,
     Father and mother you must obey;
     Love one another like sister and brother,
     And pray, young couple, come kiss one another.
                              —Colchester (Miss G. M. Frances).

III. Here stands a lady on a mountain,
     Who she is I do not know;
     All she wants is gold and silver,
     All she wants is a nice young man.

Choose you east, and choose you west,
Choose you the one as you love best.

Now Sally's got married we wish her good joy,
First a girl and then a boy ;
Twelve months a'ter a son and da'ter,
Pray young couple, kiss together.
　　　　　—Berrington (*Shropshire Folk-lore*, pp. 509, 510).

IV.　Stands a lady on the mountain,
　　　Who she is I do not know ;
　　　All she wants is gold and silver,
　　　All she wants is a nice young beau.
　　　Take her by the lily-white hand,
　　　Lead her across the water ;
　　　Give her kisses, one, two, three,
　　　For she is her mother's daughter.
　　　　　—Shipley, Horsham (*Notes and Queries*,
　　　　　　　8th series, i. 210, Miss Busk).

V.　There stands a lady on a mountain,
　　　Who she is I do not know ;
　　　All she wants is gold and silver,
　　　All she wants is a nice young man.

　　　Now she's married I wish her joy,
　　　First a girl and then a boy ;
　　　Seven years after son and daughter,
　　　Pray young couple kiss together.

　　　Kiss her once, kiss her twice,
　　　Kiss her three times three.
　　　　　—Wrotham, Kent (Miss D. Kimball).

VI.　There stands a lady on the ocean [mountain],
　　　Who she is I do not know her ;
　　　All she wants is gold or silver,
　　　All she wants is a nice young man.

　　　Choose once, choose twice,
　　　Choose three times over.

Now you're married I wish you joy,
First a girl and then a boy;
Seven years old a son and daughter,
Play and cuddle and kiss together.

Kiss her once, kiss her twice,
Kiss her three times over.   —Deptford (Miss Chase).

VII.   There stands a lady on the mountain,
Who she is I do not know:
Oh! she wants such gold and silver!
Oh! she wants such a nice young man!

Now you're married I wish you joy,
First a girl and then a boy;
Seven years after a son and a daughter,
Kiss your bride and come out of the ring.
                —Berkshire (Miss Thoyts, *Antiquary*, xxvii. 254).

(*b*) A ring is formed, one child in the centre. The ring sing the first verse, and then the centre child chooses one from the ring. The chosen pair kiss when the ring has sung the second. The first child then joins the ring, and the game begins again. In the Barnes version the centre child calls one to her from the ring by singing the second verse and naming the child she chooses.

(*c*) A version from Lady C. Gurdon's *Suffolk County Folk-lore* (p. 62) is the same as previous versions, except that it ends—   Now you're married you must be good,
Make your husband chop the wood;
Chop it fine and bring it in,
Give three kisses in the ring.

Other versions are much the same the examples given.

(*d*) This game has probably had its origin in a ballad. Miss Burne draws attention to its resemblance to the "Disdainful Lady" (*Shropshire Folk-lore*, p. 561), and Halliwell mentions a nursery rhyme (No. cccclxxix.) which is very similar. Mr. Newell (*Games*, p. 55) prints words and tune of a song which is very similar to that ballad, and he mentions the fact that he has seen it played as a round by the "Arabs of the street."

He considers it to be an old English song which has been fitted
for a ring game by the addition of a verse.

See " Lady on Yonder Hill."

Lady on Yonder Hill

  I.   Yonder stands a lovely lady,
     Whom she be I do not know ;
     I'll go court her for my beauty,
     Whether she say me yea or nay.
     Madam, to thee I humbly bow and bend.
     Sir, I take thee not to be my friend.
     Oh, if the good fairy doesn't come I shall die.
              —Derbyshire (*Folk-lore Journal*, i. 387).

  II.   There stands a lady on yonder hill,
     Who she is I cannot tell ;
     I'll go and court her for her beauty,
     Whether she answers me yes or no.
     Madam, I bow vounce to thee.
     Sir, have I done thee any harm ?
     Coxconian !
     Coxconian is not my name ; 'tis Hers and Kers, and
         Willis and Cave.
     Stab me, ha ! ha ! little I fear. Over the waters there
         are but nine, I'll meet you a man alive. Over
         the waters there are but ten, I'll meet you there
         five thousand.
     Rise up, rise up, my pretty fair maid,
     You're only in a trance ;
     Rise up, rise up, my pretty fair maid,
     And we will have a dance.
          —Lady C. Gurdon's *Suffolk County Folk-lore*, p. 65.

(*b*) In the Suffolk game the children form a ring, a boy and
girl being in the centre. The boy is called a gentleman and
the girl a lady. The gentleman commences by singing the
first verse. Then they say alternately the questions and
answers. When the gentleman says the lines commencing,
" Stab me," he pretends to stab the lady, who falls on the

ground. Then he walks round the lady and sings the last verse, " Rise up," and lifts up the lady. In the Derbyshire game only three children play, the lover, lady, and fairy. The girl stands a little distance off. The lover says the first four lines, then approaches the lady, falls on one knee, and says the next line. The lady replies, and retires further away. The lover then falls on the ground and says the next line. As this is said the good fairy appears, touches the fallen lover with her hand, and he is immediately well again.

(c) This is a curious game, and is perhaps derived from a ballad which had been popular from some more or less local circumstance, or more probably it may be a portion of an old play acted in booths at fair times by strolling players. It is not, as far as I can find out, played in any other counties. The lines—

> Over the water at the hour of ten,
> I'll meet you with five thousand men ;
> Over the water at the hour of five,
> I'll meet you there if I'm alive,

are portions of a dialogue familiar to Mr. Emslie, and also occur in some mumming plays. It may also be noted that the curing of illness or death from a stab is an incident in these plays, as is also the method of playing. The first lines are similar to those of " Lady on the Mountain," which see.

Lag

A number of boys put marbles in a ring, and then they all bowl at the ring. The one who gets nearest has the first shot at the marbles. He has the option of either " knuckling doon " and shooting at the ring from the prescribed mark, or " ligging up " (lying up)—that is, putting his taw so near the ring that if the others miss his taw, or miss the marbles in the ring, he has the game all to himself next time. If, however, he is hit by the others, he is said to be " killed."—Addy's *Sheffield Glossary*.

Lammas

A party of boys take a few straws, and endeavour to hold

one between the chin and the turned-down under-lip, pro-
nouncing the following rhyme—

> I bought a beard at Lammas fair,
> It's a' awa' but ae hair;
> Wag, beardie, wag!

He who repeats this oftenest without dropping the straw is
held to have won the game (Chambers' *Popular Rhymes*, p. 115).
This game-rhyme has an interesting reference to Lammas, and
it may also refer to the hiring of servants. Brockett (*North
Country Words*, p. 221) says, "At a fair or market where
country servants are hired, those who offer themselves stand
in the market-place with a piece of straw or green branch in
their mouths to distinguish them."

Lamploo

A goal having been selected and bounds determined, the
promoters used to prepare the others by calling at the top of
their voices—

> Lamp! Lamp! Laa-o!
> Those that don't run shan't play-o!

Then one of the "spryest" lads is elected to commence,
thus:—First touching the goal with his foot or leaning against
it, and clasping his hands so as to produce the letter W in the
dumb alphabet, he pursues the other players, who are not so
handicapped, when, if he succeeds in touching one without
unclasping his hands, they both make a rush for the goal.
Should either of the other boys succeed in overtaking one of
these before reaching that spot, he has the privilege of riding
him home pick-a-back. Then these two boys (*i.e.*, the original
pursuer and the one caught), joining hands, carry on the game
as before, incurring a similar penalty in case of being overtaken
as already described. Each successive boy, as he is touched
by the pursuers, has to make for the goal under similar risks,
afterwards clasping hands with the rest, and forming a new
recruit in the pursuing gang, in whose chain the outside players
alone have the privilege of touching and thus adding to their
numbers. Should the chain at any time be broken, or should
the original pursuer unclasp his hands, either by design or

accident, the penalty of carrying a capturer to the goal is incurred and always enforced. In West Somerset the pursuing boys after starting were in the habit of crying out the word "Brewerre" or "Brewarre;" noise appearing to be quite as essential to the game as speed.—*Somerset and Dorset Notes and Queries*, i. 186 (1888).

Another correspondent to the same periodical (i. 204) says that an almost identical game was played at the King's School, Sherborne, some fifty years ago. It was called "King-sealing," and the pursuing boy was obliged by the rules to retain his hold of the boy seized until he had uttered—

One, two, three, four, five, six, seven, eight, nine, ten.
You are one of the king-sealer's men.

If the latter succeeded in breaking away before the couplet was finished, the capture was incomplete.

The second game described is almost identical with "King Cæsar," played at Barnes.

About twenty years ago the game was common in some parts of Bedfordshire and Hertfordshire, where it was sometimes called "Chevy Chase."—*Folk-lore Journal*, vii. 233.

See "Chickidy Hand," "Hunt the Staigie," "King Cæsar," "Whiddy."

Lang Larence

That is, "Long Lawrence," an instrument marked with signs, a sort of teetotum. A "Long Lawrence" is about three inches long, something like a short ruler with eight sides; occasionally they have but four. On one side are ten x's, or crosses, forming a kind of lattice-work; on the next, to the left, three double cuts, or strokes, passing straight across in the direction of the breadth; on the third, a zig-zag of three strokes one way, and two or three the other, forming a W, with an additional stroke or a triple V; on the fourth, three single bars, one at each end and one in the middle, as in No. 2, where they are doubled; then the four devices are repeated in the same order. The game, formerly popular at Christmas, can be played by any number of persons. Each has a bank of pins or other small matters. A pool is formed; then in turn each rolls the

"Long Lawrence." If No. 1 comes up the player cries "Flush,"
and takes the pool; if No. 2, he puts down two pins; if No. 3,
he says "Lave all," and neither takes nor gives; if No. 4, he
picks up one. The sides are considered to bear the names,
"Flush," "Put doan two," "Lave all," "Sam up one." It has
been suggested that the name "Lawrence" may have arisen
from the marks scored on the instrument, not unlike the bars
of a gridiron, on which the saint perished.—Easthers's *Almondbury Glossary*.

See "Teetotum."

Leap Candle

The young girls in and about Oxford have a sport called
"Leap Candle," for which they set a candle in the middle of a
room in a candlestick, and then draw up their coats into the
form of breeches, and dance over the candle back and forth,
saying the words—

> The taylor of Bicester he has but one eye,
> He cannot cut a pair of green galagaskins
> If he were to die.

This sport, in other parts, is called "Dancing the Candle-
rush" (Aubrey's *Remaines of Gentilisme and Judaisme*, p. 45).
Halliwell (*Rhymes*, p. 65) has a rhyme—

> Jack be nimble,
> And Jack be quick,
> And Jack jump over
> The candlestick,

which may refer to this game. Northall (*Folk Rhymes*, p.
412) says in Warwickshire a similar game is called "Cock and
Breeches."

Leap-frog

One boy stoops down sideways, with his head bent towards
his body, as low as possible. This is called "Tucking in your
Tuppeny." Another boy takes a flying leap over the "frog,"
placing his hands on his back to help himself over. He then
proceeds to a distance of some four or five yards, and, in his
turn, stoops in the same manner as the first boy, as another

frog. A third boy then leaps first over frog No. 1, and then over frog No. 2, taking his place as frog No. 3, at about the same distance onwards. Any number of boys may play in the game. After the last player has taken his leap over all the frogs successively, frog No. 1 has his turn and leaps over his companions, taking his place as the last in the line of frogs. Then No. 2 follows suit, and so on, the whole line of players in course of time covering a good distance.—London (G. L. Gomme).

Leap-frog is known in Cornwall as "Leap the Long-mare" (*Folk-lore Journal*, v. 60), and in Antrim and Down as "Leap the Bullock" (Patterson's *Glossary*).

See "Accroshay," "Loup the Bullocks," "Spanish Fly."

Leap the Bullock
See "Leap-frog," "Loup the Bullocks."

Leaves are Green

> The leaves are green, the nuts are brown,
> They hang so high they will not come down ;
> Leave them alone till frosty weather,
> Then they will all come down together.
> —Berkshire (Miss Thoyts, *Antiquary*, xxvii. 254).

These lines are sung while the children dance round in a circle. When the last words are sung, the children flop down upon the ground. The tune sung is, Miss Thoyts says, that of "Nuts in May."

Lend Me your Key

> Please will you lend us your key ?
> What for ?
> Please, our hats are in the garden.
> Yes, if you won't steal any beans.
> Please, we've brought the key back ; will you lend
> us your frying-pan ?
> What to do with ?
> To fry some beans.
> Where have you got them ?
> Out of your garden.   —Earls Heaton (H. Hardy).

One child represents an old woman, and the other players carry on the dialogue with her. At the end of the dialogue the children are chased by the old woman.

See "Mother, Mother, may I go out to Play," "Witch."

Letting the Buck out

This game was played seventy years ago. A ring being formed, the "Buck" inside has to break out, and reach his "home," crying "Home!" before he can be caught and surrounded. Afterwards these words were sung—

Circle : Who comes here ?
Buck : Poor Johnny Lingo.
Circle : Don't steal none of my black sheep, Johnny Lingo,
  For if you do
  I shall put you in the pinder pin-fold.
  —Stixwold, Lincs. (Miss M. Peacock).

See "Who goes round my Stone Wall ? "

Level-coil

Nares, in his *Glossary*, says this is "a game of which we seem to know no more than that the loser in it was to give up his place to be occupied by another." Minshew gives it thus : "To play at *levell coil*, G. jouer à cul léve : *i.e.*, to play and lift up your taile when you have lost the game, and let another sit down in your place." Coles, in his *English Dictionary*, seems to derive it from the Italian *leva il culo*, and calls it also "Pitch-buttock." In his *Latin Dictionary* he has "*level-coil*, alternation, cession ;" and "to play at *level coil*, vices ludendi præbere." Skinner is a little more particular and says, "Vox tesseris globulosis ludentium propria : " an expression belonging to a game played with little round tesseræ. He also derives it from French and Italian. It is mentioned by Jonson, *Tale of a Tub*, iii. 2 :—

  "Young Justice Bramble has kept *level-coyl*
  Here in our quarters, stole away our daughter."

Gifford says that, in our old dramatists, it implies riot and disturbance. The same sport is mentioned by Sylvester, *Dubartas*, IV. iv. 2, under the name of *level-sice* :—

  "By tragick death's device
  Ambitious hearts do play at *level-sice*."

In the margin we have this explanation: "A kinde of Christmas play, wherein each hunteth the other from his seat. The name seems derived from the French *levez sus*, in English, arise up." Halliwell's *Dictionary* says that Skelton, ii. 31, spells it *levell suse*.

Libbety, Libbety, Libbety-lat

A child stands before a hassock, and as if he were going up stairs; he puts on it first his right and then his left foot, gradually quickening his steps, keeping time to the words—

Libbety, libbety, libbety-lat,
Who can do this? and who can do that?
And who can do anything better than that?
—Cornwall (*Folk-lore Journal*, v. 59).

Limpy Coley

A boy's game undescribed.—Patterson's *Antrim and Down Glossary*.

Little Dog I call you

A number of girls stand in a line with their backs to a wall. One of their number is sent away to a distance, but remains within call. Another girl, who stands in front of the line, asks the girls one by one what they would like if they could obtain their desires. After she has asked every one, she tells them to turn their faces to the wall, and calls after the girl who was sent away, saying, "Little Dog, I call you." The girl replies, "I shan't come to please you." "I'll get a stick and make you," is the rejoinder. "I don't care for that." "I've got a rice pudding for you." "I shan't come for that." "I've got a dish of bones." "I'll come for that." The Dog then comes. The girls have been previously told not to laugh whilst the one who stands out is talking to the Dog. Then the girl says to the Dog—

All the birds in the air,
All the fishes in the sea,
Come and pick me out (for example)
The girl with the golden ball.

If the girl who desired the golden ball laughs, the Dog picks her out. If nobody laughs, he guesses who the girl is that has wished for the golden ball. If the Dog guesses correctly, she goes and stands behind him, and if he guesses incorrectly she goes and stands behind the one who has been asking the questions. They continue this until they get to the last girl or girl at the end of the row, who *must* have desired to be—

> A brewer or a baker,
> Or a candlestick maker,
> Or a penknife maker.

Then the questioner says—

> All the birds in the air,
> All the fishes in the sea,
> Come pick me out
> A brewer or a baker,
> Or a candlestick maker,
> Or penknife maker.

If the Dog guesses the right one, he takes that girl on his side, she standing behind him. Then they draw a line and each side tries to pull the other over it.—Sheffield (S. O. Addy). The game, it will be seen, differs in several ways from the other games of " Fool, Fool, come to School " type. The " fool " becomes a definite Dog, and the players *wish* for any thing they choose; the Dog has apparently to find out their wishes.

See " All the Birds," " Fool, Fool."

Lobber

There are three or more players on each side, two stones or holes as stations, and one Lobber. The Lobber lobs either a stick about three inches long or a ball—(the ball seems to be a new institution, as a stick was always formerly used)—while the batsman defends the stone or hole with either a short stick or his hand. Every time the stick or ball is hit, the boys defending the stones or holes must change places. Each one is out if the stick or ball lodges in the hole or hits the stone ; or if the ball or stone is caught ; or if it can be put in the hole or hits the stone while the boys are changing places. This game is also played with two Lobbers, that lob alternately from each end. The game is won by a certain number of runs. —Ireland (*Folk-lore Journal*, ii. 264).

See " Cat," " Cudgel," " Kit-Cat," " Rounders."

Loggats

An old game, forbidden by statute in Henry VIII.'s time. It is thus played, according to Stevens. A stake is fixed in the ground; those who play throw Loggats at it, and he that is nearest the stake wins. Loggats, or loggets, are also small pieces or logs of wood, such as the country people throw at fruit that cannot otherwise be reached. "Loggats, little logs or wooden pins, a play the same with ninepins, in which the boys, however, often made use of bones instead of wooden pins" (Dean Miles' MS.; Halliwell's *Dictionary*). Strutt refers to this game (*Sports*, p. 272).

London

A diagram (see page 333) is drawn on a slate, and two children play. A piece of paper or small piece of glass or china, called a "chipper," is used to play with. This is placed at the bottom of the plan, and if of *paper*, is *blown* gently towards the top; if of glass or china, it is *nicked* with the *fingers*. The first player blows the paper, and in whichever space the paper stops makes a small round o with a slate pencil, to represent a man's head. The paper or chipper is then put into the starting-place again, and the same player blows, and makes another "man's head" in the space where the paper stops. This is continued until all the spaces are occupied. If the paper goes a second time into a space already occupied by a "head," the player adds a larger round to the "head," to represent a "body;" if a third time, a stroke is drawn for a leg, and if a fourth time, another is added for the second leg; this completes a "man." If three complete men in one space can be gained, the player makes "arms;" that is, two lines are drawn from the figures across the space to the opposite side of the plan. This occupies that space, and prevents the other player from putting any "men" in it, or adding to any already there. When all the spaces are thus occupied by one player, the game is won. Should the paper be blown on to a line or *outside* the plan, the player is out; the other player then begins, and makes as many "men" in her turn, until she goes on a line or outside. Should the paper go into "London," the player is entitled to make a "head" in every space, or to add another mark to those already there.—Westminster (A. B. Gomme).   This game resembles one described by F. H. Low in *Strand Mag.*, ii. 516.

London Bridge

—Wrotham, Kent (Miss D. Kimball).

—Rimbault's *Nursery Rhymes*, p. 34.

—Enborne School, Berks. (Miss M. Kimber).

LONDON

I.   London Bridge is broken down,
      Grant said the little bee,*
    London Bridge is broken down,
      Where I'd be.

    Stones and lime will build it up,
      Grant said the little bee,
    Stones and lime will build it up,
      Where I'd be.

    Get a man to watch all night,
      Grant said the little bee,
    Get a man to watch all night,
      Where I'd be.

* Another informant gives the refrain, " Grand says the little Dee."

Perhaps that man might fall asleep,
　　Grant said the little bee,
Perhaps that man might fall asleep,
　　Where I'd be.

Get a dog to watch all night,
　　Grant said the little bee,
Get a dog to watch all night,
　　Where I'd be.

If that dog should run away,
　　Grant said the little bee,
If that dog should run away,
　　Where I'd be.

Give that dog a bone to pick,
　　Grant said the little bee,
Give that dog a bone to pick,
　　Where I'd be.
　　　　　　—Belfast, Ireland (W. H. Patterson).

II.　London Bridge is broken down,
　　　Dance o'er my lady lee,
　　London Bridge is broken down,
　　　With a gay lady.

How shall we build it up again ?
　　Dance o'er my lady lee,
How shall we build it up again ?
　　With a gay lady.

Silver and gold will be stole away,
　　Dance o'er my lady lee,
Silver and gold will be stole away,
　　With a gay lady.

Build it up with iron and steel,
　　Dance o'er my lady lee,
Build it up with iron and steel,
　　With a gay lady.

Iron and steel will bend and bow,
 Dance o'er my lady lee,
Iron and steel will bend and bow,
 With a gay lady.

Build it up with wood and clay,
 Dance o'er my lady lee,
Build it up with wood and clay,
 With a gay lady.

Wood and clay will wash away,
 Dance o'er my lady lee,
Wood and clay will wash away,
 With a gay lady.

Build it up with stone so strong,
 Dance o'er my lady lee,
Huzza! 'twill last for ages long,
 With a gay lady.
   —[London]* (Halliwell's *Nursery Rhymes*, clii.).

III. London Bridge is broaken down,
 Is broaken down, is broaken down,
 London Bridge is broaken down,
  My fair lady.

Build it up with bricks and mortar,
Bricks and mortar, bricks and mortar,
Build it up with bricks and mortar,
 My fair lady.

Bricks and mortar will not stay,
Will not stay, will not stay,
Bricks and mortar will not stay,
 My fair lady.

Build it up with penny loaves,
Penny loaves, penny loaves,
Build it up with penny loaves,
 My fair lady.

* I have identified this with a version played at Westminster and another taught
to my children by a Hanwell girl.—A. B. G.

Penny loaves will mould away,
Mould away, mould away,
Penny loaves will mould away,
    My fair lady.

What have this poor prisoner done,
Prisoner done, prisoner done,
What have this poor prisoner done ?
    My fair lady.

Stole my watch and lost my key,
Lost my key, lost my key,
Stole my watch and lost my key,
    My fair lady.

Off to prison you must go,
You must go, you must go,
Off to prison you must go,
    My fair lady.

        —Liphook, Hants (Miss Fowler).

IV.   Where are these great baa-lambs going,
    Baa-lambs going, baa-lambs going,
    Where are these great baa-lambs going ?
       My fair lady.

We are going to London Bridge,
London Bridge, London Bridge,
We are going to London Bridge,
    My fair lady.

London Bridge is broken down,
Broken down, broken down,
London Bridge is broken down,
    My fair lady.

[Then verses follow, sung in the same way and with the same refrain, beginning with—]

    Mend it up with penny loaves.

    Penny loaves will wash away.

    Mend it up with pins and needles.

Pins and needles they will break.

Mend it up with bricks and mortar,

Bricks and mortar, that will do.

[After these verses have been sung—]

What has this great prisoner done,
Prisoner done, prisoner done,
What has this great prisoner done ?
 My fair lady.

Stole a watch and lost the key,
Lost the key, lost the key,
Stole a watch and lost the key,
 My fair lady.

Off to prison you must go,
You must go, you must go,
Off to prison you must go,
 My fair lady.
   —Hurstmonceux, Sussex (Miss Chase).

V. Over London Bridge we go,
Over London Bridge we go,
Over London Bridge we go,
 Gay ladies, gay !

London Bridge is broken down,
London Bridge is broken down,
London Bridge is broken down,
 Gay ladies, gay !

Build it up with lime and sand,
Build it up with lime and sand,
Build it up with lime and sand,
 Gay ladies, gay !

[Then follow verses sung in the same manner and with the same refrain, beginning with—]

Lime and sand will wash away.

Build it up with penny loaves.

Penny loaves 'll get stole away.

O, what has my poor prisoner done?

Robbed a house and killed a man.

What will you have to set her free?

Fourteen pounds and a wedding gown.

Stamp your foot and let her go!
—Clun (Burne's *Shropshire Folk-lore*, pp. 518–19).

VI. London Bridge is broken down,
Broken down, broken down,
London Bridge is broken down,
        My fair lady.

Build it up with iron bars,
Iron bars, iron bars,
Build it up with iron bars,
        My fair lady.

[Then follow verses with the same refrain, beginning with—]

Build it up with pins and needles.

Pins and needles rust and bend.

Build it up with penny loaves.

Penny loaves will tumble down.

Here's a prisoner I have got.

What's the prisoner done to you?

Stole my watch and broke my chain.

What will you take to let him out?

Ten hundred pounds will let him out.

Ten hundred pounds we have not got.

Then off to prison he must go.
                —Kent (Miss Dora Kimball).

VII. London Bridge is falling down,
Falling down, falling down,
London Bridge is falling down,
        My fair lady.

Build it up with mortar and bricks,
Mortar and bricks, mortar and bricks,
Build it up with mortar and bricks,
    My fair lady.

[Then follow verses in the same style and with the same refrain, beginning with—]

Bring some water, we'll wash it away.

Build it up with silver and gold.

Silver and gold will be stolen away.

We'll set a man to watch at night.

Suppose the man should fall asleep?

Give him a pipe of tobacco to smoke.

Suppose the pipe should fall and break?

We'll give him a bag of nuts to crack.

Suppose the nuts were rotten and bad?

We'll give him a horse to gallop around, &c.
      —Enborne School, Berks (M. Kimber).

VIII.   London Bridge is broken down,
     Gran says the little D,
     London Bridge is broken down,
       Fair la-dy.

Build it up with lime and stone,
Gran says the little D,
Build it up with lime and stone,
    Fair la-dy.

[Then follow verses beginning with the following lines—]

Lime and stone would waste away.

Build it up with penny loaves.

Penny loaves would be eaten away.

Build it up with silver and gold.

Silver and gold would be stolen away.

Get a man to watch all night.

If the man should fall asleep ?

Set a dog to bark all night.

If the dog should meet a bone ?

Set a cock to crow all night.

If the cock should meet a hen ?

Here comes my Lord Duke,
And here comes my Lord John ;
Let every one pass by but the very last one,
And catch him if you can.
　　　　　　—Cork (Mrs. B. B. Green).

IX. London Bridge is broken down,
　　Broken down, broken down,
　　London Bridge is broken down,
　　　　My fair lady.

[Other verses commence with one of the following lines, and are sung in the same manner—]

Build it up with penny loaves.

Penny loaves will melt away.

Build it up with iron and steel.

Iron and steel will bend and bow.

Build it up with silver and gold.

Silver and gold I have not got.

What has this poor prisoner done ?

Stole my watch and broke my chain.

How many pounds will set him free ?

Three hundred pounds will set him free.

The half of that I have not got.

Then off to prison he must go.
　　　　　　—Crockham Hill, Kent (Miss E. Chase).

(*b*) This game is now generally played like " Oranges and Lemons," only there is no " tug-of-war " at the end. Two children hold up their clasped hands to form an arch. The other children form a long line by holding to each other's dresses or waists, and run under. Those who are running under sing the first verse; the two who form the arch sing the second and alternate verses. At the words, "What has this poor prisoner done?" the girls who form the arch catch one of the line (generally the last one). When the last verse is sung the prisoner is taken a little distance away, and the game begins again. At Clun the players form a ring, moving round. They sing the first and alternate verses, and chorus, "London Bridge is broken down." Two players outside the ring run round it, singing the second and alternate verses. When singing "Penny loaves 'll get stole away," one of the two outside children goes into the ring, the other remains and continues her part, singing the next verse. When the last verse is sung the prisoner is released. The Berkshire game (Miss Kimber) is played by the children forming two long lines, each line advancing and retiring alternately while singing their parts. When the last verse is begun the children form a ring and gallop around, all singing this last verse together. In the Cork version (Mrs. Green) the children form a circle by joining hands. They march round and round, singing the verses to a sing-song tune. When singing, "If the cock should meet a hen," they all unclasp hands; two hold each other's hands and form an arch. The rest run under, saying the last verse. The "arch" lower their hands and try to catch the last child.

(c) The analysis of the game-rhymes is on pp. 342-45. It appears from this analysis that the London version is alone in its faithful reflection of an actual building episode. Three other versions introduce the incident of watching by a man, and failing him, a dog or cock; while five versions introduce a prisoner. This incident occurs the greatest number of times. It is not surprising that the London version seems to be the most akin to modern facts, being told so near the spot indicated by the verses, and on this account it cannot be considered as the oldest of the variants. There remain the other two groups. Both are distinguished by the introduction of a

ANALYSIS OF GAME-RHYMES.

No.	Belfast.	Halliwell.	Liphook.	Hurstmonceux.	Shropshire.	Kent.	Enborne.	Cork.	Crockham Hill.
1.	—	—	—	Where are these great baa-lambs going? My fair lady.	—	—	—	—	—
2.	—	—	—	We are going to L. B.	—	—	—	—	—
3.	—	—	—	—	—	—	—	—	—
4.	—	—	—	—	Over L. B. we go.	—	—	—	—
5.	L. B. is broken down.	L. B. is broken down.	L. B. is broken down.	L. B. is broken down.	L. B. is broken down.	L. B. is broken down.	—	L. B. is broken down.	L. B. is broken down.
6.	—	—	—	—	—	—	L. B. is falling down.	—	—
7.	Grant said the little bee.	—	—	—	—	—	—	Says the little D.	—
8.	—	Dance o'er my lady lee.	—	—	—	—	—	—	—
9.	—	With a gay lady.	My fair lady.	My fair lady.	Gay ladies, gay.	My fair lady.	My fair lady.	Fair lady.	My fair lady.
10.	—	—	—	—	—	—	—	—	—
11.	Where I'd be.	—	—	—	—	—	—	—	—
12.	—	How shall we build it up again?	—	—	—	—	—	—	—
13.	Stones and lime will build it up.	—	Build it up with bricks and mortar.	Mend it up with bricks and mortar.	Build it up with lime and sand.	—	Build it up with mortar and bricks.	Build it up with lime and stone.	—
14.	—	—	Bricks and mortar will not stay.	—	Lime and sand will wash away.	—	Mortar and bricks will waste away.	Lime and stone would waste away.	—

Build it up with penny loaves, Penny loaves will melt away. Build it up with silver and gold, Silver and gold I have not got.	Build it up with silver and gold. Silver and gold would be stolen away.	Build it up with silver and gold. Silver and gold will be stolen away.	Build it up with penny loaves, Penny loaves will tumble down.	Build it up with penny loaves, Penny loaves 'll get stole away.	Mend it up with penny loaves, Penny loaves will wash away.	Build it up with penny loaves, Penny loaves will mould away.	
			Build it up with pins and needles. Pins and needles rust and bend.		Mend it up with pins and needles. Pins and needles will break.		Silver and gold will be stole away. Build it up with iron and steel. Iron and steel will bend and bow.
	Set a man to watch all night.	We'll set a man to watch all night.					Build it up with wood and clay. Wood and clay will wash away. Build it up with stone so strong.
							Get a man to watch all night.

15.
16.
17.
18.
19.
20.
21.
22.
23.
24.
25.
26.

ANALYSIS OF GAME-RHYMES—*continued.*

No.	Belfast.	Halliwell.	Liphook.	Hurstmonceux.	Shropshire.	Kent.	Enborne.	Cork.	Crockham Hill.
27.	Perhaps that man might fall asleep.	—	—	—	—	—	Suppose the man should fall asleep.	If the man should fall asleep.	—
28.	—	—	—	—	—	Here's a prisoner I have got.	—	—	—
29.	—	—	What has this poor prisoner done?	What has this great prisoner done?	O, what has my poor prisoner done?	What's the prisoner done to you?	—	—	What has this poor prisoner done?
30.	—	—	Stole my watch and lost my key.	Stole a watch and lost the key.	—	Stole my watch and broke my chain.	—	—	Stole my watch and broke my chain.
31.	—	—	—	—	Robbed a house and killed a man.	—	—	—	—
32.	—	—	—	—	—	—	Give him a pipe of tobacco to smoke.	—	—
33.	—	—	—	—	—	—	Suppose the pipe should fall and break.	—	—
34	—	—	—	—	—	—	We'll give him a bag of nuts to crack.	—	—
35.	—	—	—	—	—	—	Suppose the nuts were rotten and bad.	—	—
36.	Get a dog to watch all night.	—	—	—	—	—	—	Set a dog to bark all night.	—
37.	If that dog should run away.	—	—	—	—	—	—	If the dog should meet a bone.	—

No.	A	B	C	D	E	F	G	H	I
38.									Give that dog a bone to pick.
39.		Set a cock to crow all night.							
40.		If the cock should meet a hen.							
41.	How many pounds will set him free?			What will you take to let him out?	What will you have to set her free?				
42.	Three hundred pounds will set him free.			Ten hundred pounds will let him out.	Fourteen pounds and a wedding gown.				
43.	The half of that I have not got.			Then a hundred pounds we have not got.					
44.				Then off to prison you must go.		Off to prison you must go.	Off to prison you must go.	Huzza! it will last for ages long.	
45.	Then off to prison he must go.								
46.					Stamp your foot and let her go.				
47.									
48.			We'll give him a horse to gallop around.						
49.		Here comes my lord Duke, let everyone pass by but the very last one.							

human element, one as watchman, the other as prisoner. The watchman incident approaches nearer to modern facts; the prisoner incident remains unexplained by any appeal to modern life, and it occurs more frequently than the others. In only one case, the Shropshire, is the prisoner ransomed; in the others he is sent to prison. Besides this main line of criticism brought out by the analysis there is little to note. The Hurstmonceux version begins with taking lambs over London Bridge, and the Shropshire version with the players themselves going over; but these are doubtless foreign adjuncts, because they do not properly prefix the main incident of the bridge being broken. The Belfast version has a curious line, "Grant said the little bee or dee," which the Cork version renders, "Gran says the little D." To these there is now no meaning that can be traced, but they help to prove that the rhyme originated from a state of things not understood by modern players. In all the versions with the prisoner incident it comes quite suddenly, without any previous indication, except in the Kent version, which introduces the exclamation, " Here's a prisoner I have got!" As the analysis shows the prisoner incident to be a real and not accidental part of the game, and the unmeaning expressions to indicate an origin earlier than modern players can understand, we can turn to other facts to see if the origin can be in any way traced.

(*d*) This game is universally acknowledged to be a very ancient one, but its origin is a subject of some diversity of opinion. The special feature of the rhymes is that considerable difficulty occurs in the building of the bridge by *ordinary* means, but without exactly suggesting that extraordinary means are to be adopted, a prisoner is suddenly taken. The question is, What does this indicate?

Looking to the fact of the widespread superstition of the foundation sacrifice, it would seem that we may have here a tradition of this rite. So recently as 1872, there was a scare in Calcutta when the Hooghly Bridge was being constructed. The natives then got hold of the idea that Mother Ganges, indignant at being bridged, had at last consented to submit to the insult on condition that each pier of the structure was founded on a layer of children's heads (Gomme's *Early Village Life*, p. 29). Formerly, in Siam, when a new city gate was being erected, it was customary for a number of officers to lie in wait and seize the first four or eight persons who happened to pass by, and who were then buried alive under the gate-posts to serve as guardian angels (Tylor's *Primitive Culture*, i. 97). Other instances of the same custom and belief are given in the two works from which these examples are taken; and there is a tradition about London Bridge itself, that the stones were bespattered with the blood of little children. Fitzstephen, in his well-known account of London of the twelfth century, mentions that when the Tower was built the mortar was tempered with the blood of beasts. Prisoners heads were put on the bridge after execution down to modern times, and also on city gates.

These traditions about London, when compared with the actual facts of contemporary savagery, seem to be sufficient to account for such a game as that we are now examining having originated in the foundation sacrifice. Mr. Newell, in his examination of the game, gives countenance to this theory, but he strangely connects it with other games which have a tug-of-war as the finish. Now in all the English examples it is remarkable that the tug-of-war does not appear to be a part of the game; and if this evidence be conclusive, it would appear that this incident got incorporated in America. It is this incident which Mr. Newell dwells upon in his ingenious explanation of the mythological interpretation of the game. But apart from this, the fact that the building of bridges was accompanied by the foundation sacrifice is a more likely origin for such a widespread game which is so intimately connected with a bridge.

This view is confirmed by what may be called the literary history of the game. The verses, as belonging to a game, have only recently been recorded, and how far they go back into tradition it is impossible to say. Dr. Rimbault is probably right when he states " that they have been formed by many fresh additions in a long series of years, and [the game] is perhaps almost interminable when received in all its different versions" (*Notes and Queries*, ii. 338). In *Chronicles of London Bridge*, pp. 152, 153, the author says he obtained the following note from a Bristol correspondent:—"About forty years ago, one moonlight night in the streets of Bristol, my attention was attracted by a dance and chorus of boys and girls, to which the words of this ballad gave measure. The breaking down of the Bridge was announced as the dancers moved round in a circle hand in hand, and the question, 'How shall we build it up again?' was chanted by the leader while the rest stood still." This correspondent also sent the tune the children sang, which is printed in the *Chronicles of London Bridge*. This was evidently the same game, but it would appear that the verses have also been used as a song, and it would be interesting to find out which is the more ancient of the two—the song or the game; and to do this it is necessary that we should know something of the history of the song. A correspondent of *Notes and Queries* (ii. 338) speaks of it as a "lullaby song" well known in the southern part of Kent and in Lincolnshire. In the *Gentleman's Magazine* (1823, Part II. p. 232) appeared the following interesting note:—

The projected demolition of London Bridge recalls to my mind the introductory lines of an old ballad which more than seventy years ago I heard plaintively warbled by a lady who was born in the reign of Charles II., and who lived till nearly the end of that of George II. I now transcribe the lines, not as possessing any great intrinsic merit, but in the hope of learning from some intelligent correspondent the name of the author and the story which gave rise to the ballad, for it probably originated in some accident that happened to the old bridge. The "Lady Lea" evidently refers to the river of that name, the favourite haunt of Isaac Walton, which, after fertilising the counties of Hertford, Essex, and Middlesex, glides into the Thames.

> London Bridge is broken down,
> *Dance over the Lady Lea;*
> London Bridge is broken down,
> *With a gay lady [la-dee].*

Then we must build it up again.
What shall we build it up withal ?
Build it up with iron and steel,
Iron and steel will bend and break.
Build it up with wood and stone,
Wood and stone will fall away.
Build it up with silver and gold,
Silver and gold will be stolen away.
Then we must set a man to watch,
Suppose the man should fall asleep ?
Then we must put a pipe in his mouth,
Suppose the pipe should fall and break ?
Then we must set a dog to watch,
Suppose the dog should run away ?
Then we must chain him to a post.

The two lines in *italic* are all regularly repeated after each line.—M. Green.

Another correspondent to this magazine, in the same volume, p. 507, observes that the ballad concerning London Bridge "formed, in my remembrance, part of a Christmas Carol, and commenced thus—

Dame, get up and bake your pies,
On Christmas-day in the morning.

The requisition goes on to the dame to prepare for the feast, and her answer is—

London Bridge is fallen down,
On Christ-mas day in the morning, &c.

The inference always was, that until the bridge was rebuilt some stop would be put to the Dame's Christmas operations; but why the falling of London Bridge should form part of a Christmas Carol at Newcastle-upon-Tyne I am at a loss to know." Some fragments were also printed in the *Mirror* for November 1823; and a version is also given by Ritson, *Gammer Gurton's Garland*. The *Heimskringla* (Laing, ii. 260, 261) gives an animated description of the Battle of London Bridge, when Ethelred, after the death of Sweyn, was assisted by Olaf in retaking and entering London, and it is curious that the first line of the game-rhyme appears—

> London Bridge is broken down,
> Gold is won and bright renown;
>   Shields resounding,
>   War-horns sounding,
> Hild is shouting in the din;
>   Arrows singing,
>   Mail-coats ringing,
> Odin makes our Olaf win.

If this is anything more than an accidental parallel, we come back to an historical episode wherein the breaking down and rebuilding of London Bridge occur, and it looks as if the two streams down which this tradition has travelled, namely, first, through the game, and second, through the song, both refer to the same event.

Dr. Rimbault has, in his *Nursery Rhymes*, p. 34, reconstructed a copy of the original rhyme from the versions given by Halliwell and the *Mirror*, and gives the tune to which it was sung, which is reprinted here. The tune from Kent is the one generally used in London versions. The tune of a country dance called "London Bridge" is given in Playford's *Dancing Master*, 1728 edition.

Long-duck

A number of children take hold of each other's hands and form a half-circle. The two children at one end of the line lift up their arms, so as to form an arch, and call "Bid, bid, bid," the usual cry for calling ducks. Then the children at the other end pass in order through the arch. This process is repeated, and they go circling round the field.—Addy's *Sheffield Glossary*.

See "Duck Dance."

Long Tag

See "Long Terrace."

Long-Tawl

A game at marbles where each takes aim at the other in turn, a marble being paid in forfeit to whichever of the players may make a hit.—Lowsley's *Berkshire Glossary*.

Long Terrace

Every player chooses a partner. The couples stand immediately in front of each other, forming a long line, one remaining outside of the line on the right-hand side, who is called the "Clapper." The object of the game is for the last couple to reach the top of the line, each running on different sides, and keeping to the side on which they are standing. The object of the Clapper is to hit the one running on the right side of the line, which, if he succeeds in doing, makes him the Clapper, and the Clapper takes his place. [The next *last* couple would then presumably try and reach the top.]— East Kirkby, Lincs. (Miss K. Maughan).

A similar game to this is played at Sporle, Norfolk (Miss Matthews). It is there called "Long Tag." The players stand in line behind one another, and an odd one takes her place somewhere near the front; at a given signal, such as clapping of hands, the two at the back separate and try to meet again in front before the one on the watch can catch them; they may run where they please, and when one is caught that one becomes the one "out."

See "French Jackie."

Loup the Bullocks

Young men go out to a green meadow, and there on all-fours plant themselves in a row about two yards distant from each other. Then he who is stationed farthest back in the "bullock rank" starts up and leaps over the other bullocks before him, by laying his hands on each of their backs; and when he gets over the last one leans down himself as before, whilst all the others, in rotation, follow his example; then he starts and leaps again.

I have sometimes thought that we (the Scotch) have borrowed this recreation from our neighbours of the "Green Isle," as at their wakes they have a play much of the same kind, which they call "Riding Father Doud." One of the wakers takes a stool in his hand, another mounts that one's back, then Father Doud begins rearing and plunging, and if he unhorses his rider with a dash he does well. There is another play (at these wakes) called "Kicking the Brogue," which is even ruder than "Riding Father Doud," and a third one called "Scuddieloof."—Mactaggart's *Gallovidian Encyclopædia*.

Patterson (*Antrim and Down Glossary*) mentions a game called "Leap the Bullock," which he says is the same as "Leap-frog."

Dickinson's *Cumberland Glossary Supplement*, under "Lowp," says it means a leap or jump either running or standing. The various kinds include "Catskip"—one hitch, or hop, and one jump; "Hitch steppin"—hop, step, and lowp; a hitch, a step, and a leap; "Otho"—two hitches, two steps, and a leap; "Lang spang"—two hitches, two steps, a hitch, a step, and a leap.

See "Accroshay," "Knights," "Leap-frog."

Lubin

—Hexham (Miss J. Barker).

—Doncaster (Mr. C. Bell).

—London (A. B. Gomme).

—Dorsetshire (Miss M. Kimber).

—Sporle, Norfolk (Miss Matthews).

I. Here we dance lubin, lubin, lubin,
　　Here we dance lubin light,
　Here we dance lubin, lubin, lubin,
　　On a Saturday night.

　Put all the right hands in,
　　Take all the right hands out,
　Shake all the right hands together,
　　And turn yourselves about.

　Here we dance lubin, lubin, lubin,
　　Here we dance lubin light,
　Here we dance lubin, lubin, lubin,
　　On a Saturday night.

　Put all your left hands in,
　　Take all your left hands out,
　Shake all your left hands together,
　　And turn yourselves about.

　Here we dance lubin, lubin, lubin,
　　Here we dance lubin light,

Here we dance lubin, lubin, lubin,
  On a Saturday night.

Put all your right feet in,
  Take all your right feet out,
Shake all your right feet together,
  And turn yourselves about.

Here we dance lubin, lubin, lubin,
  Here we dance lubin light,
Here we dance lubin, lubin, lubin,
  On a Saturday night.

Put all your left feet in,
  Take all your left feet out,
Shake all your left feet together,
  And turn yourselves about.

Here we dance lubin, lubin, lubin,
  Here we dance lubin light,
Here we dance lubin, lubin, lubin,
  On a Saturday night.

Put all your heads in,
  Take all your heads out,
Shake all your heads together,
  And turn yourselves about.

Here we dance lubin, lubin, lubin,
  Here we dance lubin light,
Here we dance lubin, lubin, lubin,
  On a Saturday night.

Put all the [Marys] in,
  Take all the [Marys] out,
Shake all the [Marys] together,
  And turn yourselves about.

Here we dance lubin, lubin, lubin,
  Here we dance lubin light,
Here we dance lubin, lubin, lubin,
  On a Saturday night.

Put all yourselves in,
  Take all yourselves out,
Shake all yourselves together,
  And turn yourselves about.
            —Oxford and Wakefield (Miss Fowler).

II. Now we dance looby, looby, looby,
     Now we dance looby, looby, light;
     Shake your right hand a little,
       And turn you round about.

     Now we dance looby, looby, looby;
     Shake your right hand a little,
     Shake your left hand a little,
       And turn you round about.

     Now we dance looby, looby, looby;
     Shake your right hand a little,
     Shake your left hand a little,
     Shake your right foot a little,
       And turn you round about.

     Now we dance looby, looby, looby;
     Shake your right hand a little,
     Shake your left hand a little,
     Shake your right foot a little,
     Shake your left foot a little,
       And turn you round about.

     Now we dance looby, looby, looby;
     Shake your right hand a little,
     Shake your left hand a little,
     Shake your right foot a little,
     Shake your left foot a little,
     Shake your head a little,
       And turn you round about.
            —Halliwell (*Popular Rhymes*, p. 226).

III. Fal de ral la, fal de ral la,
      Hinkumbooby round about.

Right hands in and left hands out,
Hinkumbooby round about;
Fal de ral la, fal de ral la,
Hinkumbooby round about.

Left hands in and right hands out,
Hinkumbooby round about;
Fal de ral la, fal de ral la,
Hinkumbooby round about.

Right foot in and left foot out,
Hinkumbooby round about;
Fal de ral la, fal de ral la,
Hinkumbooby round about.

Left foot in and right foot out,
Hinkumbooby round about;
Fal de ral la, &c.

Heads in and backs out,
Hinkumbooby round about;
Fal de ral la, &c.

Backs in and heads out,
Hinkumbooby round about;
Fal de ral la, &c.

A' feet in and nae feet out,
Hinkumbooby round about;
Fal de ral la, &c.

Shake hands a', shake hands a',
Hinkumbooby round about;
Fal de ral la, &c.

Good night a', good night a',
Hinkumbooby round about;
Fal de ral la, &c.
                    —Chambers (*Popular Rhymes*, pp. 137–139).

IV.   This is the way we wash our hands,
      Wash our hands, wash our hands,
      To come to school in the morning.

This is the way we wash our face,
Wash our face, wash our face,
To come to school in the morning.

Here we come dancing looby,
Lewby, lewby, li.

Hold your right ear in,
Hold your right ear out,
Shake it a little, a little,
And then turn round about.

Here we come dancing lewby,
Lewby, lewby, li, &c.
            —Eckington, Derbyshire (S. O. Addy).

  V. How do you luby lue,
      How do you luby lue,
      How do you luby lue,
      O'er the Saturday night?

      Put your right hand in,
      Put your right hand out,
      Shake it in the middle,
      And turn yourselves about.
  —Lady C. Gurdon's Suffolk *County Folk-lore*, p. 64.

[Repeat this for "left hand," "right foot," "left foot,"
"heads," and "put yourselves in."]

  VI. Can you dance looby, looby,
       Can you dance looby, looby,
       Can you dance looby, looby,
       All on a Friday night?

       You put your right foot in,
       And then you take it out,
       And wag it, and wag it, and wag it,
       Then turn and turn about.
                         Addy's *Sheffield Glossary*.

VII.   Here we dance luby, luby,
       Here we dance luby light,
       Here we dance luby, luby,
       All on a Wednesday night.
                   —Ordsall, Nottinghamshire (Miss Matthews).

VIII.   Here we go lubin loo,
        Here we go lubin li,
        Here we go lubin loo,
        Upon a Christmas night.
                   —Epworth, Doncaster (C. C. Bell).

IX.   Here we go looby loo,
      Here we go looby li,
      Here we go looby loo,
      All on a New-Year's night.
                   —Nottingham (Miss Winfield).

X.   Here we come looby, looby,
     Here we come looby light,
     Here we come looby, looby,
     All on a Saturday night.
                   —Belfast (W. H. Patterson).

XI.   Here we come looping, looping [louping ?],
      Looping all the night;
      I put my right foot in,
      I put my right foot out,
      I shake it a little, a little,
      And I turn myself about.
                   —Hexham (Miss J. Barker).

XII.   Christian was a soldier,
       A soldier, a soldier,
       Christian was a soldier, and a brave one too.
       Right hand in, right hand out,
       Shake it in the middle, and turn yourself about.
                   —Sporle, Norfolk (Miss Matthews).

XIII. Friskee, friskee, I was and I was
       A-drinking of small beer.
       Right arms in, right arms out,
       Shake yourselves a little, and little,
       And turn yourselves about.
              —Cornwall (*Folk-lore Journal*, v. p. 49).

XIV. I love Antimacassar,
       Antimacassar loves me.
       Put your left foot in,
       Put your right foot out,
       Shake it a little, a little, a little,
       And turn yourself about.
              —Dorsetshire (Miss M. Kimber).

(*b*) A ring is formed and the children dance round, singing the first verse. They then stand till, sing the next verse, and, while singing, suit the action to the word, each child turning herself rapidly round when singing the last line. The first verse is then repeated, and the fourth sung in the same way as the second, and so on.

Another way of playing is that the children do not dance round and round. They form a ring by joining hands, and they then all move in one direction, about half way round, while singing the first line, "lubin;" then back again in the opposite direction, while singing the second line, "light," still keeping the ring form, and so on for the third and fourth lines. In each case the emphasis is laid upon the "Here" of each line, the movement being supposed to answer to the "Here."

The Dorsetshire version (Miss M. Kimber) is played by the children taking hands in pairs, forming a ring, and dancing round. At Eckington (S. O. Addy) the children first pretend to wash their hands, then their face, while singing the words; then comb their hair and brush their clothes; then they join hands and dance round in a ring singing the words which follow, again suiting their actions to the words sung.

In the Scottish version a ring is formed as above. One sings, and the rest join, to the tune of "Lillibullero," the first line. As soon as this is concluded each claps his hand and wheels grotesquely, singing the second line. They then sing the third line, suiting the action to the word, still beating the time; then the second again, wheeling round and clapping hands. When they say "A' feet in, and nae feet out," they all sit down with their feet stretched into the centre of the ring.

(c) The other variants which follow the Halliwell version are limited to the first verse only, as the remainder of the lines are practically the same as those given in Miss Fowler's version which is written at length, and three or four of these apparently retain only the verse given. A London version, collected by myself, is nearly identical with that of Miss Fowler, except that the third line is "Shake your —— a little, a little," instead of as printed. This is sung to the tune given.

The incidents in this game are the same throughout. The only difference in all the versions I have collected being in the number of the different positions to be performed, most of them being for right hands, left hands, right feet, left feet, and heads; others, probably older forms, having "ears," "yourselves," &c. One version, from Eckington, Derbyshire, curiously begins with "washing hands and face," "combing hair," &c., and then continuing with the "Looby" game, an apparent "mix-up" of "Mulberry Bush" and "Looby." Three more versions, Sporle, Cornwall, and Dorsetshire, also have different beginnings, one (Dorsetshire) having the apparently unmeaning "I love Antimacassar."

(d) The origin and meaning of this game appears somewhat doubtful. It is a choral dance, and it may owe its origin to a custom of wild antic dancing in celebration of the rites of some deity in which animal postures were assumed. The Hexham version, "Here we come louping [leaping]" may probably be the oldest and original form, especially if the conjecture that this game is derived from animal rites is accepted. The term "looby," "lubin," or "luby" does not throw much light on the game. Addy (*Sheffield Glossary*) says, "Looby is an old form of the modern 'lubber,' a 'clumsy fellow,' 'a dolt.'" That a stupid or ridiculous meaning is attached to the word "looby" is also shown by one of the old penances for redeeming a forfeit, where a player has to lie stretched out on his back and declare,

> Here I lie
> The length of a looby,
> The breadth of a booby,
> And three parts of a jackass.

The Scottish forms of the game bear on the theory of the game being grotesque. The fact of the players having both their arms extended at once, one behind and one in front of them, and the more frequent spinning round, suggest this. Then, too, there is the sudden "sit down" posture, when "all feet in" is required.

In the version given by Halliwell there is more difficulty in the game, and possibly more fun. This version shows the game to be cumulative, each player having to go through an additional antic for each verse sung. This idea only needs to be carried a little further to cause the players to be ridiculous in their appearance. This version would be more difficult to perform, and they would be exhausted by the process, and the constant motion of every member of the body. Attention, too, might be drawn to the word "Hinkumbooby" occurring in Chambers's version. Newell (*Games*, p. 131) mentions that some sixty years ago the game was danced deliberately and decorously, as old fashion was, with slow rhythmical movement.

Lug and a Bite

A boy flings an apple to some distance. All present race for it. The winner bites as fast as he can, his compeers *lugging* at his ears in the meantime, who bears it as well as he can, and then he throws down the apple, when the sport is resumed (Halliwell's *Dictionary*). Brogden's *Lincolnshire Provincial Words* says "Luggery-bite" is a game boys play with fruit. One bites the fruit, and another pulls his hair until he throws the fruit away. The game is also played in Lancashire (*Reliquary*).

See "Bob-Cherry."

Luggie

A boys' game. In this game the boys lead each other about

by the "lugs," *i.e.*, ears; hence the name (Patterson's *Antrim and Down Glossary*). Jamieson says that the leader had to repeat a rhyme, and if he made a mistake, he in turn became Luggie. The rhyme is not recorded.

Luking

The West Riding name for "Knor and Spell." Playing begins at Easter.—Henderson's *Folk-lore*, p. 84.

See "Nur and Spell."

Mag

A game among boys, in which the players throw at a stone set up on edge.—Barnes (*Dorset Glossary*).

Magic Whistle

All the players but three sit on chairs, or stand in two long rows facing each other. One player sits at one end of the two rows as president; another player is then introduced into the room by the third player, who leads him up between the two rows. He is then told to kneel before the one sitting at the end of the row of players. When he kneels any ridiculous words or formula can be said by the presiding boy, and then he and those players who are nearest to the kneeling boy rub his back with their hands for two or three minutes. While they are doing this the boy who led the victim up to the president fastens a string, to which is attached a small whistle, to the victim's coat or jacket. It must be fastened in such a way that the whistle hangs loosely, and will not knock against his back. The whistle is then blown by the player who attached it, and the kneeling boy is told to rise and search for the Magic Whistle. The players who are seated in the chairs must all hold their hands in such a way that the victim suspects it is in their possession, and proceeds to search. The whistle must be blown as often as possible, and in all directions, by those players only who can do so without the victim being able to either see or feel that he is carrying the whistle with him.—London (A. B. Gomme).

This game is also called "Knight of the Whistle." The boy who is to be made a Knight of the Order of the Whistle, when led up between the two rows of players, has a cloak put round his shoulders and a cap with a feather in it on his head. The whistle is then fastened on to the cloak. This is described by the Rev. J. G. Wood (*Modern Playmate*, p. 189). Newell (*Games*, p. 122) gives this with a jesting formula of initiation into knighthood. He says it was not a game of children, but belonged to an older age.

See "Call-the-Guse."

Magical Music

A pleasant drawing-room evening amusement. — Moor's *Suffolk Words*.

Probably the same as "Musical Chairs."

Malaga, Malaga Raisins

A forfeit game. The players sat in a circle. One acquainted with the trick took a poker in his right hand, made some eccentric movements with it, passed it to his left, and gave it to his next neighbour on that side, saying, "Malaga, Malaga raisins, very good raisins I vow," and told him to do the same. Should he fail to pass it from right to left, when he in his turn gave it to his neighbour, without being told where the mistake lay, he was made to pay a forfeit.—Cornwall (*Folk-lore Journal*, v. 50).

"Malaga raisins are very good raisins, but I like Valencias better," is the saying used in the London version of this game, and instead of using a poker a paper-knife is used, and it is played at the table. Other formulæ for games of this kind are, "As round as the moon, has two eyes, a nose, and a mouth." These words are said while drawing on a table with the fore-finger of the *left* hand an imaginary face, making eyes, nose, and mouth when saying the words. The fun is caused through those players who are unacquainted with the game drawing the imaginary face with the right hand instead of the left. Another formula is to touch each finger of the right hand with the forefinger of the left hand, saying to each finger in succession, "Big Tom, Little Tom, Tommy, Tom, Tom." The secret in this case is to say, "Look here!" before commencing the formula. It is the business of those players who know the game to say the words in such a way that the uniniated imagine the saying of the words correctly with particular accents on particular words to be where the difficulty lies.   If this is well done, it diverts suspicion from the real object of these games. —A. B. Gomme.

Marbles

Brand considers that marbles had their origin in bowls, and received their name from the substance of which the bowls were formerly made.   Strutt (*Sports*, p. 384) says, "Marbles have been used as a substitute for bowls.   I believe originally nuts, round stones, or any other small things that could easily be bowled along were used as marbles."   Rogers notices "Marbles" in his *Pleasures of Memory*, l. 137 :—

> "On yon gray stone that fronts the chancel-door,
>   Worn smooth by busy feet, now seen no more,
>   Each eve we shot the marble through the ring."

Different kinds of marbles are alleys, barios, poppo, stonies. Marrididdles are marbles made by oneself by rolling and baking common clay.   By boys these are treated as spurious and are always rejected.   In barter, a bary = four stonies ; a common white alley = three stonies.   Those with pink veins being considered best.   Alleys are the most valuable and are always reserved to be used as "taws" (the marble actually used by the player).   They are said to have been formerly made of different coloured alabaster.   See also Murray's *New English Dict.*

For the different games played with marbles, see "Boss Out," "Bridgeboard," "Bun-hole," "Cob," "Hogo," "Holy Bang," "Hundreds," "Lag," "Long-Tawl," "Nine Holes," "Ring Taw."

Mary Brown

I.   Here we go round, ring by ring,
        To see poor Mary lay in the ring ;
        Rise up, rise up, poor Mary Brown,
        To see your dear mother go through the town.

   I won't rise, I won't rise [from off the ground],
        To see my poor mother go through the town.

Rise up, rise up, poor Mary Brown,
To see your dear father go through the town.

I won't rise, I won't rise [from off the ground],
To see my dear father go through the town.

Rise up, rise up, poor Mary Brown,
To see your dear sister go through the town.

I won't rise, I won't rise from off the ground,
To see my dear sister go through the town.

Rise up, rise up, poor Mary Brown,
To see your dear brother go through the town.

I won't rise, I won't rise up from off the ground,
To see my dear brother go through the town.

Rise up, rise up, poor Mary Brown,
To see your dear sweetheart go through the town.

I will rise, I will rise up from off the ground,
To see my dear sweetheart go through the town.
                              —Barnes, Surrey (A. B. Gomme).

II.   Rise up, rise up, Betsy Brown,
      To see your father go through the town.

      I won't rise up upon my feet,
      To see my father go through the street.

      Rise up, rise up, Betsy Brown,
      To see your mother go through the town.

      I won't rise up upon my feet,
      To see my mother go through the street.

[Then follow verses for sister, brother, and lover. When
this last is sung, she says—]

      I will rise up upon my feet,
      To see my lover go through the street.
                        - Ninfield, Sussex, about sixty years ago
                              (Charles Wise).

III. Rise daughter, rise daughter, off of your poor feet,
      To see your dear mother lie dead at your feet.

I won't rise, I won't rise off of my poor feet,
To see my dear mother lie dead at my feet.

Rise daughter, rise daughter, off of your poor feet,
To see your poor father lie dead at your feet.

I won't rise, I won't rise off of my poor feet,
To see my poor father lie dead at my feet.

Rise daughter, rise daughter, off of your poor feet,
To see your dear sister lie dead at your feet.

I won't rise, I won't rise off of my poor feet,
To see my poor sister lie dead at my feet.

Rise daughter, rise daughter, off of your poor feet,
To see your poor brother lie dead at your feet.

I won't rise, I won't rise off of my poor feet,
To see my poor brother lie dead at my feet.

Rise daughter, rise daughter, off of your poor feet,
To see your dear sweetheart lie dead at your feet.

I will rise, I will rise off of my poor feet,
To see my dear sweetheart lie dead at my feet.
                              —Barnes, Surrey (A. B. Gomme).

IV.   Rise daughter, rise daughter,
            Rise from off your knees,
        To see your poor father lie
            Down at yonder trees.

        I won't rise, I won't rise,
            From off my knees,
        To see my poor father lie
            Down at yonder trees.

[The verses are then repeated for mother, sister, brother,
and sweetheart.   When this is said the girl sings—]

        I will rise, I will rise,
            From off my knees,
        To see my sweetheart lie
            Down at yonder trees.
                    — Hurstmonceux, Sussex (Miss Chase).

V.   Here we all stand round the ring,
     And now we shut poor Mary in ;
     Rise up, rise up, poor Mary Brown,
     And see your poor mother go through the town.

[Then follow verses the same as in the Barnes version, No. 1,
and then—]

     Rise up, rise up, poor Mary Brown,
     To see the poor beggars go through the town.

     I will not stand up upon my feet
     To see the poor beggars go through the street.

[Two other verses are sometimes added, introducing gentleman and ladies.   All versions, however, conclude with the
girl saying—]

     Rise up, rise up, poor Mary Brown,
     And see your poor sweetheart go through the town.

     I will get up upon my feet,
     To see my sweetheart go through the street.
                         —Halliwell's *Nursery Rhymes*, p. 218.

(*b*) The children form a ring, one child laying or kneeling
down in the centre.   The ring sing the first, third, fifth, and
alternate verses; the girl in the middle answers with the
second, fourth, and so on alternately.   At the last verse the
girl jumps up and breaks through the ring by force; another
girl takes her place in the ring, and the game begins again.
The Sussex version of " Mary Brown " (Chas. Wise) is played
by the children standing in line and advancing and retiring
towards the lying or kneeling child.   The Barnes version of
" Rise, Daughter " is also played in this way.   The " daughter "
lays down, and at the end of the game joins the line, and
another lays down.   In the Hurstmonceux version, when the
last verse is sung, the girl in the middle rises and picks a
boy out of the ring; he goes in the middle with her, and they
kiss.   The version given by Halliwell is played in the same
way as the Barnes version.

(*c*) Halliwell (*Game Rhymes*, p. 219) gives a version of a

Swedish ballad or ring dance-song, entitled "Fair Gundela," he considers this may be a prototype of the English game, or that they may both be indebted to a more primitive original. The Swedish game rather gives the idea of a maiden who has sought supernatural assistance from a wise woman, or witch, to ask after the fate of those dear to her, and the English versions may also be dramatic renderings of a ballad of this character. Mr. Jacobs' *More English Fairy Tales*, p. 221, considers this game to have originated from the Tale of the "Golden Ball."

Mary mixed a Pudding up

> Mary mixed a pudding up,
> She mixed it very sweet,
> She daren't stick a knife in
> Till John came home at neet [= night].
> Taste John, taste John, don't say nay,
> Perhaps to-morrow morning will be our wedding-day.
>
> The bells shall ring and we shall sing,
> And all clap hands together (round the ring).

> > Up the lane and down,
> > It's slippery as a glass,
> > If we go to Mrs. ——
> > We'll find a nice young lass.
> > Mary with the rosy cheeks,
> > Catch her if you can ;
> > And if you cannot catch her,
> > We'll tell you her young man.
> > > —Hanging Heaton (Herbert Hardy).

A ring is formed by the children joining hands, one child in the centre. The first verse is sang. Two children from the ring go to the one in the centre and *ask* her who is her love, or as they say here [Yorks.], "who she goes with ;" after that the rest is sung.

See "All the Boys."

Merrils

See " Nine Men's Morris."

Merritot, or the Swing

This sport, which is sometimes called "Shuggy-shew" in the North of England, is described as follows by Gay:—

"On two near elms the slackened cord I hung,
Now high, now low, my Blouzalinda swung."

So Rogers, in the *Pleasures of Memory*, l. 77:—

"Soar'd in the swing, half pleas'd and half afraid,
Through sister elms that wav'd their summer shade."

Speght, in his *Glossary*, says, "'Meritot,' a sport used by children by swinging themselves in bell-ropes, or such like, till they are giddy." In *Mercurialis de Arte Gymnastica*, p. 216, there is an engraving of this exercise.

Halliwell quotes from a MS. *Yorkshire Glossary*, as follows:—"'Merrytrotter,' a rope fastened at each end to a beam or branch of a tree, making a curve at the bottom near the floor or ground in which a child can sit, and holding fast by each side of the rope, is swung backwards and forwards."

Baker (*Northamptonshire Glossary*) calls "Merrytotter" the game of "See-saw," and notes that the antiquity of the game is shown by its insertion in Pynson, "Myry totir, child's game, oscillum."

Chaucer probably alludes to it in the following lines of the *Miller's Tale*—

"What eileth you? some gay girle (God it wote)
Hath brought you thus on the merry tote."

Merry-ma-tansa

—Biggar (Wm. Ballantyne).

I.   Here we go round by jingo ring,
Jingo-ring, and jingo-ring,
Here we go round by jingo-ring,
About the merry-ma-tansa.

Come name the lad you like the best,
Like the best, like the best,
Come name the lad you like the best,
About the merry-ma-tansa.

Guess ye wha's the young gudeman,
The young gudeman, the young gudeman,
Come guess ye wha's the young gudeman
About the merry-ma-tansa.

Honey's sweet and so is he,
So is he, so is he,
Honey's sweet and so is he,
About the merry-ma-tansa.

[Or—　　Crab-apples are sour and so is he,
So is he, so is he,
Crab-apples are sour and so is he,
About the merry-ma-tansa.]

Can she bake and can she brew ?
Can she shape and can she sew,
'Boot a house can a' things do ?
About the merry-ma-tansa ?

She can bake and she can brew,
She can shape and she can sew,
'Boot a house can a' things do,
About the merry-ma-tansa.

This is the way to wash the clothes,
Wash the clothes, wash the clothes,
This is the way to wash the clothes,
About the merry-ma-tansa.

[Then follows verses for wringing clothes, ironing, baking bread, washing hands, face, combing hair, washing and sweeping the house, and a number of other things done in housekeeping. The boy then presents the girl with a ring, and they all sing—]

Now she's married in a goud ring,
A gay goud ring, a gay goud ring,
Now she's married in a goud ring,
About the merry-ma-tansa.

A gay goud ring is a dangerous thing,
A cankerous thing, a cankerous thing,
A gay goud ring is a dangerous thing,
About the merry-ma-tansa.

Now they're married we wish them joy,
Wish them joy, wish them joy,
Now they're married we wish them joy,
About the merry-ma-tansa.

Father and mother they must obey,
Must obey, must obey,
Father and mother they must obey,
About the merry-ma-tansa.

Loving each other like sister and brother,
Sister and brother, sister and brother,
Loving each other like sister and brother,
About the merry-ma-tansa.

We pray this couple may kiss thegither,
Kiss thegither, kiss thegither,
We pray this couple may kiss thegither,
About the merry-ma-tansa.

[If any lad was left without a partner, the ring sing—]

Here's a silly auld man left alone,
Left alone, left alone,
He wants a wife and can't get none,
About the merry-ma-tansa.
—Biggar (William Ballantyne).

II. Here we go the jingo-ring,
The jingo-ring, the jingo-ring,
Here we go the jingo-ring,
About the merry-ma-tansie.

Twice about, and then we fa',
Then we fa', then we fa',
Twice about, and then we fa',
About the merry-ma-tansie.

Guess ye wha's the young goodman,
The young goodman, the young goodman,
Guess ye wha's the young goodman,
About the merry-ma-tansie.

Honey is sweet, and so is he,
So is he, so is he,
Honey is sweet, and so is he,
About the merry-ma-tansie.

[Or—   Apples are sour, and so is he,
So is he, so is he,
Apples are sour, and so is he,
About the merry-ma-tansie.]

He's married wi' a gay gold ring,
A gay gold ring, a gay gold ring,
He's married wi' a gay gold ring,
About the merry-ma-tansie.

A gay gold ring's a cankerous thing,
A cankerous thing, a cankerous thing,
A gay gold ring's a cankerous thing,
About the merry-ma-tansie.

Now they're married, I wish them joy,
I wish them joy, I wish them joy,
Now they're married, I wish them joy,
About the merry-ma-tansie.

Father and mother they must obey,
Must obey, must obey,
Father and mother they must obey,
About the merry-ma-tansie.

Loving each other like sister and brother,
Sister and brother, sister and brother,
Loving each other like sister and brother,
About the merry-ma-tansie.

We pray this couple may kiss together,
Kiss together, kiss together,
We pray this couple may kiss together,
About the merry-ma-tansie.

—Chambers' *Popular Rhymes*, pp. 132–134.

(*b*) At Biggar (Mr. Ballantyne) this game was generally played on the green by boys and girls. A ring is formed by all the children but one, joining hands. The one child stands in the centre. The ring of children dance round the way of the sun, first slowly and then more rapidly. First all the children in the ring bow to the one in the centre, and she bows back. Then they dance round singing the first and second verses, the second verse being addressed to the child in the centre. She then whispers a boy's name to one in the ring. This girl then sings the third verse. None in the ring are supposed to be able to answer, and the name of the chosen boy is then said aloud by the girl who asked the question. If the name is satisfactory the ring sing the fourth verse, and the two players then retire and walk round a little. If the name given is not satisfactory the ring sing the fifth verse, and another child must be chosen. When the two again stand in the centre the boys sing the sixth verse. The girls answer with the seventh. Then all the ring sing the next verses, imitating washing clothes, wringing, ironing, baking bread, washing hands, combing hair, &c., suiting their actions to the words of the verses sung. The boy who was chosen then presents a ring, usually a blade of grass wrapped round her finger, to the girl. The ring then sing the ninth, tenth, eleventh, and twelfth verses. When all have chosen, if any lad is left without a partner, the last verse is sung.

The version recorded by Chambers is similar in action, but there are some important differences in detail. The centre child acts as mistress of the ceremonies. The ring of children dance round her, singing the verses. At the end of the first line of the second verse they all courtesy to her, and she returns the compliment. At the conclusion of this verse she selects a girl from the ring and asks her her sweetheart's name, which is imparted in a whisper. Upon this the child in the centre sings the third verse, the ring dancing round as before. If the ring approves her choice, they sing the fourth verse as in the Biggar version, and if they disapprove, the fifth. Chambers does not say whether another child is selected, if this is the case ; but it is probable, as he says, the marriage is finally concluded upon and effected by the ring singing the verses which follow. When singing the first line of the eighth verse all the ring unclasps hands for a moment, and each child performs a pirouette, clapping her hands above her head.

(c) It seems very clear from both the versions given that this is a ceremonial dance, round or at a place sacred to such ceremonies as betrothal and marriage. The version given by Chambers suggests this the more strongly, as the child in the centre acts as mistress of the ceremonies, or "go-between," the person who was the negotiator between the parents on either side in bringing a marriage about. The courtesying and bowing of those in the ring to her may show respect for this office. On the other hand, there is the more important office of priest or priestess of "the stones" suggested by the action of the game, and the reverence to the centre child may be a relic of this. The fact that she asks a girl to tell her her sweetheart's name, and then announces the name of the girl's choice for approval or disapproval by the ring in both versions, points to the time when consent by relations and friends on both sides was necessary before the marriage could be agreed upon —the inquiry regarding the qualifications of the proposed wife, the recital of her housewifely abilities, and the giving of the ring by the boy to the girl are also betrothal customs. It is to be noted that it was a popular belief in ancient times that to wed with a rush-ring was a legal marriage, without the intervention of a priest or the ceremonies of marriage. Poore, Bishop of Salisbury (circa 1217), prohibited the use of them—

"With gaudy girlonds or fresh flowers dight
        About her necke, or rings of rushes plight."
                                    —Spenser's *Queen*.

And Shakespeare alludes to the custom in the lines—"As fit as ten groats for the hand of an attorney, as Tib's rush for Tom's forefinger."—*All's Well that Ends Well.* The rejoicing and bestowal of the blessing by the ring of friends give an almost complete picture of early Scotch marriage custom. A version of this game, which appeared in the *Weekly Scotsman* of October 16, 1893, by Edgar L. Wakeman, is interesting, as it confirms the above idea, and adds one or two details which may be important, *i.e.*, the "choose your maidens one by one," and "sweep the house till the bride comes home." This game is called the "Gala Ship," and the girls, forming a ring, march round singing—

> Three times round goes the gala, gala ship,
> And three times round goes she ;
> Three times round goes the gala, gala ship,
> And sinks to the bottom of the sea.

They repeat this thrice, courtesying low. The first to courtesy is placed in the centre of the circle, when the others sing :—

> Choose your maidens one by one,
> One by one, one by one ;
> Choose your maidens one by one—
> And down goes (all courtesy)
> Merrima Tansa !

She chooses her maidens. They take her to a distance, when she is secretly told the name of her lover. The remainder of the girls imitate sweeping, and sing several stanzas to the effect that they will "sweep the house till the bride comes home," when the bride is now placed within the circle, and from a score to a hundred stanzas, with marching and various imitations of what the lucky bride accomplishes or undergoes, are sung. Each one closes with " Down goes Merrima Tansa" and the head-ducking; and this wonderful music-drama of childhood is not concluded until the christening of the bride's first-born, with—

> Next Sunday morn to church she must gae,
> A babe on her knee, the best of 'a—
> And down goes Merrima Tansa !

Jamieson gives the game as a ring within which one goes round with a handkerchief, with which a stroke is given in succession to every one in the ring; the person who strikes, or the taker, still repeating this rhyme:—

> Here I gae round the jingie ring,
> The jingie ring, the jingie ring,
> Here I gae round the jingie ring,
> And through my merry-ma-tanzie.

Then the handkerchief is thrown at one in the ring, who is obliged to take it up and go through the same process. He also mentions another account of the game which had been sent him, which describes the game as played in a similar manner to the versions given by Chambers.

Stewart, in his *Ben Nevis and Glencoe*, p. 361, records the following rhyme:—

> Here we go with merry shout,
> Up and down and round about,
> And dance a merry-ma-tandy,

but he does not describe the game in detail.

Milking Pails

—Monton, Lancashire (Miss Dendy);
London (A. B. Gomme).

—Earls Heaton, Yorks. (H. Hardy).

I. Mary's gone a-milking,
Mother, mother,
Mary's gone a-milking,
Gentle sweet mother o' mine.

Take your pails and go after her,
    Daughter, daughter,
Take your pails and go after her,
    Gentle sweet daughter o' mine.

Buy me a pair of new milking pails,
    Mother, mother,
Buy me a pair of new milking pails,
    Gentle sweet mother o' mine.

Where's the money to come from,
    Daughter, daughter,
Where's the money to come from,
    Gentle sweet daughter o' mine ?

Sell my father's feather bed,
    Mother, mother,
Sell my father's feather bed,
    Gentle sweet mother o' mine.

What's your father to sleep on,
    Daughter, daughter,
What's your father to sleep on,
    Gentle sweet daughter o' mine ?

Put him in the truckle bed,
    Mother, mother,
Put him in the truckle bed,
    Gentle sweet mother o' mine.

What are the children to sleep on,
    Daughter, daughter,
What are the children to sleep on,
    Gentle sweet daughter o' mine ?

Put them in the pig-sty,
    Mother, mother,
Put them in the pig-sty,
    Gentle sweet mother o' mine.

What are the pigs to lie in,
  Daughter, daughter,
What are the pigs to lie in,
  Gentle sweet daughter o' mine?

Put them in the washing-tubs,
  Mother, mother,
Put them in the washing-tubs,
  Gentle sweet mother o' mine.

What am I to wash in,
  Daughter, daughter,
What am I to wash in,
  Gentle sweet daughter o' mine?

Wash in the thimble,
  Mother, mother,
Wash in the thimble,
  Gentle sweet mother o' mine.

Thimble won't hold your father's shirt,
  Daughter, daughter,
Thimble won't hold your father's shirt,
  Gentle sweet daughter o' mine.

Wash in the river,
  Mother, mother,
Wash in the river,
  Gentle sweet mother o' mine.

Suppose the clothes should blow away,
  Daughter, daughter,
Suppose the clothes should blow away,
  Gentle sweet daughter o' mine?

Set a man to watch them,
  Mother, mother,
Set a man to watch them,
  Gentle sweet mother o' mine.

Suppose the man should go to sleep,
   Daughter, daughter,
Suppose the man should go to sleep,
   Gentle sweet daughter o' mine?

Take a boat and go after them,
   Mother, mother,
Take a boat and go after them,
   Gentle sweet mother o' mine.

Suppose the boat should be upset,
   Daughter, daughter,
Suppose the boat should be upset,
   Gentle sweet daughter o' mine?

Then that would be an end of you,
   Mother, mother,
Then that would be an end of you,
   Gentle sweet mother o' mine.
       —London Nursemaid, 1876 (A. B. Gomme).

II. Mary's gone a-milking, a-milking, a-milking,
    Mary's gone a-milking, mother, dear mother of mine.

Where did she get her money from, daughter, daughter?
Where did she get her money from, daughter, dear
    daughter of mine?

[Then follow verses sung in the same manner, beginning
with the following lines—]

Sold her father's feather bed, feather bed.
What will your father lie on, lie on?
Lay him in the pig-sty, pig-sty.
Where will the pigs lie, daughter?
Lay them in the wash-tub, mother.
What shall I wash in, wash in?
Wash in a thimble, mother.
A thimble won't hold my night-cap.
Wash by the sea-side, mother.

Suppose the clothes should blow away?
Get a boat and go after them, mother.
But suppose the boat should turn over?
Then that would be an end of you, mother.
                    —Bocking, Essex (*Folk-lore Record*, iii. 169).

III.   Mother, please buy me a milking-can,
            A milking-can, a milking-can!
        Mother, please buy me a milking-can,
            With a humpty-dumpty-daisy!

[Then follow verses sung in the same manner, beginning—]

Where's the money to come from, to come from?
Sell my father's feather bed.
Where's your father going to lie?
Lie on the footman's bed.
Where's the footman going to lie?
Lie in the cowshed.
Where's the cows going to lie?
Lie in the pig-sty.
Where's the pig going to lie?
Lie in the dolly-tub.
And what am I to wash in?
Wash in a thimble.
A thimble wunna hold a cap.
Wash in an egg-shell.
An egg-shell wunna hold a shirt.
Wash by the river-side.
Suppose the clothes should float away?
Get a boat and fetch them back.
Suppose the boat should overthrow?
Serve you right for going after them!
                    —Berrington, Oswestry, Chirbury (Burne's
                        Shropshire Folk-lore, p. 515).

IV.   Mother, will you buy me a milking-can,
        A milking-can, a milking-can?
        Mother, will you buy me a milking-can,
            To me, I, O, OM?

Where's the money to buy it with,
To buy it with, to buy it with,
Where's the money to buy it with,
　　　To me, I, O, OM ?

[Then the following verses—]

Sell my father's feather bed.
Where will your father sleep ?
My father can sleep in the boys' bed.
Where will the boys sleep ?
The boys can sleep in the pig-sty.
Where will the pigs sleep ?
The pigs can sleep in the wash-tub.
Where shall I wash my clothes ?
You can wash them in a thimble.
A thimble is not large enough.
You can wash them in an egg-shell.
An egg-shell would not hold them.
You can wash them by the river side.
But what if I should fall in ?
We'll get a rope and pull you out,
　　　To me, I, O, OM.　　　—Sheffield (S. O. Addy).

V.　Mother, come buy me two milking-pails,
Two milking-pails, two milking-pails,
Mother, come buy me two milking-pails,
O sweet mother o' mine.

[Then verses beginning with the following lines—]

Where shall I get my money from,
O sweet daughter o' mine ?

Sell my father's feather beds.
Where shall your father sleep ?
Sleep in the servant's bed.
Where shall the servant sleep ?
Sleep in the washing-tub.
Where shall I wash the clothes ?
Wash them in the river.

Suppose the clothes float away ?
Take a boat and go after them.
Suppose the boat upsets ?
Then you will be drownded.

—London (Miss Dendy).

VI.   Mother, come buy me a milking-can,
Milking-can, milking-can,
Mother, come buy me a milking-can,
O mother o' mine.

Where can I have my money from,
O daughter o' mine ?

Sell my father's bedsteads.
Where must your father sleep ?
Sleep in the pig-sty.
Where must the pig sleep ?
Sleep in the washing-tub.
What must I wash in ?
Wash in your thimble.
What must I sew with ?
Sew with your finger.
What will you say if I prick me ?
Serve you right, serve you right.

—Monton, Lancashire (Miss Dendy).

VII.   Mother, will you buy me a pair of milking-cans,
Milking-cans, milking-cans,
Mother, will you buy me a pair of milking-cans,
O gentle mother of mine ?

But where shall I get the money from ?
Sell my father's feather bed.
But where, O where, will your father lie ?
Father can lie in the girls' bed.
But where, O where, shall the girls then lie ?
The girls can lie in the boys' bed.
But where, O where, shall the boys lie ?
The boys may lie in the pig-sty.

Then where, O where, will the pigs lie ?
The pigs may lie in the washing-tub.
Then where, O where, shall we wash our clothes ?
We can wash by the river side.
The tide will wash the clothes away.
Get the prop and follow them.
—Sheffield (Miss Lucy Garnett).

VIII.　Mother, buy some milking-cans,
　　　Milking-cans, milking-cans.

　　　Where must our money come from ?
　　　Sell our father's feather bed.

[This goes on for many more verses, articles of furniture being mentioned in each succeeding verse.]
—Earls Heaton (Herbert Hardy).

IX.　Buy me a milking-pail, my dear mother.
　　Where's the money to come from, my dear daughter ?
　　Sell father's feather bed.
　　Where could your father sleep ?
　　Sleep in the pig-sty.
　　What's the pigs to sleep in ?
　　Put them in the washing-tub.
　　What could I wash the clothes in ?
　　Wash them in your thimble.
　　Thimble isn't big enough for baby's napkin.
　　Wash them in a saucer.
　　A saucer isn't big enough for father's shirt.
　　Wash by the river side, wash by the river side.
—Crockham Hill, Kent (Miss Chase).

X.　Please, mother, buy me a milking-can,
　　Milking-can, milking-can,
　　Please, mother, buy me a milking-can,
　　My dear mother.

　　Where can I get the money from ?
　　Sell father's feather bed.

Where shall your father sleep ?
Sleep in the boys' bed.
Where shall the boys sleep ?
Sleep in the pig-sty.
Where shall the pigs sleep ?
Sleep in the washing-tub.
What shall I wash with ?
Wash in an egg-shell.
The egg-shell will break.
Wash in a thimble.
Thimble's not big enough.
Wash by the river side.
Suppose the things should float away ?
Get a boat and go after them.
Suppose the boat should be upset ?
Then you'll be drowned,
Drowned, drowned,
Then you'll be drowned,
And a good job too.

                  —Enborne, Berks. (Miss M. Kimber).

XI.   Please, mother, buy me a milk-can,
       A milk-can, a milk-can,
          Please, mother, do.

       Where's the money coming from,
       Coming from, coming from,
          What shall I do ?

       Sell father's feather bed,
       Feather bed, feather bed,
          Please mother, do.

       Where shall the father sleep ?
       Sleep in the servants' bed.
       Where shall the servants sleep ?
       Sleep in the pig-sty.
       Where shall the pig sleep ?
       Sleep in the washing-tub.
       What shall I wash in ?
       Wash in a thimble.

The shirts won't go in.
Wash by the river side.
Supposing if I fall in ?
Good job too !
—Hartley Wintney, Winchfield, Hants (H. S. May).

XII. Mother, buy the milk-pail, mother, dear mother of mine.
Where's the money to come from, children, dear chil-
    dren of mine ?
Sell father's feather bed, mother, dear mother of mine.
Where's your father to sleep in ?
Father can sleep in the servant's bed.
Where's the servant to sleep in ?
Servant can sleep in the pig-sty.
Where's the pig to sleep in ?
The pig can sleep in the wash-tub.
Where shall we wash our clothes ?
Wash our clothes at the sea-side.
If our clothes should swim away ?
Then take a boat and go after them.
O what should we do if the boat should sink ?
O then we should all of us be at an end.
—Swaffham, Norfolk (Miss Matthews).

XIII. We want to buy a wash-pan, wash-pan, wash-pan,
We want to buy a wash-pan, early in the morning.

Where will you get the money from, money from, money
    from ?
We'll sell my father's feather bed, feather bed, feather
    bed.
Where will your father sleep ?
Father'll sleep in the boys' bed.
Where will the boys sleep ?
Boys will sleep in the girls' bed.
Where will the girls sleep ?
Girls will sleep in the pig-sty.
Where will the pigs sleep ?
Pigs will sleep in the washing-pan.
—Cowes, Isle of Wight (Miss E. Smith)

XIV. Mother, may I buy some male-scales, mother, mother ?
Mother, may I buy some male-scales, gentle mother of
 mine ?
Where will the money come from, daughter, daughter ?
Sell my father's feather bed, mother, mother.
Where will your father lie, daughter, daughter ?
Lie in the boys' bed, mother, mother.
Where will the boys lie, daughter, daughter ?
Lie in the servants' bed, mother, mother.
Where will the servants lie, daughter, daughter ?
Lie in the pig-sty, mother, mother.
Where will the pigs lie, daughter, daughter ?
Lie in the washing-tub, mother, mother.
Where will we wash our clothes, daughter, daughter ?
Wash them at the sea-side, mother, mother.
Suppose the clothes should float away, daughter,
 daughter ?
Take a boat and bring them in, mother, mother.
Suppose the boat would go too slow, daughter, daughter?
Take a steamboat and bring them in, mother, mother.
Suppose the steamboat would go too fast, daughter,
 daughter ?
Then take a rope and hang yourself, mother, mother.
—South Shields (Miss Blair, aged 9).

(*b*) One child stands apart and personates the Mother. The
other children form a line, holding hands and facing the
Mother. They advance and retire singing the first, third, and
alternate verses, while the Mother, in response, sings the
second and alternate verses. While the last verse is being
sung the children all run off; the Mother runs after them,
catches them, and beats them. Either the first or last caught
becomes Mother in next game. In the Shropshire game the
Mother should carry a stick. In the Norfolk version the
Mother sits on a form or bank, the other children advancing
and retiring as they sing. After the last verse is sung the
children try to seat themselves on the form or bank where the
Mother has been sitting. If they can thus get home without
the Mother catching them they are safe. The Kentish game is

played with two lines of children advancing and retiring. This was also the way in which the London version (A. B. Gomme) was played. In the version sent by Mr. H. S. May a ring is formed by the children joining hands. One child stands in the centre—she represents the Mother. The ring of children say the first, third, and every alternate verse. The child in the centre says the second, fourth, and alternate verses, and the game is played as above, except that when the Mother has said the last verse the children call out, "Good job, too," and run off, the Mother chasing them as above. The game does not appear to be sung.

(c) This game is somewhat of a cumulative story, having for its finish the making angry and tormenting of a mother. All the versions point to this. One interesting point, that of milk-pails, is, it will be seen, gradually losing ground in the rhymes. Milk-pails were pails of wood suspended from a yoke worn on the milkmaid's shoulders, and these have been giving place to present-day milk-cans. Consequently we find in the rhymes only four versions in which milk-pails are used. In two versions even the sense of milking-can has been lost, and the South Shields version, sent me by little Miss Blair, has degenerated into "male-scales," a thoroughly meaningless phrase. The Cowes version (Miss Smith) has arrived at "wash-pan." The "burden" of the Chirbury version is "a rea, a ria, a roses," and the Sheffield is also remarkable: the "I, O, OM" refers, probably, to something now forgotten, or it may be the "Hi, Ho, Ham!" familiar in many nursery rhymes. The game seems to point to a period some time back, when milking was an important phase of the daily life, or per-haps to the time when it was customary for the maids and women of a village to go to the hilly districts with the cows (summer shealings) for a certain period of time. The references to domestic life are interesting. The scarcity of beds, the best or feather bed, and the children's bed, seeming to be all those available. The feather bed is still a valued piece of household furniture, and is considered somewhat of the nature of a heir-loom, feather beds often descending from mother to daughter for some generations. I have been told instances of this. Gregor, in *Folk-lore of East of Scotland*, p. 52, describes the Scottish box-bed. The "truckle bed" and "footman's bed" probably refers to the small bed under a large one, which was only pulled out at night for use, and pushed under during the day. Illustrations of these beds and the children's bed are given in old tales. The proximity of the pig - sty to the house is manifest. The mention of washing-tubs calls to mind the large wooden tubs formerly always used for the family wash. Before the era of laundresses washing-tubs must have constituted an important part of the family plenishing. Washing in the rivers and streams was also a thing of frequent occurrence, hot water for the purpose of cleansing clothes not being considered necessary, or in many cases desirable. Chambers gives a version of the game (*Popular Rhymes*, p. 36) and also Newell (*Games*, p. 166). Another version from Buckingham is given by Thomas Baker in the *Midland Garner*, 1st ser., ii. 32, in which the mother desires the daughter to "milk in the washing-tub," and the words also appear very curiously tacked on to the "Three Dukes a-riding" game from Berkshire (*Antiquary*, xxvii. 195), where they are very much out of place.

Mineral, Animal, and Vegetable

A ball is thrown by one player to any one of the others. The thrower calls out at the same time either "mineral," "animal," or "vegetable," and counts from one to ten rather quickly. If the player who is touched by the ball does not name something belonging to that kingdom called before the number ten is reached, a forfeit has to be paid.—London (A. B. Gomme).

This is more usually called "Animal, Vegetable, and Mineral." See "Air, Fire, and Water."

Minister's Cat

The first player begins by saying, "The minister's cat is an ambitious cat," the next player "an artful cat," and so on, until they have all named an adjective beginning with A. The next time of going round the adjectives must begin with B, the next time C, and so on, until the whole of the alphabet has been gone through.—Forest of Dean, Gloucestershire (Miss Matthews); Anderby, Lincolnshire (Miss Peacock).

This is apparently the same game as the well-known "I love my love with an A because she is amiable." In this game every player has to repeat the same sentence, but using a different adjective, which adjective must begin with the letter A. Various sentences follow. At the next round the adjectives all begin with B; the next C, until a small story has been built up. Forfeits were exacted for every failure or mistake. The formula usually was—

I love my love with an A because she is (   ). I hate her with an A because she is (   ). I took her to the sign of the (   ), and treated her to (   ). The result was (   ).

Mollish's Land
Cornish name for "Tom Tiddler's Ground."—*Folk-lore Journal*, v. 57.

Monday, Tuesday
A game played with a ball. There are seven players, who each take a name from one of the days of the week. One (Sunday) begins by throwing the ball against a wall, calling out at the same time the name of one of the days, who has to run and catch it before it falls. If this one fails to catch the ball, the first player picks up the ball and tries to hit one of the six with it, who all endeavour to escape being hit. If the player succeeds, he again throws the ball against the wall, calling out another day of the week to catch it. If a player gets hit three times, he is out. The winner is he who has either not been hit at all or the fewest times, or who has been able to stay in the longest. The same game is played with twelve children, who are named after the twelve months of the year.—London and Barnes (A. B. Gomme); *Strand Magazine*, ii. 519 (F. H. Low).

This game belongs apparently to the ball games used for purposes of divination. Mr. Newell (*Games*, p. 181) describes a similar game to this, in which the player whose name is called drops the ball; he must pick it up as quickly as possible while the rest scatter. He then calls "Stand!"

upon which the players halt, and he flings it at whom he pleases. If he misses his aim, he must place himself in a bent position with his hands against a wall until every player has taken a shot at him. The idea of naming children after the days of the week occurs also in the games of "Gipsy," "Witch," and "Mother, Mother, the Pot boils over."

See "Ball," "Burly Whush," "Keppy Ball."

Moolie Pudding

The game of "Deadelie;" one has to run with the hands locked and "taen" the others.—Mactaggart's *Gallovidian Encyclopædia*.

See "Chickidy Hand," "Deadelie," "Hunt the Staigie," "Whiddy."

More Sacks to the Mill

A very rough game, mentioned in Dean Miles' MS., p. 180 (Halliwell's *Dictionary*). Lowsley (*Berkshire Glossary*) says this is "a favourite game with children at Christmas-time, when wishing for one of a romping character," but he does not describe it further. Northall (*English Folk Rhymes*, p. 354) says that in Warwickshire and Staffordshire boys torture an unfortunate victim by throwing him on the ground and falling atop of him, yelling out the formula, "Bags to [on] the mill." This summons calls up other lads, and they add their weight.

Mother, may I go out to Play?

I. Mother, may I go out to play?
    No, my child, it's such a wet day.
    Look how the sun shines, mother.
    Well, make three round curtseys and be off away.
        [Child goes, returns, knocks at door. Mother says,
            "Come in."]
    What have you been doing all this time?
    Brushing Jenny's hair and combing Jenny's hair.
    What did her mother give you for your trouble?
    A silver penny.
    Where's my share of it?
    Cat ran away with it.

Where's the cat ?
In the wood.
Where's the wood ?
Fire burnt it.
Where's the fire ?
Moo-cow drank it.
Where's the moo-cow ?
Butcher killed it.
Where's the butcher ?
Eating nuts behind the door, and you may have the
    nutshells.
          —London (Miss Dendy, from a maid-servant).

II.   Please, mother, may I go a-maying ?
Why, daughter, why ?
Because it is my sister's birthday.
Make three pretty curtseys and walk away.
Where is your may ?
I met puss, and puss met me, and puss took all my
    may away.
Where is puss ?
Run up the wood.
Where is the wood ?
Fire burnt it.
Where is the fire ?
Water quenched it.
Where is the water ?
Ducks have drunk it.
Where are the ducks ?
Butcher killed them.
Where is the butcher ?
Behind the churchyard, cracking nuts, and leaving
    you the shells. —Sporle, Norfolk (Miss Matthews).

III.   Please, mother, may we go out to play ?
Yes, if you don't frighten the chickens.
No, mother, we won't frighten the chickens.
    [They all go out and say, " Hush ! hush !" to
       pretended chickens.]

Where have you been ?

To grandmother's.

What for ?

To go on an errand.

What did you get ?

Some plums.

What did you do with them ?

Made a plum-pudding.

What did she give you ?

A penny.

What did you do with it ?

Bought a calf.

What did you do with it ?

Sold it.

What did you do with the money ?

Gave it to the butcher, and he gave me a penny back, and I bought some nuts with it.

What did you do with them ?

Gave them to the butcher, and he's behind the church-yard cracking them, and leaving you the shells.

—Sporle, Norfolk (Miss Matthews).

IV.   Mother, mother, may I go to play ?

No, daughter, no ! for fear you should stay.

Only as far as the garden gate, to gather flowers for my wedding day.

Make a fine curtsey and go your way.

[They all curtsey and scamper off, and proceed to plan some mischief.   Then they return.]

Now where have you been ?

Up to Uncle John's.

What for ?

Half a loaf, half a cheese, and half a pound of butter.

Where's my share ?

Up in cupboard.

'Tisn't there, then !

Then the cat eat it.

And where's the cat ?
Up on the wood [*i.e.*, the faggots].
And where's the wood ?
Fire burnt it.
Where's the fire ?
Water douted it [*i.e.*, put it out].
Where's the water ?
Ox drank it.
Where's the ox ?
Butcher killed it.
And where's the butcher ?
Behind the door cracking nuts, and you may eat
   the shells of them if you like.
                —Dorsetshire (*Folk-lore Journal*, vii. 219).

V.   Please may I go out to play ?
     How long will you stay ?
     Three hours in a day.
     Will you come when I call you ?
     No.
     Will you come when I fetch you ?
     Yes.
     Make then your curtseys and be off.

The girls then scamper off as before, and as they run about
the field keep calling out, " I won't go home till seven o'clock,
I won't go home till seven o'clock." After they have been
running about for some five or ten minutes the Mother calls
Alice (or whatever the name may be) to come home, when the
one addressed will run all the faster, crying louder than before,
" I won't go home till seven o'clock." Then the Mother commences to chase them until she catches them, and when she
gets them to any particular place in the field where the others
are playing, she says—

     Where have you been ?
     Up to grandmother's.
     What have you done that you have been away so long ?
     I have cleaned the grate and dusted the room.
     What did she give you ?

A piece of bread and cheese so big as a house, and a
    piece of plum cake so big as a mouse.
Where's my share ?
Up in higher cupboard.
It's not there.
Up in lower cupboard.
It's not there.
Then the cat have eat it.
Where's the cat ?
Up in heath.
Where's the heath ?
The fire burnt it.

[The rest is the same as in the last version, p. 393.]
                   —Dorsetshire (*Folk-lore Journal*, vii. 221–222).

VI.   Mother, mother, may I (or we) go out to play ?
       No, child ! no, child ! not for the day.
       Why, mother ? why, mother ?   I won't stay long.
       Make three pretty courtesies, and away begone.
       One for mammy, one for daddy, one for Uncle John.
       Where, child ! where, child ! have you been all the day ?
       Up to granny's.
       What have you been doing there ?

[The answer to this is often, " Washing doll's clothes," but
anything may be mentioned.]
       What did she give you ?

[The reply is again left to the child's fancy.]
       Where's my share ?
       The cat ate it [or, In the cat's belly].   What's in that
          box, mother ?
       Twopence, my child.
       What for, mother ?
       To buy a stick to beat you, and a rope to hang you, my
          child.   —Cornwall (*Folk-lore Journal*, v. 55, 56).

VII.   Grandmother, grandmother grey,
       May I go out to play ?
       No, no, no, it is a very wet day.

Grandmother, grandmother grey,
May I go out to play ?
Yes, yes, yes, if you don't frighten the geese **away.**
Children, I call you.
I can't hear you.
Where are your manners ?
In my shoe.
Who do you care for ?
Not for you.   —Earls Heaton, Yorks. (H. Hardy).

VIII.   Pray, mother, pray,
May I go out to play ?
No, daughter, no, daughter,
Not every fine day.
Why, mother, why ?
I shan't be gone long.
Make a fine curtsey
And glad git you gone.—
Wait for your sister.
                    —Hurstmonceux, Sussex (Miss Chase).

IX.   Please, mother, please, mother, may I go out to play ?
No, child, no, child, 'tis such a cold day.
Why, mother, why, mother, I won't stay long.
Make three pretty curtseys and off you run.
                    —Northants (Rev. W. D. Sweeting).

(*b*) One girl is chosen to act as " Mother," the rest of the
players pretend to be her children, and stand in front of her,
not in a line, but in a group. One of them, very frequently all
the children ask her the first question, and the Mother answers.
When she gives permission for the children to go out they all
curtsey three times, and run off and pretend to play. They
then return, and the rest of the dialogue is said, the Mother
asking the questions and the children replying. At the end of
the dialogue the Mother chases and catches them, one after the
other, pretending to beat and punish them. In the Northants
and Hurstmonceux games there appears to be no chasing. In
the London version (Miss Dendy) only two children are mentioned as playing. When the Mother is chasing the girl she

keeps asking, "Where's my share of the silver penny?" to which the girl replies, "You may have the nut-shells." In the Cornish version, when the Mother has caught one of the children, she beats her and puts her hands round the child's throat as if she were going to hang her.

(c) Miss Courtney, in *Folk-lore Journal*, v. 55, says: "I thought this game was a thing of the past, but I came across some children playing it in the streets of Penzance in 1883." It belongs to the cumulative group of games, and is similar in this respect to "Milking Pails," "Mother, Mother, the Pot boils over," &c. There seems to be no other object in the game as now played except the pleasures of teasing and showing defiance to a mother's commands, and trying to escape the consequences of disobedience by flight, in order that the mother may chase them. The idea may be that, if she is "out of breath," she cannot chastise so much. Mr. Newell (*Games*, p. 172) gives versions of a similar game.

Mother Mop

All the players, except one, stand two by two in front of each other, the inner ones forming an arch with their hands united —this is called the "oven." The odd child is "Mother Mop." She busies herself with a pretended mop, peel, &c., after the manner of old-fashioned bakers, making much ado in the valley between the rows of children. The oven soon gets demolished, and the last child vanquished becomes "Mother Mop" the next time.—Bitterne, Hants (Mrs. Byford).

It seems probable that the inner rows of children should kneel or stoop down in order that "Mother Mop" should have as much trouble as possible with her oven. The game may have lost some of its details in other directions, as there is no apparent reason why the oven is demolished or broken down.

See "Jack, Jack, the Bread's a-burning."

Mother, Mother, the Pot Boils over

A number of girls choose one of their number to represent a witch, and another to be a mother. The Witch stands near the corner of a wall, so that she can peep round. Then the

Mother counts the children by the seven days of the week, "Monday," "Tuesday," &c., and appoints another girl to act as guardian over them. She then pretends to go out washing, removing to a short distance so as to be within ear-shot of the other children. As soon as the Mother has gone, the old Witch comes and says, "Please, can I light my pipe?" Then the children say, "Yes, if you won't spit on t' hearth." She pretends to light her pipe, but spits on the hearth, and runs away with the girl called Sunday. Then the Guardian, among the confusion, pretends to rush down stairs, and, failing to find Sunday, calls out, "Mother, mother, t' pot boils over." The Mother replies, "Put your head in;" the Guardian says, "It's all over hairs;" the Mother says, "Put the dish-clout in;" the Guardian says, "It's greasy;" the Mother says, "Get a fork;" the Guardian says, "It's rusty;" the Mother says, "I'll come mysen." She comes, and begins to count the children, Monday, Tuesday, up to Saturday, and missing Sunday, asks, "Where's Sunday?" the Guardian says, "T' old Witch has fetched her." The Mother answers, "Where was you?" "Up stairs." The Mother says, "What doing?" "Making t' beds." "Why didn't you come down?" "Because I had no shoes." "Why didn't you borrow a pair?" "Because nobody would lend me a pair." "Why didn't you steal a pair." "Do you want me to get hung?" Then the Mother runs after her, and if she can catch her thrashes her for letting Sunday go. Then the Mother pretends to go out washing again, and the Witch fetches the other days of the week one by one, when the same dialogue is rehearsed.—Dronfield, Derbyshire (S. O. Addy).

This game was also played in London. The *dramatis personæ* were a mother, an eldest daughter, the younger children, a witch, and a pot was represented by another child. The Mother names the children after the days of the week. She tells her eldest daughter that she is going to wash, and that she expects her to take great care of her sisters, and to be sure and not let the old witch take them. She is also to look after the dinner, and be sure and not let the pot boil over. The Mother then departs, and stays at a little distance from the others. The eldest daughter pretends to be very busy putting the house to rights, sweeps the floor, and makes everything tidy; the younger children pretend to play, and get in the elder sister's way. She gets angry with them, and pretends to beat them. Now, the girl who personates the Witch comes and raps with her knuckles on a supposed door. The Witch stooped when walking, and had a stick to help her along.

Come in, says the eldest sister. What do you want?

Let me light my pipe at your fire? My fire's out.

Yes! if you'll not dirty the hearth.

No, certainly; I'll be careful.

While the eldest sister pretends to look on the shelf for something, the Witch "dirties" the hearth, catches hold of Monday and runs off with her; and at this moment the pot boils over. The child who is the pot makes a "hissing and fizzing" noise. The daughter calls out—

Mother, mother, the pot boils over.

Take the spoon and skim it.

Can't find it.

Look on the shelf.

Can't reach it.

Take the stool.

The leg's broke.

Take the chair.

Chair 's gone to be mended.

I suppose I must come myself?

The Mother here wrings her hands out of the water in the washing-tub and comes in. She looks about and misses Monday.

Where's Monday?

Oh, please, Mother, please, I couldn't help it; but some one came to beg a light for her pipe, and when I went for it she took Monday off.

Why, that's the witch!

The Mother pretends to beat the eldest daughter, tells her to be more careful another time, and to be sure and not let the pot boil over. The eldest daughter cries, and promises to be more careful, and the Mother goes again to the wash-tub.

The same thing occurs again.   The Witch comes and asks—
Please, will you lend me your tinder-box ?   My fire's out.
Yes, certainly, if you'll bring it back directly.
You shall have it in half-an-hour.
While the tinder-box is being looked for she runs off with
Tuesday.   Then the pot boils over, and the same dialogue is
repeated.   The Mother comes and finds Tuesday gone.   This
is repeated for all the seven children in turn, different articles,
gridiron, poker, &c., being borrowed each time.   Finally, the
eldest daughter is taken off too.   There is no one now to watch
the pot, so it boils over, and makes so much noise that the
Mother hears it and comes to see why it is.   Finding her
eldest daughter gone too, she goes after her children to the
Witch's house.   A dialogue ensues between the Witch and
the Mother.   The Mother asks—

Is this the way to the Witch's house ?
There's a red bull that way !
I'll go this way.
There's a mad cow that way !
I'll go this way.
There's a mad dog that way !

She then insists on entering the house to look for her children.   The Witch will not admit her, and says—

Your boots are too dirty.
I'll take my boots off.
Your stockings are too dirty.
I'll take them off.
Your feet are dirty.
I'll cut them off.
The blood will run over the threshold.
I'll wrap them up in a blanket.
The blood will run through.

This enrages the Mother, and she pushes her way into the
supposed house, and looks about, and calls her children.   She
goes to one and says—

This tastes like my Monday.
The Witch tells her it's a barrel of pork.

No, no, this is my Monday ; run away home.

Upon this Monday jumps up from her crouching or kneeling posture [the children were generally put by the Witch behind some chairs all close together in one corner of the room], and runs off, followed by all the others and their Mother. The Witch tries to catch one, and if successful that child becomes Witch next time.—A. B. Gomme.

A probable explanation of this game is that it illustrates some of the practices and customs connected with fire-worship and the worship of the hearth, and that the pot is a magical one, and would only boil over when something wrong had occurred and the Mother's presence was necessary. The pot boils over directly a child is taken away, and appears to cease doing this when the Mother comes in. It is remarkable, too, that the Witch should want to borrow a light from the fire; the objection to the giving of fire out of the house is a well-known and widely-diffused superstition, the possession of a brand from the house-fire giving power to the possessor over the inmates of a house. The mention of the spitting on the hearth in the Sheffield version, and dirtying the hearth in the London version, give confirmation to the theory that the desecration of the fire or hearth is the cause of the pot boiling over, and that the spirit of the hearth or fire is offended at the sacrilege. The Witch, too, may be unable to get possession of a child until she has something belonging to the house. The journey of the Mother to the Witch's house in search of her children, the obstacles put in her path, and the mention of the spilling of blood on the threshold, are incidents which have great significance. Why the "keeling" or skimming of the contents of the pot should be so difficult a task for the eldest daughter that the Mother is obliged to come herself, is not so clear; the skimming is of course to prevent the pot boiling over, and the pot may be supposed to take the place of the Mother or Guardian of the hearth, and tell when misfortune or trouble is at hand. Or the "boiling over" (which, if continued, would extinguish the fire and sully the stone) may be an offence to the hearth spirit, who ceases then to protect the inmates of the house. Fairies are said to have power over the inmates of a house when the threshold and kitchen utensils are left dirty and uncared for. Thus on the theories accompanying the ancient house ritual, this extraordinary game assumes a rational aspect, and it is not too much to suggest that this explanation is the correct one.

In the game of "Witch" practically the same incidents occur, and nearly the same dialogue, but the significant elements of pot-boiling and fire-protection do not appear in that game. It is not certain whether we have two independent games, or whether "The Witch" is this game, the incidents of pot-boiling and the fire-protection having been lost in its transmission to more modern notions. Although so closely allied, these games are not one at the present day, and are therefore treated separately. Newell (*Games*, p. 218) gives some versions of "Witch" which show a connection between that game and this. See "Keeling the Pot," "Witch."

Mount the Tin

One child throws a tin (any kind of tin will do) to some distance, and then walks towards it without looking round. The other children, in the meantime, hide somewhere near. The child who threw the tin has to guard it, and at the same time try to find those who are hiding. If he sees one he must call the name, and run to strike the tin with his foot. He does this until each one has been discovered. As they are seen they must stand out. The one who was first found has to guard the tin next time. Should one of the players be able to strike the tin while the keeper is absent, that player calls out, "Hide again." They can then all hide until the same keeper discovers them again.—Beddgelert (Mrs. Williams).

See "New Squat."

Mouse and the Cobbler

One girl stands up and personates a mother, another pretends to be a mouse, and crouches behind a chair in a corner. The mother says to another player—

Go and get your father's shirt.

This player goes to the chair to look for the shirt, and is tickled or touched by the one hiding. She rushes back and calls out—   Mother, there's a mouse.

Go and get your father's coat.

There's a mouse.

Go and get your father's watch and chain.

There's a mouse.

The Mother then goes to see herself. The second time she is scratched and chased. When caught she takes the Mouse's place.—Deptford, Kent (Miss Chase).

This is evidently the same game as "Ghost in the Garden" and "Ghost in the Copper," in a decaying stage. There is no *raison d'etre* for either mouse or cobbler. Probably these words are a corruption of the older "Ghost in the Copper."

Muffin Man

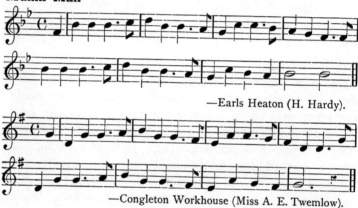

—Earls Heaton (H. Hardy).

—Congleton Workhouse (Miss A. E. Twemlow).

I.   Have you seen the muffin man, the muffin man, the
      muffin man,

    Have you seen the muffin man that lives in Drury
      Lane O ?

    Yes, I've seen the muffin man, the muffin man, the
      muffin man ;

    Yes, I've seen the muffin man who lives in Drury
      Lane O.   —Earls Heaton, Yorks. (H. Hardy).

II.   O, have you seen the muffin man,

    The muffin man, the muffin man ;

    O, have you seen the muffin man

    Who lives in Drury Lane O ?

        —N.-W. Lincolnshire (Rev. — Roberts).

III.   Have you seen the muffin girl,
  The muffin girl, the muffin girl ?
  O have you seen the muffin girl
  Down in yonder lane ?
    —Congleton Workhouse School (Miss A. E. Twemlow).

IV.   Don't you know the muffin man ?
   Don't you know his name ?
  Don't you know the muffin man
   That lives in our lane ?
  All around the Butter Cross,
   Up by St. Giles's,
  Up and down the Gullet Street,
   And call at Molly Miles's !
    —Burne's *Shropshire Folk-lore*, p. 571.

V.   Have you seen the nutting girl,
  The nutting girl, the nutting girl ?
  Have you seen the nutting girl,
   Down in yonder lane O ?
    —Holmfirth (H. Hardy).

(*b*) A ring is formed by the players joining hands ; one child, who is blindfolded and holds a stick, stands in the centre. The ring dance round, singing the verse. They then stand still, and the centre child holds out the stick and touches one of the ring. This player must take hold of the stick. Then the Muffin Man asks this player any questions he pleases, "Is the morn shining ?" "Is ink white ?" &c. The child who holds the stick answers "Yes" or "No" in a disguised voice, and the Muffin Man then guesses who it is. He is allowed three tries. If he guesses right he joins the ring, and the child who was touched takes his place in the centre. In the Yorkshire versions no questions are asked ; the blindfolded child goes to any one he can touch, and tries to guess his or her name. The other version, sent by Mr. Hardy, is played in the same way, and sung to the same tune. In the Congleton version (Miss Twemlow), the blindfolded child tries to catch one of those in the ring, when the verse is sung. The lines, with an additional four from *Shropshire Folk-lore,* are given by Miss Burne among nursery rhymes and riddles.

See "Buff with a Stick," "Dinah."

Mulberry Bush

—Miss Harrison.

Here we go round the mulberry bush,
The mulberry bush, the mulberry bush,
Here we go round the mulberry bush,
On a cold and frosty morning.

This is the way we wash our hands,
Wash our hands, wash our hands,
This is the way we wash our hands,
On a cold and frosty morning.

Here we go round the mulberry bush,
The mulberry bush, the mulberry bush,
Here we go round the mulberry bush,
On a cold and frosty morning.

This is the way we wash our clothes,
Wash our clothes, wash our clothes,
This is the way we wash our clothes,
On a cold and frosty morning.

Here we go round the mulberry bush,
The mulberry bush, the mulberry bush,
Here we go round the mulberry bush,
On a cold and frosty morning.

This is the way we go to school,
We go to school, we go to school,
This is the way we go to school,
On a cold and frosty morning.

Here we go round the mulberry bush,
The mulberry bush, the mulberry bush,
Here we go round the mulberry bush,
On a cold and frosty morning.
—Liphook, Hants (Miss Fowler).

(*b*) The children form a ring, all joining hands and dancing round while singing the first verse. When singing the last line they unclasp their hands, and each one turns rapidly round. They then sing the next verse, suiting their actions to the words they sing, again turning round singly at the last line. This is done with every alternate verse, the first verse being always sung as a chorus or dance in between the different action-verses. The verses may be varied or added to at pleasure. The actions generally consist of washing and dressing oneself, combing hair, washing clothes, baking bread, sweeping the floor, going to and returning from school, learning to read, cleaning boots, and lacing stays. When "going to school," the children walk two by two in an orderly manner; when "coming home from school," jumping and running is the style adopted; "lacing stays," the hands are put behind and moved first one and then the other, as if lacing; "this is the way the ladies walk," holding up skirts and walking primly; "gentlemen walk," walking with long strides and sticks. The dressing process and cleaning boots preceded "school."

(*c*) This game is well known, and played in almost all parts of England. It is always played in the same way. There is so little variety in the different versions that it appears unnecessary to give more than one here. In the many versions sent the only variants are: In Sporle, Norfolk, Miss Matthews says the game is sometimes called "*Ivy* Bush," or "*Ivory* Bush;" and Mr. C. C. Bell, of Epworth, sends a version, "Here we go round the Mulberry *Tree*." In Notts it is called "Holly Bush" (Miss Winfield). A version given in the *Folk-lore Record*, iv. 174, is called the "*Gooseberry* Bush," and Halliwell (*Popular Nursery Rhymes*, p. 224) records a game, the "Bramble Bush." "The bush," he says, "is often imaginative, but is sometimes represented by a child in the centre." Chambers (*Popular Rhymes*, pp. 134, 135) gives the game as a form of the "Merry-ma-tanzie "—a kind of dance. They sing while moving round to the tune of "Nancy Dawson," and stopping short with courtesy at the conclusion.

> Here we go round the mulberry bush,
> The mulberry bush, the mulberry bush,
> Here we go round the mulberry bush,
> And round the merry-ma-tanzie.

Disjoining hands, they then begin, with skirts held daintily up behind, to walk singly along, singing—

> This is the way the ladies walk,
> The ladies walk, the ladies walk ;
> This is the way the ladies walk,
> And round the merry-ma-tanzie.

At the last line they reunite, and again wheel round in a ring, singing as before—

> Here we go round the mulberry bush, &c.

After which, they perhaps simulate the walk of gentlemen, the chief feature of which is length of stride, concluding with the ring dance as before. Probably the next movement may be—

> This is the way they wash the clothes,
> Wash the clothes, wash the clothes ;
> This is the way they wash the clothes,
> And round the merry-ma-tanzie.

After which there is, as usual, the ring dance. They then represent washing, ironing clothes, baking bread, washing the house, and a number of other familiar proceedings.

Chambers quotes a fragment of this "little ballet," as practised at Kilbarchan, in Renfrewshire, which contains the following lines similar to those in this game :—

> She synes the dishes three times a day,
> Three times a day, three times a day ;
> She synes the dishes three times a day,
> Come alang wi' the merry-ma-tanzie.

> She bakes the scones three times a day,
> Three times a day, three times a day ;
> She bakes the scones three times a day,
> Come alang wi' the merry-ma-tanzie.

She ranges the stules three times a day,
Three times a day, three times a day;
She ranges the stules three times a day,
Come alang wi' the merry-ma-tanzie.

This game originated, no doubt, as a marriage dance round a sacred tree or bush. As it now exists it appears to have no other character than the performance of duties such as those enumerated in the description. In no version that I am acquainted with do the elements of love and marriage or kissing occur, otherwise the resemblance it bears to the Scotch "Merry-ma-tanzie" would suggest that it is a portion of that game. This game possesses the centre tree, which is not preserved in "Merry-ma-tansa." Trees were formerly sacred to dancing at the marriage festival, as at Polwarth in Berwickshire, where the custom once prevailed, which is not unworthy of notice. "In the midst of the village are two thorn trees near to each other; round these every newly-married pair were expected to dance with all their friends; from hence arose the old song, 'Polwarth on the Green'" (*New Statistical Account of Scotland, Polwarth, Berwickshire*, ii. 234). Holland (*Cheshire Glossary*), under "Kissing Bush," says, "A bush of holly, ivy, or other evergreens, which is hung up in farm kitchens at Christmas, and serves the purpose of mistletoe. The kissing bushes are usually prepared by the farm lads on Christmas Eve, and they are often tastefully decorated with apples, oranges, and bits of gay-coloured ribbon. I have occasionally seen them made upon a framework of hoop iron something in the form of a crown, with a socket at the bottom to hold a lighted candle." Brand (ii. 15) also describes how in Ireland men and women dance round about a bush in a large ring on the Patron Day. Newell (*Games*, p. 86), gives this game, and also mentions one in which "barberry bush" is named. The tune in all versions is the same. See "Merry ma-tansa," "Nettles."

Munshets or Munshits

Is played by two boys as follows:—One of the boys remains "at home," and the other goes out to a prescribed distance.

The boy who remains "at home" makes a small hole in the ground, and holds in his hand a stick about three feet long to strike with. The boy who is out at field throws a stick in the direction of this hole, at which the other strikes. If he hits it, he has to run to a prescribed mark and back to the hole without being caught or touched with the smaller stick by his playfellow. If he is caught, he is "out," and has to go to field. And if the boy at field can throw his stick so near to the hole as to be within the length or measure of that stick, the boy at home has to go out to field. A number of boys often play together; for any even number can play. I am told that the game was common fifty years ago. In principle it resembles cricket, and looks like the rude beginning of the game.—Addy's *Sheffield Glossary*.

See "Cat," "Cudgel," "Kit-cat," "Tip-cat."

Musical Chairs

A line of chairs is placed in a row down a room (one chair less than the number of children who are playing) in such a way that every alternate chair only is available on either side for the players to seat themselves. The children walk or dance round the chairs, keeping quite close to them. The piano or other musical instrument is played while they are dancing round. The music is continued for any length of time the player pleases, the children running round the chairs as long as the music goes on. The player stops the music suddenly, when all the children endeavour to take seats. One will be unable to find a seat, and this player remains "out." A chair is then taken away, and the music and dancing round begins again. There should always be one chair less than the number of players.—A. B. Gomme.

In Ellesmere, Miss Burne says, "Snap-tongs," called in other circles "Magic Music" or "Musical Chairs," is thus played. Five players take part; four chairs are set in the middle, and one of the players, who holds a pair of tongs, desires the others to dance round them till the clock strikes a certain hour, which is done by snapping the tongs together so many times. While they dance, a chair is taken away, and the player who cannot find a seat has to become the "snap-tongs" next time.—*Shropshire Folk-lore*, p. 525.

Nacks

A game in which pegs of wood play a similar part to the well-known object "Aunt Sally."—Robinson's *Mid Yorkshire Glossary*.

Namers and Guessers

Any number of players can play this game. Two are chosen, the one to be Namer, and the other Guesser or Witch. The rest of the players range themselves in a row. The Guesser retires out of sight or to a distance. The Namer then gives each player a secret name. When names have been given to all the players, the Namer calls on the Guesser to come, by saying—

> Witchie, witchie, yer bannocks are burnin',
> An' ready for turnin'.

Whereupon he approaches, and the Namer says—

> Come, chois me out, come, chois me in, to ——

(naming one by the assumed name). The players all shout, "Tack me, tack me," repeatedly. The Witch points to one. If the guess is correct the player goes to the Witch's side, but if it is incorrect he goes to the Namer's side. This goes on till all the players are ranged on the one side or the other. The two parties then come to a tug, with the Namer and Guesser as leaders. The gaining party then ranges itself in two lines with a space between the lines, each boy holding in his hand his cap or his handkerchief tightly plaited. The boys of the conquered side have then to run between the two lines, and are pelted by the victors. This is called, "Throuw the Muir o' Hecklepin."—Keith (Rev. W. Gregor).

This game is practically the same as "Fool, Fool, come to School," but the secret naming may indicate that this belongs to an earlier form.

See "Fool, Fool," "Hecklebirnie."

Neighbour

There is a game called "Neighbour, I torment thee," played in Staffordshire, "with two hands, and two feet, and a bob, and a nod as I do."—Halliwell's *Dictionary*.

Neiveie-nick-nack

A fireside game. A person puts a little trifle, such as a
button, into one hand, shuts it close, the other hand is also
shut; then they are both whirled round and round one another
as fast as they can, before the nose of the one who intends to
guess what hand the prize is in; and if the guesser be so fortunate as to guess the hand the prize is in, it becomes his
property; the whirling of the fists is attended with the following rhyme—

> Neiveie, neiveie, nick nack,
> What ane will ye tak,
> The right or the wrang?
> Guess or it be lang,
> Plot awa' and plan,
> I'll cheat ye gif I can.
> —Mactaggart's *Gallovidian Encyclopædia.*

The Rev. W. Gregor says at Keith this game is played at
Christmas, and by two. The stakes are commonly pins. One
player conceals a pin, or more if agreed on, in one of his (her)
hands. He then closes both hands and twirls them over each
other, in front of the other player, and repeats the words—

> Nivvie, nivvie-neek-nack,
> Filk (which) (or filk han') 'ill ye tack?
> Tack the richt, tack the left,
> An' a'll deceave ye gehn (if) I can.

The other player chooses. If he chooses the hand having the
stake, he gains it. If he does not, he forfeits the stake.
Another form of words is—

> Nivvie, nivvie-neek-nack
> Filk (which) will ye tick-tack?
> Tack ane, tack twa,
> Tack the best amo' them a'.

And—

> Nivvie, nivvie-nick-nack,
> Which han' will ye tack?
> Tack ane, tack twa,
> Tack the best amo' them a'.

Dickinson's *Cumberland Glossary* describes this as a boyish mode of casting lots. The boy says—

> Neevy, neevy-nack,
> Whether hand will ta tack,
> T' topmer or t' lowmer ?

Mr. W. H. Patterson (*Antrim and Down Glossary*) gives the rhyme as—

> Nievy, navy, nick nack,
> Which han' will ye tak',
> The right or the wrang ?
> I'll beguile ye if I can.

Chambers (*Popular Rhymes*, p. 117) gives the rhyme the same as that given by Mr. Patterson. In *Notes and Queries*, 6th Series, vii. 235, a North Yorkshire version is given as—

> Nievie, nievie, nack,
> Whether hand wilta tak,
> Under or aboon,
> For a singal half-crown ?
> Nievie, nievie, nick, nack,
> Whilk han' will thou tak ?
> Tak the richt or tak the wrang,
> I'll beguile thee if I can.

Jamieson (*Supp.*, *sub voce*) adds: "The first part of the word seems to be from neive, the fist being employed in the game." A writer in *Notes and Queries*, iii. 180, says : "The neive, though employed in the game, is not the object addressed. It is held out to him who is to guess—the conjuror—*and it is he who is addressed*, and under a conjuring name. In short (to hazard a wide conjecture, it may be) he is invoked in the person of Nic Neville (Neivi Nic), a sorcerer in the days of James VI., who was burnt at St. Andrews in 1569. If I am right, a curious testimony is furnished to his quondam popularity among the common people." It will be remembered that this game is mentioned by Scott in *St. Ronan's Well*—"Na, na, said the boy, he is a queer old cull. . . . He gave me half-a-crown yince, and forbade me to play it awa' at pitch and toss." "And you disobeyed him, of course ?" "Na, I didna disobey him—I played it awa' at 'Nievie, nievie, nick-nack.'"

See "Handy-dandy."

Nettles

> Nettles grow in an angry bush,
> An angry bush, an angry bush ;
> Nettles grow in an angry bush,
>   With my high, ho, ham !

> This is the way the lady goes,
> The lady goes, the lady goes ;
> This is the way the lady goes,
>   With my hi, ho, ham !

> Nettles grow in an angry bush, &c.

> This is the way the gentleman goes, &c.

> Nettles grow in an angry bush, &c.

> This is the way the tailor goes.
>   —Halliwell's *Nursery Rhymes*, 227.

(*b*) The children dance round, singing the first three lines, turning round and clapping hands for the fourth line. They curtsey while saying, " This is the way the lady goes," and again turn round and clap hands for the last line. The same process is followed in every verse, only varying what they act —thus, in the third verse, they bow for the gentleman—and so the amusement is protracted *ad libitum*, with shoemaking, washing clothes, ironing, churning, milking, making up butter, &c., &c.

(*c*) This game is practically the same as the " Mulberry Bush." The action is carried on in the same way, except that the children clap their hands at the fourth line, instead of each turning themselves round, as in " Mulberry Bush." The "High, ho, ham ! " termination may be the same as the " I, O, OM " of Mr. Addy's version of " Milking Pails."

See " Mulberry Bush," " When I was a Young Girl."

New Squat

A ring is made by marking the ground, and a tin placed in the middle of it. One boy acts as keeper of the tin, the other players also stand outside the ring. One of these kicks the tin out of the ring, the others then all run to hide or squat out of sight. The keeper has to replace the tin before looking for the boys. If, after that, he can spy a boy, that boy must come out and stand by the ring. When another boy is spied, he endeavours to reach the ring before the keeper does so, and kick out the tin. If he is successful, any one of the boys who is standing by, having been previously spied, is released from the keeper, and again hides. The object of the keeper is to successfully spy all the boys. When this is accomplished the last boy becomes the keeper. — Earls Heaton, Yorks. (Herbert Hardy).

See "Mount the Tin."

Nine Holes

Nine round holes are made in the ground, and a ball aimed at them from a certain distance; or the holes are made in a board with a number over each, through one of which the ball has to pass.—Forby's *Vocabulary*.

"A rural game," says Nares, "played by making nine holes in the ground, in the angles and sides of a square, and placing stones and other things upon, according to certain rules." Moor (*Suffolk Words and Phrases*) says: "This is, I believe, accurate as far as it goes, of our Suffolk game. A hole in the middle is necessary." In Norfolk, Holloway (*Dict. Prov.*) says that nine round holes are made in the ground, and a ball aimed at them from a certain distance. A second game is played with a board having nine holes, through one of which the ball must pass. Nares quotes several authors to show the antiquity of the game. He shows that the "Nine Men's Morris" of our ancestors was but another name for "Nine Holes." Nine, a favourite and mysterious number everywhere, prevails in games.

Strutt (*Sports*, p. 384) also describes the game as played in two ways—a game with bowling marbles at a wooden bridge; and another game, also with marbles, in which four, five, or six holes, and sometimes more, are made in the ground at a distance from each other, and the business of every one of the players is to bowl a marble, by a regular succession, into all the holes, and he who completes in the fewest bowls obtains

the victory. In Northamptonshire a game called " Nine Holes,"
or "Trunks," is played with a long piece of wood or bridge
with nine arches cut in it, each arch being marked with a
figure over it, from one to nine, in the following rotation—
VII., V., III., I., IX., II., IIII., VI., VIII. Each player has
two flattened balls which he aims to bowl edgeways under the
arches ; he scores the number marked over the arch he bowls
through, and he that attains to forty-five first wins the game
(Baker's *Northamptonshire Glossary*). In *Arch. Journ.*, xlix.
320, in a paper by Mr. J. T. Micklethwaite, this game is
described, and diagrams of the game given which had been
found by him cut in a stone bench in the church of Ardeley,
Hertfordshire, and elsewhere. He has also seen the game
played in London. It is evidently the same game as described
by Nares and Moor above.

See "Bridgeboard," " Nine Men's Morris."

Nine Men's Morris

In the East Riding this game is played thus : A flat piece of
wood about eight inches square is taken, and on it twenty-four
holes are bored by means of a hot skewer or piece of hot iron.

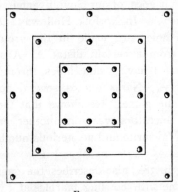

FIG. I.

Each of the two players has nine wooden pegs, which are either
coloured or shaped differently, and the object of each player is
to get three of his own pegs in a straight line (fig. 1). It is
called "Merrils."—Sheffield (S. O. Addy).

Cotgrave's *Dictionarie*, 1632, says: "*Merelles*, le jeu de merelles, the boyish game called merrils, or fiue-pennie morris. Played here most commonly with stones, but in France with pawns or men made of purpose, and termed merelles." Strutt (*Sports*, p. 317) says: "This was why the game received this name. It was formerly called 'Nine Men's Morris' and 'Five-penny Morris,' and is a game of some antiquity. It was certainly much used by the shepherds formerly, and continues to be used by them and other rustics to the present hour." An illustration of the form of the merelle table and the lines upon it, as it appeared in the fourteenth century, is given by him, and he observes that the lines have not been varied. The black spots at every angle and intersection of the lines are the places for the men to be laid upon. The men are different in form and colour for distinction's sake, and from the moving these men backwards and forwards, as though they were dancing a morris, I suppose the pastime received the name of "Nine Men's Morris," but why it should have been called "Five-penny Morris" I do not know. The manner of playing is briefly thus:—Two persons, having each of them nine pieces or men, lay them down alternately, one by one, upon the spots, and the business of either party is to prevent his antagonist from placing three of his pieces so as to form a row of three without the intervention of an opponent piece. If a row be formed, he that made it is at liberty to take up one of his competitor's pieces from any part he thinks most to his own advantage, excepting he has made a row, which must not be touched, if he have another piece upon the board that is not a component part of that row. When all the pieces are laid down they are played backwards and forwards in any direction that the lines run, but can only move from one spot to another at one time. He that takes off all his antagonist's pieces is the conqueror. The rustics, when they have not materials at hand to make a table, cut the lines in the same form upon the ground and make a small hole for every dot. They then collect stones of different forms or colours for the pieces, and play the game by depositing them in the holes in the same manner that they are set

over the dots on the table.   Hence Shakespeare, describing the
effects of a wet and stormy season, says—

> " The folds stand empty in the drowned field,
>   And crows are fatted with the murrain flock—
>   The Nine Men's Morris is filled up with mud."
>   —*Midsummer Night's Dream*, act ii. sc. 2.

Miss Baker (*Northamptonshire Glossary*), in describing
" Merell" or " Morris," says:—" On the inclosing of open
fields this game was transferred to a board, and continues a
fireside recreation of the agricultural labourer.   It is often
called by the name of ' Mill' or ' Shepherd's Mill.' "   She says
the mode of playing now observed is this.   Each of the players
has nine pieces, or men, differing in colour, or material, from
his adversary, for distinction's sake ; which they lay down on
the spots alternately, one by one, each endeavouring to prevent
his opponent from placing three of his pieces in a line, as
whichever does so is entitled to take off any one of his antagonist's men where he pleases, without breaking a row of three,
which must not be done whilst there is another man on the
board.   After all the pieces are placed on the board, they are
moved alternately backwards and forwards along the lines ;
and as often as either of the players succeeds in accomplishing
a row of three, he claims one of his antagonist's men, which is
placed in the pound (the centre), and he who takes the most
pieces wins the game.   It is played on a board whereon are
marked three squares, one being denominated the pound.   It
is sometimes played with pegs, bits of paper, or wood, or
stone.   It is called " Peg Morris " by Clare, the Northamptonshire poet.

The ancient game of " Nine Men's Morris " is yet played by
the boys of Dorset.   The boys of a cottage, near Dorchester,
had a while ago carved a " Marrel " pound on a block of stone
by the house.   Some years ago a clergyman of one of the
upper counties wrote that in the pulling down of a wall in his
church, built in the thirteenth century, the workmen came to a
block of stone with a " Marrel's " pound cut on it.   " Merrels "
the game was called by a mason.—Barnes' *Additional Glossary ;
Folk-lore Journal*, vii. 233.

" ' Nine Men's Morris,' in Gloucestershire called ' Ninepenny Morris,' was," says a correspondent in the *Midland Garner*, "largely practised by boys and even older people over thirty years ago, but is now, as far as I know, entirely disused. Two persons play. Each must have twelve pegs, or twelve pieces of anything which can be distinguished. The Morris was usually marked on a board or stone with chalk, and consists of twenty-four points. The pegs are put down one at a time alternately upon any point upon the Morris, and the first person who makes a consecutive row of three impounds one of his opponent's pegs. The pegs must only be moved on the lines. The game is continued until one or other of the players has only two pegs left, when the game is won" (1st ser., i. 20). Another correspondent in the same journal (ii. 2) says, "The game was very generally played in the midland counties under the name of 'Merrilpeg' or 'Merelles.' The twelve pieces I have never seen used, though I have often played with nine. We generally used marbles or draught pieces, and not pegs."

The following are the accounts of this game given by the commentators on Shakespeare :—

" In that part of Warwickshire where Shakespeare was educated, and the neighbouring parts of Northamptonshire, the shepherds and other boys dig up the turf with their knives to represent a sort of imperfect chess-board. It consists of a square, sometimes only a foot diameter, sometimes three or four yards. Within this is another square, every side of which is parallel to the external square ; and these squares are joined by lines drawn from each corner of both squares, and the middle of each line. One party, or player, has wooden pegs, the other stones, which they move in such a manner as to take up each other's men, as they are called, and the area of the inner square is called the pound, in which the men taken up are impounded. These figures are by the country people called *nine men's morris*, or *merrils ;* and are so called because each party has nine men. These figures are always cut upon the green turf, or leys as they are called, or upon the grass at the end of ploughed lands, and in rainy seasons never fail to be choked up with mud " (Farmer). "*Nine men's morris* is a game still played by the shepherds, cow-keepers, &c., in the midland counties, as follows:—A figure (of squares one within another) is made on the ground by cutting out the turf; and two persons take each nine stones, which they place by turns in the angles, and afterwards move alternately, as at chess or draughts. He who can play three in a straight line may then take off any one of his adversary's, where he pleases, till one, having lost all his men, loses the game " (Alchorne).

The following is the account of this game given by Mr. Douce in the *Illustrations of Shakespeare and of Ancient Manners*, 1807, i. 184:—"This game was sometimes called the *nine men's merrils* from *merelles*, or *mereaux*, an ancient French word for the jettons, or counters, with which it was played. The other term, *morris*, is probably a corruption suggested by the sort of dance which, in the progress of the game, the counters performed. In the French *merelles* each party had three counters only, which were to be placed in a line in order to win the game. It appears to have been the *tremerel* mentioned in an old fabliau. See *Le Grand, Fabliaux et Contes*, ii. 208. Dr. Hyde thinks the morris, or merrils, was known during the time that the Normans continued in possession of England, and that the name was afterwards corrupted into *three men's morals*, or *nine men's morals*. If this be true,

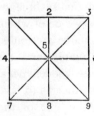

FIG. 2.

the conversion of *morrals* into *morris*, a term so very familiar to the country people, was extremely natural. The Doctor adds, that it was likewise called *nine-penny* or *nine-pin miracle, three-penny morris, five-penny morris, nine-penny morris*, or *three-pin, five-pin*, and *nine-pin morris*, all corruptions of *three-pin*, &c., *merels* " (Hyde's *Hist. Nederluddi*, p. 202). Nares says the simpler plan here represented (fig. 2), which he had also seen cut on small boards, is more like the game than the one referred to in the variorem notes of Shakespeare.

Forby has, "*Morris*, an ancient game, in very common

modern use. In Shakespeare it is called 'nine men's *morris*,' from its being played with nine men, as they were then, and still are called. We call it simply *morris*. Probably it took the name from a fancied resemblance to a dance, in the motions of the men. Dr. Johnson professes that he knew no more of it than that it was some rustic game. Another commentator speaks of it as common among shepherds' boys in some parts of Warwickshire. It cannot well be more common there than here, and it is not particularly rustic. Shepherds' boys and other clowns play it on the green turf, or on the bare ground ; cutting or scratching the lines, on the one or the other. In either case it is soon filled up with mud in wet weather. In towns, porters and other labourers play it, at their leisure hours, on the flat pavement, tracing the figure with chalk. It is also a domestic game ; and the figure is to be found on the back of some draught-boards. But to compare *morris* with that game, or with chess, seems absurd ; as it has a very distant resemblance, if any at all, to either, in the lines, or in the rules of playing. On the ground, the men are pebbles, broken tiles, shells, or potsherds ; on a table, the same as are used at draughts or backgammon. In Nares it is said to be the same as nine-holes. With us it is certainly different." Cope (*Hampshire Glossary*) says that "Nine Men's Morrice" is a game played with counters. He does not describe it further. Atkinson (*Glossary of Cleveland Dialect*) says under "Merls," the game of "Merelles," or "Nine Men's Morris." Toone (*Etymological Dictionary*) describes it as a game played on the green sward, holes being cut thereon, into which stones were placed by the players. Stead's *Holderness Glossary* calls it "Merrils," and describes it as a game played on a square board with eighteen pegs, nine on each side, called in many parts "Nine Men's Morrice." See also *Sussex Arch. Collections*, xxv. 234, and a paper by Mr. J. T. Micklethwaite (*Arch. Journ.*, xlix. 322), where diagrams of this game are given which have been found cut in several places on the benches of the cloisters at Gloucester, Salisbury, and elsewhere.

See "Noughts and Crosses."

Nip-srat-and-bite

A children's game, in which nuts, pence, gingerbread, &c.,
are squandered.—Addy's *Sheffield Glossary*.

Nitch, Notch, No-Notch

Children cut a number of slices from an apple, extending
from the eye to the tail, broader on the outside than on the
inner, which reaches nearly to the core; one piece has a part
cut out, making a notch—this is called "Notch;" another is
not cut at all—this is called "No-Notch;" while a third has
an incision made on it, but not cut out—this is called "Nitch."
The pieces when thus marked are replaced, and the game
consists in one child holding the apple, and pointing to one
of the pieces, asking another child which he will have, "Nitch,
Notch, or No-Notch;" if he guesses right, he has it and eats
it; if wrong, the other eats it.—Sussex (Holloway's *Dict. of
Provincialisms*).

Not

A game where the parties, ranged on opposite sides, with
each a bat in their hands, endeavour to strike a ball to opposite
goals. The game is called "Not," from the ball being made of
a knotty piece of wood.—Gloucestershire (Holloway's *Dict. of
Provincialisms*).

See "Hawkey."

Noughts and Crosses

This game is played on slates by school-children. The
accompanying diagram is drawn on the slate, and a certain

figure (generally twenty) is agreed upon as
"game." There are two players, one takes
noughts [o], the other crosses [×]. The
three places drawn on the slate above the
diagram are for the players each to put down
marks or numbers for the games they win,
the centre place being for "Old Nick," or
"Old Tom." The object of the game is for
each player to occupy three contiguous places in a row or line
with either noughts or crosses, and to prevent his opponent

from doing so. The diagram is of course empty when play begins. One player commences by putting his mark into either of the vacant places he prefers, the other player then places his in another, wherever he thinks he has the best opportunity to prevent his opponent getting a "three," and at the same time to get a three himself; then the first player plays again, and so on alternately until all the squares are occupied, or until one of the players has a "three" in line. If neither player gets a "three," the game is won by "Old Nick," and one is scored to his name. In the diagram the result of the game is shown when won by "Old Nick." Whichever player first wins a game adds "Old Nick's" score to his own. In some games "Old Nick" keeps all he wins for himself, and then most frequently wins the game.—London (A. B. Gomme).

See "Corsicrown," "Kit-Cat-Cannio," "Nine Men's Morris."

Nur and Spel

A boys' game in Lincolnshire, somewhat similar to "Trap Ball." It is played with a "kibble," a "nur," and a "spell." By striking the end of the spell with the kibble, the nur, of course, rises into the air, and the art of the game is to strike it with the kibble before it reaches the ground. He who drives it the greatest distance wins the game.—Halliwell's *Dictionary*.

Strutt (*Sports and Pastimes*, p. 109) describes this game as "Northern-spell," played with a trap, and the ball is stricken with a bat or bludgeon. The contest between the players is simply who shall strike the ball to the greatest distance in a given number of strokes. The length of each stroke is measured before the ball is returned, by means of a cord made fast at one end near the trap, the other being stretched into the field by a person stationed there for that purpose, who adjusts it to the ball wherever it may lie.

In a work entitled the *Costumes of Yorkshire* this game is described and represented as "Nor and Spell." The little wooden ball used in this game is in Yorkshire called the "Nor," and the receptacle in which it is placed the "Spell." Peacock

(*Manley and Corringham Glossary*) gives "knur," (1) a hard wooden ball, (2) the head. Addy (*Sheffield Glossary*) says "knur" is a small round ball, less than a billiard ball. It is put into a cup fixed on a spring which, being touched, causes the ball to rise into the air, when it is struck by a trip-stick, a slender stick made broad and flat at one end. The "knur" is struck by the broad part. The game is played on Shrove Tuesday. Brogden (*Provincial Words of Lincolnshire*) gives it under "Bandy." It is called "Knur, Spell, and Kibble" in S.-W. Lincolnshire.—Cole's *Glossary*.

The following letter relating to this game is extracted from the *Worcestershire Chronicle*, September 1847, in Ellis's edition of Brand:—" Before the commons were taken in, the children of the poor had ample space wherein to recreate themselves at cricket, *nurr*, or any other diversion ; but now they are driven from every green spot, and in Bromsgrove here, the nailor boys, from the force of circumstances, have taken possession of the turnpike road to play the before-mentioned games, to the serious inconvenience of the passengers, one of whom, a woman, was yesterday knocked down by a *nurr* which struck her in the head."

Brockett says of this game, as played in Durham : It is called "Spell and Ore," Teut. "spel," a play or sport; and Germ. "knorr," a knot of wood or ore. The recreation is also called "Buckstick, Spell, and Ore," the buckstick with which the ore is struck being broad at one end like the butt of a gun (*North Country Words*). In Yorkshire it is "Spell and Nurr," or "Knur," the ore or wooden ball having been, perhaps, originally the knurl or knot of a tree. The *Whitby Glossary* also gives this as "Spell and Knor," and says it is known in the South as "Dab and Stick." The author adds, "May not 'tribbit,' or 'trevit,' be a corruption of 'three feet,' the required length of the stick for pliable adaptation ? "

Robinson (*Mid-Yorkshire Glossary*), under "Spell and Nur," says : "A game played with a wooden ball and a stick fitted at the striking end with a club-shaped piece of wood. The 'spell' made to receive and spring the ball for the blow at a touch, is a simple contrivance of wood an inch or so in breadth

and a few inches long. . . . The players, who usually go in and
out by turns each time, after a preliminary series of tippings of
the spell with the stick in one hand, and catches of the ball
with the other, in the process of calculating the momentum
necessary for reach of hand, are also allowed two trial 'rises'
in a striking attitude, and distance is reckoned by scores of
yards. The long pliable stick, with a loose club end, used in
the game, is called the 'tribit' or 'trivit' stick. . . . The trevit
is, in fact, the trap itself, and the trevit-stick the stick with
which the trap is struck." The tribbit-stick is elsewhere called
"primstick," "gelstick," "buckstick," "trippit," and "trevit."
Atkinson says that "spell" is O.N., "spill" meaning a play or
game, and the probability is that the game is a lineal descendant
from the Ball-play of the Old Danes, or Northmen, and Ice-
landers. "Spell and knor" is a corruption of "spell a' knor," the
play at ball. Nurspel is simply ball-play, therefore which name,
taken in connection with the fact that the game is elsewhere
called "Spell and Knor," and not "Knor and Spell," is significant. There is one day in the year, Shrove Tuesday, when the
play is customarily practised, though not quite exclusively.—
Atkinson's *Cleveland Glossary*.

Easther (*Almondbury Glossary*) describes it as played with a
wooden ball, a spel, and a pommel. Two may play, or two
sides. When a player goes in he drives the knor for, say, 100
yards, *i.e.*, five score, and he reckons five. Each person has
the same number of strokes previously agreed upon, but generally only one innings. The "spell" is a kind of stage with
three or four feet, to drive it into the ground. On the top of
this stage is a spring made of steel, containing a cup to receive
the "knor," which is about one or two inches in diameter, and
is made of holly or box. The spring is kept down by a sneck,
which is tapped by the pommel when the knor is intended to be
struck. The pommel is thus formed—the driving part is frequently of ash-root or owler, in shape like half a sugar-loaf
split lengthwise, but only three or four inches long, and the
handle is of ash, wrapped with a wax band where held, which
is in one hand only.

See "Kibel and Nerspel," "Trap Ball," "Trippit and Coit."

Nuts in May

—Shropshire (Miss Burne).

I. Here we come gathering nuts in May,
    Nuts in May, nuts in May,
    Here we come gathering nuts in May,
    On a fine summer morning.

    Whom will you have for nuts in May,
    Nuts in May, nuts in May?
    Whom will you have for nuts in May,
    On a fine summer morning?

    We'll have —— for nuts in May,
    Nuts in May, nuts in May,
    We'll have -—— for nuts in May,
    On a fine summer morning.

    Who will you send to fetch her [*or* him] away,
    To fetch her away, to fetch her away?
    Who will you send to fetch her away,
    On a fine summer morning?

    We'll send —— to fetch her away,
    Fetch her away, fetch her away,
    We'll send —— to fetch her away,
    On a fine summer morning.
                —Liphook and Winterton, Hants (Miss Fowler).

II. Here we come gathering nuts and May
    [Nuts and May, nuts and May],
    Here we come gathering nuts and May,
    On a cold and frosty morning.

    Pray who will you gather for nuts and May,
    Pray who will you gather for nuts and May,
    On a cold and frosty morning?

We'll gather —— for nuts and May,
We'll gather —— for nuts and May,
On a cold and frosty morning.

Pray who will you send to take her away,
Pray who will you send to take her away,
On a cold and frosty morning?

We'll send —— to take her away,
We'll send —— to take her away,
On a cold and frosty morning.
                              —Penzance (Mrs. Mabbott).

III.   Here we come gathering nuts in May,
         Nuts in May, nuts in May,
         Here we come gathering nuts in May,
             May, May, May.

       Who will you have for nuts in May,
       Nuts in May, nuts in May?
       Who will you have for nuts in May,
             May, May, May?

       [Bessie Stewart] for nuts in May,
       Nuts in May, nuts in May,
       [Bessie Stewart] for nuts in May,
             May, May, May.

       Very well, very well, so you may,
       So you may, so you may,
       Very well, very well, so you may,
             May, may, may.

       Whom will you have to take her away,
       Take her away, take her away?
       Whom will you have to take her away,
             Way, way, way?

       —— —— to take her away,
       Take her away, take her away,
       —— —— to take her away,
             Way, way, way.   —Belfast (W. H. Patterson).

IV. Here we come gathering nuts in May,
Nuts in May, nuts in May,
Here we come gathering nuts in May,
On a cold and frosty morning.

Where do you gather your nuts in May?
On Galloway Hill we gather our nuts.
Who will you gather for nuts in May?
We'll gather —— for nuts in May.
Who will you send to fetch her away?
We'll send —— to fetch her away.
—Bocking, Essex (*Folk-lore Record*, iii. 169).

V. Here we go gathering nuts away,
Nuts away, nuts away,
Here we go gathering nuts away,
On a cold and frosty morning.

[Then follow verses beginning—]

Whose nuts shall we gather away?
We'll gather [Minnie Brown's] nuts away.
Whom shall we send to fetch them away?

[And the final verse is—]

We'll send [Johnny Cope] to fetch them away,
Fetch them away, fetch them away,
We'll send [Johnny Cope] to fetch them away,
On a cold and frosty morning.
—Newbury, Berks (Mrs. S. Batson).

VI. Who will go gathering nuts in May,
Nuts in May, nuts in May?
Who will go gathering nuts in May,
At five o'clock in the morning?
—N.-W. Lincolnshire (Rev. — Roberts).

VII. Here we come gathering nuts in May,
Nuts in May, nuts in May,
Here we come gathering nuts in May,
On a cold and frosty morning.

Who will you have for your nuts in May,
Nuts in May, nuts in May?
Who will you have for your nuts in May,
On a cold and frosty morning?

We will have a girl for nuts in May,
Nuts in May, nuts in May,
We will have a girl for nuts in May,
On a cold and frosty morning.
—Earls Heaton, Yorks. (Herbert Hardy).

VIII.   Here we come gathering nuts in May,
Nuts in May, nuts in May,
Here we come gathering nuts in May,
This cold frosty morning.

Who will you have for your nuts in May,
Nuts in May, nuts in May?
Who will you have for your nuts in May,
This cold frosty morning?

We will have —— for our nuts in May,
Nuts in May, nuts in May,
We will have —— for our nuts in May,
This cold frosty morning.

Who will you have to pull her away,
Pull her away, pull her away?
Who will you have to pull her away,
This cold frosty morning?

We will have —— to pull her away,
Pull her away, pull her away,
We will have —— to pull her away,
This cold frosty morning.
—Settle, Yorks. (Rev. W. S. Sykes).

IX.   Here we come gathering nuts to-day,
Nuts to-day, nuts to-day,
Here we come gathering nuts to-day,
So early in the morning.

Pray, whose nuts will you gather away,
Gather away, gather away?
Pray, whose nuts will you gather away,
So early in the morning?

We'll gather Miss A——'s nuts away,
Nuts away, nuts away,
We'll gather Miss A——'s nuts away,
So early in the morning.

Pray, who will you send to take them away,
To take them away, take them away?
Pray, who will you send to take them away,
So early in the morning?

We'll send Miss B—— to take them away,
To take them away, take them away,
We'll send Miss B—— to take them away,
So early in the morning.

        —Symondsbury, Dorsetshire (*Folk-lore Journal*,
                     vii. 226-7).

(*b*) The children form in two lines of equal length, facing one another, with sufficient space between the lines to admit of their walking in line backwards and forwards towards and away from each other, as each line sings the verses allotted to it (fig. 1). The first line sings the first, third, and fifth verses, and the opposite line the second and fourth. At the end of the fifth verse

Fig 1   Fig 2

a handkerchief or other mark is laid on the ground, and the two children (whose names have been mentioned, and who are as evenly matched as possible), take each other's right hand and endeavour to pull each other over the handkerchief to their own side (fig. 2). The child who is pulled over the handkerchief becomes the "captured nut," and joins the side of her capturers. Then the game begins again by the second line singing the first, third, and fifth verses, while advancing to gather or capture the "nuts," the first line responding with the second and fourth verses, and the same finish as before. Then the first line begins the game, and so on until all the children are in this way matched one against the other.

(c) Other versions have been sent me, with slight variations: NUTS IN MAY, with the verses ending, "On a fine summer morning," from Lincoln and Nottinghamshire (Miss M. Peacock); "So early in the morning," Sporle, Norfolk (Miss Matthews); "Six o'clock in the morning," Nottingham (Miss Wenfield); "On a cold and frosty morning," East Kirkby, Lincolnshire (Miss K. Maughan); Barnes (A. B. Gomme), Colchester (Miss G. M. Frances). NUTS AND MAY: "On a bright and sunny morning" (Mr. C. C. Bell); "On a cold and frosty morning," Forest of Dean (Miss Matthews); "Every night and morning," Gainford, Durham (Miss Edleston); "We've picked [Sally Gray] for nuts in May," "All on a summer's morning," Sheffield (Mr. S. O. Addy). A version by Miss Kimber (Newbury, Berks, and Marlborough, Wilts) ends each verse, "Nuts and May." In other respects these variants are practically the same. Printed versions not given above are Hersham, Surrey (*Folk-lore Record*, v. 85); Burne's *Shropshire Folk-lore*, p. 516; Sulhampstead, Berks (*Antiquary*, vol. xxvii., Miss E. E. Thoyts); and Dorsetshire, "Gathering nuts away" (*Folk-lore Journal*, vii. 225). From Longcot, Berks, a version sent me by Miss I. Barclay has no fourth line to the verses.

(d) This game is probably, unless we except "Mulberry Bush," the most popular and the most widely played of any singing game. It might almost be called universal. This is shown by the fact that there are few counties where it is not known, and also that important variants, either in the words or in the method of playing, are rarely met with. In all the versions which have been sent there are only the following variations in the words, and these are principally in the refrain, or last line of each verse: "On a cold and frosty morning" ends by far the greater number of versions; "On a fine summer's morning," "So early in the morning," "All on a summer's morning," "Five o'clock in the morning," "On a cold and sunny morning," coming next in number.   The Belfast version ends, "May! May! May!" and a Newbury and Marlborough fourth line is simply a repetition of the second, "Nuts in May, nuts in May."

In the first line of the verse the only important variant seems to be the Symondsbury "Gathering nuts away" and "Gathering nuts to-day."   "Gathering nuts away" also occurs in one version from Newbury (Berks), "Nuts and May" appearing in the larger number after the more usual "Nuts in May."   In only one version is a specific place mentioned for the gathering. This is in the Bocking version, where Galloway Hill is named, in reply to the unusual question, "Where do you gather your nuts in May?"   A player is usually gathered for "Nuts in May."   In three or four cases only is this altered to gathering a player's "nuts away," which is obviously an alteration to try and make the action coincide exactly with the words.   The game is always played in "lines," and the principal incidents running throughout all the versions are the same, *i.e.*, one player is selected by one line of players from their opponents' party.   The "selected" one is refused by her party unless some one from the opposite side can effect her capture by a contest of strength.   In all versions but two or three this contest takes place between the two; in one or two all the players join in the trial of strength.   In another instance there appears to be no contest, but the selected player crosses over to the opposite side.   Two important incidents occur in the Bocking and Symondsbury versions.   In the Bocking game the side which is victorious has the right to begin the next game first: this also occurs in the Barnes version.   In Symondsbury, when one child is drawn over the boundary line by one from the opposite side she has to be "crowned" immediately.   This is done by the conqueror putting her hand on the captured one's head.   If this is not done at once the captured one is at liberty to return to her own side.   In some versions (Shropshire and London) the player who is selected for "Nuts" is always captured by the one sent to fetch her. Some Barnes children also say that this is the proper way to play. When boys and girls play the boys are always sent to "fetch away" the girls. In Sheffield (a version collected by Mr. S. O. Addy) a boy is chosen to fetch the girl away; and in the Earls Heaton version the line runs, "We'll have a girl for nuts in May."

(e) There is some analogy in the game to marriage by capture, and to the marriage customs practised at May Day festivals and gatherings. For the evidence for marriage by capture in the game there is no element of love or courtship, though there is the obtaining possession of a member of an opposing party. But it differs from ordinary contest-games in the fact that one party does not wage war against another party for possession of a particular piece of ground, but individual against individual for the possession of an individual. That the player sent to fetch the selected girl is expected to conquer seems to be implied—first, by a choice of a certain player being made to effect the capture; secondly, by the one sent "to fetch" being always successful; and thirdly, the "crowning" in the Symondsbury game. Through all the games I have seen played this idea seems to run, and it exactly accords with the conception of marriage by capture. For examples of the actual survivals in English, Scottish, Welsh, and Irish customs of marriage by capture see Gomme's *Folk-lore Relics of Early Village Life*, pp. 204–210.

The question is, How does this theory of the origin of the game fit in with the term "Nuts in May"? I attribute this to the gathering by parties of young men of bunches of May at the May festivals and dances, to decorate not only the May-pole, May "kissing-bush," but the doors of houses. "Knots of May" is a term used by children, meaning bunches of May. Thus, a note by Miss Fowler in the MS. of the games she had collected says, "In Bucks the children speak of 'knots of May,' meaning each little bunch of hawthorn blossom." The gathering of bunches of May by parties of young men and maidens to make the May-bush round which the May Day games were held, and dancing and courting, is mentioned by Wilde (*Irish Popular Superstitions*, p. 52), the game being "Dance in the

Ring." Holland (*Cheshire Glossary*) says, "May birches were branches of different kinds of trees fastened over doors of houses and on the chimney on the eve of May Day. They were fastened up by parties of young men who went round for the purpose, and were intended to be symbolical of the character of the inmates." I remember one May Day in London, when the "May girls" came with a garland and short sticks decorated with green and bunches of flowers, they sang—

> Knots of May we've brought you,
> Before your door it stands;
> It is but a sprout, but it's well budded out
> By the work of the Lord's hands,

and a Miss Spencer, who lived near Hampton (Middlesex), told me that she well remembered the May girls singing the first verse of this carol, using "knots" instead of the more usual word "branch" or "bunch," and that she knew the small bunch of May blossom by the name of "knots" of May, "bringing in knots of May" being a usual expression of children.

The association of May—whether the month, or the flower, or both—with the game is very strong, the refrain "cold and frosty morning," "all on a summer's morning," "bright summer's morning," "so early in the morning," also being characteristic of the early days of May and spring, and suggests that the whole day from early hours is given up to holiday. The familiar nursery rhyme given by Halliwell—

> Here we come a-piping,
> First in spring and then in May,

no doubt also refers to house-to-house visiting of May.

The connection between the May festival and survival in custom of marriage by capture is well illustrated by a passage from Stubbe's *Anatomie of Abuses*, p. 148. He says: "Against May Day, Whitsonday, or other time, euery Parishe, Towne and Village assemble themselves together, bothe men women and children, olde and yong, . . . and either goyng all together or diuidyng themselues into companies, they goe some to the Woodes and groves where they spend all the night in plesant pastimes; and in the morning they return bringing with them birch and branches of trees to deck their assemblies withall . . . and then they fall to daunce about it like as the heathen people did. . . . I have heard it credibly reported (and that *viva voce*) by men of great grauitie and reputation, that of fortie, threescore or a hundred maides going to the wood ouer night, there haue scaresly the third part of them returned home againe undefiled." Herrick's *Hesperides* also describes the festival, and the custom of courting and marriage at the same time.

The tune sung to this game appears to be the same in every version.

CATALOG OF DOVER BOOKS

CATALOGUE OF DOVER BOOKS

Americana

THE EYES OF DISCOVERY, J. Bakeless. A vivid reconstruction of how unspoiled America appeared to the first white men. Authentic and enlightening accounts of Hudson's landing in New York, Coronado's trek through the Southwest; scores of explorers, settlers, trappers, soldiers. America's pristine flora, fauna, and Indians in every region and state in fresh and unusual new aspects. "A fascinating view of what the land was like before the first highway went through," Time. 68 contemporary illustrations, 39 newly added in this edition. Index. Bibliography. x + 500pp. 5⅜ x 8. **T761 Paperbound $2.00**

AUDUBON AND HIS JOURNALS, J. J. Audubon. A collection of fascinating accounts of Europe and America in the early 1800's through Audubon's own eyes. Includes the Missouri River Journals —an eventful trip through America's untouched heartland, the Labrador Journals, the European Journals, the famous "Episodes", and other rare Audubon material, including the descriptive chapters from the original letterpress edition of the "Ornithological Studies", omitted in all later editions. Indispensable for ornithologists, naturalists, and all lovers of Americana and adventure. 70-page biography by Audubon's granddaughter. 38 illustrations. Index. Total of 1106pp. 5⅜ x 8. **T675 Vol I Paperbound $2.00**
T676 Vol II Paperbound $2.00
The set $4.00

TRAVELS OF WILLIAM BARTRAM, edited by Mark Van Doren. The first inexpensive illustrated edition of one of the 18th century's most delightful books is an excellent source of first-hand material on American geography, anthropology, and natural history. Many descriptions of early Indian tribes are our only source of information on them prior to the infiltration of the white man. "The mind of a scientist with the soul of a poet," John Livingston Lowes. 13 original illustrations and maps. Edited with an introduction by Mark Van Doren. 448pp. 5⅜ x 8. **T13 Paperbound $2.00**

GARRETS AND PRETENDERS: A HISTORY OF BOHEMIANISM IN AMERICA, A. Parry. The colorful and fantastic history of American Bohemianism from Poe to Kerouac. This is the only complete record of hoboes, cranks, starving poets, and suicides. Here are Pfaff, Whitman, Crane, Bierce, Pound, and many others. New chapters by the author and by H. T. Moore bring this thorough and well-documented history down to the Beatniks. "An excellent account," N. Y. Times. Scores of cartoons, drawings, and caricatures. Bibliography. Index. xxviii + 421pp. 5⅝ x 8⅜. **T708 Paperbound $1.95**

THE EXPLORATION OF THE COLORADO RIVER AND ITS CANYONS, J. W. Powell. The thrilling first-hand account of the expedition that filled in the last white space on the map of the United States. Rapids, famine, hostile Indians, and mutiny are among the perils encountered as the unknown Colorado Valley reveals its secrets. This is the only uncut version of Major Powell's classic of exploration that has been printed in the last 60 years. Includes later reflections and subsequent expedition. 250 illustrations, new map. 400pp. 5⅝ x 8⅜. **T94 Paperbound $2.00**

THE JOURNAL OF HENRY D. THOREAU, Edited by Bradford Torrey and Francis H. Allen. Henry Thoreau is not only one of the most important figures in American literature and social thought; his voluminous journals (from which his books emerged as selections and crystalliza-tions) constitute both the longest, most sensitive record of personal internal development and a most penetrating description of a historical moment in American culture. This present set, which was first issued in fourteen volumes, contains Thoreau's entire journals from 1837 to 1862, with the exception of the lost years which were found only recently. We are reissuing it, complete and unabridged, with a new introduction by Walter Harding, Secretary of the Thoreau Society. Fourteen volumes reissued in two volumes. Foreword by Henry Seidel Canby. Total of 1888pp. 8⅜ x 12¼. **T312-3 Two volume set, Clothbound $20.00**

GAMES AND SONGS OF AMERICAN CHILDREN, collected by William Wells Newell. A remarkable collection of 190 games with songs that accompany many of them; cross references to show similarities, differences among them; variations; musical notation for 38 songs. Textual dis-cussions show relations with folk-drama and other aspects of folk tradition. Grouped into categories for ready comparative study: Love-games, histories, playing at work, human life, bird and beast, mythology, guessing-games, etc. New introduction covers relations of songs and dances to timeless heritage of folklore, biographical sketch of Newell, other pertinent data. A good source of inspiration for those in charge of groups of children and a valuable reference for anthropologists, sociologists, psychiatrists. Introduction by Carl Withers. New indexes of first lines, games. 5⅜ x 8½. xii + 242pp. **T354 Paperbound $1.65**

CATALOGUE OF DOVER BOOKS

GARDNER'S PHOTOGRAPHIC SKETCH BOOK OF THE CIVIL WAR, Alexander Gardner. The first published collection of Civil War photographs, by one of the two or three most famous photographers of the era, outstandingly reproduced from the original positives. Scenes of crucial battles: Appomattox, Manassas, Mechanicsville, Bull Run, Yorktown, Fredericksburg, etc. Gettysburg immediately after retirement of forces. Battle ruins at Richmond, Petersburg, Gaines'Mill. Prisons, arsenals, a slave pen, fortifications, headquarters, pontoon bridges, soldiers, a field hospital. A unique glimpse into the realities of one of the bloodiest wars in history, with an introductory text to each picture by Gardner himself. Until this edition, there were only five known copies in libraries, and fewer in private hands, one of which sold at auction in 1952 for $425. Introduction by E. F. Bleiler. 100 full page 7 x 10 photographs (original size). 224pp. 8½ x 10¾.   T476 Clothbound **$6.00**

A BIBLIOGRAPHY OF NORTH AMERICAN FOLKLORE AND FOLKSONG, Charles Haywood, Ph.D. The only book that brings together bibliographic information on so wide a range of folklore material. Lists practically everything published about American folksongs, ballads, dances, folk beliefs and practices, popular music, tales, similar material—more than 35,000 titles of books, articles, periodicals, monographs, music publications, phonograph records. Each entry complete with author, title, date and place of publication, arranger and performer of particular examples of folk music, many with Dr. Haywood's valuable criticism, evaluation. Volume I, "The American People," is complete listing of general and regional studies, titles of tales and songs of Negro and non-English speaking groups and where to find them, Occupational Bibliography including sections listing sources of information, folk material on cowboys, riverboat men, 49ers, American characters like Mike Fink, Frankie and Johnnie, John Henry, many more. Volume II, "The American Indian," tells where to find information on dances, myths, songs, ritual of more than 250 tribes in U.S., Canada. A monumental product of 10 years' labor, carefully classified for easy use. "All students of this subject . . . will find themselves in debt to Professor Haywood," Stith Thompson, in American Anthropologist. ". . . a most useful and excellent work," Duncan Emrich, Chief Folklore Section, Library of Congress, in "Notes." Corrected, enlarged republication of 1951 edition. New Preface. New index of composers, arrangers, performers. General index of more than 15,000 items. Two volumes. Total of 1301pp. 6⅛ x 9¼.   T797-798 Clothbound **$12.50**

INCIDENTS OF TRAVEL IN YUCATAN, John L. Stephens. One of first white men to penetrate interior of Yucatan tells the thrilling story of his discoveries of 44 cities, remains of once-powerful Maya civilization. Compelling text combines narrative power with historical significance as it takes you through heat, dust, storms of Yucatan; native festivals with brutal bull fights; great ruined temples atop man-made mounds. Countless idols, sculptures, tombs, examples of Mayan taste for rich ornamentation, from gateways to personal trinkets, accurately illustrated, discussed in text. Will appeal to those interested in ancient civilizations, and those who like stories of exploration, discovery, adventure. Republication of last (1843) edition. 124 illustrations by English artist, F. Catherwood. Appendix on Mayan architecture, chronology. Two volume set. Total of xxviii + 927pp.
Vol I T926 Paperbound **$2.00**
Vol II T927 Paperbound **$2.00**
The set **$4.00**

A GENIUS IN THE FAMILY, Hiram Percy Maxim. Sir Hiram Stevens Maxim was known to the public as the inventive genius who created the Maxim gun, automatic sprinkler, and a heavier-than-air plane that got off the ground in 1894. Here, his son reminisces—this is by no means a formal biography—about the exciting and often downright scandalous private life of his brilliant, eccentric father. A warm and winning portrait of a prankish, mischievous, impious personality, a genuine character. The style is fresh and direct, the effect is unadulterated pleasure. "A book of charm and lasting humor . . . belongs on the 'must read' list of all fathers," New York Times. "A truly gorgeous affair," New Statesman and Nation. 17 illustrations, 16 specially for this edition. viii + 108pp. 5⅜ x 8½.
T948 Paperbound **$1.00**

HORSELESS CARRIAGE DAYS, Hiram P. Maxim. The best account of an important technological revolution by one of its leading figures. The delightful and rewarding story of the author's experiments with the exact combustibility of gasoline, stopping and starting mechanisms, carriage design, and engines. Captures remarkably well the flavor of an age of scoffers and rival inventors not above sabotage; of noisy, uncontrollable gasoline vehicles and incredible mobile steam kettles. ". . . historic information and light humor are combined to furnish highly entertaining reading," New York Times. 56 photographs, 12 specially for this edition. xi + 175pp. 5⅜ x 8½.   T964 Paperbound **$1.35**

BODY, BOOTS AND BRITCHES: FOLKTALES, BALLADS AND SPEECH FROM COUNTRY NEW YORK, Harold W. Thompson. A unique collection, discussion of songs, stories, anecdotes, proverbs handed down orally from Scotch-Irish grandfathers, German nurse-maids, Negro workmen, gathered from all over Upper New York State. Tall tales by and about lumbermen and pirates, canalers and injun-fighters, tragic and comic ballads, scores of sayings and proverbs all tied together by an informative, delightful narrative by former president of New York Historical Society. ". . . a sparkling homespun tapestry that every lover of Americana will want to have around the house," Carl Carmer, New York Times. Republication of 1939 edition. 20 line-drawings. Index. Appendix (Sources of material, bibliography). 530pp. 5⅜ x 8½.   T411 Paperbound **$2.00**

Art, History of Art, Antiques, Graphic Arts, Handcrafts

ART STUDENTS' ANATOMY, E. J. Farris. Outstanding art anatomy that uses chiefly living objects for its illustrations. 71 photos of undraped men, women, children are accompanied by carefully labeled matching sketches to illustrate the skeletal system, articulations and movements, bony landmarks, the muscular system, skin, fasciae, fat, etc. 9 x-ray photos show movement of joints. Undraped models are shown in such actions as serving in tennis, drawing a bow in archery, playing football, dancing, preparing to spring and to dive. Also discussed and illustrated are proportions, age and sex differences, the anatomy of the smile, etc. 8 plates by the great early 18th century anatomic illustrator Siegfried Albinus are also included. Glossary. 158 figures, 7 in color. x + 159pp. 5⅝ x 8⅜. T744 Paperbound **$1.45**

AN ATLAS OF ANATOMY FOR ARTISTS, F Schider. A new 3rd edition of this standard text enlarged by 52 new illustrations of hands, anatomical studies by Cloquet, and expressive life studies of the body by Barcsay. 189 clear, detailed plates offer you precise information of impeccable accuracy. 29 plates show all aspects of the skeleton, with closeups of special areas, while 54 full-page plates, mostly in two colors, give human musculature as seen from four different points of view, with cutaways for important portions of the body. 14 full-page plates provide photographs of hand forms, eyelids, female breasts, and indicate the location of muscles upon models. 59 additional plates show how great artists of the past utilized human anatomy. They reproduce sketches and finished work by such artists as Michelangelo, Leonardo da Vinci, Goya, and 15 others. This is a lifetime reference work which will be one of the most important books in any artist's library. "The standard reference tool," AMERICAN LIBRARY ASSOCIATION. "Excellent," AMERICAN ARTIST. Third enlarged edition. 189 plates, 647 illustrations. xxvi + 192pp. 7⅞ x 10⅝. T241 Clothbound **$6.00**

AN ATLAS OF ANIMAL ANATOMY FOR ARTISTS, W. Ellenberger, H. Baum, H. Dittrich. The largest, richest animal anatomy for artists available in English. 99 detailed anatomical plates of such animals as the horse, dog, cat, lion, deer, seal, kangaroo, flying squirrel, cow, bull, goat, monkey, hare, and bat. Surface features are clearly indicated, while progressive beneath-the-skin pictures show musculature, tendons, and bone structure. Rest and action are exhibited in terms of musculature and skeletal structure and detailed cross-sections are given for heads and important features. The animals chosen are representative of specific families so that a study of these anatomies will provide knowledge of hundreds of related species. "Highly recommended as one of the very few books on the subject worthy of being used as an authoritative guide," DESIGN. "Gives a fundamental knowledge," AMERICAN ARTIST. Second revised, enlarged edition with new plates from Cuvier, Stubbs, etc. 288 illustrations. 153pp. 11⅜ x 9. T82 Clothbound **$6.00**

THE HUMAN FIGURE IN MOTION, Eadweard Muybridge. The largest selection in print of Muybridge's famous high-speed action photos of the human figure in motion. 4789 photographs illustrate 162 different actions: men, women, children—mostly undraped—are shown walking, running, carrying various objects, sitting, lying down, climbing, throwing, arising, and performing over 150 other actions. Some actions are shown in as many as 150 photographs each. All in all there are more than 500 action strips in this enormous volume, series shots taken at shutter speeds of as high as 1/6000th of a second! These are not posed shots, but true stopped motion. They show bone and muscle in situations that the human eye is not fast enough to catch. Earlier, smaller editions of these prints have brought $40 and more on the out-of-print market. "A must for artists," ART IN FOCUS. "An unparalleled dictionary of action for all artists," AMERICAN ARTIST. 390 full-page plates, with 4789 photographs. Printed on heavy glossy stock. Reinforced binding with headbands. xxi + 390pp. 7⅞ x 10⅝. T204 Clothbound **$10.00**

ANIMALS IN MOTION, Eadweard Muybridge. This is the largest collection of animal action photos in print. 34 different animals (horses, mules, oxen, goats, camels, pigs, cats, guanacos, lions, gnus, deer, monkeys, eagles—and 21 others) in 132 characteristic actions. The horse alone is shown in more than 40 different actions. All 3919 photographs are taken in series at speeds up to 1/6000th of a second. The secrets of leg motion, spinal patterns, head movements, strains and contortions shown nowhere else are captured. You will see exactly how a lion sets his foot down; how an elephant's knees are like a human's—and how they differ; the position of a kangaroo's legs in mid-leap; how an ostrich's head bobs; details of the flight of birds—and thousands of facets of motion only the fastest cameras can catch. Photographed from domestic animals and animals in the Philadelphia zoo, it contains neither semiposed artificial shots nor distorted telephoto shots taken under adverse conditions. Artists, biologists, decorators, cartoonists, will find this book indispensable for understanding animals in motion. "A really marvelous series of plates," NATURE (London). "The dry plate's most spectacular early use was by Eadweard Muybridge," LIFE. 3919 photographs; 380 full pages of plates. 440pp. Printed on heavy glossy paper. Deluxe binding with headbands. 7⅞ x 10⅝. T203 Clothbound **$10.00**

CATALOGUE OF DOVER BOOKS

THE 100 GREATEST ADVERTISEMENTS, WHO WROTE THEM AND WHAT THEY DID, J. L. Watkins. 100 (plus 13 added for this edition) of most successful ads ever to appear. "Do You Make These Mistakes in English," "They laughed when I sat down," "A Hog Can Cross the Country," "The Man in the Hathaway Shirt," over 100 more ads that changed habits of a nation, gave new expressions to the language, built reputations. Also salient facts behind ads, often in words of their creators. "Useful . . , valuable . . . enlightening," Printers' Ink. 2nd revised edition. Introduction. Foreword by Raymond Rubicam. Index. 130 illustrations. 252pp. 7¾ x 10¾. T540 Paperbound **$2.25**

THE DIDEROT PICTORIAL ENCYCLOPEDIA OF TRADES AND INDUSTRY, MANUFACTURING AND THE TECHNICAL ARTS IN PLATES SELECTED FROM "L'ENCYCLOPEDIE OU DICTIONNAIRE RAISONNE DES SCIENCES, DES ARTS, ET DES METIERS" OF DENIS DIDEROT, edited with text by C. Gillispie. The first modern selection of plates from the high point of 18th century French engraving, Diderot's famous Encyclopedia. Over 2000 illustrations on 485 full-page plates, most of them original size, illustrating the trades and industries of one of the most fascinating periods of modern history, 18th century France. These magnificent engravings provide an invaluable source of fresh, copyright-free material to artists and illustrators, a lively and accurate social document to students of cultures, an outstanding find to the lover of fine engravings. The plates teem with life, with men, women, and children performing all of the thousands of operations necessary to the trades before and during the early stages of the industrial revolution. Plates are in sequence, and show general operations, closeups of difficult operations, and details of complex machinery. Such important and interesting trades and industries are illustrated as sowing, harvesting, beekeeping, cheesemaking, operating windmills, milling flour, charcoal burning, tobacco processing, indigo, fishing, arts of war, salt extraction, mining, smelting iron, casting iron steel, extracting mercury, zinc, sulphur, copper, etc., slating, tinning, silverplating, gilding, making gunpowder, cannons, bells, shoeing horses, tanning, papermaking, printing, dying, and more than 40 other categories. Besides being a work of remarkable beauty and skill, this is also one of the largest collections of working figures in print. 920pp. 9 x 12. Heavy library cloth. T421 Two volume set **$18.50**

THE HANDBOOK OF PLANT AND FLORAL ORNAMENT, R. G. Hatton. One of the truly great collections of plant drawings for reproduction: 1200 different figures of flowering or fruiting plants—line drawings that will reproduce excellently. Selected from superb woodcuts and copperplate engravings appearing mostly in 16th and 17th century herbals including the fabulously rare "Kreuter Büch" (Bock) "Cruijde Boeck" (Dodoens), etc. Plants classified according to botanical groups. Also excellent reading for anyone interested in home gardening or any phase of horticulture. Formerly "The Craftsman's Plant-Book: or Figures of Plants." Introductions. Over 1200 illustrations. Index. 548pp. 6⅛ x 9¼. T649 Paperbound **$2.98**

HANDBOOK OF ORNAMENT, F. S. Meyer. One of the largest collections of copyright-free traditional art in print. It contains over 3300 line cuts from Greek, Roman, Medieval, Islamic, Renaissance, Baroque, 18th and 19th century sources. 180 plates illustrate elements of design with networks, Gothic tracery, geometric elements, flower and animal motifs, etc., while 100 plates illustrate decorative objects: chairs, thrones, daises, cabinets, crowns, weapons, utensils, vases, jewelry, armor, heraldry, bottles, altars, and scores of other objects. Indispensable for artists, illustrators, designers, handicrafters, etc. Full text. 3300 illustrations. xiv + 548pp. 5⅜ x 8. T302 Paperbound **$2.25**

COSTUMES OF THE GREEKS AND ROMANS, Thomas Hope. Authentic costumes from all walks of life in Roman, Greek civilizations, including Phrygia, Egypt, Persia, Parthia, Etruria, in finely drawn, detailed engravings by Thomas Hope (1770-1831). Scores of additional engravings of ancient musical instruments, furniture, jewelry, sarcophagi, other adjuncts to ancient life. All carefully copied from ancient vases and statuary. Textual introduction by author. Art and advertising personnel, costume and stage designers, students of fashion design will find these copyright-free engravings a source of ideas and inspiration and a valuable reference. Republication of 1st (1812) edition. 300 full-page plates, over 700 illustrations. xliv + 300pp. 5⅝ x 8⅜. T21 Paperbound **$2.00**

PRINCIPLES OF ART HISTORY, H. Wölfflin. Analyzing such terms as "baroque," "classic," "neoclassic," "primitive," "picturesque," and 164 different works by artists like Botticelli, van Cleve, Dürer, Hobbema, Holbein, Hals, Rembrandt, Titian, Brueghel, Vermeer, and many others, the author establishes the classifications of art history and style on a firm, concrete basis. This classic of art criticism shows what really occurred between the 14th century primitives and the sophistication of the 18th century in terms of basic attitudes and philosophies. "A remarkable lesson in the art of seeing," SAT. REV. OF LITERATURE. Translated from the 7th German edition. 150 illustrations. 254pp. 6⅛ x 9¼. T276 Paperbound **$2.00**

AFRICAN SCULPTURE, Ladislas Segy. First publication of a new book by the author of critically acclaimed AFRICAN SCULPTURE SPEAKS. It contains 163 full-page plates illustrating masks, fertility figures, ceremonial objects, etc., representing the culture of 50 tribes of West and Central Africa. Over 85% of these works of art have never been illustrated before, and each is an authentic and fascinating tribal artifact. A 34-page introduction explains the anthropological, psychological, and artistic values of African sculpture. "Mr. Segy is one of its top authorities," NEW YORKER. 164 full-page photographic plates. Bibliography. 244pp. 6 x 9. T396 Paperbound **$2.00**

CATALOGUE OF DOVER BOOKS

SHAKER FURNITURE, E. D. Andrews and F. Andrews. The most illuminating study on what many scholars consider the best examples of functional furniture ever made. Includes the history of the sect and the development of Shaker style. The 48 magnificent plates show tables, chairs, cupboards, chests, boxes, desks, beds, woodenware, and much more, and are accompanied by detailed commentary. For all antique collectors and dealers, designers and decorators, historians and folklorists. "Distinguished in scholarship, in pictorial illumination, and in all the essentials of fine book making," Antiques. 3 Appendixes. Bibliography. Index. 192pp. 7⅞ x 10¾.   T679 Paperbound **$2.00**

JAPANESE HOMES AND THEIR SURROUNDINGS, E. S. Morse. Every aspect of the purely traditional Japanese home, from general plan and major structural features to ceremonial and traditional appointments—tatami, hibachi, shoji, tokonoma, etc. The most exhaustive discussion in English, this book is equally honored for its strikingly modern conception of architecture. First published in 1886, before the contamination of the Japanese traditions, it preserves the authentic features of an ideal of construction that is steadily gaining devotees in the Western world. 307 illustrations by the author. Index. Glossary. xxxvi + 372pp. 5⅝ x 8⅜.   T746 Paperbound **$2.00**

COLONIAL LIGHTING, Arthur H. Hayward. The largest selection of antique lamps ever illustrated anywhere, from rush light-holders of earliest settlers to 1880's—with main emphasis on Colonial era. Primitive attempts at illumination ("Betty" lamps, variations of open wick design, candle molds, reflectors, etc.), whale oil lamps, painted and japanned hand lamps, Sandwich glass candlesticks, astral lamps, Bennington ware and chandeliers of wood, iron, pewter, brass, crystal, bronze and silver. Hundreds of illustrations, loads of information on colonial life, customs, habits, place of acquisition of lamps illustrated. A unique, thoroughgoing survey of an interesting aspect of Americana. Enlarged (1962) edition. New Introduction by James R. Marsh. Supplement "Colonial Chandeliers," photographs with descriptive notes. 169 illustrations, 647 lamps. xxxi + 312pp. 5⅝ x 8¼.   T975 Paperbound **$2.00**

CHINESE HOUSEHOLD FURNITURE, George N. Kates. The first book-length study of authentic Chinese domestic furniture in Western language. Summarizes practically everything known about Chinese furniture in pure state, uninfluenced by West. History of style, unusual woods used, craftsmanship, principles of design, specific forms like wardrobes, chests and boxes, beds, chairs, tables, stools, cupboards and other pieces. Based on author's own investigation into scanty Chinese historical sources and surviving pieces in private collections and museums. Will reveal a new dimension of simple, beautiful work to all interior decorators, furniture designers, craftsmen. 123 illustrations; 112 photographs. Bibliography. xiii + 205pp. 5¼ x 7¾.   T958 Paperbound **$1.50**

ART AND THE SOCIAL ORDER, Professor D. W. Gotshalk, University of Illinois. One of the most profound and most influential studies of aesthetics written in our generation, this work is unusual in considering art from the relational point of view, as a transaction consisting of creation-object-apprehension. Discussing material from the fine arts, literature, music, and related disciplines, it analyzes the aesthetic experience, fine art, the creative process, art materials, form, expression, function, art criticism, art and social· life and living. Graceful and fluent in expression, it requires no previous background in aesthetics and will be read with considerable enjoyment by anyone interested in the theory of art. "Clear, interesting, the soundest and most penetrating work in recent years," C. J. Ducasse, Brown University. New preface by Professor Gotshalk. xvi + 248pp. 5⅝ x 8½.
T294 Paperbound **$1.50**

FOUNDATIONS OF MODERN ART, A. Ozenfant. An illuminating discussion by a great artist of the interrelationship of all forms of human creativity, from painting to science, writing to religion. The creative process is explored in all facets of art, from paleolithic cave painting to modern French painting and architecture, and the great universals of art are isolated. Expressing its countless insights in aphorisms accompanied by carefully selected illustrations, this book is itself an embodiment in prose of the creative process. Enlarged by 4 new chapters. 226 illustrations. 368pp. 6⅛ x 9¼.   T215 Paperbound **$1.95**

VITRUVIUS: TEN BOOKS ON ARCHITECTURE. Book by 1st century Roman architect, engineer, is oldest, most influential work on architecture in existence; for hundreds of years his specific instructions were followed all over the world, by such men as Bramante, Michelangelo, Palladio, etc., and are reflected in major buildings. He describes classic principles of symmetry, harmony; design of treasury, prison, etc.; methods of durability; much more. He wrote in a fascinating manner, and often digressed to give interesting sidelights, making this volume appealing reading even to the non-professional. Standard English translation, by Prof. M. H. Morgan, Harvard U. Index. 6 illus. 334pp. 5⅜ x 8.   T645 Paperbound **$2.00**

THE BROWN DECADES, Lewis Mumford. In this now classic study of the arts in America, Lewis Mumford resurrects the "buried renaissance" of the post-Civil War period. He demonstrates that it contained the seeds of a new integrity and power and documents his study with detailed accounts of the founding of modern architecture in the work of Sullivan, Richardson, Root, Roebling; landscape development of Marsh, Olmstead, and Eliot; the graphic arts of Homer, Eakins, and Ryder. 2nd revised enlarged edition. Bibliography. 12 illustrations. Index. xiv + 266pp. 5⅜ x 8.   T200 Paperbound **$1.65**

History, Political Science

THE POLITICAL THOUGHT OF PLATO AND ARISTOTLE, E. Barker. One of the clearest and most accurate expositions of the corpus of Greek political thought. This standard source contains exhaustive analyses of the "Republic" and other Platonic dialogues and Aristotle's "Politics" and "Ethics," and discusses the origin of these ideas in Greece, contributions of other Greek theorists, and modifications of Greek ideas by thinkers from Aquinas to Hegel. "Must" reading for anyone interested in the history of Western thought. Index. Chronological Table of Events. 2 Appendixes. xxiv + 560pp. 5⅜ x 8.   T521 Paperbound **$1.85**

THE IDEA OF PROGRESS, J. B. Bury. Practically unknown before the Reformation, the idea of progress has since become one of the central concepts of western civilization. Prof. Bury analyzes its evolution in the thought of Greece, Rome, the Middle Ages, the Renaissance, to its flowering in all branches of science, religion, philosophy, industry, art, and literature, during and following the 16th century. Introduction by Charles Beard. Index. xl + 35/pp. 5⅜ x 8.   T40 Paperbound **$1.95**

THE ANCIENT GREEK HISTORIANS, J. B. Bury. This well known, easily read work covers the entire field of classical historians from the early writers to Herodotus, Thucydides, Xenophon, through Poseidonius and such Romans as Tacitus, Cato, Caesar, Livy. Scores of writers are studied biographically, in style, sources, accuracy, structure, historical concepts, and influences. Recent discoveries such as the Oxyrhinchus papyri are referred to, as well as such great scholars as Nissen, Gomperz, Cornford, etc. "Totally unblemished by pedantry." Outlook. "The best account in English," Dutcher, A Guide to Historical Lit. Bibliography, Index. x + 281pp. 5⅜ x 8.   T397 Paperbound **$1.50**

HISTORY OF THE LATER ROMAN EMPIRE, J. B. Bury. This standard work by the leading Byzantine scholar of our time discusses the later Roman and early Byzantine empires from 395 A.D. through the death of Justinian in 565, in their political, social, cultural, theological, and military aspects. Contemporary documents are quoted in full, making this the most complete reconstruction of the period and a fit successor to. Gibbon's "Decline and Fall." "Most unlikely that it will ever be superseded," Glanville Downey, Dumbarton Oaks Research Lib. Geneological tables. 5 maps. Bibliography. Index. 2 volumes total of 965pp. 5⅜ x 8.
T398, 399 Two volume set, Paperbound **$4.00**

A HISTORY OF ANCIENT GEOGRAPHY, E. H. Bunbury. Standard study, in English, of ancient geography; never equalled for scope, detail. First full account of history of geography from Greeks' first world picture based on mariners, through Ptolemy. Discusses every important map, discovery, figure, travel expedition, war, conjecture, narrative, bearing on subject. Chapters on Homeric geography, Herodotus, Alexander expedition, Strabo, Pliny, Ptolemy, would stand alone as exhaustive monographs. Includes minor geographers, men not usually regarded in this context: Hecataeus, Pytheas, Hipparchus, Artemidorus, Marinus of Tyre, etc. Uses information gleaned from military campaigns such as Punic Wars, Hannibal's passage of Alps, campaigns of Lucullus, Pompey, Caesar's wars, the Trojan War. New introduction by W. H. Stahl, Brooklyn College. Bibliography. Index. 20 maps. 1426pp. 5⅜ x 8.
T570-1, clothbound, 2-volume set **$12.50**

POLITICAL PARTIES, Robert Michels. Classic of social science, reference point for all later work, deals with nature of leadership in social organization on government and trade union levels. Probing tendency of oligarchy to replace democracy, it studies need for leadership, desire for organization, psychological motivations, vested interests, hero worship, reaction of leaders to power, press relations, many other aspects. Trans. by E. & C. Paul. Introduction. 447pp. 5⅜ x 8.   T569 Paperbound **$2.00**

A HISTORY OF HISTORICAL WRITING, Harry Elmer Barnes. Virtually the only adequate survey of the whole course of historical writing in a single volume. Surveys developments from the beginnings of historiographies in the ancient Near East and the Classical World, up through the Cold War. Covers major historians in detail, shows interrelationship with cultural background, makes clear individual contributions, evaluates and estimates importance; also enormously rich upon minor authors and thinkers who are usually passed over. Packed with scholarship and learning, clear, easily written. Indispensable to every student of history. Revised and enlarged up to 1961. Index and bibliography. xv + 442pp. 5⅜ x 8½.
T104 Paperbound **$2.25**

Teach Yourself

These British books are the most effective series of home study books on the market! With no outside help they will teach you as much as is necessary to have a good background in each subject, in many cases offering as much material as a similar high school or college course. They are carefully planned, written by foremost British educators, and amply provided with test questions and problems for you to check your progress; the mathematics books are especially rich in examples and problems. Do not confuse them with skimpy outlines or ordinary school texts or vague generalized popularizations; each book is complete in itself, full without being overdetailed, and designed to give you an easily-acquired branch of knowledge.

TEACH YOURSELF ALGEBRA, P. Abbott. The equivalent of a thorough high school course, up through logarithms. 52 illus. 307pp. 4¼ x 7. T680 Clothbound **$2.00**

TEACH YOURSELF GEOMETRY, P. Abbott. Plane and solid geometry, covering about a year of plane and six months of solid. 268 illus. 344pp. 4½ x 7. T681 Clothbound **$2.00**

TEACH YOURSELF TRIGONOMETRY, P. Abbott. Background of algebra and geometry will enable you to get equivalent of elementary college course. Tables. 102 illus. 204pp. 4½ x 7. T682 Clothbound **$2.00**

TEACH YOURSELF THE CALCULUS, P. Abbott. With algebra and trigonometry you will be able to acquire a good working knowledge of elementary integral calculus and differential calculus. Excellent supplement to any course textbook. 380pp. 4¼ x 7. T683 Clothbound **$2.00**

TEACH YOURSELF THE SLIDE RULE, B. Snodgrass. Basic principles clearly explained, with many applications in engineering, business, general figuring, will enable you to pick up very useful skill. 10 illus. 207pp. 4¼ x 7. T684 Clothbound **$2.00**

TEACH YOURSELF MECHANICS, P. Abbott. Equivalent of part course on elementary college level, with lever, parallelogram of force, friction, laws of motion, gases, etc. Fine introduction before more advanced course. 163 illus. 271pp. 4½ x 7. T685 Clothbound **$2.00**

TEACH YOURSELF ELECTRICITY, C. W. Wilman. Current, resistance, voltage, Ohm's law, circuits, generators, motors, transformers, etc. Non-mathematical as much as possible. 115 illus. 184pp. 4¼ x 7. T230 Clothbound **$2.00**

TEACH YOURSELF HEAT ENGINES E. DeVille. Steam and internal combustion engines; non-mathematical introduction for student, for layman wishing background, refresher for advanced student. 76 illus. 217pp. 4¼ x 7. T237 Clothbound **$2.00**

TEACH YOURSELF TO PLAY THE PIANO, King Palmer. Companion and supplement to lessons or self study. Handy reference, too. Nature of instrument, elementary musical theory, technique of playing, interpretation, etc. 60 illus. 144pp. 4¼ x 7. T959 Clothbound **$2.00**

TEACH YOURSELF HERALDRY AND GENEALOGY, L. G. Pine. Modern work, avoiding romantic and overpopular misconceptions. Editor of new Burke presents detailed information and commentary down to present. Best general survey. 50 illus. glossary; 129pp. 4¼ x 7. T962 Clothbound **$2.00**

TEACH YOURSELF HANDWRITING, John L. Dumpleton. Basic Chancery cursive style is popular and easy to learn. Many diagrams. 114 illus. 192pp. 4¼ x 7. T960 Clothbound **$2.00**

TEACH YOURSELF CARD GAMES FOR TWO, Kenneth Konstam. Many first-rate games, including old favorites like cribbage and gin and canasta as well as new lesser-known games. Extremely interesting for cards enthusiast. 60 illus. 150pp. 4¼ x 7. T963 Clothbound **$2.00**

TEACH YOURSELF GUIDEBOOK TO THE DRAMA, Luis Vargas. Clear, rapid survey of changing fashions and forms from Aeschylus to Tennessee Williams, in all major European traditions: Plot summaries, critical comments, etc. Equivalent of a college drama course; fine cultural background 224pp. 4¼ x 7. T961 Clothbound **$2.00**

TEACH YOURSELF THE ORGAN, Francis Routh. Excellent compendium of background material for everyone interested in organ music, whether as listener or player. 27 musical illus. 158pp. 4¼ x 7. T977 Clothbound **$2.00**

TEACH YOURSELF TO STUDY SCULPTURE, William Gaunt. Noted British cultural historian surveys culture from Greeks, primitive world, to moderns. Equivalent of college survey course. 23 figures, 40 photos. 158pp. 4¼ x 7. T976 Clothbound **$2.00**

Miscellaneous

THE COMPLETE KANO JIU-JITSU (JUDO), H. I. Hancock and K. Higashi. Most comprehensive guide to judo, referred to as outstanding work by Encyclopaedia Britannica. Complete authentic Japanese system of 160 holds and throws, including the most spectacular, fully illustrated with 487 photos. Full text explains leverage, weight centers, pressure points, special tricks, etc.; shows how to protect yourself from almost any manner of attack though your attacker may have the initial advantage of strength and surprise. This authentic Kano system should not be confused with the many American imitations. xii + 500pp. 5⅜ x 8.
T639 Paperbound **$2.00**

THE MEMOIRS OF JACQUES CASANOVA. Splendid self-revelation by history's most engaging scoundrel—utterly dishonest with women and money, yet highly intelligent and observant. Here are all the famous duels, scandals, amours, banishments, thefts, treacheries, and imprisonments all over Europe: a life lived to the fullest and recounted with gusto in one of the greatest autobiographies of all time. What is more, these Memoirs are also one of the most trustworthy and valuable documents we have on the society and culture of the extravagant 18th century. Here are Voltaire, Louis XV, Catherine the Great, cardinals, castrati, pimps, and pawnbrokers—an entire glittering civilization unfolding before you with an unparalleled sense of actuality. Translated by Arthur Machen. Edited by F. A. Blossom. Introduction by Arthur Symons. Illustrated by Rockwell Kent. Total of xlviii + 2216pp. 5⅜ x 8.
T338 Vol I   Paperbound **$2.00**
T339 Vol II   Paperbound **$2.00**
T340 Vol III Paperbound **$2.00**
The set **$6.00**

BARNUM'S OWN STORY, P. T. Barnum. The astonishingly frank and gratifyingly well-written autobiography of the master showman and pioneer publicity man reveals the truth about his early career, his famous hoaxes (such as the Fejee Mermaid and the Woolly Horse), his amazing commercial ventures, his fling in politics, his feuds and friendships, his failures and surprising comebacks. A vast panorama of 19th century America's mores, amusements, and vitality. 66 new illustrations in this edition. xii + 500pp. 5⅜ x 8.
T764 Paperbound **$1.65**

THE STORY OF THE TITANIC AS TOLD BY ITS SURVIVORS, ed. by Jack Winocour. Most significant accounts of most overpowering naval disaster of modern times: all 4 authors were survivors. Includes 2 full-length, unabridged books: "The Loss of the S.S. Titanic," by Laurence Beesley, "The Truth about the Titanic," by Col. Archibald Gracie; 6 pertinent chapters from "Titanic and Other Ships," autobiography of only officer to survive, Second Officer Charles Lightoller; and a short, dramatic account by the Titanic's wireless operator, Harold Bride. 26 illus. 368pp. 5⅜ x 8.
T610 Paperbound **$1.50**

THE PHYSIOLOGY OF TASTE, Jean Anthelme Brillat-Savarin. Humorous, satirical, witty, and personal classic on joys of food and drink by 18th century French politician, litterateur. Treats the science of gastronomy, erotic value of truffles, Parisian restaurants, drinking contests; gives recipes for funny omelette, pheasant, Swiss fondue, etc. Only modern translation of original French edition. Introduction. 41 illus. 346pp. 5⅝ x 8⅜.
T591 Paperbound **$1.50**

THE ART OF THE STORY-TELLER, M. L. Shedlock. This classic in the field of effective story-telling is regarded by librarians, story-tellers, and educators as the finest and most lucid book on the subject. The author considers the nature of the story, the difficulties of communicating stories to children, the artifices used in story-telling, how to obtain and maintain the effect of the story, and, of extreme importance, the elements to seek and those to avoid in selecting material. A 99-page selection of Miss Shedlock's most effective stories and an extensive bibliography of further material by Eulalie Steinmetz enhance the book's usefulness. xxi + 320pp. 5⅜ x 8.
T635 Paperbound **$1.50**

CREATIVE POWER: THE EDUCATION OF YOUTH IN THE CREATIVE ARTS, Hughes Mearns. In first printing considered revolutionary in its dynamic, progressive approach to teaching the creative arts; now accepted as one of the most effective and valuable approaches yet formulated. Based on the belief that every child has something to contribute, it provides in a stimulating manner invaluable and inspired teaching insights, to stimulate children's latent powers of creative expression in drama, poetry, music, writing, etc. Mearns's methods were developed in his famous experimental classes in creative education at the Lincoln School of Teachers College, Columbia Univ. Named one of the 20 foremost books on education in recent times by National Education Association. New enlarged revised 2nd edition. Introduction. 272pp. 5⅜ x 8.
T490 Paperbound **$1.65**

FREE AND INEXPENSIVE EDUCATIONAL AIDS, T. J. Pepe, Superintendent of Schools, Southbury, Connecticut. An up-to-date listing of over 1500 booklets, films, charts, etc. 5% costs less than 25¢; 1% costs more; 94% is yours for the asking. Use this material privately, or in schools from elementary to college, for discussion, vocational guidance, projects. 59 categories include health, trucking, textiles, language, weather, the blood, office practice, wild life, atomic energy, other important topics. Each item described according to contents, number of pages or running time, level. All material is educationally sound, and without political or company bias. 1st publication. Second, revised edition. Index. 244pp. 5⅜ x 8.
T663 Paperbound **$1.50**

THE ROMANCE OF WORDS, E. Weekley. An entertaining collection of unusual word-histories that tracks down for the general reader the origins of more than 2000 common words and phrases in English (including British and American slang): discoveries often surprising, often humorous, that help trace vast chains of commerce in products and ideas. There are Arabic trade words, cowboy words, origins of family names, phonetic accidents, curious wanderings, folk-etymologies, etc. Index. xiii + 210pp. 5⅜ x 8. T710 Paperbound **$1.25**

PHRASE AND WORD ORIGINS: A STUDY OF FAMILIAR EXPRESSIONS, A. H. Holt. One of the most entertaining books on the unexpected origins and colorful histories of words and phrases, based on sound scholarship, but written primarily for the layman. Over 1200 phrases and 1000 separate words are covered, with many quotations, and the results of the most modern linguistic and historical researches. "A right jolly book Mr. Holt has made," N. Y. Times. v + 254pp. 5⅜ x 8. T758 Paperbound **$1.35**

AMATEUR WINE MAKING, S. M. Tritton. Now, with only modest equipment and no prior knowledge, you can make your own fine table wines. A practical handbook, this covers every type of grape wine, as well as fruit, flower, herb, vegetable, and cereal wines, and many kinds of mead, cider, and beer. Every question you might have is answered, and there is a valuable discussion of what can go wrong at various stages along the way. Special supplement of yeasts and American sources of supply. 13 tables. 32 illustrations. Glossary. Index. 239pp. 5½ x 8½. T514 Clothbound **$4.00**

SAILING ALONE AROUND THE WORLD. Captain Joshua Slocum. A great modern classic in a convenient inexpensive edition. Captain Slocum's account of his single-handed voyage around the world in a 34 foot boat which he rebuilt himself. A nearly unparalleled feat of seamanship told with vigor, wit, imagination, and great descriptive power. "A nautical equivalent of Thoreau's account," Van Wyck Brooks. 67 illustrations. 308pp. 5⅜ x 8. T326 Paperbound **$1.00**

TREASURY OF THE WORLD'S COINS, Fred Reinfeld. The finest general introduction to numismatics, non-technical, thorough, always fascinating. Coins of Greece, Rome, modern countries of every continent, primitive societies, such oddities as the 50 lb. stone money of Yap, the nail coinage of New England; all mirror man's economy, customs, religion, politics, philosophy, and art. An entertaining, absorbing study, and a novel view of history. Over 750 illustrations. Table of value of coins illustrated. List of U.S. coin clubs. Bibliographic material. Index. 224pp. 6½ x 9¼. T457 Paperbound **$1.75**

HOAXES, C. D. MacDougall. Shows how art, science, history, journalism can be perverted for private purposes. Hours of delightful entertainment and a work of scholarly value, .this often shocking book tells of the deliberate creation of nonsense news, the Cardiff giant, Shakespeare forgeries, the Loch Ness monster, Biblical frauds, political schemes, literary hoaxers like Chatterton, Ossian, the disumbrationist school of painting, the lady in black at Valentino's tomb, and over 250 others. It will probably reveal the truth about a few things you've believed, and help you spot more readily 'the editorial "gander" and planted publicity release. "A stupendous collection . . . and shrewd analysis." New Yorker. New revised edition. 54 photographs. Index. 320pp. 5⅜ x 8. T465 Paperbound **$1.75**

A HISTORY OF THE WARFARE OF SCIENCE WITH THEOLOGY IN CHRISTENDOM, A. D. White. Most thorough account ever written of the great religious-scientific battles shows gradual victory of science over ignorant, harmful beliefs. Attacks on theory of evolution; attacks on Galileo; great medieval plagues caused by belief in devil-origin of disease; attacks on Franklin's experiments with electricity; the witches of Salem; scores more that will amaze you. Author, co-founder and first president of Cornell U., writes with vast scholarly background, but in clear, readable prose. Acclaimed as classic effort in America to do away with superstition. Index. Total of 928pp. 5⅜ x 8. T608 Vol I Paperbound **$1.85**
T609 Vol II Paperbound **$1.85**

THE SHIP OF FOOLS, Sebastian Brant. First printed in 1494 in Basel, this amusing book swept Europe, was translated into almost every important language, and was a best-seller for centuries. That it is still living and vital is shown by recent developments in publishing. This is the only English translation of this work, and it recaptures in lively, modern verse all the wit and insights of the original, in satirizations of foibles and vices: greed, adultery, envy, hatred, sloth, profiteering, etc. This will long remain the definitive English edition, for Professor Zeydel has provided biography of Brant, bibliography, publishing history, influences, etc. Complete reprint of 1944 edition. Translated by Professor E. Zeydel, University of Cincinnati. All 114 original woodcut illustrations. viii + 399pp. 5½ x 8⅝. T266 Paperbound **$2.00**

ERASMUS, A STUDY OF HIS LIFE, IDEALS AND PLACE IN HISTORY, Preserved Smith. This is the standard English biography and evaluation of the great Netherlands humanist Desiderius Erasmus. Written by one of the foremost American historians it covers all aspects of Erasmus's life, his influence in the religious quarrels of the Reformation, his overwhelming role in the field of letters, and his importance in the emergence of the new world view of the Northern Renaissance. This is not only a work of great scholarship, it is also an extremely interesting, vital portrait of a great man. 8 illustrations. xiv + 479pp. 5⅝ x 8½. T331 Paperbound **$2.00**

CATALOGUE OF DOVER BOOKS

CHRONICLES OF THE HOUSE OF BORGIA, Frederick Baron Corvo (Frederick W. Rolfe). In the opinion of many this is the major work of that strange Edwardian literary figure, "Baron Corvo." It was Corvo's intention to investigate the notorious Borgias, from their first emergence in Spain to the Borgia saint in the 16th century and discover their true nature, disregarding both their apologists and their enemies. How well Corvo succeeded is questionable in a historical sense, but as a literary achievement and as a stylistic triumph the "Chronicles" has been a treasured favorite for generations. All the fabulous intrigues and devious currents and countercurrents of the Renaissance come vividly to life in Corvo's work, which is peopled with the notorious and notable personages of Italy and packed with fascinating lore. This is the first complete reprinting of this work, with all the appendices and illustrations. xxi + 375pp. 5⅝ x 8½.   T275 Paperbound **$2.00**

ERROR AND ECCENTRICITY IN HUMAN BELIEF, Joseph Jastrow. A thoroughly enjoyable exposé, by a noted psychologist, of the ineradicable gullibility of man. Episodes throughout history —180 A.D. to 1930—that will shock and amuse by revelations of our tendency to fashion belief from desire not reason: the case of "Patience Worth," Ozark woman taking down novels from dictation of 17th-century girl from Devon; "Taxil," perhaps greatest hoaxer of all time; the odic force of Baron Reichenbach; Charles Richet, Nobel Laureate, accepting brazen trickeries of Eusapia Palladino; dozens of other lunacies, crank theories, public tricksters and frauds. For anyone who likes to read about the aberrations of his race. Formerly "Wish and Wisdom." 58 illustrations; 22 full-page plates. Index. xiv + 394pp. 5⅜ x 8½.   T986 Paperbound **$1.85**

FADS AND FALLACIES IN THE NAME OF SCIENCE, Martin Gardner. Formerly entitled IN THE NAME OF SCIENCE, this is the standard account of various cults, quack systems, and delusions which have masqueraded as science: hollow earth fanatics, Reich and orgone sex energy, dianetics, Atlantis, multiple moons, Forteanism, flying saucers, medical fallacies like iridiagnosis, zone therapy, etc. A new chapter has been added on Bridey Murphy, psionics, and other recent manifestations in this field. This is a fair, reasoned appraisal of eccentric theory which provides excellent inoculation against cleverly masked nonsense. "Should be read by everyone, scientist and non-scientist alike," R. T. Birge, Prof. Emeritus of Physics, Univ. of California; Former President, American Physical Society. Index. x + 365pp. 5⅜ x 8.
                                                                      T394 Paperbound **$1.50**

MONEY CONVERTER AND TIPPING GUIDE FOR EUROPEAN TRAVEL, C. Vomacka. A small, convenient handbook crammed with information on currency regulations and tipping for every European country including the Iron Curtain countries, plus Israel, Egypt, and Turkey. Currency conversion tables for every country from U.S. to foreign and vice versa. The only source of such information as phone rates, postal rates, clothing sizes, what and when to tip, duty-free imports, and dozens of other valuable topics. Always kept up to date. 128 pp. 3½ x 5¼.
                                                                      T260 Paperbound **75¢**

HOW ADVERTISING IS WRITTEN—AND WHY, Aesop Glim. The best material from the famous "Aesop Glim" column in Printer's Ink. Specific, practical, constructive comments and criticisms on such matters as the aims of advertising, importance of copy, art of the headline, adjusting "tone of voice," creating conviction, etc. Timely, effective, useful. Written for the person interested in advertising profession, yet it has few equals as a manual for effective writing of any kind. Revised edition. 150pp. 5⅜ x 8.   T782 Paperbound **$1.25**

THE WORLD'S GREAT SPEECHES, edited by Lewis Copeland and Lawrence Lamm. 255 speeches ranging over scores of topics and moods (including a special section of "Informal Speeches" and a fine collection of historically important speeches of the U.S.A. and other western hemisphere countries), present the greatest speakers of all time from Pericles of Athens to Churchill, Roosevelt, and Dylan Thomas. Invaluable as a guide to speakers, fascinating as history both past and contemporary, much material here is available elsewhere only with great difficulty. 3 indices: Topic, Author, Nation. xx + 745pp. 5⅜ x 8. T468 Paperbound **$2.75**

Pets

CARE AND FEEDING OF BUDGIES (SHELL PARRAKEETS), C. H. Rogers. Sources of information and supply. Index. 40 illustrations. 93pp. 5 x 7¼.   T937 Paperbound **65¢**

THE CARE AND BREEDING OF GOLDFISH, Anthony Evans. Hundreds of important details about indoor and outdoor pools and aquariums; the history, physical features and varieties of goldfish; selection, care, feeding, health and breeding—with a special appendix that shows you how to build your own goldfish pond. Enlarged edition, newly revised. Bibliography. 22 full-page plates; 4 figures. 129pp. 5 x 7¼.   T935 Paperbound **75¢**

OBEDIENCE TRAINING FOR YOUR DOG, C. Wimhurst. You can teach your dog to heel, retrieve, sit, jump, track, climb, refuse food, etc. Covers house training, developing a watchdog, obedience tests, working trials, police dogs. "Proud to recommend this book to every dog owner who is attempting to train his dog," says Blanche Saunders, noted American trainer, in her Introduction. Index. 34 photographs. 122pp. 5 x 7¼.   T938 Paperbound **75¢**

Dover Classical Records

Now available directly to the public exclusively from Dover: top-quality recordings of fine classical music for only $2 per record! Originally released by a major company (except for the previously unreleased Gimpel recording of Bach) to sell for $5 and $6, these records were issued under our imprint only after they had passed a severe critical test. We insisted upon:

First-rate music that is enjoyable, musically important and culturally significant.

First-rate performances, where the artists have carried out the composer's intentions, in which the music is alive, vigorous, played with understanding and sympathy.

First-rate sound—clear, sonorous, fully balanced, crackle-free, whir-free.

Have in your home music by major composers, performed by such gifted musicians as Elsner, Gitlis, Wührer, the Barchet Quartet, Gimpel. Enthusiastically received when first released, many of these performances are definitive. The records are not seconds or remainders, but brand new pressings made on pure vinyl from carefully chosen master tapes. "All purpose" 12" monaural 33⅓ rpm records, they play equally well on hi-fi and stereo equipment. Fine music for discriminating music lovers, superlatively played, flawlessly recorded: there is no better way to build your library of recorded classical music at remarkable savings. There are no strings; this is not a come-on, not a club, forcing you to buy records you may not want in order to get a few at a lower price. Buy whatever records you want in any quantity, and never pay more than $2 each. Your obligation ends with your first purchase. And that's when ours begins. Dover's money-back guarantee allows you to return any record for any reason, even if you don't like the music, for a full, immediate refund, no questions asked.

MOZART: STRING QUARTET IN A MAJOR (K.464); STRING QUARTET IN C MAJOR ("DISSONANT", K.465), Barchet Quartet. The final two of the famed Haydn Quartets, high-points in the history of music. The A Major was accepted with delight by Mozart's contemporaries, but the C Major, with its dissonant opening, aroused strong protest. Today, of course, the remarkable resolutions of the dissonances are recognized as major musical achievements. "Beautiful warm playing," MUSICAL AMERICA. "Two of Mozart's loveliest quartets in a distinguished performance," REV. OF RECORDED MUSIC. (Playing time 58 mins.) HCR 5200 **$2.00**

MOZART: QUARTETS IN G MAJOR (K.80); D MAJOR (K.155); G MAJOR (K.156); C MAJOR (K157), Barchet Quartet. The early chamber music of Mozart receives unfortunately little attention. First-rate music of the Italian school, it contains all the lightness and charm that belongs only to the youthful Mozart. This is currently the only separate source for the composer's work of this time period. "Excellent," HIGH FIDELITY. "Filled with sunshine and youthful joy; played with verve, recorded sound live and brilliant," CHRISTIAN SCI. MONITOR. (Playing time 51 mins.) HCR 5201 **$2.00**

MOZART: SERENADE #9 IN D MAJOR ("POSTHORN", K.320); SERENADE #6 IN D MAJOR ("SERENATA NOTTURNA", K.239), Pro Musica Orch. of Stuttgart, under Edouard van Remoortel. For Mozart, the serenade was a highly effective form, since he could bring to it the immediacy and intimacy of chamber music as well as the free fantasy of larger group music. Both these serenades are distinguished by a playful, mischievous quality, a spirit perfectly captured in this fine performance. "A triumph, polished playing from the orchestra," HI FI MUSIC AT HOME. "Sound is rich and resonant, fidelity is wonderful," REV. OF RECORDED MUSIC. (Playing time 51 mins.) HCR 5202 **$2.00**

MOZART: DIVERTIMENTO IN E FLAT MAJOR FOR STRING TRIO (K.563); ADAGIO AND FUGUE IN F MINOR FOR STRING TRIO (K.404a), Kehr Trio. The Divertimento is one of Mozart's most beloved pieces, called by Einstein "the finest, most perfect trio ever heard." It is difficult to imagine a music lover who will not be delighted by it. This is the only recording of the lesser known Adagio and Fugue, written in 1782 and influenced by Bach's Well-Tempered Clavichord. "Extremely beautiful recording, strongly recommended," THE OBSERVER. "Superior to rival editions," HIGH FIDELITY. (Playing time 51 mins.) HCR 5203 **$2.00**

SCHUMANN: KREISLERIANA (OP.16); FANTASY IN C MAJOR ("FANTASIE," OP.17), Vlado Perlemuter, Piano. The vigorous Romantic imagination and the remarkable emotional qualities of Schumann's piano music raise it to special eminence in 19th century creativity. Both these pieces are rooted to the composer's tortuous romance with his future wife, Clara, and both receive brilliant treatment at the hands of Vlado Perlemuter, Paris Conservatory, proclaimed by Alfred Cortot "not only a great virtuoso but also a great musician." "The best Kreisleriana to date," BILLBOARD. (Playing time 55 mins.) HCR 5204 **$2.00**

SCHUMANN: TRIO #1, D MINOR; TRIO #3, G MINOR, Trio di Bolzano. The fiery, romantic, melodic Trio #1, and the dramatic, seldom heard Trio #3 are both movingly played by a fine chamber ensemble. No one personified Romanticism to the general public of the 1840's more than did Robert Schumann, and among his most romantic works are these trios for cello, violin and piano. "Ensemble and overall interpretation leave little to be desired," HIGH FIDELITY. "An especially understanding performance," REV. OF RECORDED MUSIC. (Playing time 54 mins.) HCR 5205 **$2.00**

CATALOGUE OF DOVER BOOKS

SCHUBERT: SONATA IN C MINOR; SONATA IN B MAJOR (OP.177), Wührer, piano. Schubert's sonatas retain the structure of the classical form, but delight listeners with romantic freedom and a special melodic richness. The C Minor, one of the Three Grand Sonatas, is a product of the composer's maturity. The B Major was not published until 15 years after his death. "Remarkable interpretation, reproduction of the first rank," DISQUES. "A superb pianist for music like this, musicianship, sweep, power, and an ability to integrate Schubert's measures such as few pianists have had since Schnabel," Harold Schonberg. (Playing time 49 mins.)
HCR 5207 **$2.00**

STRAVINSKY: VIOLIN CONCERTO IN D MAJOR, Gitlis, Concerts Colonne Orch. under Byrns; DUO CONCERTANT, Gitlis, Zelka; JEU DE CARTES, Bamberg Symphony under Hollreiser. Igor Stravinsky is probably the most important composer of this century, and these three works are among the most significant of his works during his neoclassical period of the 1930's. The Violin Concerto is one of the few modern classics. Jeu de Cartes, a ballet score, bubbles with gaiety, color and melodiousness. "Imaginatively played and beautifully recorded," E. T. Canby, HARPERS MAGAZINE. "Gitlis is excellent, Hollreiser beautifully worked out," HIGH FIDELITY. (Playing time 55 mins.)
HCR 5208 **$2.00**

GEMINIANI: SIX CONCERTI GROSSI (OP.3), Barchet, Quartet, Helma Elsner, Harpsichord, Pro Musica String Orch. of Stuttgart under Reinhardt. Francesco Geminiani (1687-1762) has been rediscovered in the same musical exploration that revealed Scarlatti, Vivaldi and Corelli. In form he is more sophisticated than the earlier Italians, but his music delights modern listeners with its combination of contrapuntal techniques and the full harmonies and rich melodies characteristic of Italian music. This is the only recording of the six 1733 concerti: D Major, B Flat Minor, E Minor, G Minor, E Minor (bis), and D Minor. "I warmly recommend it, spacious, magnificent, I enjoyed every bar," C. Cudworth, RECORD NEWS. "Works of real charm, recorded with understanding and style," ETUDE. (Playing time 52 mins.)
HCR 5209 **$2.00**

TELEMANN: 12 FANTASIES FOR HARPSICHORD, Helma Elsner, Harpsichord. Until recently, Georg Philip Telemann (1681-1767) was one of the mysteriously neglected great men of music. Recently he has received the attention he deserves. Intent upon grafting Italian melodic richness and French delicacy onto German solidity, he created music that delights modern listeners with its freshness and originality. "This is another blessing of the contemporary LP output. Miss Elsner plays with considerable sensitivity and a great deal of understanding," REV. OF RECORDED MUSIC. "Fine recorded sound," Harold Schonberg. "Recommended warmly, very high quality," DISQUES. (Playing time 50 mins.)
HCR 5210 **$2.00**

BARTOK: VIOLIN CONCERTO; SONATA FOR UNACCOMPANIED VIOLIN, Gitlis, Pro Musica Orch. of Vienna under Hornstein. Both these works are outstanding examples of Bartok's final period, and they show his powers at their fullest. The Violin Concerto is, in the opinion of many authorities, Bartok's finest work, and the Sonata, his last work, is "a masterpiece" (F. Sackville West). "Wonderful, finest performances of both Bartok works I have ever heard," GRAMOPHONE. "Gitlis makes such potent and musical sense out of these works that I suspect many general music lovers [not otherwise in sympathy with modern music] will discover to their amazement that they like it. Exceptionally good sound," AUDITOR. (Playing time 54 mins.)
HCR 5211 **$2.00**

J. S. BACH: PARTITAS #3 IN E MAJOR & #2 IN D MINOR FOR UNACCOMPANIED VIOLIN, Gimpel, violin. Bach's works for unaccompanied violin fall within the same era as produced the Brandenburg Concerti, the Orchestral Suites, and the first part of the Well-Tempered Clavichord. The D Minor is considered one of Bach's masterpieces; the E Major is a buoyant work with exceptionally interesting bariolage effects. This is the first release of a truly memorable recording by Bronislaw Gimpel, "as a violinist, the equal of the greatest" (P. Leron, in OPERA, Paris). (Playing time 53 mins.)
HCR 5212 **$2.00**

SCHUBERT: QUINTET IN A MAJOR ("TROUT", OP.114), Wührer, Barchet, Reimann, Hirschfelder, Kruger; NOCTURNE IN E FLAT MAJOR (OP.148), Wührer, Barchet, Reimann. If there is a single piece of chamber music that is a universal favorite, it is probably Schubert's "Trout" Quintet. Delightful melody, harmonic resources, musical exuberance are its characteristics. The Nocturne is an exquisite piece with a deceptively simple theme and harmony. "The best Trout on the market—Wührer is a fine Vienese-style Schubertian, and his spirit infects the Barchets," ATLANTIC MONTHLY. "Exquisitely recorded," ETUDE. (Playing time 44 mins.)
HCR 5206 **$2.00**

This is only a partial listing of Dover's classical music records. Write to us for complete listings.

New Books

101 PATCHWORK PATTERNS, Ruby Short McKim. With no more ability than the fundamentals of ordinary sewing, you will learn to make over 100 beautiful quilts: flowers, rainbows, Irish chains, fish and bird designs, leaf designs, unusual geometric patterns, many others. Cutting designs carefully diagrammed and described, suggestions for materials, yardage estimates, step-by-step instructions, plus entertaining stories of origins of quilt names, other folklore. Revised 1962. 101 full-sized patterns. 140 illustrations. Index. 128pp. 7⅞ x 10¾.
T773 Paperbound **$1.85**

ESSENTIAL GRAMMAR SERIES
By concentrating on the essential core of material that constitutes the semantically most important forms and areas of a language and by stressing explanation (often bringing parallel English forms into the discussion) rather than rote memory, this new series of grammar books is among the handiest language aids ever devised. Designed by linguists and teachers for adults with limited learning objectives and learning time, these books omit nothing important, yet they teach more usable language material and do it more quickly and permanently than any other self-study material. Clear and rigidly economical, they concentrate upon immediately usable language material, logically organized so that related material is always presented together. Any reader of typical capability can use them to refresh his grasp of language, to supplement self-study language records or conventional grammars used in schools, or to begin language study on his own. Now available:

ESSENTIAL GERMAN GRAMMAR, Dr. Guy Stern & E. F. Bleiler. Index. Glossary of terms. 128pp. 4½ x 6⅜.
T422 Paperbound **75¢**

ESSENTIAL FRENCH GRAMMAR, Dr. Seymour Resnick. Index. Cognate list. Glossary. 159pp. 4½ x 6⅜.
T419 Paperbound **75¢**

ESSENTIAL ITALIAN GRAMMAR, Dr. Olga Ragusa. Index. Glossary. 111pp. 4½ x 6⅜.
T779 Paperbound **75¢**

ESSENTIAL SPANISH GRAMMAR, Dr. Seymour Resnick. Index. 50-page cognate list. Glossary. 138pp. 4½ x 6⅜.
T780 Paperbound **75¢**

PHILOSOPHIES OF MUSIC HISTORY: A Study of General Histories of Music, 1600-1960, Warren D. Allen. Unquestionably one of the most significant documents yet to appear in musicology, this thorough survey covers the entire field of historical research in music. An influential masterpiece of scholarship, it includes early music histories; theories on the ethos of music; lexicons, dictionaries and encyclopedias of music; musical historiography through the centuries; philosophies of music history; scores of related topics. Copiously documented. New preface brings work up to 1960. Index. 317-item bibliography. 9 illustrations; 3 full-page plates. 5⅜ x 8½. xxxiv + 382pp.
T282 Paperbound **$2.00**

MR. DOOLEY ON IVRYTHING AND IVRYBODY, Finley Peter Dunne. The largest collection in print of hilarious utterances by the irrepressible Irishman of Archey Street, one of the most vital characters in American fiction. Gathered from the half dozen books that appeared during the height of Mr. Dooley's popularity, these 102 pieces are all unaltered and uncut, and they are all remarkably fresh and pertinent even today. Selected and edited by Robert Hutchinson. 5⅜ x 8½. xii + 244p.
T626 Paperbound **$1.00**

TREATISE ON PHYSIOLOGICAL OPTICS, Hermann von Helmholtz. Despite new investigations, this important work will probably remain preeminent. Contains everything known about physiological optics up to 1925, covering scores of topics under the general headings of dioptrics of the eye, sensations of vision, and perecptions of vision. Von Helmholtz's voluminous data are all included, as are extensive supplementary matter incorporated into the third German edition, new material prepared for 1925 English edition, and copious textual annotations by J. P. C. Southall. The most exhaustive treatise ever prepared on the subject, it has behind it a list of contributors that will never again be duplicated. Translated and edited by J. P. C. Southall. Bibliography. Indexes. 312 illustrations. 3 volumes bound as 2. Total of 1749pp. 5⅜ x 8.
S15-16 Two volume set, Clothbound **$15.00**

THE ARTISTIC ANATOMY OF TREES, Rex Vicat Cole. Even the novice with but an elementary knowledge of drawing and none of the structure of trees can learn to draw, paint trees from this systematic, lucid instruction book. Copiously illustrated with the author's own sketches, diagrams, and 50 paintings from the early Renaissance to today, it covers composition; structure of twigs, boughs, buds, branch systems; outline forms of major species; how leaf is set on twig; flowers and fruit and their arrangement; etc. 500 illustrations. Bibliography. Indexes. 347pp. 5⅜ x 8.
T1016 Clothbound **$4.50**

CATALOGUE OF DOVER BOOKS

HOW PLANTS GET THEIR NAMES, L. H. Bailey. In this basic introduction to botanical nomenclature, a famed expert on plants and plant life reveals the confusion that can result from misleading common names of plants and points out the fun and advantage of using a sound, scientific approach. Covers every aspect of the subject, including an historical survey beginning before Linnaeus systematized nomenclature, the literal meaning of scores of Latin names, their English equivalents, etc. Enthusiastically written and easy to follow, this handbook for gardeners, amateur horticulturalists, and beginning botany students is knowledgeable, accurate and useful. 11 illustrations. Lists of Latin, English botanical names. 192pp. 5⅜ x 8½.
T796 Paperbound **$1.15**

PIERRE CURIE, Marie Curie. Nobel Prize winner creates a memorable portrait of her equally famous husband in a fine scientific biography. Recounting his childhood, his haphazard education, and his experimental research (with his brother) in the physics of crystals, Mme. Curie brings to life the strong, determined personality of a great scientist at work and discusses, in clear, straightforward terms, her husband's and her own work with radium and radioactivity. A great book about two very great founders of modern science. Includes Mme. Curie's autobiographical notes. Translated by Charlotte and Vernon Kellogg. viii + 120pp. 5⅜ x 8½.
T199 Paperbound **$1.00**

STYLES IN PAINTING: A Comparative Study, Paul Zucker. Professor of Art History at Cooper Union presents an important work of art-understanding that will guide you to a fuller, deeper appreciation of masterpieces of art and at the same time add to your understanding of how they fit into the evolution of style from the earliest times to this century. Discusses general principles of historical method and aesthetics, history of styles, then illustrates with more than 230 great paintings organized by subject matter so you can see at a glance how styles have changed through the centuries. 236 beautiful halftones. xiv + 338pp. 5⅝ x 8½.
T760 Paperbound **$2.00**

NEW VARIORUM EDITION OF SHAKESPEARE
One of the monumental feats of Shakespeare scholarship is the famous New Variorum edition, containing full texts of the plays together with an entire reference library worth of historical and critical information: all the variant readings that appear in the quartos and folios; annotations by leading scholars from the earliest days of Shakespeare criticism to the date of publication; essays on meaning, background, productions by Johnson, Addison, Fielding, Lessing, Hazlitt, Coleridge, Ulrici, Swinburne, and other major Shakespeare critics; original sources of Shakespeare's inspiration. For the first time, this definitive edition of Shakespeare's plays, each printed in a separate volume, will be available in inexpensive editions to scholars, to teachers and students, and to every lover of Shakespeare and fine literature. Now ready:

KING LEAR, edited by Horace Howard Furness. Bibliography. List of editions collated in notes. viii + 503pp. 5⅜ x 8½.
T1000 Paperbound **$2.25**

MACBETH, edited by Horace Howard Furness Jr. Bibliography. List of editions collated in notes. xvi + 562pp. 5⅜ x 8½.
T1001 Paperbound **$2.25**

ROMEO AND JULIET, edited by Horace Howard Furness. Bibliography. List of editions collated in notes. xxvi + 480pp. 5⅜ x 8½.
T1002 Paperbound **$2.25**

OTTHELLO, edited by Horace Howard Furness. Bibliography. List of editions collated in notes. x + 471pp. 5⅜ x 8½.
T1003 Paperbound **$2.25**

HAMLET, edited by Horace Howard Furness. Bibliography. List of editions collated in notes. Total of 926pp. 5⅜ x 8½.
T1004-1005 Two volume set, Paperbound **$4.50**

THE GARDENER'S YEAR, Karel Capek. The author of this refreshingly funny book is probably best known in U. S. as the author of "R. U. R.," a biting satire on the machine age. Here, his satiric genius finds expression in a wholly different vein: a warm, witty chronicle of the joys and trials of the amateur gardener as he watches over his plants, his soil and the weather from January to December. 59 drawings by Joseph Capek add an important second dimension to the fun. "Mr. Capek writes with sympathy, understanding and humor," NEW YORK TIMES. "Will delight the amateur gardener, and indeed everyone else," SATURDAY REVIEW. Translated by M. and R. Weatherall. 59 illustrations. 159pp. 4½ x 6½.
T1014 Paperbound **$1.00**

THE ADVANCE OF THE FUNGI, E. C. Large. The dramatic story of the battle against fungi, from the year the potato blight hit Europe (1845) to 1940, and of men who fought and won it: Pasteur, Anton de Bary, Tulasne, Berkeley, Woronin, Jensen, many others. Combines remarkable grasp of facts and their significance with skill to write dramatic, exciting prose. "Philosophically witty, fundamentally thoughtful, always mature," NEW YORK HERALD TRIBUNE. "Highly entertaining, intelligent, penetrating," NEW YORKER. Bibliography. 64 illustrations. 6 full-page plates. 488pp. 5⅜ x 8½.
T437 Paperbound **$2.25**

THE PAINTER'S METHODS AND MATERIALS, A. P. Laurie. Adviser to the British Royal Academy discusses the ills that paint is heir to and the methods most likely to counteract them. Examining 48 masterpieces by Fra Lippo Lippi, Millais, Boucher, Rembrandt, Romney, Van Eyck, Velazquez, Michaelangelo, Botticelli, Frans Hals, Turner, and others, he tries to discover how special and unique effects were achieved. Not conjectural information, but certain and authoritative. Beautiful, sharp reproductions, plus textual illustrations of apparatus and the results of experiments with pigments and media. 63 illustrations and diagrams. Index. 250pp. 5⅜ x 8.
T1019 Clothbound **$3.75**

CATALOGUE OF DOVER BOOKS

CHANCE, LUCK AND STATISTICS, H. C. Levinson. The theory of chance, or probability, and the science of statistics presented in simple, non-technical language. Covers fundamentals by analyzing games of chance, then applies those fundamentals to immigration and birth rates, operations research, stock speculation, insurance rates, advertising, and other fields. Excellent course supplement and a delightful introduction for non-mathematicians. Formerly "The Science of Chance." Index. xiv + 356pp. 5⅜ x 8.   T1007 Paperbound **$1.75**

THROUGH THE ALIMENTARY CANAL WITH GUN AND CAMERA: A Fascinating Trip to the Interior, George S. Chappell. An intrepid explorer, better known as a major American humorist, accompanied by imaginary camera-man and botanist, conducts this unforgettably hilarious journey to the human interior. Wildly imaginative, his account satirizes academic pomposity, parodies cliché-ridden travel literature, and cleverly uses facts of physiology for comic purposes. All the original line drawings by Otto Soglow are included to add to the merriment. Preface by Robert Benchley. 17 illustrations. xii + 116pp. 5⅜ x 8½.   T376 Paperbound **$1.00**

TALKS TO TEACHERS ON PSYCHOLOGY and to Students on Some of Life's Ideals, William James. America's greatest psychologist invests these lectures with immense personal charm, invaluable insights, and superb literary style. 15 Harvard lectures, 3 lectures delivered to students in New England touch upon psychology and the teaching of art, stream of consciousness, the child as a behaving organism, education and behavior, association of ideas, the gospel of relaxation, what makes life significant, and other related topics. Interesting, and still vital pedagogy. x + 146pp. 5⅜ x 8½.   T261 Paperbound **$1.00**

A WHIMSEY ANTHOLOGY, collected by Carolyn Wells. Delightful verse on the lighter side: logical whimsies, poems shaped like decanters and flagons, lipograms and acrostics, alliterative verse, enigmas and charades, anagrams, linguistic and dialectic verse, tongue twisters, limericks, travesties, and just about very other kind of whimsical poetry ever written. Works by Edward Lear, Gelett Burgess, Poe, Lewis Carroll, Henley, Robert Herrick, Christina Rossetti, scores of other poets will entertain and amuse you for hours. Index. xiv + 221pp. 5⅜ x 8½.   T1020 Paperbound **$1.25**

LANDSCAPE PAINTING, R. O. Dunlop. A distinguished modern artist is a perfect guide to the aspiring landscape painter. This practical book imparts to even the uninitiated valuable methods and techniques. Useful advice is interwoven throughout a fascinating illustrated history of landscape painting, from Ma Yüan to Picasso. 60 half-tone reproductions of works by Giotto, Giovanni Bellini, Piero della Francesca, Tintoretto, Giorgione, Raphael, Van Ruisdael, Poussin, Gainsborough, Monet, Cezanne, Seurat, Picasso, many others. Total of 71 illustrations, 4 in color. Index. 192pp. 7⅜ x 10.   T1018 Clothbound **$6.00**

PRACTICAL LANDSCAPE PAINTING, Adrian Stokes. A complete course in landscape painting that trains the senses to perceive as well as the hand to apply the principles underlying the pictorial aspect of nature. Author fully explains tools, value and nature of various colors, and instructs beginners in clear, simple terms how to apply them. Places strong emphasis on drawing and composition, foundations often neglected in painting texts. Includes pictorial-textual survey of the art from Ancient China to the present, with helpful critical comments and numerous diagrams illustrating every stage. 93 illustrations. Index. 256pp. 5⅜ x 8.   T1017 Clothbound **$3.75**

PELLUCIDAR, THREE NOVELS: AT THE EARTH'S CORE, PELLUCIDAR, TANAR OF PELLUCIDAR, Edgar Rice Burroughs. The first three novels of adventure in the thrill-filled world within the hollow interior of the earth. David Innes's mechanical mole drills through the outer crust and precipitates him into an astonishing world. Among Burroughs's most popular work. Illustrations by J. Allan St. John. 5⅜ x 8½.   T1051 Paperbound **$2.00**
                                                                                 T1050 Clothbound **$3.75**

JOE MILLER'S JESTS OR, THE WITS VADE-MECUM. Facsimile of the first edition of famous 18th century collection of repartees, bons mots, puns and jokes, the father of the humor anthology. A first-hand look at the taste of fashionable London in the Age of Pope. 247 entertaining anecdotes, many involving well-known personages such as Colley Cibber, Sir Thomas More, Rabelais, rich in humor, historic interest. New introduction contains biographical information on Joe Miller, fascinating history of his enduring collection, bibliographical information on collections of comic material. Introduction by Robert Hutchinson. 96pp. 5⅜ x 8½.
                                                                                 Paperbound **$1.00**

THE HUMOROUS WORLD OF JEROME K. JEROME. Complete essays and extensive passages from nine out-of-print books ("Three Men on Wheels," "Novel Notes," "Told After Supper," "Sketches in Lavender, Blue and Green," "American Wives and Others," 4 more) by a highly original humorist, author of the novel "Three Men in a Boat." Human nature is JKJ's subject: the problems of husbands, of wives, of tourists, of the human animal trapped in the drawing room. His sympathetic acceptance of the shortcomings of his race and his ability to see humor in almost any situation make this a treasure for those who know his work and a pleasant surprise for those who don't. Edited and with an introduction by Robert Hutchinson. xii + 260pp. 5⅜ x 8½.   T58 Paperbound **$1.00**

CATALOGUE OF DOVER BOOKS

GEOMETRY OF FOUR DIMENSIONS, H. P. Manning. Unique in English as a clear, concise introduction to this fascinating subject. Treatment is primarily synthetic and Euclidean, although hyperplanes and hyperspheres at infinity are considered by non-Euclidean forms. Historical introduction and foundations of 4-dimensional geometry; perpendicularity; simple angles; angles of planes; higher order; symmetry; order, motion; hyperpyramids, hypercones, hyperspheres; figures with parallel elements; volume, hypervolume in space; regular polyhedroids. Glossary of terms. 74 illustrations. ix + 348pp. 5⅜ x 8. S182 Paperbound **$1.95**

PAPER FOLDING FOR BEGINNERS, W. D. Murray and F. J. Rigney. A delightful introduction to the varied and entertaining Japanese art of origami (paper folding), with a full, crystal-clear text that anticipates every difficulty; over 275 clearly labeled diagrams of all important stages in creation. You get results at each stage, since complex figures are logically developed from simpler ones. 43 different pieces are explained: sailboats, frogs, roosters, etc. 6 photographic plates. 279 diagrams. 95pp. 5⅝ x 8⅜. T713 Paperbound **$1.00**

SATELLITES AND SCIENTIFIC RESEARCH, D. King-Hele. An up-to-the-minute non-technical account of the man-made satellites and the discoveries they have yielded up to September of 1961. Brings together information hitherto published only in hard-to-get scientific journals. Includes the life history of a typical satellite, methods of tracking, new information on the shape of the earth, zones of radiation, etc. Over 60 diagrams and 6 photographs. Mathematical appendix. Bibliography of over 100 items. Index. xii + 180pp. 5⅜ x 8½. T703 Paperbound **$2.00**

LOUIS PASTEUR, S. J. Holmes. A brief, very clear, and warmly understanding biography of the great French scientist by a former Professor of Zoology in the University of California. Traces his home life, the fortunate effects of his education, his early researches and first theses, and his constant struggle with superstition and institutionalism in his work on microorganisms, fermentation, anthrax, rabies, etc. New preface by the author. 159pp. 5⅜ x 8. T197 Paperbound **$1.00**

THE ENJOYMENT OF CHESS PROBLEMS, K. S. Howard. A classic treatise on this minor art by an internationally recognized authority that gives a basic knowledge of terms and themes for the everyday chess player as well as the problem fan: 7 chapters on the two-mover; 7 more on 3- and 4-move problems; a chapter on selfmates; and much more. "The most important one-volume contribution originating solely in the U.S.A.," Alain White. 200 diagrams. Index. Solutions, viii + 212pp. 5⅜ x 8. T742 Paperbound **$1.25**

SAM LOYD AND HIS CHESS PROBLEMS, Alain C. White. Loyd was (for all practical purposes) the father of the American chess problem and his protégé and successor presents here the diamonds of his production, chess problems embodying a whimsy and bizarre fancy entirely unique. More than 725 in all, ranging from two-move to extremely elaborate five-movers, including Loyd's contributions to chess oddities—problems in which pieces are arranged to form initials, figures, other by-paths of chess problem found nowhere else. Classified according to major concept, with full text analyzing problems, containing selections from Loyd's own writings. A classic to challenge your ingenuity, increase your skill. Corrected republication of 1913 edition. Over 750 diagrams and illustrations. 744 problems with solutions. 471pp. 5⅜ x 8½. T928 Paperbound **$2.00**

FABLES IN SLANG & MORE FABLES IN SLANG, George Ade. 2 complete books of major American humorist in pungent colloquial tradition of Twain, Billings. 1st reprinting in over 30 years includes "The Two Mandolin Players and the Willing Performer," "The Base Ball Fan Who Took the Only Known Cure," "The Slim Girl Who Tried to Keep a Date that was Never Made," 42 other tales of eccentric, perverse, but always funny characters. "Touch of genius," H. L. Mencken. New introduction by E. F. Bleiler. 86 illus. 208pp. 5⅜ x 8. T533 Paperbound **$1.00**

FARES, PLEASE! by J. A. Miller. Authoritative, comprehensive, and entertaining history of local public transit from its inception to its most recent developments: trolleys, horsecars, streetcars, buses, elevateds, subways, along with monorails, "road-railers," and a host of other extraordinary vehicles. Here are all the flamboyant personalities involved, the vehement arguments, the unusual information, and all the nostalgia. "Interesting facts brought into especially vivid life," N. Y. Times. New preface. 152 illustrations, 4 new. Bibliography. xix + 204pp. 5⅜ x 8. T671 Paperbound **$1.50**

Dover publishes books on art, music, philosophy, literature, languages, history, social sciences, psychology, handcrafts, orientalia, puzzles and entertainments, chess, pets and gardens, books explaining science, intermediate and higher mathematics mathematical physics, engineering, biological sciences, earth sciences, classics of science, etc. Write to:

Dept. catrr.
Dover Publications, Inc.
180 Varick Street, N. Y. 14, N. Y.